Hands-On Microservices – C# 8 and .NET Core 3
Third Edition

Refactor your monolith architecture into microservices using Azure

Gaurav Aroraa
Ed Price

Packt>

BIRMINGHAM - MUMBAI

Hands-On Microservices with C# 8 and .NET Core 3
Third Edition

Copyright © 2020 Packt Publishing

All rights reserved. No part of this book may be reproduced, stored in a retrieval system, or transmitted in any form or by any means, without the prior written permission of the publisher, except in the case of brief quotations embedded in critical articles or reviews.

Every effort has been made in the preparation of this book to ensure the accuracy of the information presented. However, the information contained in this book is sold without warranty, either express or implied. Neither the authors, nor Packt Publishing or its dealers and distributors, will be held liable for any damages caused or alleged to have been caused directly or indirectly by this book.

Packt Publishing has endeavored to provide trademark information about all of the companies and products mentioned in this book by the appropriate use of capitals. However, Packt Publishing cannot guarantee the accuracy of this information.

Commissioning Editor: Richa Tripathi
Acquisition Editor: Denim Pinto
Content Development Editor: Tiksha Abhimanyu Lad
Senior Editor: Afshaan Khan
Technical Editor: Romy Dias
Copy Editor: Safis Editing
Project Coordinator: Francy Puthiry
Proofreader: Safis Editing
Indexer: Priyanka Dhadke
Production Designer: Nilesh Mohite

First published: June 2017
Second edition: December 2017
Third edition: March 2020

Production reference: 2100620

Published by Packt Publishing Ltd.
Livery Place
35 Livery Street
Birmingham
B3 2PB, UK.

ISBN 978-1-78961-794-8

www.packt.com

To my younger sister, Preeti, who always inspires me with her positive attitude toward life. I have learned a lot from her on how to be positive in life: how to achieve your goals in life even when there are obstacles preventing you from reaching them.

– Gaurav Aroraa

Packt>

Packt.com

Subscribe to our online digital library for full access to over 7,000 books and videos, as well as industry leading tools to help you plan your personal development and advance your career. For more information, please visit our website.

Why subscribe?

- Spend less time learning and more time coding with practical eBooks and Videos from over 4,000 industry professionals

- Improve your learning with Skill Plans built especially for you

- Get a free eBook or video every month

- Fully searchable for easy access to vital information

- Copy and paste, print, and bookmark content

Did you know that Packt offers eBook versions of every book published, with PDF and ePub files available? You can upgrade to the eBook version at www.packt.com and as a print book customer, you are entitled to a discount on the eBook copy. Get in touch with us at customercare@packtpub.com for more details.

At www.packt.com, you can also read a collection of free technical articles, sign up for a range of free newsletters, and receive exclusive discounts and offers on Packt books and eBooks.

Foreword

Microservices is more than just a buzzword. They represent a fresh new way of thinking about systems architecture that builds upon the designs and layering of the last two decades, combined with the real-world experiences of building large scalable systems at a size we once thought impossible.

We've all learned about three-tiered architecture: we design our systems with the single responsibility principle, and we have tried different ways to scale and deploy our systems. Microservices combines the best of all these worlds. It aims to build systems that separate responsibility appropriately; that manage, version, and deploy services individually; and that elastically scale, backed by the power of the cloud.

This new generation of cloud-native applications needed a new way of thinking about architecture. Gaurav and Ed have put together a journey that walks you through the process of creating effective microservices, using C# 8 and the new open source, cross-platform .NET Core.

The book covers everything that you'll need, from architecture, an introduction to containers, and how services communicate, to the concepts behind a service mesh. Everything is backed by practical examples in real-world use cases, including IoT.

I'm thrilled that you're coming along this journey with us, and I'm excited to see what you'll be able to build with this new knowledge.

Scott Hanselman
Partner Program Manager
.NET Open Source

Contributors

About the authors

Gaurav Aroraa is a serial entrepreneur and start-up mentor. He has done an M.Phil in computer science. He is a Microsoft MVP award recipient. He is a lifetime member of the Computer Society of India (CSI), is an advisory member and senior mentor at IndiaMentor, is certified as a Scrum trainer/coach, is ITIL-F certified, and is PRINCE-F and PRINCE-P certified. He is an open source developer and a contributor to the Microsoft TechNet community. Recently, Gaurav was awarded "Icon of the year – excellence in Mentoring Technology Startups" for 2018-19 by Radio City, a Jagran initiative, for his extraordinary work during his 22-year career in the industry in the field of technology mentoring.

> *In life, it's hard to understand things when you don't find support. My family is one such support system and I am the luckiest to have them. I would like to thank my wife, Shuby Aroraa, and my little angel, Aarchi Arora, who gave me permission to write and invest time in this book.*
>
> *A special thanks to the Packt team (especially Tiksha, Afshaan, and Richa) and Andreas Helland. Also, a big thanks to Ed Price (my coauthor) and Scott Hanselman.*

Ed Price is a senior program manager in engineering at Microsoft, with an MBA in technology management. He has run Microsoft customer feedback programs for Azure Development, Service Fabric, IoT, and Visual Studio. He was also a technical writer at Microsoft for 6 years, helped to lead TechNet Wiki, and now leads efforts to publish key guidance from AzureCAT (Customer Advisory Team), especially in the development of microservices. He is the coauthor of *Learn to Program with Small Basic*.

About the reviewer

Andreas Helland has a degree in software engineering and over 20 years of experience in building products and services. He has worked both with the development side and the infrastructure side and holds a number of Microsoft certifications across various skill sets. This also led him to become an early adopter of Azure. After building up his knowledge working in the telecommunications industry, he switched to consulting, and currently works as an architect for Capgemini where he assists customers on how to utilize the cloud in the best ways possible. He specializes in Azure Active Directory and works closely with the Identity teams at Microsoft, both in testing new services and providing feedback based on learnings from the field.

> *I have to thank my family for allowing me to spend so much time "in my lab" working on my pet projects as well as being more or less understanding of why a home needs proper IT infrastructure. I've also been lucky with having employers that have given me great freedom to work with the things I've wanted to and letting me "go crazy" with the Microsoft tech stack. My output is certainly not a result purely based on what I put in.*

Packt is searching for authors like you

If you're interested in becoming an author for Packt, please visit authors.packtpub.com and apply today. We have worked with thousands of developers and tech professionals, just like you, to help them share their insight with the global tech community. You can make a general application, apply for a specific hot topic that we are recruiting an author for, or submit your own idea.

Table of Contents

Preface   1
Chapter 1: An Introduction to Microservices   7
   Technical requirements   8
   The origin of microservices   8
   Discussing microservices   10
   Exploring monolithic architecture   10
      Service-oriented architecture   12
         Understanding services   13
   Understanding microservice architecture   16
      Messaging in microservices   18
         Synchronous messaging   18
         Asynchronous messaging   19
         Message formats   19
   Using microservices   20
   The workings of microservice architecture   20
   The advantages of microservices   21
   SOA versus microservices   22
   The prerequisites of microservice architecture   23
   Understanding the problems with the monolithic architectural style   24
      The challenges in standardizing a .NET stack   25
         Fault tolerance   26
      The scaling property of a system   27
         Vertical scaling or scale-up   27
         Horizontal scaling or scale-out   28
         Deployment challenges   28
         Organizational alignment   29
         Modularity   30
         Big database   31
   Prerequisites for microservices   31
      Functional overview of the application   33
         Solutions for the current challenges   34
         Handling deployment problems   35
         Making better monolithic applications   35
            Introducing dependency injections   35
            Database refactoring   40
            Database sharding and partitioning   41
            DevOps culture   43
            Automation   43
            Testing   43
            Versioning   44
            Deployment   44

Table of Contents

Identifying decomposition candidates within monolithic — 45
- Important microservices advantages — 46
  - Technology independence — 46
  - Interdependency removal — 46
  - Alignment with business goals — 47
  - Cost benefits — 47
  - Easy scalability — 47
  - Security — 48
    - Data management — 48
    - Integrating monolithic applications with microservices — 49
- **An overview of Azure Service Fabric** — 50
- **Summary** — 52
- **Questions** — 52

Chapter 2: Refactoring the Monolith — 53
- **Technical requirements** — 53
- **Understanding the current and new technology stack** — 54
  - Discussion – current stack (C#, EF, and SQL Server) — 54
    - C# 8 — 54
    - Entity Framework Core — 55
    - Visual Studio 2019 — 55
    - Microsoft SQL Server — 55
  - New features in .NET Core — 56
  - New features in C# 8.0 — 63
    - Enabling support for the C# 8.0 language using Visual Studio — 63
    - Indices and ranges — 65
    - The readonly members — 69
    - Default interface methods — 70
- **The size of microservices** — 71
- **What makes a good service?** — 72
- **DDD and its importance for microservices** — 73
  - Domain model design — 73
  - Importance for microservices — 74
- **Understanding the concept of seam** — 75
  - Module interdependency — 75
  - Technology — 76
  - Team structure — 76
  - Databases — 77
  - Master data — 80
  - Transactions — 81
- **Communication between microservices** — 82
  - The benefits of the API gateway for microservices — 83
  - API gateway versus API management — 84
- **Revisiting the FlixOne case study** — 84
  - Prerequisites — 85
  - Transitioning to our product service — 85
  - Migrations — 87

[ii]

Code migration	87
Creating our project	88
Adding the model	91
Adding a repository	94
Registering repositories	96
Adding a product controller	97
The ProductService API	98
Adding EF Core support	99
EF Core DbContext	99
EF Core migrations	101
Database migration	102
Revisiting repositories and the controller	102
Introducing ViewModel	103
Revisiting ProductController	105
Adding Swagger support	106
Summary	**109**
Questions	**109**
Further reading	**110**
Chapter 3: Effective Communication between Services	**111**
Technical requirements	**111**
Understanding communication between services	**112**
Styles of collaboration	114
Learning about integration patterns	**118**
The API gateway	118
The event-driven pattern	122
Event-sourcing pattern	124
Eventual consistency pattern	125
Compensating transactions	126
Competing consumers	126
Understanding Azure Service Fabric	**127**
Service Fabric architecture	127
Discussing the orchestrator	130
Service Fabric programming models overview	130
Implementing information on competing consumers	131
Azure Service Bus	131
Azure message queues	133
Implementing information on Service Fabric	133
Prerequisites	133
Sending messages to the queue	138
Adding configuration settings	140
Receiving messages from the queue	142
Implementing information on containers	143
Containers on Service Fabric	144
Prerequisites	144
Execution	144
Microservices with Kubernetes	**145**

[iii]

An overview of Azure Kubernetes Service (AKS) 145
Important concepts 146
Ease of deploying and managing microservices 146
The sidecar pattern 148
When to use the sidecar pattern 149
Best practices to be observed 150
The ambassador pattern 150
When to use the ambassador pattern 151
Best practices to be observed 152
Considering IoT when building microservices apps 152
An overview of IoT Hub 154
An overview of IoT Edge 155
Summary 156
Questions 156
Further reading 156

Chapter 4: Testing Microservices with the Microsoft Unit Testing Framework 157
Technical requirements 158
Testing the microservice application 158
Handling testing challenges with microservices 159
Understanding testing strategies 160
Testing pyramid 161
Types of microservice tests 162
Unit testing 162
Component (service) testing 163
Integration testing 163
Contract testing 164
Consumer-driven contracts 164
How to implement a consumer-driven test 165
How Pact-net-core helps us achieve our goal 165
Performance testing 167
End-to-end (UI/functional) testing 167
Sociable versus isolated unit tests 168
Stubs and mocks 168
Testing the microservice application 169
Getting ready for the test project 170
Unit tests 172
Integration tests 175
Summary 180
Questions 181
Further reading 181

Chapter 5: Deploying Microservices with Docker 183
Technical requirements 184
Monolithic application deployment challenges 185
Understanding the deployment terminology 186

[iv]

Prerequisites for successful microservice deployments	188
Isolation requirements for microservice deployment	189
The need for a new deployment paradigm	191
The way out – containers	192
What are containers?	192
Suitability of containers over virtual machines	192
Transformation of the operation team's mindset	194
Containers are new binaries	194
Does it work on your machine? Let's ship your machine!	195
Introducing Docker	195
Deploying a sample application	197
Microservice deployment example using Docker	198
Setting up Docker on your machine	198
Prerequisites	198
Creating an ASP.NET Core web application	200
Summary	205
Questions	205
Further reading	206
Chapter 6: Securing Microservices Using Azure Active Directory	207
Technical requirements	208
Security in monolithic applications	209
Security in microservices	210
Why won't a traditional .NET auth mechanism work?	210
JSON Web Tokens	212
Working with OAuth 2.0	214
Exploring OpenID Connect	216
Understanding Azure Active Directory	217
Microservice Auth example with OpenID Connect, OAuth 2.0, and Azure AD	218
Registering our application with the Azure AD tenant	219
Generating AppKey for FlixOne.BookStore.Web	225
Configuring Visual Studio solution projects	227
Generating client certificates on IIS Express	229
Running both applications	230
Managing Azure API Management as an API gateway	232
An example of a rate limit and quota policy	235
Understanding container security	236
Other security best practices	237
Summary	238
Questions	238
Further reading	238
Chapter 7: Monitoring Microservices	239
Technical requirements	240

[v]

Setting up .NET Core 3.1	241
A valid Azure account	241
Beginning with instrumentation and telemetry	241
Instrumentation	242
Telemetry	242
The need for monitoring	243
Health monitoring	243
Availability monitoring	244
SLA monitoring	244
Performance monitoring	245
Security monitoring	245
Auditing sensitive data and critical business transactions	246
End user monitoring	246
Troubleshooting system failures	246
Understanding the monitoring challenges	247
Scaling issues	247
DevOps mindset	248
Data flow visualization	248
Testing monitoring tools	249
Working on monitoring strategies	249
Application/system monitoring	249
Real user monitoring	250
Semantic monitoring and synthetic transactions	250
Profiling	250
Endpoint monitoring	251
Understanding logging	252
Logging challenges	252
Logging strategies	253
Centralized logging	253
Using a correlation ID in logging	254
Semantic logging	254
Monitoring on Azure	255
Microsoft Azure Diagnostics	256
Storing diagnostic data using Azure storage	257
Using the Azure portal	258
Defining an Azure storage account	259
Azure storage schema for diagnostic data	259
Introduction to Application Insights	261
Monitoring our FlixOne application	262
Other microservice monitoring solutions	277
A brief overview of the ELK stack	277
Elasticsearch	277
Logstash	277
Kibana	278
Splunk	278
Alerting	279

Reporting	279
Summary	280
Questions	280
Further reading	281
Chapter 8: Scaling Microservices with Azure	**283**
Technical requirements	284
Getting an overview of scalability	284
Scaling infrastructure	284
Vertical scaling (scaling up)	285
Horizontal scaling (scaling out)	285
Understanding microservice scalability	286
The Scale Cube model of scalability	286
Scaling of the x axis	287
Scaling of the z axis	288
Scaling of the y axis	288
Characteristics of a scalable microservice	289
Implementing scaling infrastructure	291
Scaling virtual machines using scale sets	292
Autoscaling	293
Container scaling using Docker Swarm	294
Scaling service design	295
Data persistence model design	295
Caching mechanism	296
CacheCow	297
Azure Cache for Redis	298
Redundancy and fault tolerance	299
Circuit breakers	299
Closed state	301
Open state	301
Half-Open state	301
Service discovery	301
Summary	302
Questions	303
Further reading	303
Chapter 9: Introduction to Reactive Microservices	**305**
Technical requirements	306
Installing Visual Studio 2019	306
Understanding reactive microservices	307
Responsiveness	307
Resilience	308
Autonomy	308
Message-driven – a core of reactive microservices	309
Making code reactive	310
Understanding event communication	311

Security — 312
    Message-level security — 312
Scalability — 313
Communication resilience — 313
Managing data — 314
Trying out the coding of reactive microservices — 317
    Creating the project — 318
        Communicating between the application and the database — 325
    Client – coding it down — 328
Summary — 329
Questions — 330
Further reading — 330

Chapter 10: Design Patterns and Best Practices — 331
Technical requirements — 331
    Installing Visual Studio 2019 — 332
The Aggregator pattern — 332
    Pros and cons — 333
    Best practices to be observed — 334
    The problem and its solution – example in FlixOne — 334
    Implementing the solution — 335
        The Common folder — 337
        The Controllers folder — 338
        The Models folder — 340
        The Persistence folder — 342
        The Services folder — 343
The Shared Data microservices pattern — 345
    Pros and cons of the pattern — 346
    Best practices to be observed — 347
    The problem and its solution – example in FlixOne — 347
    Implementing the solution — 349
        The Extensions folder — 350
        The Models folder — 352
        The Persistence folder — 356
        The Controllers folder — 359
The Anti-Corruption Layer pattern — 361
    Pros and cons — 362
    Best practices to be observed — 363
    Problem and its solution – the need for the Anti-Corruption Layer pattern — 363
    Implementing the solution — 364
        The BL folder — 365
            The Models folder — 365
        The DAL folder — 368
            The Contexts folder — 369
            The Repository folder — 369
        The Services folder — 370
            The Controllers folder — 370

Summary	372
Further reading	372
Chapter 11: Building a Microservice Application	**373**
Technical requirements	374
Installing Visual Studio 2019	374
Setting up Azure	375
Revisiting the monolithic architecture style and SOA	375
Introducing the strangler pattern	378
Understanding the business needs of an application	379
Revisiting the application	383
Building the application	384
Summary	386
Chapter 12: Microservices Architecture Summary	**387**
Technical requirements	387
Understanding architectures before microservices	388
Monolithic architecture	388
Challenges in standardizing the .NET stack	389
Scaling	389
Service-oriented architecture	389
Microservice-style architecture	390
Messaging in microservices	391
Understanding how monolith transitioning works	391
Integration techniques	392
Deployment	393
Testing microservices	393
Security	394
Monitoring the application	395
Monitoring challenges	397
Scale	397
Component lifespan	397
Information visualization	398
Understanding monitoring strategies	398
Understanding scalability	399
Infrastructure scaling	399
Service design	400
An overview of reactive microservices	400
Building a greenfield application	401
Scoping our services	401
The book-listing microservice	402
The book-searching microservice	402
The shopping-cart microservice	402
The order microservice	403
User authentication	403
Synchronous versus asynchronous	404

The book-catalog microservice	405
The shopping-cart microservice	406
The order microservice	407
The user-authentication microservice	407
An overview of cloud-native microservices	**408**
Summary	**410**

Appendix
411

Assessments
431

Other Books You May Enjoy
441

Index
445

Preface

The purpose of this book is to give you a broad understanding of microservices in modern software development while also diving into more detail with specific examples using .NET Core APIs. This book covers the theory of microservices followed by a high-level understanding of the patterns used to develop an imaginary application, where we'll cover the concepts used in solutions that can be easily configured to run in the cloud or on-premises.

Notably, microservice architecture does have critical advantages—particularly in regard to empowering the agile improvement and conveyance of complex venture applications.

However, there is no clear or practical advice on how to implement microservices in the Microsoft ecosystem, especially on how to take advantage of Azure and the .NET Core framework. This book tries to fill that void.

Although many aspects of the microservice architecture do not require a detailed explanation, we try to sum up these concepts and provide Microsoft docs links for further reading. Throughout the book, until we start developing our imaginary application, we will cover every part that is required to develop a microservice architecture-based application.

Starting with a simple API project and monolith application, the book describes various steps that you can perform to transition to microservices. To make the code examples simpler, the book uses .NET Core APIs throughout. The last chapter includes an application that shows the crux of the complete book.

Who this book is for

The target audience of this book includes application developers who want to find a one-stop shop of best practices for architecting a high-performing application in the Azure cloud. This book applies to all developers of Azure. It is also aimed at developers who want to learn about and understand microservice architecture and implement it in their .NET Core applications. This book has been written/updated in such a way that novice-to-advanced-level users will be covered. It's ideal for developers who are completely new to microservices or only have a theoretical understanding of this architectural approach and want to gain a practical perspective in order to better manage the complexity of their application.

What this book covers

Chapter 1, *An Introduction to Microservices*, discusses the basics of microservices, reviews a monolith application, and uncovers its limitations. You will also learn how to start the transition to a microservices architecture.

Chapter 2, *Refactoring the Monolith*, discusses the current stack of the application. It also covers the features of .NET Core and C#8, demonstrates how to implement separate microservices, and looks at communication between microservices.

Chapter 3, *Effective Communication between Services*, covers communication between services, including synchronous and asynchronous communication, and an overview of Azure Service Bus. Additionally, the chapter examines integration with the help of an integration pattern. An overview of Azure Service Fabric is followed by a look at Docker and containers, as well as an overview of Azure Kubernetes Service, IoT Hub, and IoT Edge.

Chapter 4, *Testing Microservices with the Microsoft Unit Testing Framework*, covers various types of services and their differences. Here you will implement testing approaches using the Microsoft Unit Testing Framework, Moq, and the ASP.NET Core API.

Chapter 5, *Deploying Microservices with Docker*, covers the deployment paradigm and explains deployment terminology.

Chapter 6, *Securing Microservices Using Azure Active Directory*, uncovers the concept of securing microservices by deploying a sample application using Azure Active Directory.

Chapter 7, *Monitoring Microservices*, covers instrumentation and telemetry, followed by monitoring strategies, logging, and monitoring in the cloud.

Chapter 8, *Scaling Microservices with Azure*, explores scalability, infrastructure scaling, and microservices scaling. The chapter also presents an overview of Azure Redis Cache.

Chapter 9, *Introduction to Reactive Microservices*, introduces you to reactive microservices with the help of code examples.

Chapter 10, *Design Patterns and Best Practices*, covers high-level patterns to help build microservices, as well as Aggregator, DDD, API gateways, the Shared Data microservices pattern, the anti-corruption layer pattern, and BFF.

Chapter 11, *Building a Microservice Application*, examines the various approaches that are available to develop a real-world application.

`Chapter 12`, *Microservices Architecture Summary*, looks at how applications could evolve in the future by following the microservices approach.

`Appendix`, explains about the API Gateway pattern and the Backends to Frontends pattern, in terms of their pros and cons, to help us understand their best practices.

To get the most out of this book

This book assumes that you have some familiarity with SOA, RESTful web services, APIs, server/client architectures, .NET Core, ASP.NET Core, and C#. This book covers advanced topics, basic concepts, and an overview of technologies such as Kubernetes and IoT Edge. The book's contents are designed to get you started with the development of a microservices-based application. It can also be used as a comprehensive guide. Using a toolbox analogy, the book provides a large number of tools for the modern application developer, progressing from low-level code design to higher-level architecture, as well as important concepts, patterns, and best practices commonly used today for the development of microservices-based applications.

This book will cover the following main points:

- The details of microservices, including in-depth details of monolith versus SOA versus microservices architectures
- Examples using C#8 and ASP.NET Core 3
- An overview of the current application stack and the new stack to develop microservices via an imaginary application
- In-depth discussion of design patterns and best practices using demo application

You need to install Visual Studio 2019 (Community edition preferably) with the latest update. All code examples have been tested using .NET Core 3.1 on Windows OS. However, they should work with future version releases too.

Software/Hardware covered in the book	OS requirements
ASP.NET Core 3.1	Windows
C# 8	Windows
SQL Server 2008R2	Windows
SQL Server 2017	Windows

If you are using the digital version of this book, we advise you to type the code yourself or access the code via the GitHub repository (link available in the next section). Doing so will help you avoid any potential errors related to copy/pasting of code.

Preface

> Few of the code example uses Angular 8 to showcase the UI part. There is no code for these component as these are only for UI and you would require to setup Angular 8 on your Windows OS.

Download the example code files

You can download the example code files for this book from your account at `www.packt.com`. If you purchased this book elsewhere, you can visit `www.packt.com/support` and register to have the files emailed directly to you.

You can download the code files by following these steps:

1. Log in or register at `www.packt.com`.
2. Select the **SUPPORT** tab.
3. Click on **Code Downloads & Errata**.
4. Enter the name of the book in the **Search** box and follow the onscreen instructions.

Once the file is downloaded, please make sure that you unzip or extract the folder using the latest version of:

- WinRAR/7-Zip for Windows
- Zipeg/iZip/UnRarX for Mac
- 7-Zip/PeaZip for Linux

The code bundle for the book is also hosted on GitHub at `https://github.com/PacktPublishing/Hands-On-Microservices-with-CSharp-8-and-.NET-Core-3-Third-Edition`. In case there's an update to the code, it will be updated on the existing GitHub repository.

We also have other code bundles from our rich catalog of books and videos available at `https://github.com/PacktPublishing/`. Check them out!

Download the color images

We also provide a PDF file that has color images of the screenshots/diagrams used in this book. You can download it here: `https://static.packt-cdn.com/downloads/9781789617948_ColorImages.pdf`

Conventions used

There are a number of text conventions used throughout this book.

`CodeInText`: Indicates code words in text, database table names, folder names, filenames, file extensions, pathnames, dummy URLs, user input, and Twitter handles. Here is an example: "The preceding code declares two `readonly` properties with preassigned values."

A block of code is set as follows:

```
Range book = 1..4;
var res = Books[book] ;
Console.WriteLine($"\tElement of array using Range: Books[{book}] => {Books[book]}");
```

When we wish to draw your attention to a particular part of a code block, the relevant lines or items are set in bold:

```
private static readonly int num1=5;
private static readonly int num2=6;
```

Any command-line input or output is written as follows:

```
dotnet --info
```

Bold: Indicates a new term, an important word, or words that you see on screen. For example, words in menus or dialog boxes appear in the text like this. Here is an example: "Select **System info** from the **Administration** panel."

> Warnings or important notes appear like this.

> Tips and tricks appear like this.

[5]

Get in touch

Feedback from our readers is always welcome.

General feedback: If you have questions about any aspect of this book, mention the book title in the subject of your message and email us at `customercare@packtpub.com`.

Errata: Although we have taken every care to ensure the accuracy of our content, mistakes do happen. If you have found a mistake in this book, we would be grateful if you would report this to us. Please visit `www.packt.com/submit-errata`, selecting your book, clicking on the Errata Submission Form link, and entering the details.

Piracy: If you come across any illegal copies of our works in any form on the internet, we would be grateful if you would provide us with the location address or website name. Please contact us at `copyright@packt.com` with a link to the material.

If you are interested in becoming an author: If there is a topic that you have expertise in and you are interested in either writing or contributing to a book, please visit `authors.packtpub.com`.

Reviews

Please leave a review. Once you have read and used this book, why not leave a review on the site that you purchased it from? Potential readers can then see and use your unbiased opinion to make purchase decisions, we at Packt can understand what you think about our products, and our authors can see your feedback on their book. Thank you!

For more information about Packt, please visit `packt.com`.

An Introduction to Microservices

The focus of this chapter is to get you acquainted with microservices. Slicing your application into a number of services is neither a feature of **service-oriented architecture** (**SOA**) nor microservices. However, microservices combines service design with best practices from the SOA world, along with a few emerging practices, such as isolated deployment, semantic versioning, providing lightweight services, and service discovery in polyglot programming. We implement microservices to satisfy business features, reducing the time to market and increasing flexibility.

We will cover the following topics in this chapter:

- The origin of microservices
- Discussing microservices
- Understanding the microservice architecture
- The advantages of microservices
- SOA versus microservices
- Understanding the problems with the monolithic architectural style
- The challenges in standardizing a .NET stack
- An overview of Azure Service Fabric

In this chapter, we will become familiar with the problems that arise from having a layered monolithic architecture. We will also discuss the solutions available for these problems in the monolithic world. By the end of the chapter, we will be able to break down a monolithic application into a microservice architecture.

Technical requirements

This chapter contains various code examples to explain the concepts. The code is kept simple and is just for demo purposes.

To run and execute the code, you will need the following prerequisites:

- Visual Studio 2019
- .NET Core 3.1

To install and run these code examples, you need to install Visual Studio 2019 (the preferred IDE). To do so, download Visual Studio 2019 (the Community edition, which is free) from the download link mentioned in the installation instructions: `https://docs.microsoft.com/en-us/visualstudio/install/install-visual-studio`. Multiple versions are available for the Visual Studio installation. We are using Visual Studio for Windows.

If you do not have .NET Core 3.1 installed, you can download it from the following link: `https://www.microsoft.com/net/download/windows`.

> The complete source code is available here: `https://github.com/PacktPublishing/Hands-On-Microservices-with-CSharp-8-and-.NET-Core-3-Third-Edition/tree/master/Chapter%2001`

The origin of microservices

Before we discuss the details, we should explore the origin of microservices or any new framework, language, and so on. Microservices is a buzzword, and we should be aware of how this architectural style evolved to the point that it is now trending. There are several reasons to familiarize yourself with the origin of any language or framework. The most important things to know are as follows:

- How the specific language or framework came into context.
- Who is behind the new trending architectural style of microservices?
- What and where it was founded.

Now let's discuss the origin of microservices. The term **microservices** was used for the first time in mid-2011 at a workshop for software architects. In March 2012, James Lewis presented some of his ideas about microservices. By the end of 2013, various groups from the IT industry started having discussions about microservices, and by 2014, the concept had become popular enough to be considered a serious contender for large enterprises.

There is no official definition available for microservices. The understanding of the term is purely based on use cases and discussions held in the past.

In 2014, James Lewis and Martin Fowler came together and provided a few real-world examples as well as presenting microservices (refer to `http://martinfowler.com/microservices/`).

> The development of a single application by combining small services (running on their processes) is called a microservice architectural style. Each service carries business capabilities and is independently deployed. Moreover, these services can be written in different languages and have different database storage.

The official Microsoft document page for microservices (refer to `https://docs.microsoft.com/en-us/azure/architecture/guide/architecture-styles/microservices`) defines the microservices architectural style as follows:

> *"Microservices architecture is a bunch of services, where each service is independently deployed and should implement a single business capability."*

It is very important that you see all the attributes Lewis and Fowler defined here. They defined microservices as an architectural style that developers can utilize to develop a single application with the business logic spread across a bunch of small services, each having their own persistent storage functionality. Also, note its attributes: it can be independently deployable, can run in its own process, is a lightweight communication mechanism, and can be written in different programming languages.

We want to emphasize this specific definition since it is the crux of the whole concept. As we move along, all the pieces will fit together by the time we finish this book. For now, we will look at microservices in detail.

Discussing microservices

We have gone through a few definitions of microservices; now let's discuss them in detail.

In short, a microservice architecture removes most of the drawbacks of SOA. It is also more code-oriented than SOA services (we will discuss this in detail in the coming sections).

Before we move on to understanding the architecture, let's discuss the two important architectures that led to its existence:

- The monolithic architecture style
- SOA

Most of us know that when we develop an enterprise application, we have to select a suitable architectural style. Then, at various stages, the initial pattern is further improved and adapted with changes that cater to various challenges, such as deployment complexity, a large code base, and scalability issues. This is exactly how the monolithic architecture style evolved into SOA, and then led to microservices.

Exploring monolithic architecture

The monolithic architectural style is a traditional architecture type that has been widely used in the IT industry. The term monolithic is not new and is borrowed from the Unix world. In Unix, most commands exist as a standalone program whose functionality is not dependent on any other program. As seen in the following diagram, we can have different components in the application, including the following:

- **User interface**: This handles all of the user interactions while responding with HTML, JSON, or any other preferred data interchange format (in the case of web services).
- **Business logic**: This includes all the business rules applied to the input being received in the form of user input, events, and the database.
- **Database access**: This houses the complete functionality for accessing the database for the purpose of querying and persisting objects. A widely accepted rule is that it is utilized through business modules and never directly through user-facing components.

Software built using this architecture is self-contained. We can imagine a single .NET assembly that contains various components, as depicted in the following diagram:

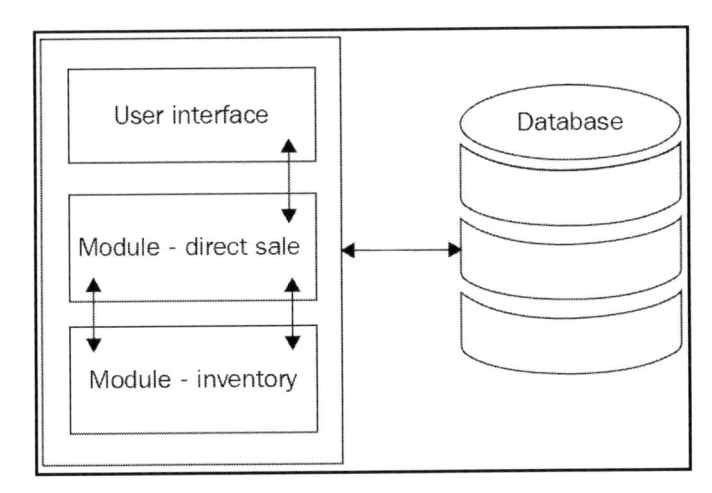

```
┌─────────────────────────────┐
│  ┌───────────────────┐      │       ┌──────────────┐
│  │  User interface   │      │       │   Database   │
│  └─────────▲─────────┘      │       ╞══════════════╡
│            ▼                │       │              │
│  ┌───────────────────┐      │◄─────►╞══════════════╡
│  │ Module - direct sale │   │       │              │
│  └──▲──────────────▲──┘     │       └──────────────┘
│     ▼              ▼        │
│  ┌───────────────────┐      │
│  │ Module - inventory │     │
│  └───────────────────┘      │
└─────────────────────────────┘
```

As the software is self-contained here, its components are interconnected and interdependent. Even a simple code change in one of the modules may break a major functionality in other modules. This would result in a scenario in which we'd need to test the whole application. With the business depending critically on its enterprise application frameworks, this amount of time could prove to be very critical.

Having all the components tightly coupled poses another challenge: whenever we execute or compile such software, all the components should be available or the build will fail. Refer to the previous diagram, which represents a monolithic architecture and is a self-contained or a single .NET assembly project. However, monolithic architectures might also have multiple assemblies. This means that even though a business layer (assembly, data access layer assembly, and so on) is separated, all of them will come together and run as one process at runtime.

A user interface depends on other components' direct sales and inventory in a manner similar to all other components that depend upon each other. In this scenario, we would not be able to execute this project in the absence of any one of these components. The process of upgrading them would be more complex, as we would have to consider other components that require code changes too. This would result in more development time than is required for the actual change.

Deploying such an application would become another challenge. During deployment, we would have to make sure that every component was deployed properly. If we didn't do this, we may end up facing a lot of issues in our production environments.

An Introduction to Microservices

If we develop an application using the monolithic architecture style, as discussed previously, we might face the following challenges:

- **Large code base**: This is a scenario where the code lines outnumber the comments by a great margin. As components are interconnected, we would have to deal with a repetitive code base.
- **Too many business modules**: This is in regard to modules within the same system.
- **Code base complexity**: This results in a higher chance of code breaking due to the fix required in other modules or services.
- **Complex code deployment**: You may come across minor changes that would require whole system deployment.
- **One module failure affecting the whole system**: This is with regard to modules that depend on each other.
- **Scalability**: This is required for the entire system and not just the modules in it.
- **Intermodule dependency**: This is due to tight coupling. This results in heavy changes if required for an operation of any of the modules.

> Tight coupling is a scenario in which one class is intended for many responsibilities, or in other words, when classes (mostly a group of classes) are dependent on each other.

- **Spiraling development time**: This is due to code complexity and interdependency.
- **Inability to easily adapt to new technology**: In this case, the entire system would need to be upgraded.

As discussed earlier, if we want to reduce development time, ease deployment, and improve the maintainability of software for enterprise applications, we should avoid traditional or monolithic architecture. Therefore, we will look at SOA.

Service-oriented architecture

In the previous section, we discussed the monolithic architecture and its limitations. We also discussed why it does not fit into our enterprise application requirements. To overcome these issues, we should take a modular approach where we can separate the components so that they come out of the self-contained or single .NET assembly. A system that uses a service or multiple services in the fashion depicted in the previous diagram is called a **service-oriented architecture** (**SOA**).

> The main difference between SOA and monolithic architecture is not one or multiple assemblies. As the service in SOA runs as a separate process, SOA scales better in comparison.

Let's discuss modular architecture, that is, SOA. This is a famous architectural style where enterprise applications are designed as a collection of services. These services may be RESTful or ASMX web services. To understand SOA in more detail, let's discuss services first.

Understanding services

Services, in this case, are an essential concept of SOA. They can be a piece of code, a program, or software that provides functionality to other system components. This piece of code can interact directly with the database or indirectly through another service. Furthermore, it can be consumed by clients directly, where the client may be a website, desktop app, mobile app, or any other device app. The following diagram shows that services can be consumed by various clients via the web, desktop, mobile, or any other devices. Services can be with or without database support at the backend:

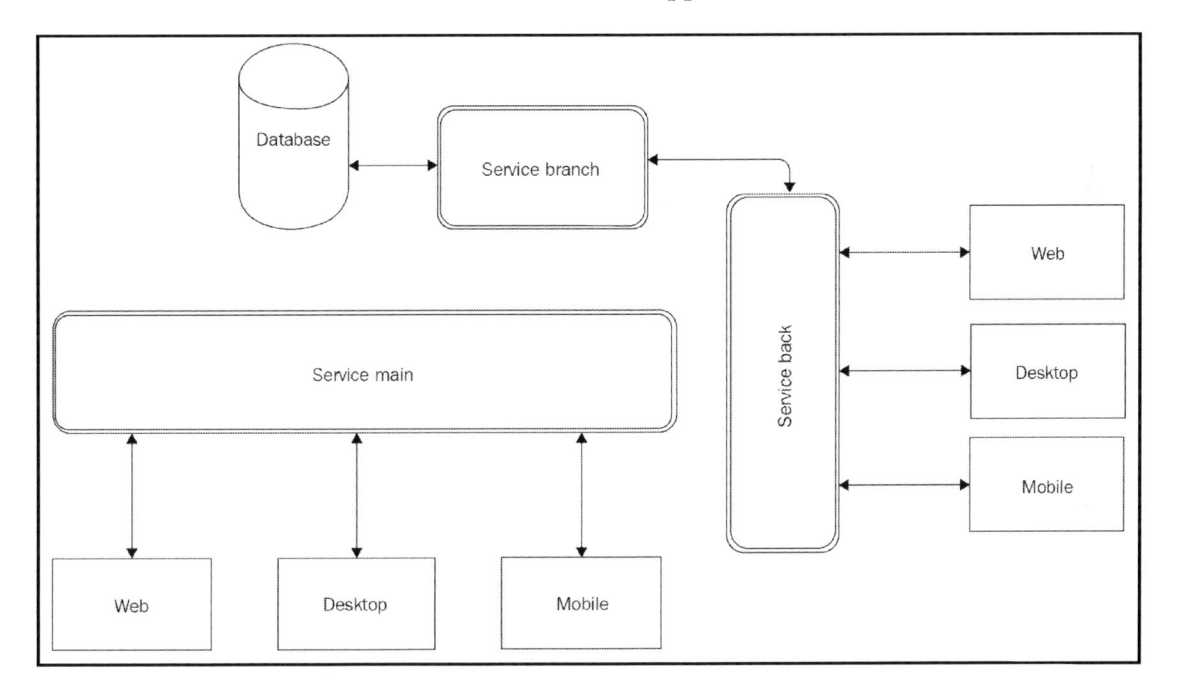

An Introduction to Microservices

A service refers to a type of functionality exposed for consumption by other systems (generally referred to as **clients/client applications**). As mentioned earlier, this can be represented by a piece of code, a program, or software. Such services are exposed over the HTTP transport protocol as a general practice. However, the HTTP protocol is not a limiting factor, and a protocol can be picked as deemed fit for the scenario.

In the following diagram, **Service - direct selling** is directly interacting with the **Database** and three different clients, namely, **Web**, **Desktop**, and **Mobile**, are consuming the service. On the other hand, we have clients consuming **Service - partner selling**, which is interacting with **Service - channel partners** for database access.

A product selling service is a set of services that interact with client applications and provide database access directly or through another service, in this case, **Service – Channel partners**. In the case of **Service – direct selling**, shown in the following diagram, it is providing the functionality to a web store, a desktop application, and a mobile application. This service is further interacting with the database for various tasks, namely, fetching and persisting data.

Normally, services interact with other systems via a communication channel, generally the HTTP protocol. These services may or may not be deployed on the same or single servers:

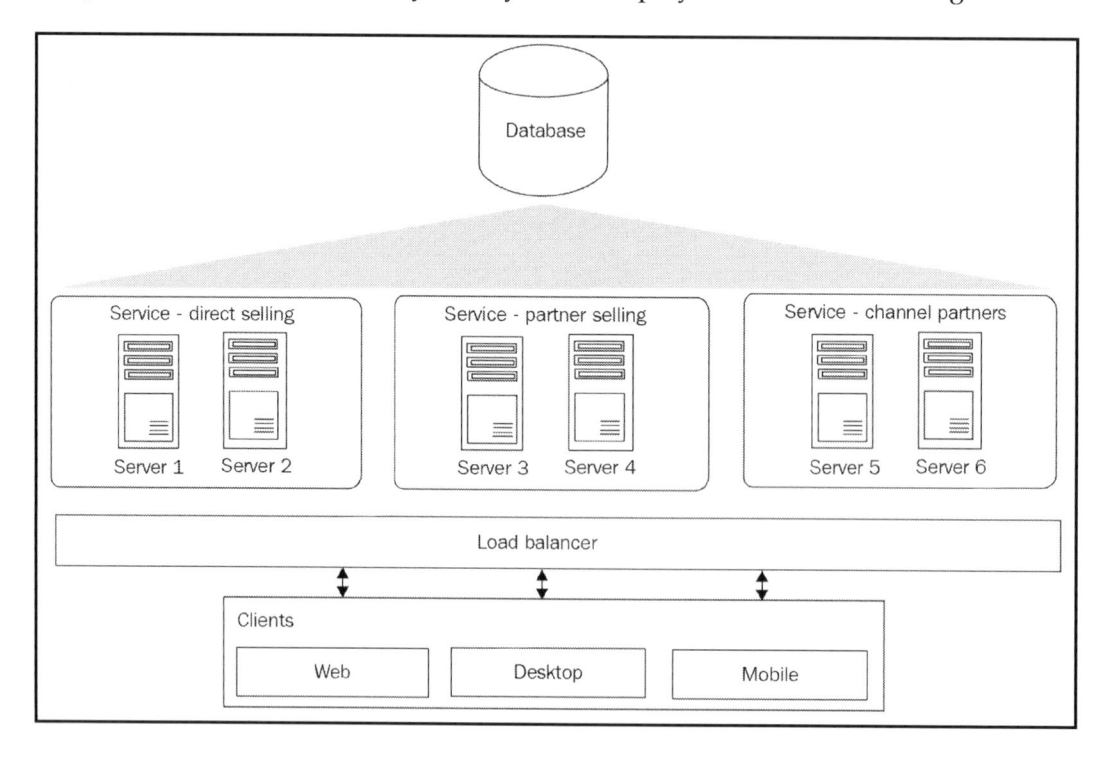

Chapter 1

In the previous diagram, we have projected an SOA example scenario. There are many fine points to note here, so let's get started. First, our services can be spread across different physical machines. Here, **Service - direct selling** is hosted on two separate machines. It is possible that instead of the entire business functionality, only a part of it will reside on **Server 1** and the remaining part on **Server 2**. Similarly, **Service - partner selling** appears to have the same arrangement on **Server 3** and **Server 4**. However, it doesn't stop **Service - channel partners** from being hosted as a complete set on both **Server 5** and **Server 6**.

We will discuss SOA in detail in the following sections.

Let's recall monolithic architecture. In this case, we did not use it because it restricts code reusability; it is a self-contained assembly, and all the components are interconnected and interdependent. For deployment, in this case, we will have to deploy our complete project after we select the SOA (refer to the previous diagram and the subsequent discussion). Now, because of the use of this architectural style, we have the benefit of code reusability and easy deployment. Let's examine this in the light of the previous diagram:

- **Reusability**: Multiple clients can consume the service. This can also be simultaneously consumed by other services. For example, `OrderService` is consumed by web and mobile clients. `OrderService` can now also be used by the Reporting Dashboard UI.
- **Stateless**: Services do not persist in any state between requests from the client. This means that the service doesn't know or care that the subsequent request has come from the client that has/hasn't made the previous request.
- **Contract-based:** Interfaces make any service technology-agnostic on both sides of implementation and consumption. They also serve to make it immune to the code updates in the underlying functionality.
- **Scalability**: A system can be scaled up, and the SOA can be individually clustered with the appropriate load balancing.
- **Upgradeability**: It is very easy to roll out new functionalities or introduce new versions of the existing functionality. The system doesn't stop you from keeping multiple versions of the same business functionality.

This section covered SOA, and we have also discussed the concept of services and how they impact architecture. Next, we will move on to learn all about microservice architecture.

Understanding microservice architecture

Microservice architecture is a way to develop a single application containing a set of smaller services. These services are independent of each other and run in their own processes. An important advantage of these services is that they can be developed and deployed independently. In other words, we can say that microservices are a way to segregate our services so that they can be handled completely independently of each other in the context of design, development, deployment, and upgrades.

In a monolithic application, we have a self-contained assembly of a user interface, direct sales, and inventory. In microservice architecture, the parts of the services of the application change to the following depiction:

Here, business components have been segregated into individual services. These independent services are now the smaller units that existed earlier within the self-contained assembly in the monolithic architecture. Both direct sales and inventory services are independent of each other, with the dotted lines depicting their existence in the same ecosystem, not yet bound within a single scope.

Refer to the following diagram, depicting user interaction with different APIs:

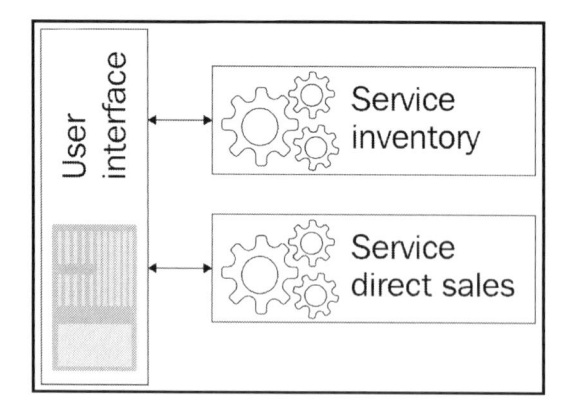

Chapter 1

From the previous diagram, it's clear that our user interface can interact with any services. There is no need to intervene with any service when a UI calls it. Both services are independent of each other, without being aware of when the other one would be called by the user interface. Both services are liable for their own operations and not for any other part of the whole system. Although we are much closer to the layout of our intended microservice architecture. Note that the previous representation of the layout is not entirely a complete visualization of the intended microservice architecture.

> **TIP**
> In microservice architecture, services are small, independent units with their own persistent stores.

Now let's apply this final change so that each service will have its own database persisting the necessary data. Refer to the following diagram:

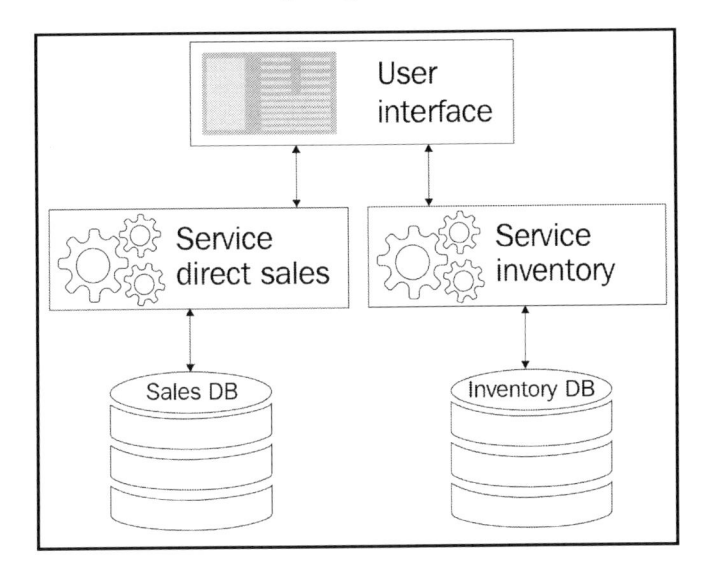

Here, the **User interface** is interacting with the services, which have their own independent storage. In this case, when a user interface calls the service for direct sales, the business flow for direct sales is executed independently of any data or logic contained within the inventory service.

[17]

An Introduction to Microservices

The solution provided by the use of microservices has a lot of benefits, including the following:

- **A smaller code base**: Each service is small and therefore easier to develop and deploy as a unit.
- **The ease of an independent environment**: With the separation of services, all developers work independently, deploy independently, and no one is concerned about module dependency.

With the adoption of microservice architecture, monolithic applications are now harnessing the associated benefits, as they can now be scaled easily and deployed independently using a service.

Messaging in microservices

It is very important to carefully consider the choice of messaging mechanism when dealing with microservice architecture. If this aspect is ignored, it can compromise the entire purpose of designing a microservice architecture. In monolithic applications, this is not a concern, as the business functionality of the components gets invoked through function calls. On the other hand, this happens via a loosely coupled web service-level messaging feature in which services are primarily based on SOAP. In the case of the microservice messaging mechanism, this should be simple and lightweight.

There are no set rules for making a choice between the various frameworks or protocols for microservice architecture. However, there are a few points worth considering here. First, it should be simple enough to implement, without adding any complexity to your system. Second, it should be very lightweight, keeping in mind the fact that the microservice architecture could heavily rely on interservice messaging. Let's move ahead and consider our choices for both synchronous and asynchronous messaging, along with the different messaging formats.

Synchronous messaging

Synchronous messaging is when a timely response is expected from service by a system, and the system waits until a response is received from the service. What's left is the most sought-after choice in the case of microservices. This is simple and supports an HTTP request-response, thereby leaving little room to look for an alternative. This is also one of the reasons that most implementations of microservices use HTTP (API-based styles).

Asynchronous messaging

Asynchronous messaging is when a system does not immediately expect a timely response from the service, and the system can continue processing without blocking that call.

Let's incorporate this messaging concept into our application and see how it would change the working and look of our application:

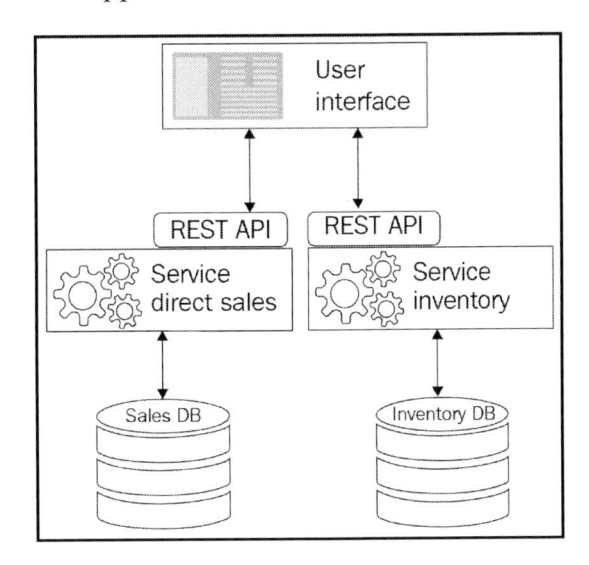

In the preceding diagram, the user would get a response while the system is interacting with the **Sales DB** and/or **Inventory DB** service(s) and fetch or push the data to their respective databases. The calls from the user (via the **User interface**) to respective services would not block new calls from the same or different users.

Message formats

Over the past few years, working with MVC and the like has got me hooked on the JSON format. You could also consider XML. Both formats would be fine on HTTP with the API style resource. Binary message formats are also available if you need to use one. We are not recommending any particular format; you can go ahead with your preferred message format.

Using microservices

Tremendous patterns and architectures have been explored by the community, with some gaining popularity. With each solution having its own advantages and disadvantages, it has become increasingly important for companies to quickly respond to fundamental demands, such as scalability, high performance, and easy deployment. Any single aspect failing to be fulfilled in a cost-effective manner could easily impact large businesses negatively, making a big difference between a profitable and a non-profitable venture.

> We will discuss scalability in detail in `Chapter 8`, *Scaling Microservices with Azure*.

With the help of this architectural style, stakeholders can ensure that their designs are protected against the problems mentioned previously. It is also important to consider the fact that this objective is met in a cost-effective manner while respecting the time involved.

Let's see how microservice architecture works.

The workings of microservice architecture

Microservice architecture is an architectural style that structures an application as a collection of loosely coupled services. These services can intercommunicate or be independent of each other. The overall working architecture of a microservice-based application depends on the various patterns that are used to develop the application. For example, microservices could be based on backend or frontend patterns. We will discuss various patterns in `Chapter 10`, *Design Patterns and Best Practices*.

Up until this point, we have discussed various aspects of microservice architecture, and we can now depict how it works; we can use any combination according to our design approach or predict a pattern that would fit. Here are some benefits of working with microservice architecture:

- In the current era of programming, everyone is expected to follow all of the SOLID principles. Almost all languages are **object-oriented programming (OOP)**.

- It is the best way is to expose functionality to other, or external, components in a way that allows any other programming language to use that functionality without adhering to any specific user interfaces (that is, services such as web services, APIs, REST services, and so on).
- The whole system works according to a type of collaboration that is not interconnected or interdependent.
- Every component is liable for its own responsibilities. In other words, components are responsible for only one functionality.
- It segregates code with a separation concept, and segregated code is reusable.

The advantages of microservices

Now let's explore and discuss various factors as advantages of microservices over the SOA and monolithic architectures:

- **Cost-effective to scale**: You don't need to invest a lot to make the entire application scalable. In terms of a shopping cart, we could simply load balance the product search module and the order-processing module while leaving out less frequently used operational services, such as inventory management, order cancellation, and delivery confirmation.
- **Clear code boundaries**: The code should match an organization's departmental hierarchies. With different departments sponsoring product development in large enterprises, this can be a huge advantage.
- **Easier code changes**: The code is done in a way that is not dependent on the code of other modules and only achieves isolated functionality. If done right, then the chances of a change in a microservice affecting another microservice are minimal.
- **Easy deployment**: Since the entire application is more like a group of ecosystems that are isolated from each other, deployment can be done one microservice at a time, if required. Failure in any one of these would not bring the entire system down.
- **Technology adaptation**: You could port a single microservice or a whole bunch of them overnight to a different technology, without your users even knowing about it. Remember to maintain those service contracts.

- **Distributed system**: The meaning is implied here, but a word of caution is necessary. Make sure that your asynchronous calls are used well and synchronous ones are not really blocking the whole flow of information. Use data partitioning well. We will come to this a little later, in the *Data partition* section of this chapter, so don't worry for now.
- **Quick market response**: The world being competitive is a definite advantage. Users tend to quickly lose interest if you are slow to respond to new feature requests or the adoption of new technology within your system.

So far, we have covered SOA and microservice architecture. We have discussed each in detail. We also saw how each is independent. In the next section, we will understand the differences between microservices and SOA.

SOA versus microservices

You'll get confused between microservices and SOA if you don't have a complete understanding of both. On the surface, the microservice features and advantages sound almost like a slender version of SOA, with many experts suggesting that there is, in fact, no need for an additional term such as **microservices** and that SOA can fulfill all the attributes laid out by microservices. However, this is not the case. There are enough differences to isolate them technologically.

The underlying communication system of SOA inherently suffers from the following problems:

- The fact that a system developed in SOA depends upon its components, which are interacting with each other. So, no matter how hard you try, it is eventually going to face a bottleneck in the message queue.
- Another focal point of SOA is imperative monogramming. With this, we lose the path to make a unit of code reusable with respect to OOP.

We all know that organizations are spending more and more on infrastructure. The bigger the enterprise is, the more complex the question of the ownership of the application being developed. With an increasing number of stakeholders, it becomes impossible to accommodate all of their ever-changing business needs.

Chapter 1

> In SOA, the development of services can be managed and organized within multiple teams. On the other hand, services can be developed, operated, and deployed independently when working with microservices. This helps to deploy new versions of services easily.
>
> SOA uses an **enterprise service bus** (**ESB**) for communication; an ESB can be the reason for communication failures and can impact the entire application. This could happen in a scenario where one service is slowing down and communication is delayed, hampering the workings of the entire application. On the other hand, it would not be a problem in microservices; in the case of independent services, if one service is down, then only that microservice will be affected. In the case of interdependent services, if one of the services is down, then only a particular service(s) will be affected. The other microservices will continue to handle requests.
>
> Data storage is common/sharable in the case of SOA. On the other hand, each service can have independent data storage in microservices.

This is where microservices clearly stand apart. Although cloud development is not in the current scope of our discussion, it won't harm us to say that the scalability, modularity, and adaptability of microservice architecture can be easily extended with the use of cloud platforms. It's time for a change.

Let's look at the prerequisites of microservice architecture.

The prerequisites of microservice architecture

It is important to understand the resulting ecosystem from a microservice architecture implementation. The impact of microservices is not just pre-operational in nature. The changes in any organization opting for microservice architecture are so profound that if they are not well prepared to handle them, it won't be long before advantages turn into disadvantages.

After the adoption of microservice architecture is agreed upon, it would be wise to have the following prerequisites in place:

- **Deployment and QA**: Requirements will become more demanding, with a quicker turnaround from development requirements. This will require you to deploy and test as quickly as possible. If it is just a small number of services, then this will not be a problem. However, if the number of services is increasing, it could very quickly challenge the existing infrastructure and practices. For example, your QA and staging environment may no longer suffice to test the number of builds that come back from the development team.
- **A collaboration platform for the development and operations team**: As the application goes to the public domain, it won't be long before the age-old script of development versus QA is played out again. The difference this time would be that the business would be at stake. So, you need to be prepared to quickly respond in an automated manner to identify the root cause when required.
- **A monitoring framework**: With the increasing number of microservices, you will quickly need a way to monitor the functioning and health of the entire system for any possible bottlenecks or issues. Without any means of monitoring the status of the deployed microservices and the resultant business function, it would be impossible for any team to take a proactive deployment approach.

This section explained the prerequisites of a microservice architecture-based application. With them in place, the next section will help us understand the problems with a monolithic .NET stack-based application.

Understanding the problems with the monolithic architectural style

In this section, we will discuss all the problems with the monolithic .NET stack-based application. In a monolithic application, the core problem is this: scaling monolithic applications is difficult. The resultant application ends up having a very large code base and poses challenges with regard to maintainability, deployment, and modifications. In the coming sections, we will learn about scaling, and then we will move on to deployment challenges by following scaling properties.

The challenges in standardizing a .NET stack

In monolithic application technology, stack dependency stops the introduction of the latest technologies from the outside world. The present stack poses challenges, as a web service itself will suffer from them:

- **Security**: There is no way to identify the user via web services due to there being no clear consensus on a strong authentication scheme. Just imagine a banking application sending unencrypted data containing user credentials. All airports, cafes, and public places offering free Wi-Fi could easily become victims of increased identity theft and other cybercrimes.
- **Response time**: Though the web services themselves provide some flexibility in the overall architecture, it quickly diminishes because of the long processing time taken by the service itself. So, there is nothing wrong with the web service in this scenario. It is a fact that a monolithic application involves a huge amount of code; complex logic makes the response time of a web service long, and therefore unacceptable.
- **Throughput rate**: This is on the higher side, and as a result, hampers subsequent operations. It is not a bad idea for a checkout operation to rely on a call to the inventory web service that has to search for a few million records. However, when the same inventory service feeds the main product searching for the entire portal, it could result in a loss of business. One service call failure out of 10 calls would mean a 10% lower conversion rate for the business.
- **Frequent downtime**: As the web services are part of the whole monolithic ecosystem, they are bound to be down and unavailable each time there is an upgrade or an application failure. This means that the presence of any B2B dependency from the outside world on the application's web services would further complicate decision-making, thereby causing downtime. This makes the smaller upgrades of the system look expensive; thus, it further increases the backlog of the pending system upgrades.
- **Technology adoption**: In order to adopt or upgrade a technology stack, it would require the whole application to be upgraded, tested, and deployed, since modules are interdependent and the entire code base of the project would be affected. Consider the payment gateway module using a component that requires a compliance-related framework upgrade. The development team has no option but to upgrade the framework itself and carefully go through the entire code base to identify any code breaks preemptively. Of course, this would still not rule out a production crash, but this can easily make even the best of architects and managers lose sleep.

- **Availability**: A percentage of time during which a service is operating.
- **Response time**: The time a service takes to respond.
- **Throughput**: The rate of processing requests.

Fault tolerance

Monolithic applications have high module interdependency, as they are tightly coupled. The different modules utilize functionality in such an intra-module manner that even a single module failure brings the system down, due to its cascading effect. We all know that a user not getting results for a product search would be far less severe than the entire system coming down to its knees.

Decoupling using web services has been traditionally attempted at the architecture level. For database-level strategies, ACID has been relied upon for a long time. Let's examine both of these points further:

- **Web services**: In the current monolithic application, the customer experience is degraded due to using web services. Even as a customer tries to place an order, reasons, such as the long response time of web services or even a complete failure of the service itself, result in a failure to place the order successfully. Not even a single failure is acceptable, as users tend to remember their last experience and assume a possible repeat. Not only does this result in the loss of possible sales, but also the loss of future business prospects. Web service failures can cause a cascading failure in the system that relies on them.
- **ACID**: ACID is the acronym for **atomicity, consistency, isolation, and durability**; it's an important concept in databases. It is in place, but whether it's a boon or a bane is to be judged by the sum total of the combined performance. It takes care of failures at the database level, and there is no doubt that it does provide some insurance against database errors that creep in. At the same time, every ACID operation hampers/delays operations by other components/modules. The point at which it causes more harm than benefit needs to be judged very carefully.

The monolithic application that will be transitioned to microservices has various challenges related to security, response time, scalability, and moreover, its modules are highly dependent on each other. These are all big challenges while trying to deal with a standard application, but especially a monolithic application, which is supposed to be used for a high volume of users. The main and important point here for our monolithic application is scalability, which will be discussed in the next section.

The scaling property of a system

Factors, such as the availability of different means of communication, easy access to information, and open-world markets, are resulting in businesses growing rapidly and diversifying at the same time. With this rapid growth, there is an ever-increasing need to accommodate an increasing client base. Scaling is one of the biggest challenges that any business faces while trying to cater to an increased user base.

Scalability describes the capability of a system/program to handle an increasing workload. In other words, scalability refers to the ability of a system/program to scale.

Before starting the next section, let's discuss scaling in detail, as this will be an integral part of our exercise, as we work on transitioning from monolithic architecture to microservices.

There are two main strategies or types of scalability:

1. Vertical scaling or scale-up
2. Horizontal scaling or scale-out

We can scale our application by adopting one of these types of strategies. Let's discuss more about these two types of scaling and see how we can scale our application.

Vertical scaling or scale-up

In vertical scaling, we analyze our existing application to find the parts of the modules that cause the application to slow down, due to a longer execution time. Making the code more efficient could be one strategy, so that less memory is consumed. This exercise of reducing memory consumption could be for a specific module or the whole application. On the other hand, due to obvious challenges involved with this strategy, instead of changing the application, we could add more resources to our existing IT infrastructure, such as upgrading the RAM or adding more disk drives. Both these paths in vertical scaling have a limit to the extent to which they can be beneficial. After a specific point in time, the resulting benefit will plateau. It is important to keep in mind that this kind of scaling requires downtime.

Horizontal scaling or scale-out

In horizontal scaling, we dig deep into modules that show a higher impact on the overall performance for factors such as high concurrency; this will enable our application to serve our increased user base, which is now reaching the million mark. We also implement load balancing to process a greater amount of work. The option of adding more servers to the cluster does not require downtime, which is a definite advantage. Each case is different, so whether the additional costs of power, licenses, and cooling are worthwhile, and up to what point, will be evaluated on a case-by-case basis.

> Scaling will be covered in detail in `Chapter 8`, *Scaling Microservices with Azure*.

Deployment challenges

The current application also has deployment challenges. It was designed as a monolithic application, and any change in the order module would require the entire application to be deployed again. This is time-consuming, and the whole cycle would have to be repeated with every change, meaning that this could be a frequent cycle. Scaling could only be a distant dream in such a scenario.

As discussed with regard to scaling current applications that have deployment challenges that require us to deploy the entire assembly, the modules are interdependent, and this is a single assembly application of .NET. The deployment of the entire application in one go also makes it mandatory to test the entire functionality of our application. The impact of such an exercise would be huge:

- **High-risk deployment**: Deploying an entire solution or application in one go poses a high risk, as all modules would be deployed even for a single change in one of the modules.
- **Longer testing time**: As we have to deploy the complete application, we will have to test the functionality of the entire application. We can't go live without testing. Due to higher interdependency, the change might cause a problem in some other module.
- **Unplanned downtime**: Complete production deployment needs code to be fully tested, and hence we need to schedule our production deployment. This is a time-consuming task that results in long downtime. While it is planned downtime, during this time, both business and customers will be affected due to the unavailability of the system; this could cause revenue loss to the business.

- **Production bugs**: A bug-free deployment would be the dream for any project manager. However, this is far from reality and every team dreads this possibility of a buggy deployment. Monolithic applications are no different from this scenario, and the resolution of production bugs is easier said than done. The situation can only become more complex with a previous bug remaining unresolved.

Organizational alignment

In a monolithic application, having a large code base is not the only challenge that you'll face. Having a large team to handle such a code base is one more problem that will affect the growth of the business and application.

To align an organization, the most concerning factor is the goal of the team. It is very important that a team goal should be the same for all team members:

- **The same goal**: In a team, all the team members have the same goal, which is timely and bug-free delivery at the end of each day. However, having a large code base in the current application means that the monolithic architectural style will not be comfortable territory for the team members. With team members being interdependent due to the interdependent code and associated deliverables, the same effect that is experienced in the code is present in the development team as well. Here, everyone is just scrambling and struggling to get the job done. The question of helping each other out or trying something new does not arise. In short, the team is not a self-organizing one.

> Roy Osherove defined three stages of a team as: **survival phase**—no time to learn, **learning phase**—learning to solve your own problems, and **self-organizing phase**—facilitate, and experiment.

- **A different perspective**: The development team takes too much time for deliverables for reasons such as feature enhancement, bug fixes, or module interdependency, preventing easy development. The QA team is dependent upon the development team, and the development team has its own problems. The QA team is stuck once developers start working on bugs, fixes, or feature enhancements. There is no separate environment or build available for a QA team to proceed with their testing. This delay hampers the overall delivery, and customers or end users will not get the new features or fixes on time.

Modularity

In respect to our monolithic application where we may have an `Order` module, a change in the `Order` module affects the `Stock` module, and so on. It is the absence of modularity that results in such a condition.

This also means that we can't reuse the functionality of a module within another module. The code is not decomposed into structured pieces that could be reused to save time and effort. There is no segregation within the code modules, and hence no common code is available.

The business is growing and its customers are growing in leaps and bounds. New or existing customers from different regions have different preferences when it comes to the use of the application. Some like to visit the website, but others prefer to use mobile apps. The system is structured in a way that means that we can't share the components across a website and a mobile app. This makes introducing a mobile/device app for the business a challenging task. The business is therefore affected as companies lose out owing to customers preferring mobile apps.

The difficulty is in replacing the application components that are using third-party libraries, an external system such as payment gateways, and an external order-tracking system. It is a tedious job to replace the old components in the currently styled monolithic architectural application. For example, if we consider upgrading the library of our module that is consuming an external order-tracking system, then the whole change would prove to be very difficult. Furthermore, it would be an intricate task to replace our payment gateway with another one.

In any of the previous scenarios, whenever we upgraded the components, we upgraded everything within the application, which called for the complete testing of the system and required a lot of downtime. Apart from this, the upgrade would possibly result in production bugs, which would require repeating the whole cycle of development, testing, and deployment.

Big database

Our current application has a mammoth database, containing a single schema with plenty of indexes. This structure poses a challenging job when it comes to fine-tuning performance:

- **Single schema**: All the entities in the database are clubbed under a single schema named `dbo`. This again hampers the business, owing to the confusion with the single schema regarding various tables that belong to different modules. For example, customer and supplier tables belong to the same schema, that is, `dbo`.
- **Numerous stored procedures**: Currently, the database has a large number of stored procedures, which also contain a sizeable chunk of the business logic. Some of the calculations are being performed within the stored procedures. As a result, these stored procedures prove to be a baffling task to tend to when it comes to optimizing them or breaking them down into smaller units.

Whenever deployment is planned, the team will have to look closely at every database change. This, again, is a time-consuming exercise that will often turn out to be more complex than the build and deployment exercise itself.

A big database has its own limitations. In our monolithic application, we have a single schema database. This has a lot of stored procedure and functions; all this has an impact on the performance of the database.

In the coming section, we will discuss various solutions and other approaches to overcome these problems. But before that, we need to know the prerequisites of microservices before digging into this architectural style.

Prerequisites for microservices

To gain a better understanding of microservices, let's look at an imaginary example of FlixOne Inc. With this example as our base, we can discuss all the concepts in detail and see what it looks like to be ready for microservices.

An Introduction to Microservices

FlixOne is an e-commerce player that is spread all over India. They are growing at a very fast pace and diversifying their business at the same time. They have built their existing system on .NET Framework, and this is a traditional three-tier architecture. They have a massive database that is central to this system, and there are peripheral applications in their ecosystem. One such application is for their sales and logistics team, and it happens to be an Android app. These applications connect to their centralized data center and face performance issues. FlixOne has an in-house development team supported by external consultants. Refer to the following diagram:

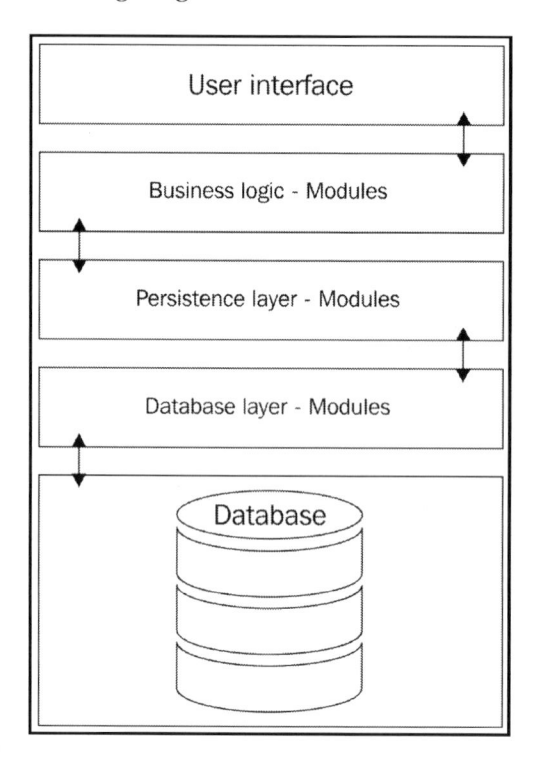

```
┌─────────────────────────────────────────┐
│         User interface                  │
│              ▲                          │
│              ▼                          │
│         Business logic - Modules        │
│              ▲                          │
│              ▼                          │
│         Persistence layer - Modules     │
│              ▲                          │
│              ▼                          │
│         Database layer - Modules        │
│              ▲                          │
│              ▼                          │
│              ⌢ Database ⌢               │
└─────────────────────────────────────────┘
```

The previous diagram depicts a broader sense of our current application, which is a single .NET assembly application. Here, we have the user interfaces we use to search and order products, track the order, and check out. Now look at the following diagram:

Chapter 1

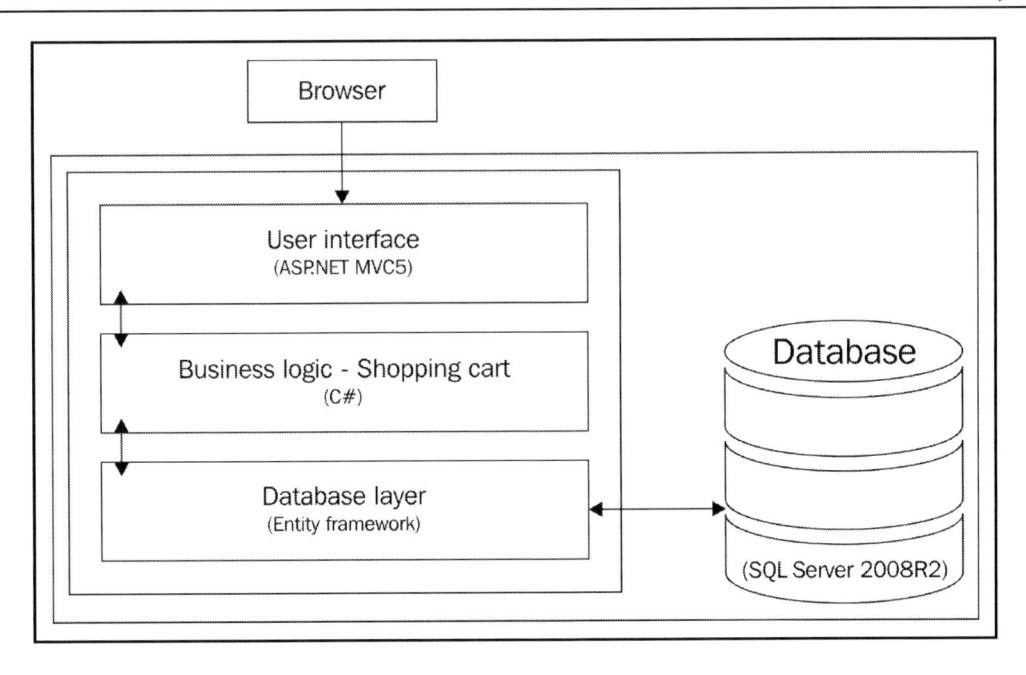

The previous diagram depicts our **Shopping cart** module only. The application is built with C#, MVC5, and Entity Framework, and it has a single project application. This diagram is just a pictorial overview of the architecture of our application. This application is web-based and can be accessed from any browser. Initially, any request that uses the HTTP protocol will land on the user interface that is developed using MVC5 and jQuery. For cart activities, the UI interacts with the **Shopping cart** module, which is a business logic layer that interacts with the database layer (written in C#). We are storing data within the database (SQL Server 2008R2).

Functional overview of the application

Here, we are going to understand the functional overview of the FlixOne bookstore application. This is only for the purpose of visualizing our application. The following is a simplified functional overview of the application that shows the process from **Home page** to **Checkout**:

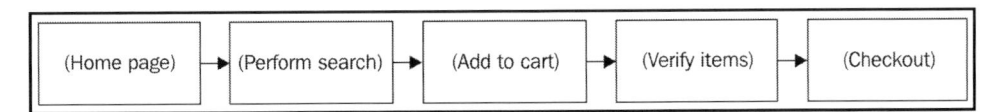

[33]

In the current application, the customer lands on the home page, where they see featured/highlighted books. They also have the option to search for a book item. After getting the desired result, the customer can choose book items and add them to their shopping cart. Customers can verify the book items before the final checkout. As soon as the customer decides to check out, the existing cart system redirects them to an external payment gateway for the specified amount you need to pay for the book items in the shopping cart.

As discussed previously, our application is a monolithic application; it is structured to be developed and deployed as a single unit. This application has a large code base that is still growing. Small updates need to deploy the whole application at once.

In this section, we have discussed the functional overview of the application. We still need to analyze and address the challenges and find the best solution for the current challenges. So, let's discuss those things next.

Solutions for the current challenges

The business is growing rapidly, so we decide to open our e-commerce website in 20 more cities. However, we are still facing challenges with the existing application and struggling to serve the existing user base properly. In this case, before we start the transition, we should make our monolithic application ready for its transition to microservices.

In the very first approach, the **Shopping cart** module will be segregated into smaller modules, then you'll be able to make these modules interact with each other, as well as external or third-party software:

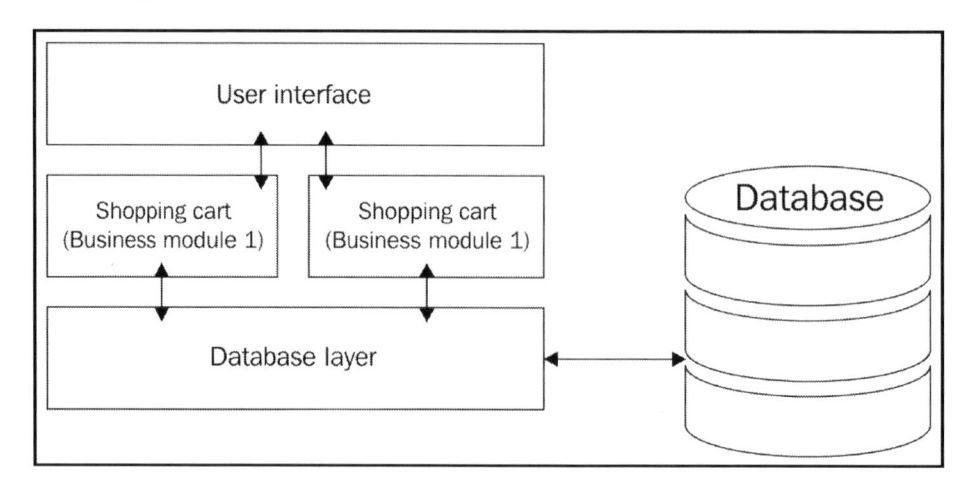

This proposed solution is not sufficient for our existing application, though developers would be able to divide the code and reuse it. However, the internal processing of the business logic would remain the same in the way it would interact with the UI or the database. The new code would interact with the UI and the database layer, with the database still remaining as the same old single database. With our database remaining undivided and as tightly coupled layers, the problem of having to update and deploy the whole code base would still remain. So, this solution is not suitable for resolving our problem.

Handling deployment problems

In the previous section, we discussed the deployment challenges we will face with the current .NET monolithic application. In this section, let's take a look at how we can overcome these challenges by making or adapting a few practices within the same .NET stack.

With our .NET monolithic application, our deployment is made up of XCOPY deployments. After dividing our modules into different submodules, we can adapt to deployment strategies with the help of these. We can simply deploy our business logic layer or some common functionality. We can adapt to continuous integration and deployment. The XCOPY deployment is a process where all the files are copied to the server; it is mostly used for web projects.

Making better monolithic applications

Now that we understand all the challenges with our existing monolithic application, our new application should serve us better with new changes. As we are expanding, we can't miss the opportunity to get new customers. If we do not overcome a challenge, then we will lose business opportunities as well. Let's discuss a few points to solve these problems.

Introducing dependency injections

Our modules are interdependent, so we are facing issues, such as the reusability of code and unresolved bugs due to changes in one module. These are deployment challenges. To tackle these issues, let's segregate our application in such a way that we will be able to divide modules into submodules. We can divide our Order module so that it will implement the interface, and this can be initiated from the constructor.

An Introduction to Microservices

> **Dependency injection** (**DI**) is a design pattern and provides a technique so that you can make a class independent of its dependencies. It can be achieved by decoupling an object from its creation.

Here is a short code snippet that shows how we can apply this to our existing monolithic application. The following code example shows our `Order` class, where we use constructor injection:

```
using System;
using System.Collections.Generic;
using FlixOne.BookStore.Models;

namespace FlixOne.BookStore.Common
{
    public class Order : IOrder
    {
        private readonly IOrderRepository _orderRepository;
        public Order() => _orderRepository = new OrderRepository();
        public Order(IOrderRepository orderRepository) => _orderRepository = orderRepository;
        public IEnumerable<OrderModel> Get() => _orderRepository.GetList();
        public OrderModel GetBy(Guid orderId) => _orderRepository.Get(orderId);
    }
}
```

> **Inversion of control**, or **IoC**, is the way in which objects do not create other objects on whom they rely to do their work.

In the previous code snippet, we abstracted our `Order` module in such a way that it could use the `IOrder` interface. Afterward, our `Order` class implements the `IOrder` interface, and with the use of inversion of control, we create an object, as this is resolved automatically with the help of inversion of control.

Chapter 1

Furthermore, the code snippet for `IOrderRepository` is as follows:

```csharp
using FlixOne.BookStore.Models;
using System;
using System.Collections.Generic;

namespace FlixOne.BookStore.Common
{
    public interface IOrderRepository
    {
        IEnumerable<OrderModel> GetList();
        OrderModel Get(Guid orderId);
    }
}
```

We have the following code snippet for `OrderRepository`, which implements the `IOrderRepository` interface:

```csharp
using System;
using System.Collections.Generic;
using System.Linq;
using FlixOne.BookStore.Models;

namespace FlixOne.BookStore.Common
{
    public class OrderRepository : IOrderRepository
    {
        public IEnumerable<OrderModel> GetList() => DummyData();
        public OrderModel Get(Guid orderId) => DummyData().FirstOrDefault(x => x.OrderId == orderId);
    }
}
```

In the preceding code snippet, we have a method called `DummyData()`, which is used to create `Order` data for our sample code.

The following is a code snippet showing the `DummyData()` method:

```csharp
private IEnumerable<OrderModel> DummyData()
        {
            return new List<OrderModel>
            {
                new OrderModel
                {
                    OrderId = new Guid("61d529f5-a9fd-420f-84a9-
                                       ab86f3eaf8ad"),
                    OrderDate = DateTime.Now,
                    OrderStatus = "In Transit"
```

[37]

An Introduction to Microservices

```
                },
                ...
            };
    }
```

Here, we are trying to showcase how our `Order` module gets abstracted. In the previous code snippet, we returned default values (using sample data) for our order just to demonstrate the solution to the actual problem.

Finally, our presentation layer (the MVC controller) will use the available methods, as shown in the following code snippet:

```
using FlixOne.BookStore.Common;
using System;
using System.Web.Mvc;

namespace FlixOne.BookStore.Controllers
{
    public class OrderController : Controller
    {
        private readonly IOrder _order;
        public OrderController() => _order = new Order();
        public OrderController(IOrder order) => _order = order;
        // GET: Order
        public ActionResult Index() => View(_order.Get());
        // GET: Order/Details/5
        public ActionResult Details(string id)
        {
            var orderId = Guid.Parse(id);
            var orderModel = _order.GetBy(orderId);
            return View(orderModel);
        }
    }
}
```

The following diagram is a class diagram that depicts how our interfaces and classes are associated with each other and how they expose their methods, properties, and so on:

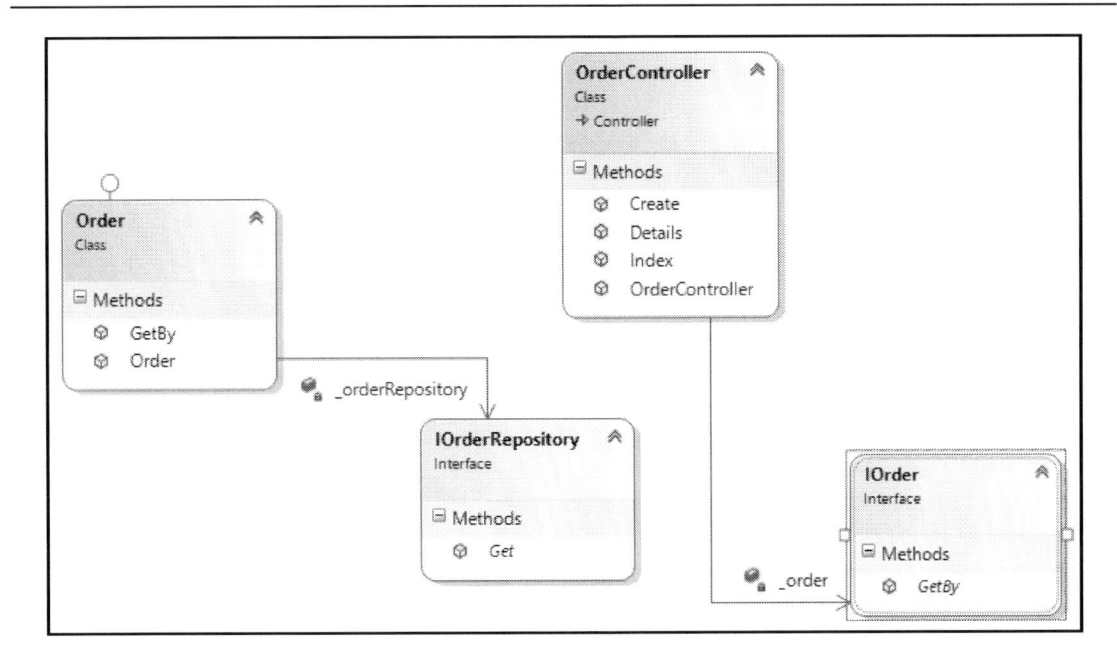

Chapter 1

```
Order                              OrderController
Class                              Class
                                   → Controller
⊟ Methods
   ⊗ GetBy                         ⊟ Methods
   ⊗ Order                            ⊗ Create
                                      ⊗ Details
              _orderRepository        ⊗ Index
                                      ⊗ OrderController

                    IOrderRepository
                    Interface                        IOrder
                                                     Interface
                    ⊟ Methods
                       ⊗ Get                         ⊟ Methods
                                       _order           ⊗ GetBy
```

Here, we again used constructor injection where `IOrder` passed and got the `Order` class initialized. Consequently, all the methods are available within our controller.

Getting this far means we have overcome a few problems, including the following:

- **Reduced module dependency**: With the introduction of `IOrder` in our application, we have reduced the interdependency of the `Order` module. This way, if we are required to add or remove anything to or from this module, then other modules will not be affected, as `IOrder` is only implemented by the `Order` module. Let's say we want to make an enhancement to our `Order` module; this would not affect our `Stock` module. This way, we reduce module interdependency.
- **Introducing code reusability**: If you are required to get the order details of any application modules, you can easily do so using the `IOrder` type.
- **Improvements in code maintainability**: We have now divided our modules into submodules or classes and interfaces. We can now structure our code in such a manner that all the types (that is, all the interfaces) are placed under one folder and follow the structure for the repositories. With this structure, it will be easier for us to arrange and maintain code.
- **Unit testing**: Our current monolithic application does not have any kind of unit testing. With the introduction of interfaces, we can now easily perform unit testing and adopt the system of test-driven development with ease.

Database refactoring

As discussed in the previous section, our application database is huge and depends on a single schema. This huge database should be considered while refactoring. To refactor our application database, we follow these points:

- **Schema correction**: In general practice (not required), our schema depicts our modules. As discussed in previous sections, our huge database has a single schema (which is now dbo), and every part of the code or table should not be related to dbo. There might be several modules that will interact with specific tables. For example, our Order module should contain some related schema names, such as Order. So, whenever we need to use the tables, we can use them with their own schema, instead of a general dbo schema. This will not impact any functionality related to how data is retrieved from the database, but it will have structured or arranged our tables in such a way that we will be able to identify and correlate each and every table with their specific modules. This exercise will be very helpful when we are in the stage of transitioning a monolithic application to microservices. Refer to the following diagram depicting the **Order schema** and **Stock schema** of the database:

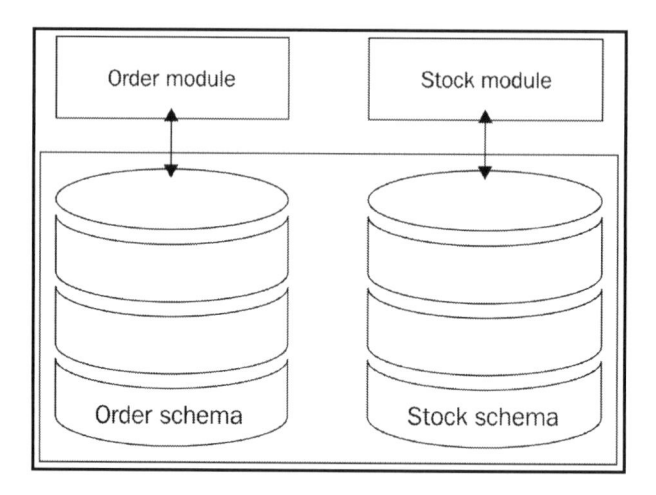

In the previous diagram, we see how the database schema is separated logically. It is not separated physically as our **Order schema** and **Stock schema** belong to the same database. Consequently, here, we will separate the database schema logically, not physically.

We can also take the example of our users; not all users are an admin or belong to a specific zone, area, or region. However, our user table should be structured in such a way that we should be able to identify the users by the table name or the way they are structured. Here, we can structure our user table on the basis of regions. We should map our user table to a region table in such a way that it should not impact or make any changes to the existing code base.

- **Moving the business logic to code from stored procedures**: In the current database, we have thousands of lines of stored procedure with a lot of business logic. We should move the business logic to our code base. In our monolithic application, we are using Entity Framework; here, we can avoid the creation of stored procedures, and we can write all of our business logic as code.

Database sharding and partitioning

When it comes to database sharding and partitioning, we choose database sharding. Here, we will break it into smaller databases. These smaller databases will be deployed on a separate server:

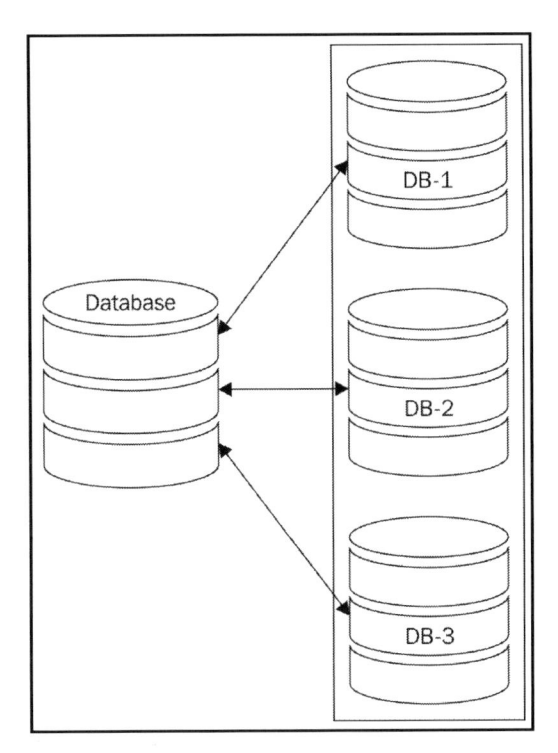

An Introduction to Microservices

In general, database sharding is simply defined as a shared-nothing partitioning scheme for large databases. This way, we can achieve a new level of high performance and scalability. The word sharding comes from shard and spreading, which means dividing a database into chunks (shards) and spreading it to different servers.

> **TIP**
> Sharding can come in different forms. One would be splitting customers and orders into different databases, but one could also split customers into multiple databases for optimization. For instance, customers A-G, customers H-P, and customers Q-Z (based on surname).

The previous diagram is a pictorial overview of how our database is divided into smaller databases. Take a look at the following diagram:

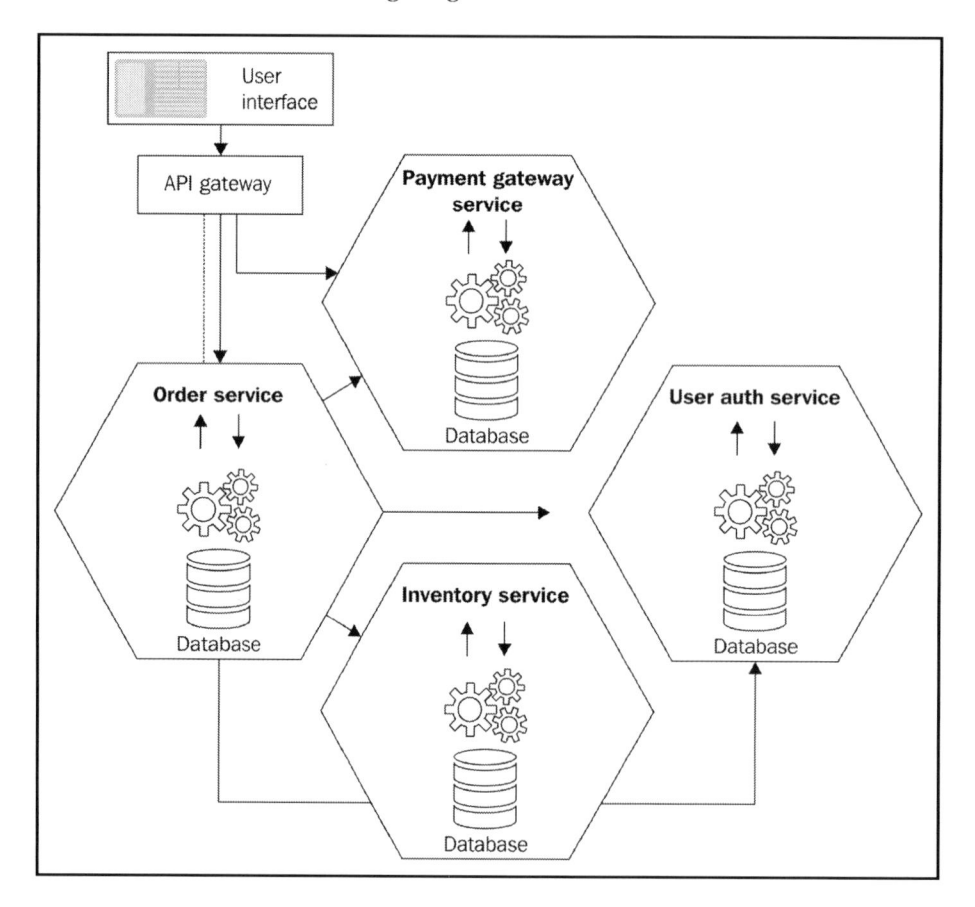

The preceding diagram illustrates that our application now has a smaller database or each service has its own database.

DevOps culture

In the previous sections, we discussed the challenges and problems faced by the team. Here, we'll propose a solution for the DevOps team: the collaboration of the development team with another operational team should be emphasized. We should also set up a system where development, QA, and the infrastructure teams work in collaboration.

Automation

Infrastructure setup can be a very time-consuming job, and developers remain idle while the infrastructure is being readied for them. They will take some time before joining the team and contributing. The process of infrastructure setup should not stop a developer from becoming productive, as it will reduce overall productivity. This should be an automated process. With the use of Chef or PowerShell, we can easily create our virtual machines and quickly ramp up the developer count as and when required. This way, our developers can be ready to start work on day one of joining the team.

Chef is a DevOps tool that provides a framework to automate and manage your infrastructure. PowerShell can be used to create our Azure machines and to set up Azure DevOps (formerly TFS).

Testing

We are going to introduce automated testing as a solution to the problems that we faced while testing during deployment. In this part of the solution, we have to divide our testing approach as follows:

- Adopt **test-driven development (TDD)**. With TDD, a developer writes the test before its actual code. In this way, they will test their own code. The test is another piece of code that can validate whether the functionality is working as intended. If any functionality is found to not satisfy the test code, the corresponding unit test fails. This functionality can be easily fixed as you know this is where the problem is. In order to achieve this, we can utilize frameworks, such as MS tests or unit tests.
- The QA team can use scripts to automate their tasks. They can create scripts by utilizing QTP or the Selenium framework.

Versioning

The current system does not have any kind of versioning system, so there is no way to revert if something happens during a change. To resolve this issue, we need to introduce a version control mechanism. In our case, this should be either Azure DevOps or Git. With the use of version control, we can now revert our change if it is found to break some functionality or introduce any unexpected behavior in the application. We now have the capability of tracking the changes being made by the team members working on this application, at an individual level. However, in the case of our monolithic application, we did not have the capability to do this.

Deployment

In our application, deployment is a huge challenge. To resolve this, we'll introduce **continuous integration** (**CI**). In this process, we need to set up a CI server. With the introduction of CI, the entire process is automated. As soon as the code is checked in by any team member, using version control Azure DevOps or Git, in our case, the CI process kicks into action. This ensures that the new code is built and unit tests are run along with the integration test. In the scenario of a successful build or otherwise, the team is alerted to the outcome. This enables the team to quickly respond to the issue.

Next, we move onto continuous deployment. Here, we introduce various environments, namely, a development environment, a staging environment, a QA environment, and so on. Now, as soon as the code is checked in by any team member, CI kicks into action. This invokes the unit/integration test suites, builds the system, and pushes it out to the various environments we have set up. This way, the turnaround time for the development team to provide a suitable build for QA is reduced to a minimum.

As a monolith application, we have various challenges related to deployment that affect the development team as well. We have discussed CI/CD and seen how deployment works.

The next section covers identifying decomposition candidates within a monolith architecture, which can cause problems.

Identifying decomposition candidates within monolithic

We have now clearly identified the various problems that the current FlixOne application architecture and its resultant code are posing for the development team. We also understand which business challenges the development team is not able to take up and why.

It is not that the team is not capable enough—it is just the code. Let's move ahead and check out the best strategy to zero in on the various parts of the FlixOne application that we need to move to the microservice-styled architecture. We need to know that we have a candidate with a monolith architecture, which poses problems in one of the following areas:

- **Focused deployment**: Although this comes at the final stage of the whole process, it demands more respect, and rightly so. It is important to understand here that this factor shapes and defines the whole development strategy from the initial stages of identification and design. Here's an example of this: the business is asking you to resolve two problems of equal importance. One of the issues might require you to perform testing for many more associated modules, and the resolution for the other might allow you to get away with limited testing. Having to make such a choice would be wrong, and a business shouldn't have the option to do so.
- **Code complexity**: Having smaller teams is the key here. You should be able to assign small development teams for a change that is associated with a single functionality. Small teams are comprised of one or two members. Any more than this and a project manager will be needed. This means that something is more interdependent across modules than it should be.
- **Technology adoption**: You should be able to upgrade components to a newer version or a different technology without breaking anything. If you have to think about the components that depend on technology, you have more than one candidate. Even if you have to worry about the modules that this component depends on, you'll still have more than one candidate. I remember one of my clients who had a dedicated team to test out whether the technology being released was a suitable candidate for their needs. I learned later that they would actually port one of the modules and measure the performance impact, effort requirement, and turnaround time of the whole system. I don't agree with this, though.

- **High resources**: In my opinion, everything in a system, from memory, CPU time, and I/O requirements, should be considered a module. If any one of the modules takes more time, and/or occurs more frequently, it should be singled out. In any operation that involves higher-than-normal memory, the processing time blocks the delay and the I/O keeps the system waiting; this would be good in our case.
- **Human dependency**: If moving team members across modules seems like too much work, you have more candidates. Developers are smart, but if they struggle with large systems, it is not their fault. Break the system down into smaller units, and the developers will be both more comfortable and more productive.

This section helped us understand the problems that a monolithic architecture faces. Next, we will move on to some advantages of this architecture.

Important microservices advantages

We have performed the first step of identifying our candidates for moving to microservices. It will be worthwhile to go through the corresponding advantages that microservices provide. Let's understand them in the following sections.

Technology independence

With each of the microservices being independent of each other, we now have the power to use different technologies for each microservice. The payment gateway could be using the latest .NET Framework, whereas the product search could be shifted to any other programming language.

The entire application could be based on a SQL Server for data storage, whereas the inventory could be based on NoSQL. The flexibility is limitless.

Interdependency removal

Since we try to achieve isolated functionality within each microservice, it is easy to add new features, fix bugs, or upgrade technology within each one. This will have no impact on other microservices. Now you have vertical code isolation that enables you to perform all of this and still be as fast with the deployments.

This doesn't end here. The FlixOne team now has the ability to release a new option for the payment gateway, alongside the existing one. Both payment gateways could coexist until both the team and the business owners are satisfied with the reports. This is where the immense power of this architecture comes into play.

Alignment with business goals

It is not necessarily the business owner's concern to understand that certain features are harder or more time-consuming to address. Their responsibility is to keep driving and growing the business. The development team should become a support network for achieving the business goals, not a roadblock.

It is extremely important to understand that quickly responding to business needs and adapting to marketing trends are not by-products of microservices, but goals.

The capability to achieve these goals with smaller teams only makes microservices more suitable for business owners.

Cost benefits

Each microservice becomes an investment for the business, since it can easily be consumed by other microservices, without having to redo the same code again and again. Every time a microservice is reused, time is saved by avoiding the testing and deployment of that part.

The user experience is enhanced, since the downtime is either eliminated or reduced to a minimum.

Easy scalability

With vertical isolation in place and each microservice rendering a specific service to the whole system, it is easy to scale. Not only is the identification easier for the scaling candidates, but the cost is less. This is because we only scale a part of the whole microservice ecosystem.

This exercise can be cost-intensive for the business. Consequently, the prioritization of which microservice is to be scaled first can now be a choice for the business team; this decision no longer has to be a choice for the development team.

Security

Security is similar to what is provided by the traditional layered architecture; microservices can be secured as easily. Different configurations can be used to secure different microservices. You can have a part of the microservice ecosystem behind firewalls and another part for user encryption. Web-facing microservices can be secured differently from the rest of the microservices. You can suit your needs as per choice, technology, or budget.

Data management

It is common to have a single database in the majority of monolithic applications. And almost always, there is a database architect or a designated owner responsible for its integrity and maintenance. The path to any application enhancement that requires a change in the database has to go via this route. For me, it has never been an easy task. This further slows down the process of application enhancement, scalability, and technology adoption.

Because each microservice has its own *independent* database, the decision-making related to changes required in the database can be easily delegated to the respective team. We don't have to worry about the impact on the rest of the system, as there will not be any.

At the same time, this separation of the database brings forth the possibility for the team to become self-organized. They can now start experimenting.

For example, the team can now consider using Azure Table storage or Azure Cache for Redis to store the massive product catalog instead of the database, as is being done currently. Not only can the team now experiment, but their experience can also easily be replicated across the whole system, as required by other teams in the form of a schedule convenient to them.

In fact, nothing is stopping the FlixOne team now from being innovative and using a multitude of technologies available at the same time, then comparing performance in the real world and making a final decision. Once each microservice has its own database, this is how FlixOne will look:

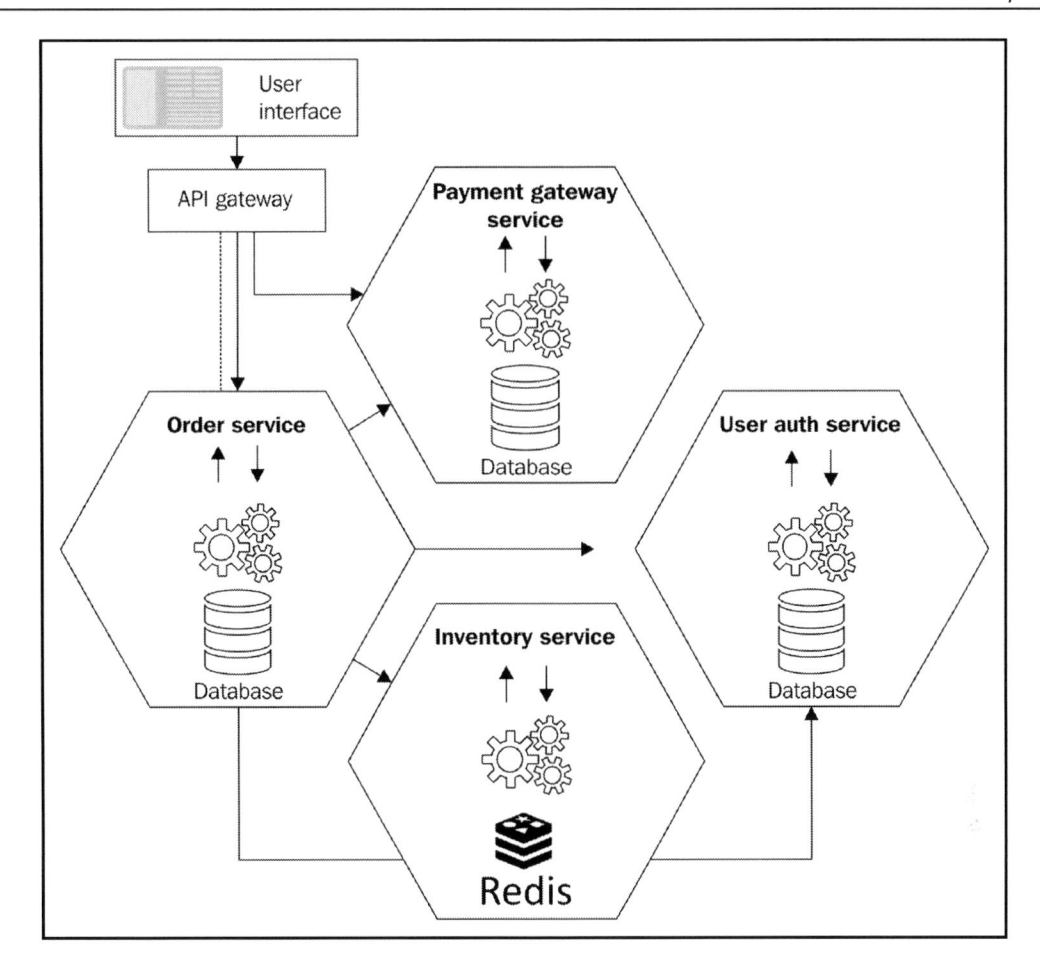

In the preceding image, each service has its own database and has scalability; the inventory service has caching (Redis server).

Integrating monolithic applications with microservices

Whenever a choice is made to move away from monolithic architecture in favor of microservice-styled architecture, the time and cost axis of the initiative will pose some resistance. A business evaluation might rule against moving some parts of the monolithic application that do not make a business case for the transition.

It would have been a different scenario if we were developing the application from the beginning. However, this is also the power of microservices, in my opinion. The correct evaluation of the entire monolithic architecture can safely identify the monolithic parts to be ported later.

We must safeguard against the risk of integration to ensure that these isolated parts do not cause a problem to other microservices in the future.

While we discussed various parts of the monolithic application, our goal was to create them collaboratively, so that they can communicate with each other on the patterns followed by the application based on the microservice architectural style. To achieve this, there would be a need for various patterns and the technology stack in which the original monolithic application was developed. For example, if we have used the event-driven pattern, our monolithic application should adhere to this pattern in such a way that it consumes and publishes the events. To implement or obey this pattern, we should manage the code of our monolithic application, which basically includes the development efforts to make the changes in the existing code.

Similarly, if there is a need to use the API Gateway pattern, then we should make sure that our gateway should suffice, so that it communicates with the monolith application. To achieve this could be a bit complex or tricky, where the existing monolithic application does not have such functionality to expose web services (RESTful). This would also put pressure on the development team to make changes in the existing code to make the application viable to fit the standard of a gateway. There would be a great chance to make code changes to add or update the RESTful services because these services could be easily consumed by the gateway. To overcome this overburden, we can create a separate microservice so that we can avoid major changes in the source code.

We discussed the integration of monolithic applications in this section, with the help of various approaches, such as the domain-driven pattern, the API Gateway pattern, and so on. The next section discusses Azure Service Fabric.

An overview of Azure Service Fabric

When we talk about microservices in the .NET Core world, Azure Service Fabric is a name that is widely used for microservices. In this section, we will discuss Fabric services.

This is a platform that helps us with easy packaging, deployment, and managing scalable and reliable microservices (the container is also like Docker). Sometimes it is difficult to focus on your main responsibility as a developer, because of complex infrastructural problems. With the help of Azure Service Fabric, developers need not worry about infrastructure issues. Azure Service Fabric provides various technologies and comes as a bundle that has the power of Azure SQL Database, Cosmos DB, Microsoft Power BI, Azure Event Hubs, Azure IoT Hub, and many more core services.

According to the official documentation (https://docs.microsoft.com/en-us/azure/service-fabric/service-fabric-overview), we can define Azure Service Fabric as follows:

- **Service fabric—any OS, any cloud**: You just need to create a cluster of service fabric and this will run on Azure (cloud) or on-premises, on Linux, or on a Windows server. Moreover, you can also create clusters on other public clouds.
- **Service fabric**: Stateless and stateful microservices. With the help of service fabric, you can build applications as stateless or stateful.

According to its official documentation (https://docs.microsoft.com/en-us/azure/service-fabric/), we can define stateless microservices as follows:

> "Stateless microservices are not in the mutable state outside a request and its response from the service, for example Azure Cloud Services worker roles (Cloud Services should be avoided during development of new services). Stateful microservices are in a mutable state beyond the request and its response."

Full support for application lifecycle management: With the help of service fabric, get the support of a full application lifecycle that includes development, deployment, and so on.

You can develop a scalable application. For more information on this, refer to: https://docs.microsoft.com/en-us/azure/service-fabric/service-fabric-application-lifecycle.

You can develop highly reliable, stateless, and stateful microservices.

> Cloud Services should be avoided during the development of new services.

There are different service fabric programming models available that are beyond the scope of this chapter. For more information, refer to: https://docs.microsoft.com/en-us/azure/service-fabric/service-fabric-choose-framework.

The aim of this section was to give an overview of Azure Service Fabric followed by stateless microservices. We have seen that Azure Service Fabric supports in developing scalable applications.

Summary

In this chapter, we discussed the microservice architectural style in detail, its history, and how it differs from its predecessors, monolithic architecture, and SOA. We further defined the various challenges that monolithic architecture faces when dealing with large systems. Scalability and reusability are some definite advantages that SOA provides over monolithic architecture.

We also discussed the limitations of monolithic architecture, including scaling problems by implementing a real-life monolithic application. The microservice architecture style resolves all of these issues by reducing code interdependency and isolating the dataset size that any one of the microservices work upon. We utilized dependency injection and database refactoring for this. We also further explored automation, CI, and deployment. These easily allow the development team to let the business sponsor choose which industry trends to respond to first. This results in cost benefits, better business response, timely technology adoption, effective scaling, and the removal of human dependency. Finally, we discussed Azure Service Fabric and got an idea about Service Fabric and its different programming models.

In the next chapter, we will go ahead and transition our existing application to microservice-style architecture and put our knowledge to the test. We will transition our monolithic application to microservices by discussing the new technology stack (C#, EF, and so on). We will also cover the concept of seam and discuss microservice communication.

Questions

1. What are microservices?
2. Can you define Azure Service Fabric?
3. What is database sharding?
4. What is TDD and why should developers adopt this?
5. Can you elaborate on dependency injection (DI)?

2
Refactoring the Monolith

In the previous chapter, we discussed the problems of a layered monolith architecture. This chapter aims to discuss the transitioning of monolithic- to microservices-based applications. We will start this chapter with a discussion of our new tech stack (C# and Entity Framework), then move on to the features of a good service and how we can refactor them from an existing system and build separate microservices for products and orders.

We will cover the following topics:

- Understanding the current and new technology stack
- The size of microservices
- What makes a good service?
- Understanding the concept of seam
- Communication between microservices
- Revisiting the FlixOne case study

Technical requirements

This chapter contains various code examples that explain the concepts. The code is kept simple and is just for demo purposes.

To run and execute the code, the following are prerequisites:

- Visual Studio 2019
- .NET Core 3.1

To run these code examples, you need to install Visual Studio 2019 (the preferred IDE). To do so, download Visual Studio 2019 from the download link mentioned in the installation instructions: https://docs.microsoft.com/en-us/visualstudio/install/install-visual-studio. Multiple versions of Visual Studio are available for installation, including Visual Studio Community, a free version. We are using Visual Studio for Windows.

If you do not have .NET Core 3.1 installed, you can download it from this link: https://www.microsoft.com/net/download/windows.

> The complete source code is available here: https://github.com/PacktPublishing/Hands-On-Microservices-with-CSharp-8-and-.NET-Core-3-Third-Edition/tree/master/Chapter%2002

Understanding the current and new technology stack

Before we proceed with the concepts to implement microservices, it is worth mentioning the core concepts, languages, and tools that we'll be using to implement these microservices. In this chapter, we will get an overview of these topics.

Discussion – current stack (C#, EF, and SQL Server)

In this section, we will discuss the technology stack that we're using in our demo application.

C# 8

C# is a programming language developed by Microsoft, and the current release at the time of writing this book is C# 8. This object-oriented and component-oriented language started in 2002. The current version has various new features, such as ValueTuple, deconstructors, pattern matching, and the switch statement local function.

We won't go into the details of these features, as it's beyond the scope of this book. Refer to https://docs.microsoft.com/en-us/dotnet/csharp/whats-new/ for more details.

Entity Framework Core

Entity Framework Core (EF Core) is a cross-platform version of Microsoft Entity Framework, which is one of the most popular **Object-Relational Mappers (ORMs)**.

> ORM is a technique that helps you to query and manipulate data, according to the required business output.

EF Core supports various databases. A complete list of databases is available here: https://docs.microsoft.com/en-us/ef/core/providers/index. The current version of EF Core (at the time of writing) is 3.1 (https://devblogs.microsoft.com/dotnet/announcing-entity-framework-core-3-1-and-entity-framework-6-4/).

Visual Studio 2019

Visual Studio is one of the best IDEs, created by Microsoft. It enables developers to work in various ways using popular languages, such as C#, VB.NET, and F#. The current release of Visual Studio 2019 is VS16.4 (https://docs.microsoft.com/en-us/visualstudio/releases/2019/release-notes). To find the most recent version of Visual Studio, check the official page: https://docs.microsoft.com/en-us/visualstudio/install/update-visual-studio?view=vs-2019.

> An IDE is an integrated development environment, a software application that provides a facility for programmers to write programs by using programming languages. For more information, visit https://en.wikipedia.org/wiki/Integrated_development_environment.

Microsoft also released Visual Studio for macOS, and Visual Studio has many new features. For more information, please refer to https://www.visualstudio.com/vs/whatsnew/. In this book, all the examples are written using Visual Studio 2019. You can also download the Community edition, which is free, at the following link: https://www.visualstudio.com/.

Microsoft SQL Server

Microsoft SQL Server (MSSQL) is a software application that is a relational database management system. It is mainly used as database software to store and retrieve data; it is built on top of **Structured Query Language (SQL)**: http://searchsqlserver.techtarget.com/definition/SQL.

The current release—that is, SQL Server 2019—is more robust and can be used on Windows and Linux. You can get SQL Server 2019 from here: https://www.microsoft.com/en-IN/sql-server/sql-server-2019. Please note that we will use SQL Server 2008 R2 or later in this book.

Before we get started with the book's hands-on instructions, let's learn about the new features in .NET Core and C# 8.0 that we will leverage in this book. The following two sections will be more like an exploration of *New Features in .NET Core 3.1* and *New Features in C# 8.0*. We will add in-depth details and instructions for those features. You can skip these sections if you are aware of the new features already.

New features in .NET Core

In the previous section, we gave an overview of the current technology stack. The aim of this and the next section is to provide a brief run-through of the expected features of the upcoming technology stack (.NET Core 3.1 and C# 8.0) and take advantage of the new features in our code examples. Please note that, at the time of writing this book, .NET Core 3.1 has just released.

The release of .NET Core 3.1 is a small release that consists of fixes of the earlier release of .NET Core 3.0. So, in this section, we will focus on discussing the new features of .NET Core 3.0.

> .NET Core 3.1 is announced as a Long Term Support (LTS) release for three years.

.NET Core 3.0 should excite developers of desktop applications. This release comes with the biggest enhancements, and it now supports the development of Windows desktop applications. Currently, this enhancement is only for users who work on Windows machines, as the support is limited to Windows only. The support includes the development of Windows Forms and Windows Presentation Foundation (WPF) applications.

I assume that you've installed .NET Core 3.1; if you haven't yet, please revisit the *Technical requirements* section.

Chapter 2

To validate the installation of .NET Core 3.1, you can check the information on the currently installed version of .NET Core. To do this, open Command Prompt and type the following command:

```
dotnet --info
```

The preceding command will tell you the complete information about the installed .NET Core version, as shown in the following screenshot:

```
Microsoft Windows [Version 10.0.14393]
(c) 2016 Microsoft Corporation. All rights reserved.

C:\Users\aroraG>dotnet --info
.NET Core SDK (reflecting any global.json):
 Version:   3.1.100
 Commit:    cd82f021f4

Runtime Environment:
 OS Name:     Windows
 OS Version:  10.0.14393
 OS Platform: Windows
 RID:         win10-x64
 Base Path:   C:\Program Files\dotnet\sdk\3.1.100\

Host (useful for support):
  Version: 3.1.0
  Commit:  65f04fb6db
```

The preceding screenshot shows information about all of the available .NET Core versions. Our version of .NET Core is **3.1.100**.

Now let's see how we can leverage the new features we mentioned earlier. If you want to develop Windows Desktop applications, then you can create both WPF and Windows Forms applications, by using **Command Line Interface (CLI)** `dotnet` commands or Visual Studio 2019.

To start with the CLI, follow these steps:

1. Open your Command Prompt or Windows PowerShell (we'll use PowerShell).
2. Go to your desired folder (where you want to create a new project)—in our case, we will use the `Chapter02` folder.
3. Pass the following command to create a Windows Forms application:

   ```
   dotnet new winforms
   ```

[57]

Refactoring the Monolith

The preceding code snippet says the following:

- `dotnet new`: This initializes a valid .NET Core project.
- `winforms`: This is a template that is being called on the initialization of a valid .NET Core project.

> **TIP**
> If you want to use the VB language instead of C#, you just need to pass the preceding command with the language as `dotnet new winforms -lang VB`.

The preceding command is processed and creates a **Windows Forms** application, using the `WinForms` template. The following screenshot depicts the creation of the project steps:

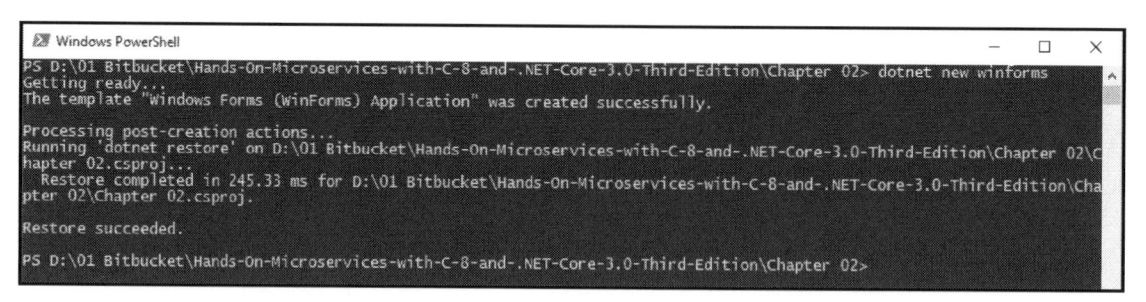

```
PS D:\01 Bitbucket\Hands-On-Microservices-with-C-8-and-.NET-Core-3.0-Third-Edition\Chapter 02> dotnet new winforms
Getting ready...
The template "Windows Forms (WinForms) Application" was created successfully.

Processing post-creation actions...
Running 'dotnet restore' on D:\01 Bitbucket\Hands-On-Microservices-with-C-8-and-.NET-Core-3.0-Third-Edition\Chapter 02\Chapter 02.csproj...
  Restore completed in 245.33 ms for D:\01 Bitbucket\Hands-On-Microservices-with-C-8-and-.NET-Core-3.0-Third-Edition\Chapter 02\Chapter 02.csproj.

Restore succeeded.

PS D:\01 Bitbucket\Hands-On-Microservices-with-C-8-and-.NET-Core-3.0-Third-Edition\Chapter 02>
```

We have created a `WinForms` application. To run this project, pass the following command:

dotnet run

The preceding command will run the project and show the output of the project. We did not add anything, so we will see the blank Windows Form, as shown in the following screenshot:

```
PS D:\01 Bitbucket\Hands-On-Microservices-with-C-8-and-.NET-Core-3.0-Third-Edition\Chapter 02\WinFormsSample\WinFormsSample> dotnet run
```

[Form1]

[58]

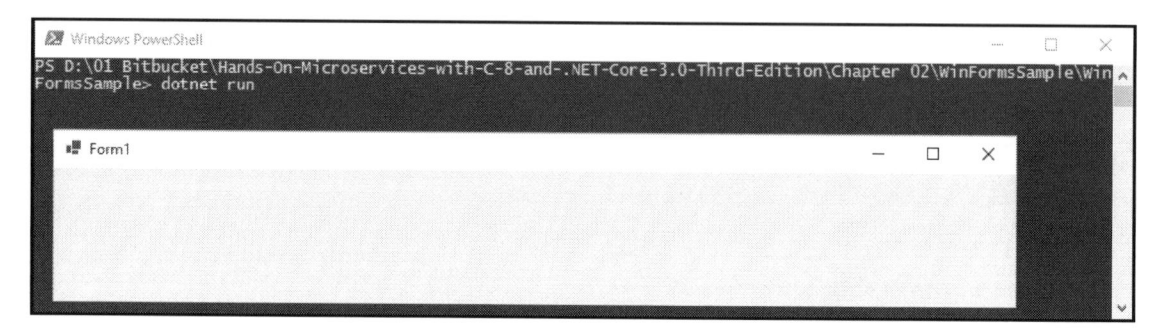

4. Pass the following command to create a Windows Forms application:

   `dotnet new wpf`

The preceding command creates a WPF application, using the `wpf` template. The following screenshot shows the steps to create the application:

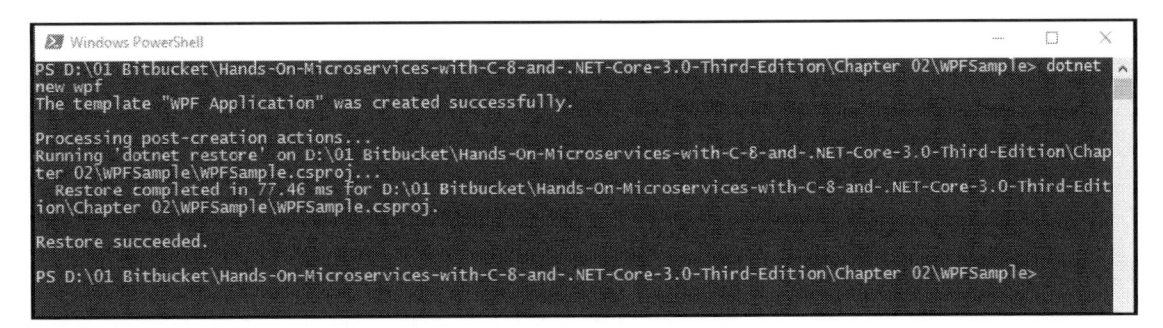

```
Windows PowerShell
PS D:\01 Bitbucket\Hands-On-Microservices-with-C-8-and-.NET-Core-3.0-Third-Edition\Chapter 02\WPFSample> dotnet new wpf
The template "WPF Application" was created successfully.

Processing post-creation actions...
Running 'dotnet restore' on D:\01 Bitbucket\Hands-On-Microservices-with-C-8-and-.NET-Core-3.0-Third-Edition\Chapter 02\WPFSample\WPFSample.csproj...
  Restore completed in 77.46 ms for D:\01 Bitbucket\Hands-On-Microservices-with-C-8-and-.NET-Core-3.0-Third-Edition\Chapter 02\WPFSample\WPFSample.csproj.

Restore succeeded.

PS D:\01 Bitbucket\Hands-On-Microservices-with-C-8-and-.NET-Core-3.0-Third-Edition\Chapter 02\WPFSample>
```

We have created a `wpf` application. To run this project, pass the following command:

   `dotnet run`

The preceding command will run the project and show the output of the project. We did not add anything, so we will see the blank WPF Form, as shown in the following screenshot:

```
Windows PowerShell
PS D:\01 Bitbucket\Hands-On-Microservices-with-C-8-and-.NET-Core-3.0-Third-Edition\Chapter 02\WPFSample> dotnet run

     MainWindow
```

You can use more templates with `dotnet new` commands; if you are not sure about the template name, just pass the following command:

   `dotnet new -l`

Refactoring the Monolith

The preceding command gives you a list of all the available templates in tabular form. Refer to the following screenshot, which shows the available templates:

```
Templates                                          Short Name           Language          Tags
-------------------------------------------------  -------------------  ----------------  -------------------------------------
Console Application                                console              [C#], F#, VB      Common/Console
Class library                                      classlib             [C#], F#, VB      Common/Library
WPF Application                                    wpf                  [C#], VB          Common/WPF
Windows Forms (WinForms) Application               winforms             [C#], VB          Common/WinForms
Worker Service                                     worker               [C#]              Common/Worker/Web
Unit Test Project                                  mstest               [C#], F#, VB      Test/MSTest
NUnit 3 Test Project                               nunit                [C#], F#, VB      Test/NUnit
NUnit 3 Test Item                                  nunit-test           [C#], F#, VB      Test/NUnit
xUnit Test Project                                 xunit                [C#], F#, VB      Test/xUnit
Razor Component                                    razorcomponent       [C#]              Web/ASP.NET
Razor Page                                         page                 [C#]              Web/ASP.NET
MVC ViewImports                                    viewimports          [C#]              Web/ASP.NET
MVC ViewStart                                      viewstart            [C#]              Web/ASP.NET
Blazor (server-side)                               blazorserverside     [C#]              Web/Blazor
ASP.NET Core Empty                                 web                  [C#], F#          Web/Empty
ASP.NET Core Web App (Model-View-Controller)       mvc                  [C#], F#          Web/MVC
ASP.NET Core Web App                               webapp               [C#]              Web/MVC/Razor Pages
ASP.NET Core with Angular                          angular              [C#]              Web/MVC/SPA
ASP.NET Core with React.js                         react                [C#]              Web/MVC/SPA
ASP.NET Core with React.js and Redux               reactredux           [C#]              Web/MVC/SPA
Razor Class Library                                razorclasslib        [C#]              Web/Razor/Library/Razor Class Library
ASP.NET Core Web API                               webapi               [C#], F#          Web/WebAPI
ASP.NET Core gRPC Service                          grpc                 [C#]              Web/gRPC
dotnet gitignore file                              gitignore                              Config
global.json file                                   globaljson                             Config
NuGet Config                                       nugetconfig                            Config
Dotnet local tool manifest file                    tool-manifest                          Config
Web Config                                         webconfig                              Config
Solution File                                      sln                                    Solution
Protocol Buffer File                               proto                                  Web/gRPC
```

The preceding screenshot shows the available pre-installed templates; if you want to install any additional templates, you can use the `dotnet new -i <Tempate>` command. The previous snapshot contains the following:

- `Templates`: This is the complete name of the template.
- `Short Name`: This is the template name that is used with the `dotnet new` command.
- `Language`: This is the programming language that supports the template. The default language for the template is shown in the brackets, `[ ]`.
- `Tags`: This represents the type of template. For example, the `Web` tag refers to an **ASP.NET Core** (web) project template.

Chapter 2

The `dotnet new` commands have various options, as mentioned in the following table:

Option	Description	Syntax
`-h, --help`	This provides help for the command and information about the command and its utilization.	`dotnet new -h`
`-l, --list`	This gives the complete list of templates.	`dotnet new wpf -l` `dotnet new -l`
`-n, --name`	This is the project/application name that is created by using a specific template. If no name is specified, then the name of the current folder is used.	`dotnet new wpf -n "MyProjName"`
`-i, --install`	This installs a new template.	`dotnet new -i Microsoft.AspNetCore.Blazor.Templates::3.0.0`
`-lang, --language`	This specifies the language to create a project in.	`dotnet new winforms -lang VB`

If you're using VS16.4 and have an earlier version of .NET Core 3.0 and/or .NET Core 3.1 installed, then you might see the following screen. In this case, versions, `WinForms`, and `WPF` designer support are not available. If you try to open the project we created previously, you will notice a designer error, as shown in the following screenshot. This error occurs when you try to open the design layout of **Form1**:

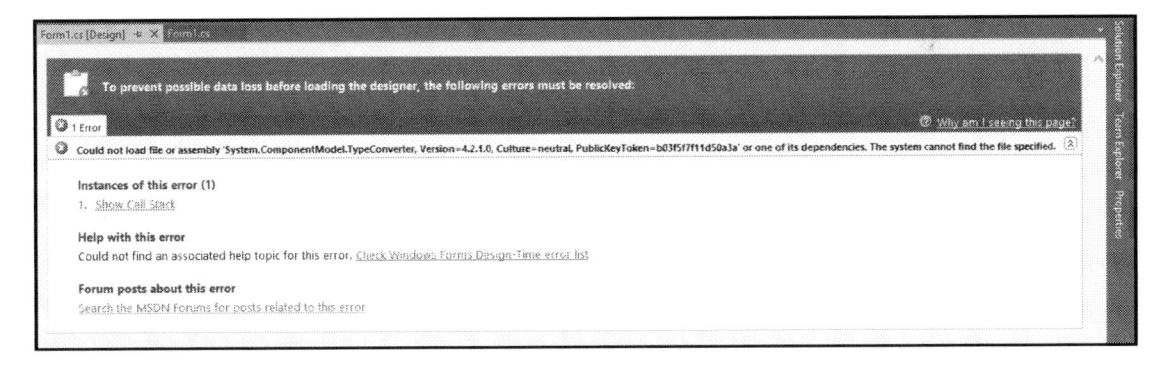

[61]

Refactoring the Monolith

The issue shown in the previous screenshot can be worked around with the help of a classic designer (.NET Framework). With this workaround, we would see a designer and could arrange or design the layout of our forms. This topic is beyond the scope of this book, so we won't go into more detail.

> To get more details and to know how we can fix the designer issue, you can refer to the official GitHub repository: `https://github.com/dotnet/winforms/blob/master/Documentation/winforms-designer.md`.

This fix is shipped with Visual Studio Preview (at the time of writing this book); you need at least VS16.5 to view the designer of WinForms or WPF. You can check by installing VS16.5. To make sure you marked the preview SDK from Visual Studio Options, go to the settings in **Tools | Options | Environment | Preview Features**, and then make sure you checked **Use the preview Windows Form designer for .NET Core apps**, as shown in the following snapshot:

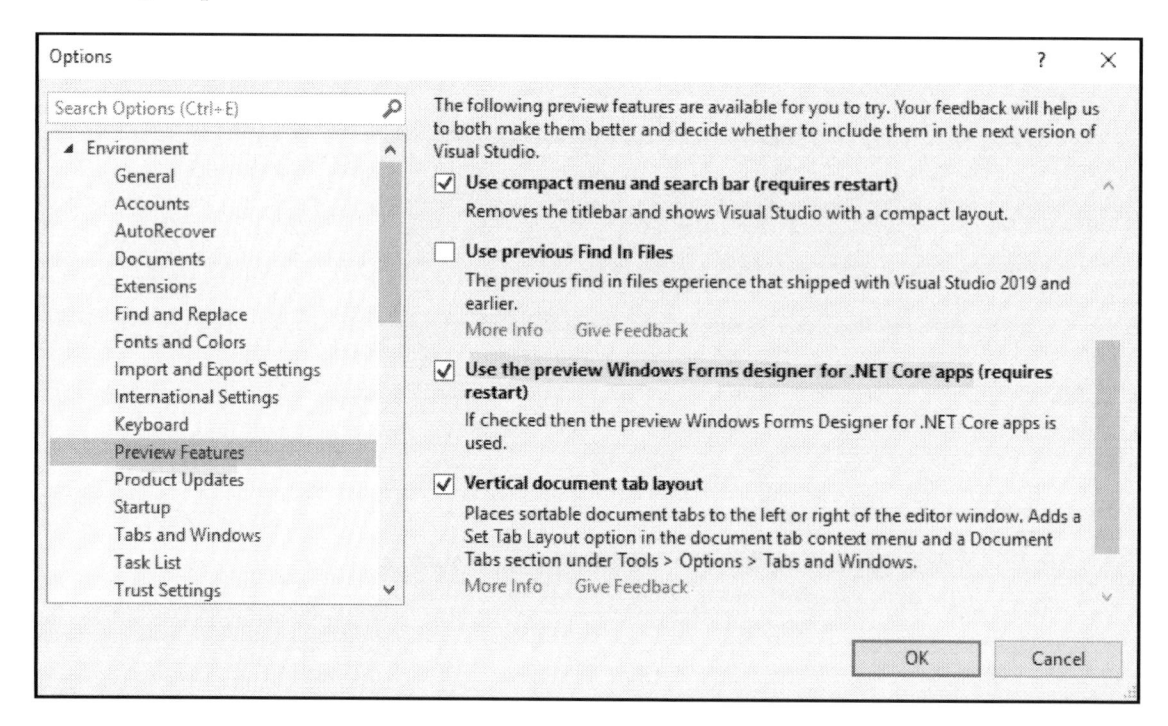

You would need to restart Visual Studio, open the Windows Project, and then click **Shift+F7** on the name of the file that you want to open in the designer.

New features in C# 8.0

In this section, we will discuss the new features of C# 8.0 that are yet to be released (at the time of writing this book). In our code examples, we use the latest preview of C# 8.0.

Before we start discussing the new features, we should first enable the support for the C#8.0 language.

Enabling support for the C# 8.0 language using Visual Studio

If you do not have the latest installation of Visual Studio (refer to *Technical requirements*), follow these steps to enable support for C# 8.0:

Open the project properties, then the **Build** tab, and then click on the **Advanced...** button, near the bottom of the page. Select **C# 8.0 (beta)**, as shown in the following screenshot, or whatever the latest version is from the **Language version** drop-down list, under the **General** group. The following screenshot illustrates every step:

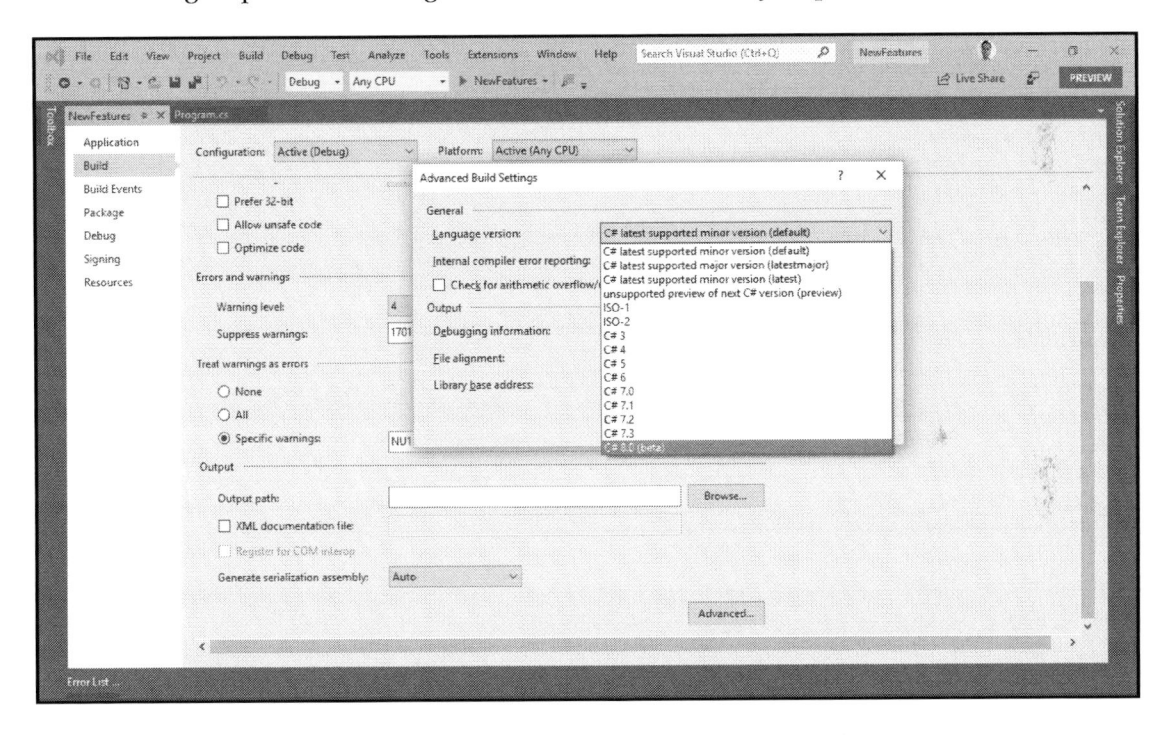

Refactoring the Monolith

If you have the latest version of Visual Studio installed, you will see the following window:

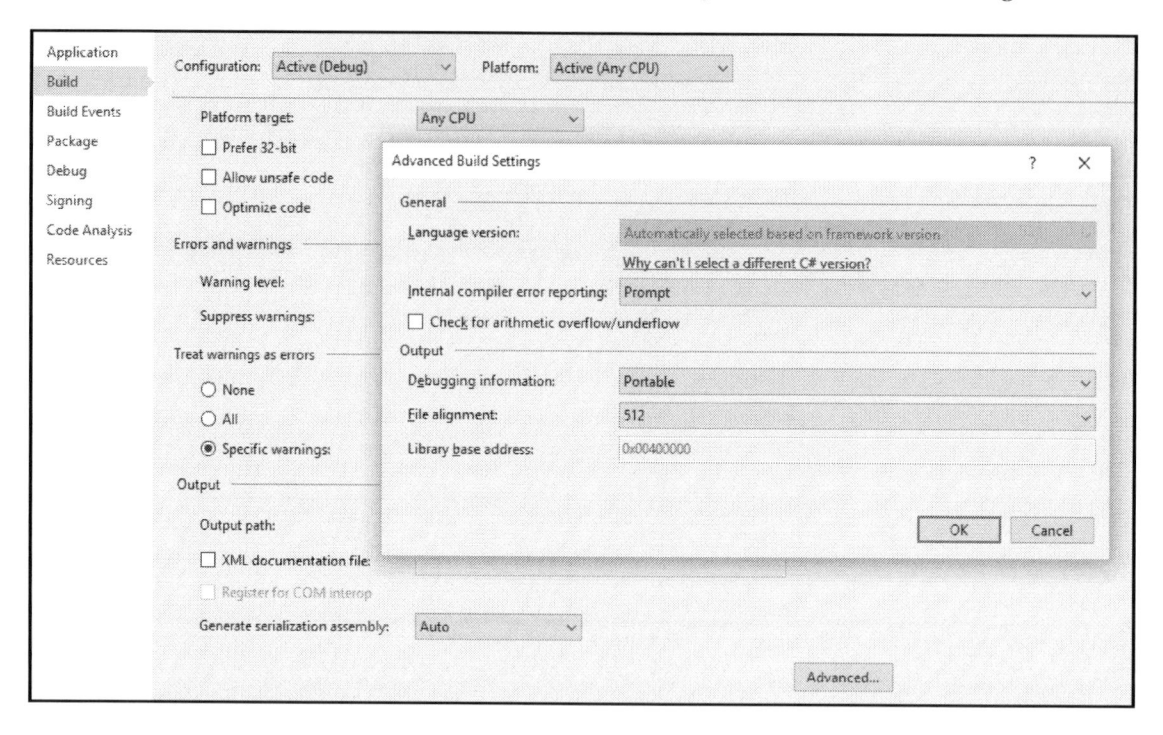

As per the preceding screenshot, Visual Studio does not allow us to change/select the C# version. This is because the C# version has already been selected. The C# compiler has identified the default language version for us, based on the framework we are targeting for our project.

The following table shows how the compiler picks the default version:

Target framework	C# language version
.NET Core 3.x	8.0
.NET Core 2.x	7.3
.NET Standard (all versions)	7.3
.NET Framework (all versions)	7.3

> If a project targets a preview framework, then the compiler accepts all of the language syntaxes from the latest preview version.

Now that's done, let's discuss the new features of C# 8.0.

Indices and ranges

As a new feature, now developers can easily get element values of an array based on its index or a specified range. This is possible with the introduction of two operators: the ^ operator represents the index from the end, and the .. operator represents the range. The following screenshot represents our array of book names:

```
New features of C#8.0
------------------------

Name                        index from start    index from end
-----------------------------------------------------------------

Microservices               0                   6
Design Patterns             1                   5
Test Driven Development     2                   4
Data Sciences               3                   3
Functional Programming      4                   2
Concurrent Programming      5                   1
```

The previous screenshot displays the values of every element of Books [], along with the index position.

> To showcase the feature, we have created a console app, using Visual Studio 2019.

In an earlier version of C#, you could only get the value of the first element of an array by its first index; in that case, we would write the following code:

```
Console.WriteLine($"\tFirst element of array (index from start): Books{{0}} => {Books[0]}");
```

With the help of a new feature of C# 8.0, now you can get the element value using the ^ operator, and it takes the index and counts from the end. Our Books[] array has a total length of 6. Hence, to get the value of the first element, we would write the following code:

```
Console.WriteLine($"\tFirst element of array (index from end): Books{{^6}} => {Books[^6]}");
```

Refactoring the Monolith

Now, run the code and you will get the output shown in the following screenshot:

```
Indices and Ranges
------------------------

-----------------------------------------------------------------
Name                         Index from start    Index from end
-----------------------------------------------------------------
Microservices                0                   6
Design Patterns              1                   5
Test Driven Development      2                   4
Data Sciences                3                   3
Functional Programming       4                   2
Concurrent Programming       5                   1
-----------------------------------------------------------------

First element of array (index from start): Books{0} => Microservices
First element of array (index from end): Books{^6} => Microservices
```

In earlier versions of C#, when we needed the values of all of the elements of an array, we would have to iterate the array's elements, starting from the 0th index up to the array's length. In C# 8.0, we can use a range when we need to print the values of an array, within a range from the start index value to the end index value. With the help of the `..` operator, now we can get the values of `Book []` in this way: `Book [1..4]`.

To use this feature, let's write the following code:

```
//Print using range
Range book = 1..4;
var res =  Books[book] ;
Console.WriteLine($"\tElement of array using Range: Books[{book}] => {Books[book]}");
```

In the previous code, we have declared a `book` variable with a range value of 1 to 4, and then we have used that variable to print the values of `Books[]` within the range. Run the code and see the output; the output is shown in the following screenshot:

[66]

```
Indices and Ranges
-----------------------------------

Name                          Index from start    Index from end
-----------------------------------------------------------------

Microservices                 0                   6
Design Patterns               1                   5
Test Driven Development       2                   4
Data Sciences                 3                   3
Functional Programming        4                   2
Concurrent Programming        5                   1
-----------------------------------------------------------------

First element of array (index from start): Books[0] => Microservices
First element of array (index from end): Books[^6] => Microservices
Element of array using Range: Books[1..4] => System.String[]
```

In the highlighted line of the previous screenshot, you might have noticed that our output is not as expected; we got `System.String[]` as an output, but we're expecting the values of the array. The preceding output is correct—we stored the values of `Books[]` in a new variable, `book`, and we have to iterate the variable to get the values.

To verify this, run the preceding code in debug mode (from Visual Studio 2019), by pressing the *F5* function key or by using the menu options: **Debug** | **Start Debugging**. Make sure you have put a break-point at the right place to see the debug results. The following screenshot was captured during debugging:

```
27      }
28      Console.WriteLine($"\t{Replicate('-', 65)}\n");
29      //Print index 0
30      Console.WriteLine($"\tFirst element of array (index from start): Books[0] => {Books[0]}");
31      Console.WriteLine($"\tFirst element of array (index from end): Books[^6] => {Books[^6]}");
32      //Print using range
33      Range book = 1..4;
34      var res = Books[book] ;
35      Console.WriteLine($"\tElement of array using Range: Books[{book}] => {res}");
36
37      }
38
                                                                    res {string[3]}
                                                                    ● [0] Q ▼ "Design Patterns"
                                                                    ● [1] Q ▼ "Test Driven Development"
                                                                    ● [2] Q ▼ "Data Sciences"
39      private static string Replicate(char repl = '-', int length = 5) => new string
40      }
41    }
42
```

Refactoring the Monolith

To get the values, we have modified the preceding code, and the following is the code to get the output:

```
//Print using range
Range book = 1..4;
var books =  Books[book] ;
Console.WriteLine($"\n\tElement of array using Range: Books[{book}] => {books}\n");
foreach (var b in books)
{
    Console.WriteLine($"\t{b}");
}
```

Now, run the preceding code, and you should see the output shown in the following screenshot:

```
Indices and Ranges
--------------------------


--------------------------------------------------------------
Name                        Index from start    Index from end
--------------------------------------------------------------

Microservices               0                   6
Design Patterns             1                   5
Test Driven Development     2                   4
Data Sciences               3                   3
Functional Programming      4                   2
Concurrent Programming      5                   1
--------------------------------------------------------------

First element of array (index from start): Books[0] => Microservices
First element of array (index from end): Books[^6] => Microservices

Element of array using Range: Books[1..4] => System.String[]

Design Patterns
Test Driven Development
Data Sciences
```

The previous screenshot gives us the exact output, as per our range. There are more indices and range scenarios, but we are not covering everything, as it is not in the scope of this book.

The readonly members

With this feature, we can now define a `readonly` member in a struct. This means the member can't be modified, and it can't be changed from any member functions. The values of `static readonly` members can be only changed from static constructor at runtime. The importance of the `readonly` field as being unmodifiable is that it will help avoid any accidental changes or wrong assignment throughout the code. This is also important in scenarios where we have a default value and would like to change the field at runtime.

The following code defines `readonly` members:

```
private static readonly int num1=5;
private static readonly int num2=6;
```

The preceding code declares two `readonly` members with pre-assigned values. You can write a method to use these members' values—something like `public static int Add => num1 + num2;`.

Run the code, and you should see the output shown in the following screenshot:

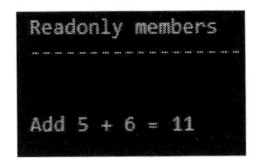

```
Readonly members
-----------------------

Add 5 + 6 = 11
```

The previous screenshot shows the output of our `Add` method. This method should not be declared as read-only, otherwise, it will give you an error. For example, the following code would give you an error:

```
public readonly static int Add => num1 + num2;
```

The preceding code would not work, and it would give you an error if you built the code. Consider the following screenshot:

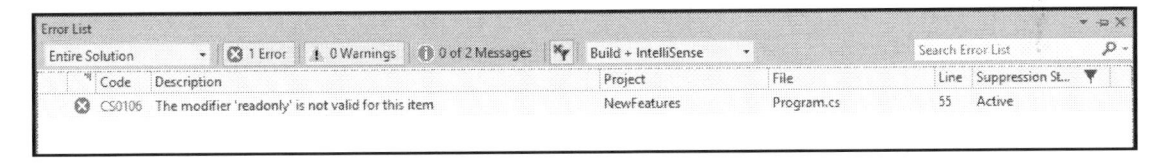

Code	Description	Project	File	Line	Suppression St...
CS0106	The modifier 'readonly' is not valid for this item	NewFeatures	Program.cs	55	Active

You will see a message, as shown in the preceding screenshot.

Default interface methods

With this feature, now, developers can add methods with a body in the interfaces. Earlier we had to explicitly write the functionality of the interface methods in the subsequent classes. But now, we will get the advantage of these default interface methods from which we can get pre-defined results while these methods are being called in the subsequent class. Consider the following code for a better understanding of this feature:

```
public interface IProduct
{
    public int Id { get; set; }
    public string Name { get; set; }
    public decimal Price { get; set; }
    public string ProductDesc() => $"Book:{Name} has Price:{Price}";
}
```

In the previous code, we declared an IProduct interface that has the following:

- Id: This is a unique product ID.
- Name: This is the product name.
- Price: This is the product price.
- ProductDesc: This is the default method of our interface, and it always produces the result; in our case, it will return string as the result of this method. Also, this method is available to all classes that implement the IProduct interface.

Let's implement the IProduct interface on our Product class. Consider the following code:

```
public class Product : IProduct
{
    public Product(int id, string name, decimal price)
    {
        Id = id;
        Name = name;
        Price = price;
    }
    public int Id { get; set; }
    public string Name { get; set; }
    public decimal Price { get; set; }
}
```

Our `Product` class has not defined anything extra, apart from the properties of the `IProduct` interface. There is no extra method in this class. The `ProductDesc()` method is available for this class. Consider the following code, and let's consume this default method in our code:

```
IProduct product = new Product(1, "Design Patterns", 350.00M);
Console.WriteLine($"\t{product.ProductDesc()}");
```

In the preceding code, we declared a `product` variable of the `IProduct` type, and then simply called the `ProductDesc()` method. This produces the output shown in the following screenshot:

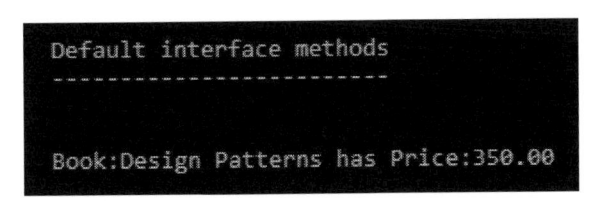

```
Default interface methods
-----------------------------

Book:Design Patterns has Price:350.00
```

The `ProductDesc()` method that is defined in the `IProduct` interface worked for our `Product` class.

In this section, we discussed a few features of C# 8.0. Please note that we've also added features that have been released with C# 8.0 Preview 5. We then updated features using C#8.0; there is a chance that a few features might be excluded or more features will be added in the official release of C# 8.0. Here, I provided an overview of the expected features of C# 8.0, but for a complete reference of these features, I suggest checking the official documentation of the C# language.

Now, let's look at the sizes of microservices in detail and how that contributes to building them.

The size of microservices

Before we start building our microservices, we should be clear about a few of their basic aspects, such as what factors to consider when sizing our microservices and how to ensure that they are isolated from the rest of the system.

As the name suggests, microservices should be micro. But what is micro? Microservices are all about size and granularity. To understand this better, let's consider the application discussed in `Chapter 1`, *An Introduction to Microservices*.

We want the teams working on this project to stay synchronized at all times with respect to their code. Staying synchronized is even more important when we release the complete project. We first needed to decompose our application and its specific parts into smaller functionalities/segments of the main service. Let's discuss the factors that need to be considered for the high-level isolation of microservices:

- **Risks due to requirement changes**: Changes in the requirements of one microservice should be independent of other microservices. In such cases, we will isolate/split our software into smaller services in such a way that, if there are any requirement changes in one service, they will be independent of another microservice.
- **Functionality changes**: We will isolate the functionalities that are rarely changed from the dependent functionalities that can be frequently modified. For example, in our application, the customer module notification functionality will rarely change. However, its related modules, such as Order, are more likely to have frequent business changes as part of their life cycle.
- **Team changes**: We should also consider isolating modules in such a way that one team can work independently of all the other teams. If the process of making a new developer productive—regarding the tasks in such modules—is not dependent on people outside the team, this means we are well placed.
- **Technology changes**: Technology use needs to be isolated vertically within each module. A module should not be dependent on a technology or component from another module. We should strictly isolate the modules developed in different technologies or stacks, or look at moving them to a common platform as a last resort.

Our primary goal should not be to make services as small as possible. Instead, our goal should be to isolate the identified bounded context and keep it small.

Now we know what the size of a microservice is. Next, let's learn what makes a good service.

What makes a good service?

Before microservices were conceptualized, whenever we thought of enterprise application integration, middleware looked like the most feasible option. Software vendors offered **Enterprise Service Bus (ESB)**, and this was one of the best options for middleware.

Besides considering these solutions, our main priority should be architectural features. When microservices arrived, middleware was no longer a consideration. Rather, the focus shifted to the contemplation of business problems and how to tackle those problems with the help of the architecture.

To make a service that can be used and maintained easily by developers and users, the service must have the following features (we can also consider these as characteristics of good services):

- **Standard data formats**: Good services should follow standardized data formats, while exchanging services or systems with other components. The most popular data formats used in the .NET stack are XML and JSON.
- **Standard communication protocol**: Good services should obey standard communication formats, such as SOAP and REST.
- **Loose coupling**: One of the most important characteristics of a good service is that it follows loose coupling. When services are loosely coupled, we don't have to worry about changes. Changes in one service will not impact other services.

This section helped us to understand what makes a service good and how. We will next cover domain-driven design and its importance for microservices.

DDD and its importance for microservices

Domain-Driven Design (**DDD**) is a method and a process for designing complex systems. In this section, we will briefly discuss DDD and how it is important in the context of microservices.

Domain model design

The main objective of domain design is to understand the exact domain problems and then draft a model that can be written in any language or set of technologies. For example, in our FlixOne bookstore application, we need to understand order management and stock management.

Here are a few characteristics of the domain-driven model:

- A domain model should focus on a specific business model and not multiple business models.
- It should be reusable.

- It should be designed so that it can be called in a loosely coupled way, unlike the rest of the system.
- It should be designed independently of persistence implementations.
- It should be pulled out from a project to another location, so it should not be based on any infrastructure framework.

Next, let's see how this model is important for microservices.

Importance for microservices

DDD is the blueprint and can be implemented by microservices. In other words, once DDD is done, we can implement it using microservices. This is just like how, in our application, we can easily implement order services, inventory services, tracking services, and so on.

Once you have dealt with the transition process to your satisfaction, a simple exercise should be performed. This will help you to verify that the size of the microservice is small enough. Every system is unique and has its own complexity level. Considering these levels of your domain, you need to have a baseline for the maximum number of domain objects that can talk to each other. If any service fails this evaluation criterion, then you have a possible candidate to evaluate your transition once again. However, don't get into this exercise with a specific number in mind; you can always go easy. As long as you have followed all of the steps correctly, the system should be fine for you.

If you feel that this baseline process is difficult for you to achieve, you can take another route by going through all of the interfaces and classes in each microservice. Considering all of the steps we have followed, and the industry-standard coding guidelines, anybody new to the system should be able to make sense of its purpose.

You can also perform another simple test to check whether the correct vertical isolation of the services was achieved. You can deploy each one of them and make them live with the rest of the services that are still unavailable. If your service goes live and continues listening for incoming requests, you can pat yourself on the back.

There are many benefits that can be derived from the isolated deployment capability. The capability to just deploy them independently allows the host in them to enter its own independent processes. It also allows you to harness the power of the cloud and any other hybrid models of hosting that you can think of. You are free to independently pick different technologies for each one of them as well.

After understanding DDD, we can now move on to the concept of seam.

Understanding the concept of seam

At the very core of microservices, lies the capability to work on a specific functionality in isolation from the rest of the system. This translates into all of the advantages discussed earlier, such as reduced module dependency, code reusability, easier code maintenance, and better deployment.

In my opinion, the same attributes, which were attained with the implementation of microservices, should be maintained during the process of implementation. Why should the whole process of moving monoliths to microservices be painful and not be as rewarding as using the microservices themselves? Just remember that the transition can't be done overnight and will require meticulous planning. Many capable solution architects have differed in their approaches when presenting their highly capable teams. The answer lies not just in the points already mentioned, but in the risk to the business itself.

This is very well attainable. However, we must identify our method correctly to achieve it. Otherwise, there is a possibility that the whole process of transitioning a monolithic application to microservices could be a dreadful one. Let's see how this is done.

Module interdependency

This should always be the starting point when trying to transition a monolithic application into a microservice-style architecture. Identify and pick up those parts of the application that are least depended on by other modules and have the least dependency on them as well.

It is very important to understand that, by identifying such parts of the application, you are not just trying to pick up the least challenging parts to deal with. However, at the same time, you have identified seams, which are the most easily visible parts to change. These are parts of the application where we will perform the necessary changes first. This allows us to completely isolate this part of the code from the rest of the system. It should be ready to become a part of the microservice or to be deployed in the final stage of this exercise.

Even though the seams have been identified, the capability to achieve microservice-style development is still a little further away. In this section, we covered the concept of a seam, and then we saw what module interdependency is. This is a good start. However, microservices-based applications require more patterns, and we need to understand the technology. In the coming section, we will discuss the technology.

Technology

A two-pronged approach is required here. First, you must identify what different features of the application's base framework are being utilized. The differentiation could be, for example, an implementation based on a heavy dependency on certain data structures, the interprocess communication being performed, or the activity of report generation. This is the easy part.

However, as the second step, I recommend that you become more confident and pick up the pieces of code that use a type of technology that is different from what is being used currently. For example, there could be a piece of code relying on simple data structures or XML-based persistence. Identify such baggage in the system and mark it for a transition. A lot of prudence is required in this twin-pronged approach. Making a selection that is too ambitious could set you on a path similar to what we have been trying to avoid altogether.

Some of these parts might not look like very promising candidates for the final microservice-style architecture application. They should still be dealt with now. In the end, they will allow you to easily perform the transition. The technology and framework play an important role in the development of any application, but the technology is most important when we are dealing with applications that are based on the microservices architectural style.

This section explained the technology; in the next section, we will discuss the team structure.

Team structure

With every iteration of this identification process being executed, this factor becomes more and more important. There could be teams that are differentiated on various grounds, such as their technical skill set, geographical location, or security requirements (employees versus freelancers).

If there is a part of the functionality that requires a specific skill set, then you could be looking at another probable seam candidate. Teams can be composed of varying degrees of these differentiation factors. As part of the transition to microservices, the clear differentiation that could enable them to work independently could further optimize their productivity.

This can also provide a benefit in the form of safeguarding the intellectual property of the company; outsourcing to consultants for specific parts of the application is not uncommon. The capability to allow consultants or partners to help you only on a specific module makes the process simpler and more secure.

The team and its members are very important to the execution of any application. In the case of a microservices-based application, we have the flexibility for teams where anyone can work on individual services without interfering with others' tasks or activities. To see how this happens, in the next section, we will discuss databases.

Databases

The heart and soul of any enterprise system is its database. This is the biggest asset of the system on any given day. It is also the most vulnerable part of the whole system in such an exercise. (No wonder database architects can sound mean and intrusive whenever you ask them to make even the smallest change.) Their domain is defined by database tables and stored procedures.

The health of their domain is also judged by referential integrity and the time it takes to perform various transactions. I don't blame architects for overdoing it anymore. They have a reason for this: their past experiences. It's time to change that. Let me tell you, this won't be easy, as we will have to utilize a completely different approach to handling data integrity when we embark on this path.

You might think that the easiest approach is to divide the whole database in one go, but that is not the case. This could lead us to the situation we have been trying to avoid all along. Let's look at how to go about doing this more efficiently.

As you continue picking up pieces after the module dependency analysis, identify the database structures that are being used to interact with the database. There are two steps that you need to perform here. First, check whether you can isolate the database structures in your code to be broken down, and then align this with the newly defined vertical boundaries. Secondly, identify what it would take to break down the underlying database structure as well.

Don't worry yet if breaking down the underlying data structure seems difficult. If it appears that it involves other modules that you haven't started to move to microservices, this is a good sign. Don't let the database changes define the modules that you would pick and migrate to a microservice-style architecture; keep it the other way round. This ensures that, when a database change is picked up, the code that depends on the change is already ready to absorb the change.

This ensures that you don't pick up the battle of data integrity while you are already occupied with modifying the code that will rely on this part of the database. Nevertheless, such database structures should draw your attention so that the modules that depend on them are picked next. This will allow you to easily complete the move to microservices for all of the associated modules in one go. Refer to the following diagram:

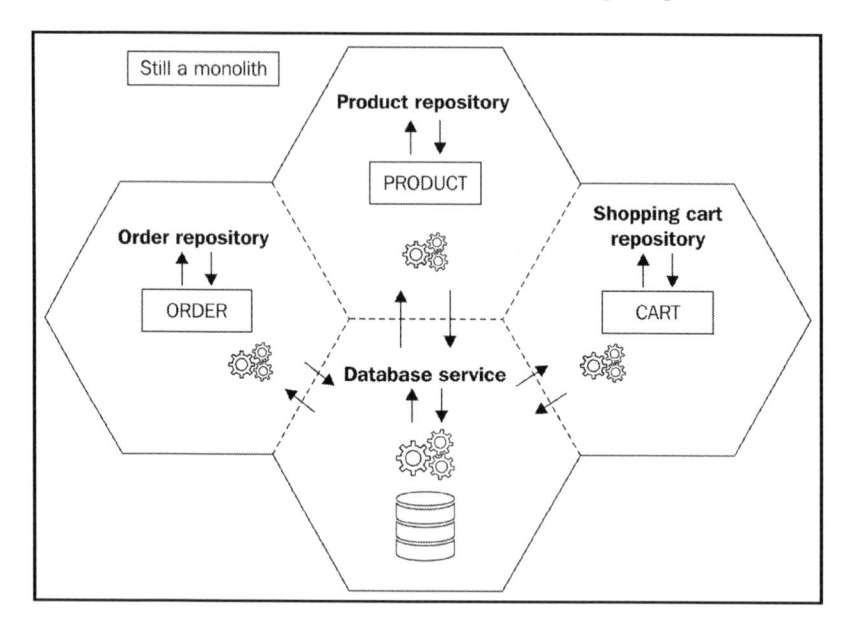

Here, we have not broken the database yet. Instead, we have simply separated our database access part into layers, as part of the first step.

What we have done here is mapped the code data structure to the database so that they no longer depend on each other. Let's see how this step will work out when we remove foreign key relationships.

If we can transition the code structures being used to access the database along with the database structure, we will save time. This approach might differ from system to system and can be affected by our personal bias. If your database structure changes seem to be impacting modules that are yet to be marked for transition, move on for now.

You also need to understand what kind of changes are acceptable when you break down this database table or when you merge it with another partial structure. The most important thing is to not shy away from breaking those foreign key relationships. This might sound like a big difference from our traditional approach to maintaining data integrity.

However, removing your foreign key relationships is the most fundamental challenge when restructuring your database to suit the microservice architecture. Remember that a microservice is meant to be independent of other services. If there are foreign key relationships with other parts of the system, this makes it dependent on the services that own that part of the database. Refer to the following diagram:

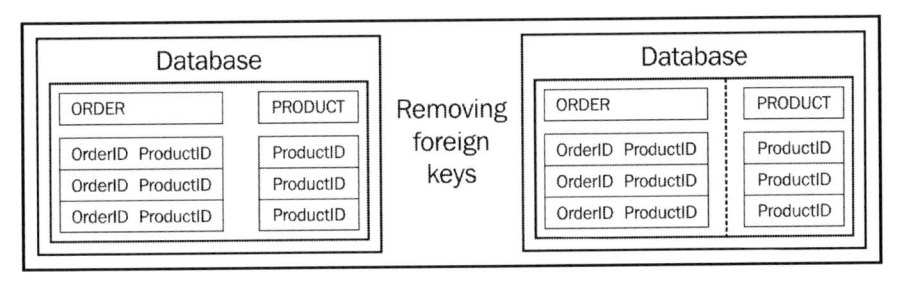

As part of step two, we have kept the foreign key fields in the database tables, but we have removed the foreign key constraint. Consequently, the **ORDER** table still holds information about **ProductID**, but the foreign key relation is broken now. Refer to the following diagram:

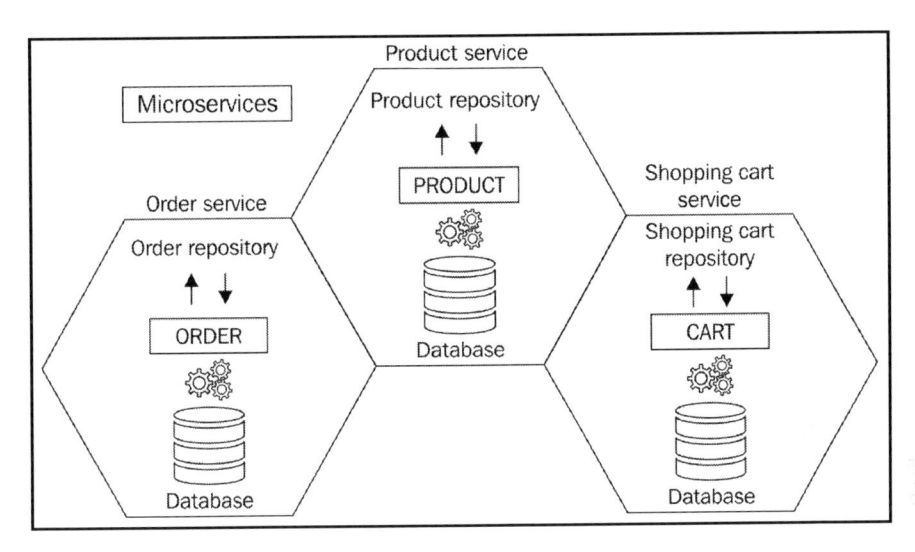

This is what our microservice-style architecture would finally look like. The central database would be moved away, in favor of each service having its own database. So, by separating the data structures in the code and by removing foreign key relationships, we've prepared to finally make the change. The connected boundaries of microservices in the preceding diagram signify interservice communication.

Refactoring the Monolith

With the two steps performed, your code is now ready to split **ORDER** and **PRODUCT** into separate services, with each having their own database.

If the discussions here have left you bewildered about all of the transactions that have been safely performed up until now, you are not alone. This outcome of the challenge with the transactions is not a small one by any means, and it deserves focused attention. We'll cover this in detail a bit later.

In this section, we discussed a database that we called the **main storage** of the application. We can also break down a single database into small databases that can be used per service, so we can say there is one database per service.

Before we go further, there is another part that becomes a no man's land in the database. This is master data, or static data, as some may call it.

Master data

Handling master data is about your personal choice and system-specific requirements. If you see that the master data is not going to change for ages and occupies an insignificant amount of records, you are better off with the configuration files or even code enumerations.

This requires someone to push out the configuration files once in a while when the changes do happen. However, this still leaves a gap in the future. As the rest of the system would depend on this one module, it would be responsible for these updates. If this module does not behave correctly, other parts of the system relying on it could also be impacted negatively.

Another option is to wrap up the master data in a separate service altogether. Having the master data delivered through a service would provide the advantage of the services knowing the change instantly and understanding the capability to consume it as well.

The process of requesting this service might not be much different from the process of reading configuration files, when required. It might be slower, but it is to be done only as many times as necessary.

Moreover, you could also support different sets of master data. It would be fairly easy to maintain product sets that differ every year. With the microservice architecture style, it is always a good idea to be independent of any kind of outside reliance in the future.

In this section, we have discussed master data. Transactions play an important role when we interact with data, so in the next section, we will discuss them.

Transactions

With our foreign keys gone and the database split into smaller parts, we need to devise our own mechanisms for handling data integrity. Here, we need to factor in the possibility that not all services will successfully go through a transaction, in the scope of their respective data stores.

A good example is a user ordering a specific product. At the time the order is accepted, there is a sufficient quantity available to be ordered. However, by the time the order is logged, the product service cannot log the order for some reason. We don't know yet whether it is due to an insufficient quantity or some other communication fault within the system. There are two possible options here. Let's discuss them one by one.

The first option is to try again and perform the remaining part of the transaction sometime later. This would require us to orchestrate the whole transaction in a way that tracks individual transactions across services. So, every transaction, which leads to transactions being performed for more than one service, must be tracked. If one of them does not go through, it deserves a retry. This might work for long-lived operations.

However, for other operations, this could cause a real problem. If the operation is not long-lived and you still decide to retry, the outcome will result in either locking out other transactions or making the transaction wait—meaning it is impossible to complete it.

Another option is canceling the entire set of transactions that is spread across various services. This means that a single failure at any stage of the entire set of transactions would result in the reversal of all of the previous transactions.

This is one area where maximum prudence would be required, and it would be time well invested. A stable outcome is only guaranteed when the transactions are planned out well in any microservice-style architecture application.

Transactions are very important when we work with database operations; these operations could be fetch, insert, and so on. With the help of transactions, we can roll back the complete operation within the flow that is in the scope of transactions, if any operation fails.

Now, let's move on to understanding communication between microservices.

Communication between microservices

In the preceding section, we separated our Order module into **Order services** and discussed how we can break down the foreign key relationship between the ORDER and PRODUCT tables.

In a monolithic application, we have a single repository that queries the database to fetch the records from both the ORDER and PRODUCT tables. However, in our upcoming microservice application, we will segregate repositories between **Order service** and **Product service**. With each service having its respective database, each one would access its own database only. **Order service** would only be able to access the order **Database**, whereas **Product service** would be able to access the product **Database** only. **Order service** should not be allowed to access the product **Database** and vice versa.

> We will discuss communication between microservices in Chapter 3, *Effective Communication between Services*, in detail.

The following diagram shows the interaction with different services, using the **API gateway**:

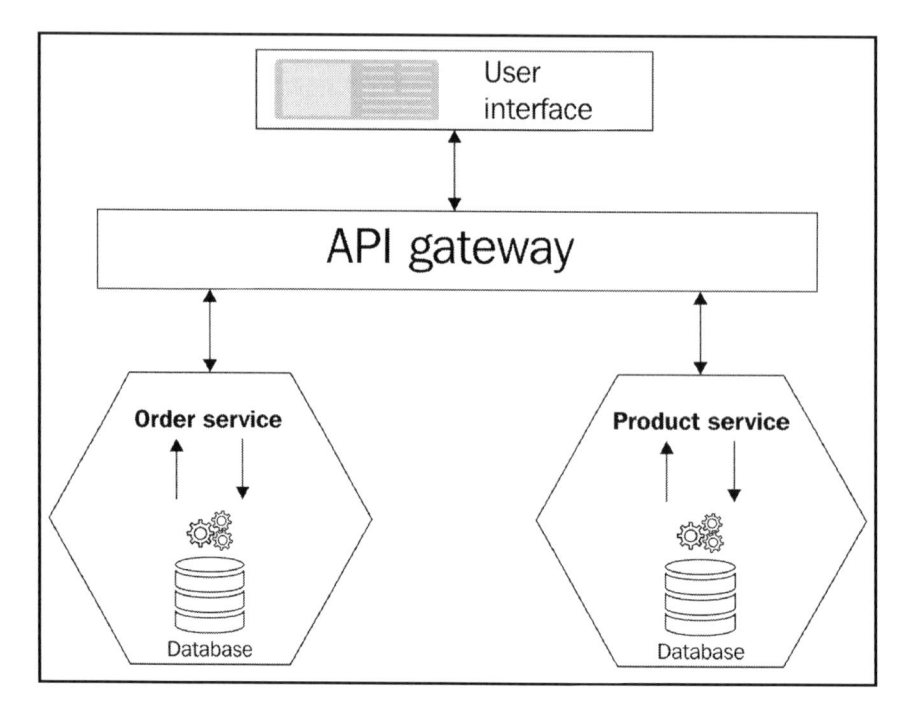

In the preceding diagram, we can see that our UI is interacting with **Order Service** and **Product service** via the **API gateway**. Both of the services are physically separated from each other, and there is no direct interaction between these services. Communication performed in this manner is also referred to as communication that is based on the **API gateway** pattern.

The API gateway is nothing but a middle-tier from which the UI can interact with the microservices. It also provides a simpler interface and makes the process of consuming these services simpler. It provides a different level of granularity to different clients, as required (browser and desktop).

We can say that it provides coarse-grained APIs to mobile clients and fine-grained APIs to desktop clients, and it can use a high-performance network underneath its hood, to provide some serious throughput.

We can easily define granularity as the following (also, see `https://softwareengineering.stackexchange.com/questions/385313/what-is-granularity`):

> "...a system is broken down into small parts; large systems can further be broken or torn down to finer parts."

The benefits of the API gateway for microservices

There is no doubt that the API gateway is beneficial for microservices. With an API gateway, you can do the following:

- Invoke services through the API gateway
- Reduce round trips between the client and the application
- The client can access different APIs in one place, as segregated by the gateway

It provides flexibility to clients in such a manner that they can interact with different services, as they need to and when they need to. This way, there is no need to expose complete/all services at all. The API gateway is a component of complete API management. In our solution, we will use Azure API Management, and we will explain it further in `Chapter 3`, *Effective Communication between Services*.

API gateway versus API management

In the preceding section, we discussed how the API gateway hides the actual APIs from its clients and then simply redirects the calls to the actual API from these clients. The API management solution provides a complete management system to manage all of the APIs of its external consumers. All API management solutions, such as Azure API Management (https://docs.microsoft.com/en-us/azure/api-management/), provide various capabilities and functionalities, such as the following:

- Design
- Development
- Security
- Publishing
- Scalability
- Monitoring
- Analysis
- Monetization

Next, let's revisit the FlixOne case study for better understanding.

Revisiting the FlixOne case study

In the preceding chapter, we looked at an example of an imaginary company, FlixOne Inc., which operates in the e-commerce domain and has its own .NET monolithic application: the FlixOne bookstore.

We have already discussed the following:

- How to segregate the code
- How to segregate the database
- How to denormalize the database
- How to begin transitioning
- The available refactoring approaches

The preceding points are important, as we are transitioning our monolithic application to a microservices-based application. In `Chapter 1`, *An Introduction to Microservices*, we already discussed why we want to build microservices-based applications. The demand of the application, frequent updates, and 100% uptime (the availability of the application) are required to compete in the existing e-commerce market.

In the next sections, we will start transitioning a .NET monolith to a microservices application.

Prerequisites

We will use the following tools and technologies while transitioning our monolithic application to a microservice-style architecture:

- Visual Studio 2019 or later
- C# 8.0
- ASP.NET Core MVC/Web API
- Entity Framework Core
- SQL Server 2008 R2 or later

Transitioning to our product service

We already have our product module in place. We are going to pull back this module now and start with a new ASP.NET Core MVC project. To do this, follow all of the steps we discussed in the preceding sections and in `Chapter 1`, *An Introduction to Microservices*. Let's examine the technology and database we will use:

- **Technology stack**: We have already selected this for our product service; we will go with ASP.NET Core, C#, **Entity Framework (EF)**, and so on. Microservices can be written using different technology stacks and can be consumed by clients that are created by different technologies. For our product service, we will go with ASP.NET Core.
- **Database**: We have already discussed this in `Chapter 1`, *An Introduction to Microservices*, when we discussed a monolithic application and segregating its database. Here, we will go with SQL Server, and the database schema will be `Product` instead of `dbo`.

Refactoring the Monolith

Our product database is segregated. We will use this database in our product service, as shown in the following screenshot:

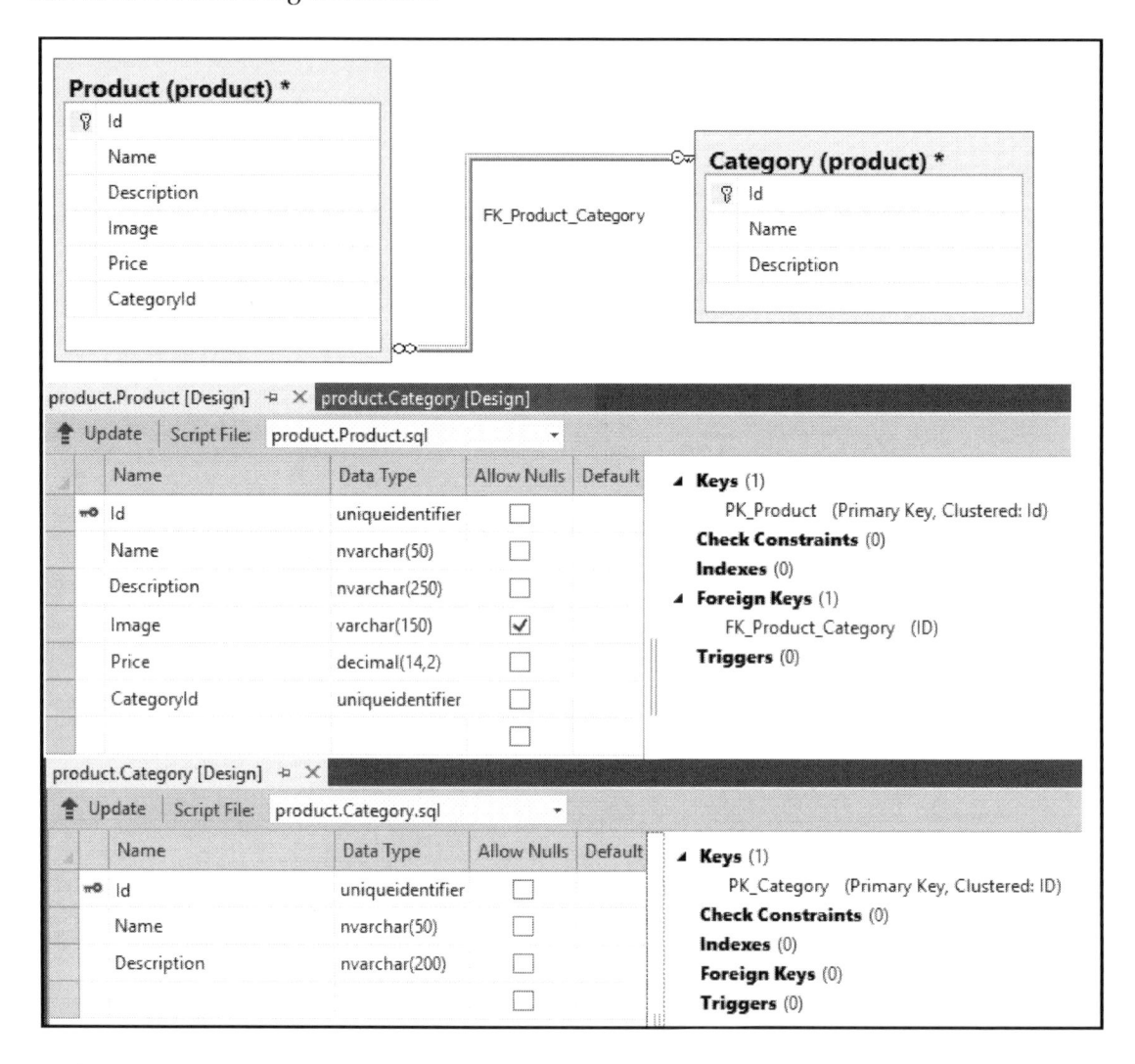

We have created a separated product database for our product service. We did not migrate the entire data set. In the following sections, we will discuss product database migration as well.

Migration is important, as we have numerous existing records of FlixOne bookstore customers. We can't ignore these records, and they need to be migrated to our modified structure. Let's get started.

Migrations

In the preceding section, we separated our product database to ensure that it would only be used by our product service. We also selected a technology stack of our choice to build our microservice (product service).

In this section, we will discuss how we can migrate both our existing code and database to ensure that they fit right in with our new architectural style.

Code migration

Code migration does not involve just pulling out a few layers of code from the existing monolithic application and then bundling it with our newly created **Product service**. To achieve this, you'll need to implement all that you have learned, up until now. In the existing monolithic application, we have a single repository, which is common to all modules. However, for microservices, we will create repositories for each module separately and keep them isolated from each other:

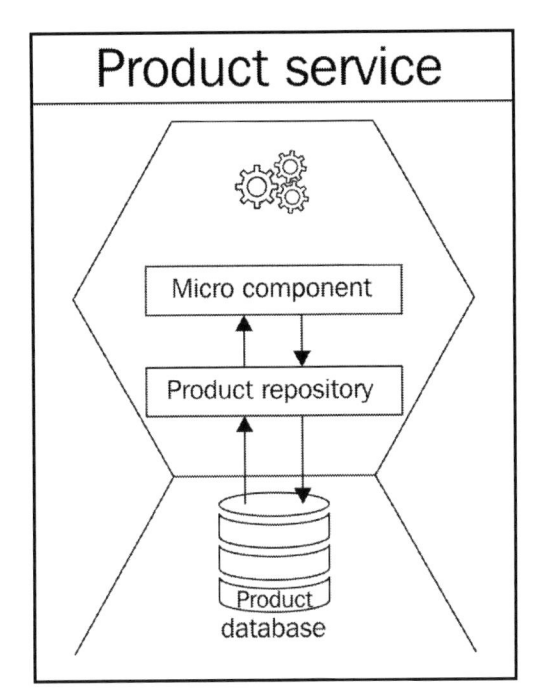

Refactoring the Monolith

In the preceding diagram, the **Product service** has a **Product repository**, which further interacts with its designated data store, named **Product database**. We will now discuss microcomponents a bit more. They are nothing but isolated parts of the application (microservice), namely, common classes and business functionalities. It is worthwhile noting here that the **Product repository** itself is a microcomponent in the world of microservices.

In our final product service, which is to be done in ASP.NET Core, we will work with a model and controller to create our RESTful API. Let's describe both of these briefly:

- **Model**: This is an object that represents the data in the product service. In our case, the identified models are stacked into product and category fields. In our code, models are nothing but a set of simple C# classes. When we talk in terms of EF Core, they are commonly referred to as **Plain Old CLR Objects** (**POCOs**). POCOs are nothing but simple entities without any data access functionality.
- **Controller**: This is a simple C# class that inherits an abstract class controller of the `Microsoft.AspNetCore.Mvc` namespace. It handles HTTP requests and is responsible for the creation of the HTTP response to be sent back. In our product service, we have a product controller that handles everything.

Let's follow a step-by-step approach to create our product service.

Creating our project

As already decided in the previous sections, we will create `ProductService` in ASP.NET Core 3.0 or C# 8.0, using Visual Studio. Let's look at what steps are required to do this:

1. Start Visual Studio.
2. Create a new project by navigating to **File | New | Project**.
3. From the template options available, select **ASP.NET Core Web Application**, and then click **Next**. The following screenshot shows the **Create a new project** window:

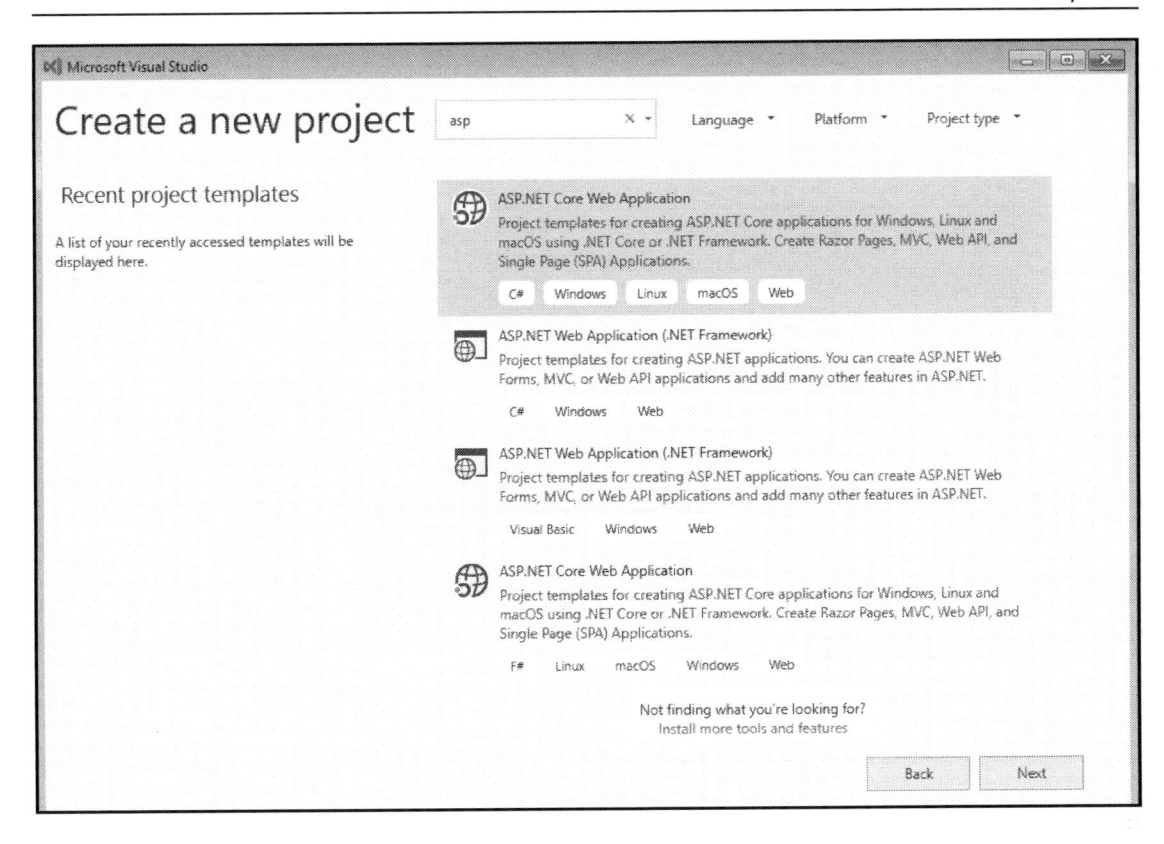

4. Enter the project name as `FlixOne.BookStore.ProductService`, and click **OK**.

Refactoring the Monolith

5. From the template screen, select **Web Application (Model-View-Controller)** and make sure you selected **.NET Core** and **ASP.NET Core 3.1** from the options, as shown in the following screenshot:

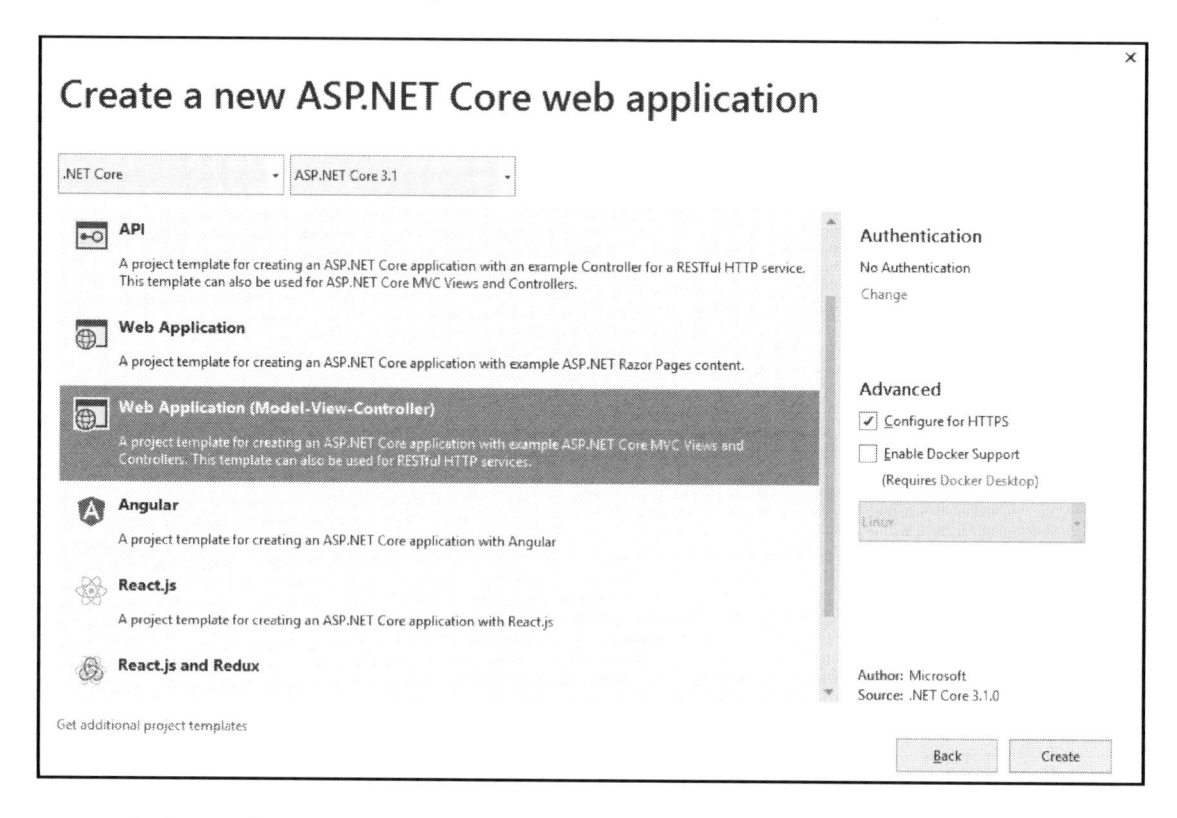

6. Leave the rest of the options as the default and click **Create**. The new solution should look like the following screenshot:

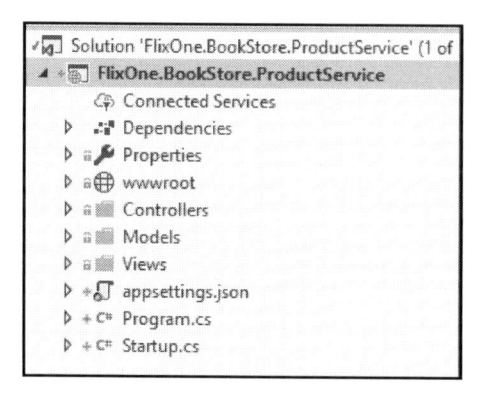

Chapter 2

7. From the **Solution Explorer**, right-click (or press *Alt + Enter*) on the project and click **Properties**.
8. From the **Properties** window, click **Build | Advance**. The **Language version** is automatically selected, based on the framework version. Our framework is .NET Core 3.0, so our language should be C# 8.0, as shown in the following screenshot:

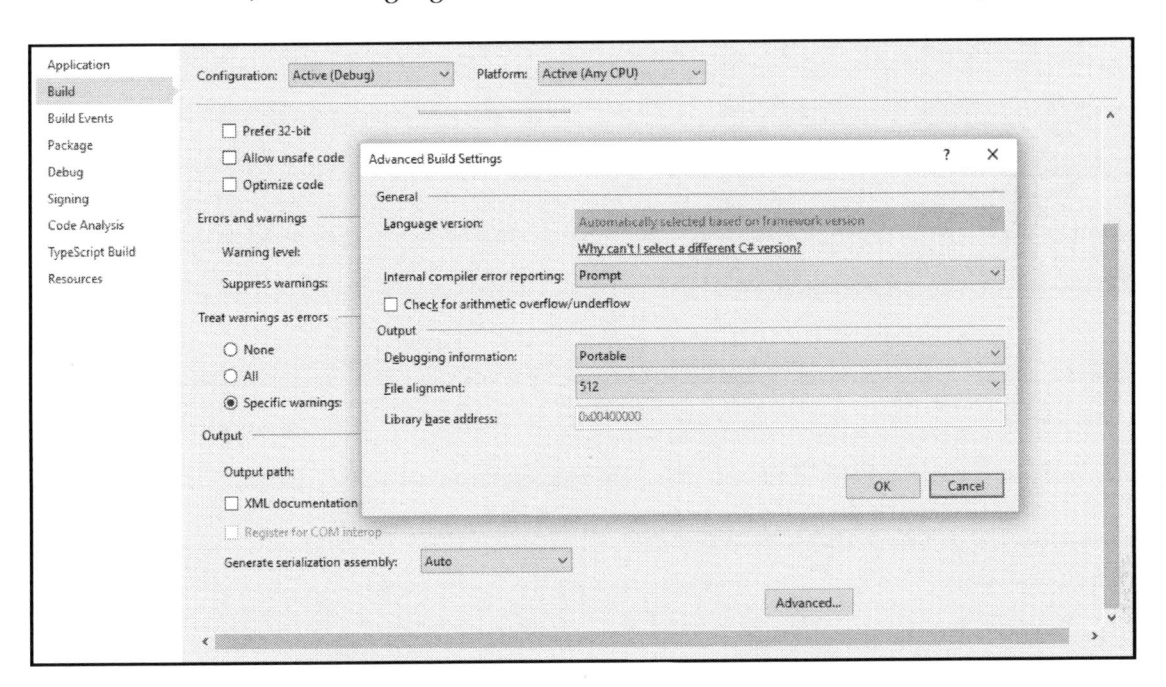

> Please make sure you select the latest version of C# 8.0. The use of older versions might be troublesome.

Adding the model

In our monolithic application, we do not have any model classes yet. So, let's go ahead and add a new model, as required.

[91]

Refactoring the Monolith

To add the new model, add a new folder and name it `Models`, if does not exist in the project. In the **Solution Explorer**, right-click on the project, and then click **Add | New Folder**:

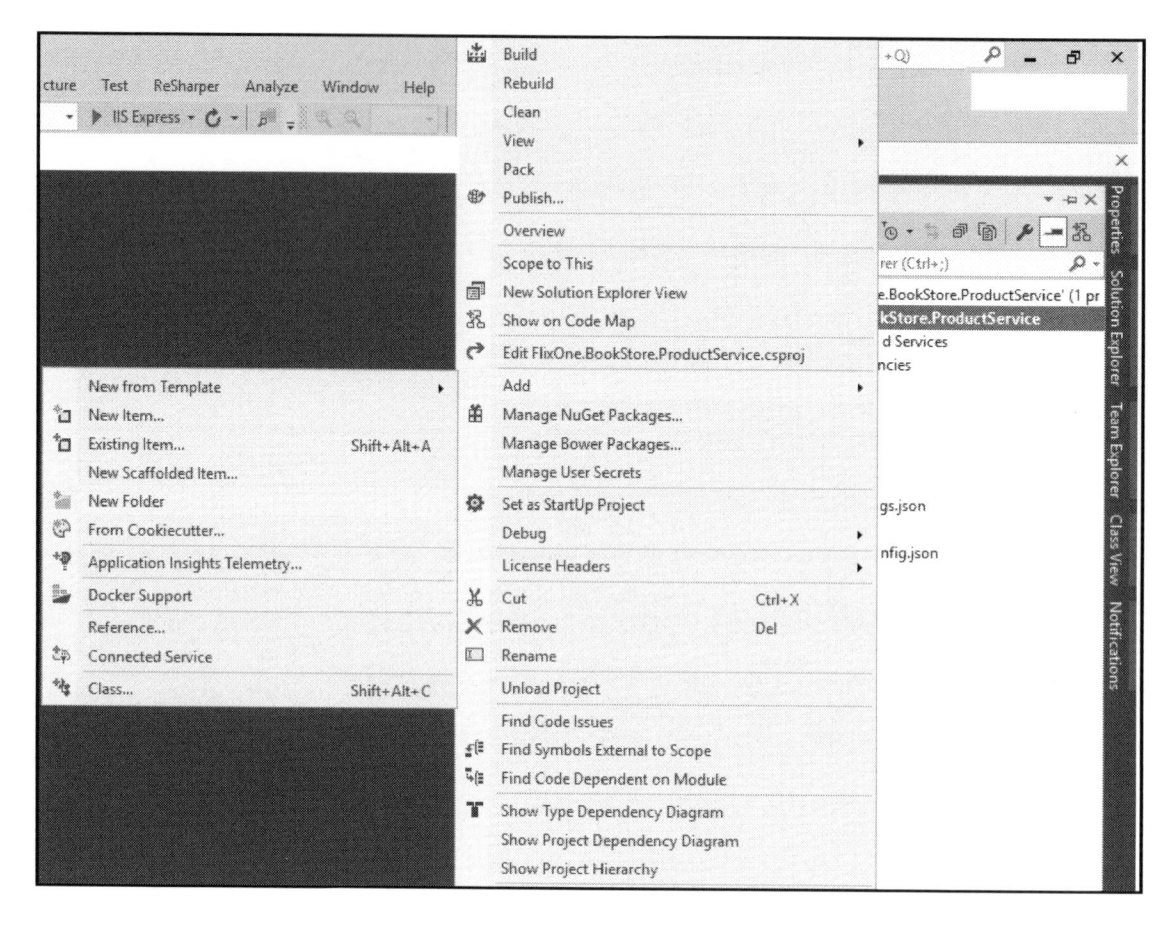

There is no hard and fast rule for putting all of the model classes in a folder named `Models`. As a matter of fact, we can put our model classes anywhere in the project in our application. We follow this practice because it becomes self-explanatory from folder names. At the same time, it easily identifies that this folder is for the model classes.

To add new `Product` and `Category` classes (these classes will represent our POCOs), do the following:

1. Right-click on the `Models` folder and choose **Add | New Item | Class** and name it `Product`; repeat this step, add another class, and name it `Category`.

2. Now, add the properties that depict our product database column name to the `Product` and `Category` tables respectively.

> There is no restriction, regarding having the property name match the table column name. It is just a general practice.

The following code snippet depicts what our `Product` model class will look like:

```
using System;
namespace FlixOne.BookStore.ProductService.Models
{
    public class Product
    {
        public Guid Id { get; set; }
        public string Name { get; set; }
        public string Description { get; set; }
        public string Image { get; set; }
        public decimal Price { get; set; }
        public Guid CategoryId { get; set; }
        public virtual Category Category { get; set; }
    }
}
```

The preceding code example represents a product model, and it contains the following:

- `Id` is a **Globally Unique Identifier (GUID)** and represents a record ID.
- `Name` is a string-type property and holds a product name.
- `Description` is a string-type property and holds a complete description of a product.
- `Image` is a string-type property and holds a Base64 string.
- `Price` is a decimal-type property and holds the price of a product.
- `CategoryId` is the GUID; it holds a record ID of a category of the product.
- `Category` is a virtual property and contains complete information on the category of the product.

The following code snippet shows what our `Category.cs` model class will look like:

```
using System;
using System.Collections.Generic;
namespace FlixOne.BookStore.ProductService.Models
{
    public class Category
```

```
    {
        public Category()
        {
            Products = new List<Product>();
        }
        public Guid Id { get; set; }
        public string Name { get; set; }
        public string Description { get; set; }
        public IEnumerable<Product> Products { get; set; }
    }
}
```

The preceding code represents our category model, which contains the following:

- `Id` is a GUID and represents a record ID.
- `Name` is a string type property and holds a category name.
- `Description` is a string type property and holds a complete description of the category.
- `Products` is a collection of all the products that belong to the category of the current record.

Let's add a repository into our code examples, so that we can make a few realistic database calls.

Adding a repository

In our monolithic application, we have a common repository throughout the project. In `ProductService`, by virtue of following all of the principles learned up until now, we will create microcomponents, which means separate repositories encapsulating the data layer.

> A repository is nothing but a simple C# class that contains the logic to retrieve data from the database and map it to the model.

Adding a repository is as simple as following these steps:

1. Create a new folder, and then name it `Persistence`.
2. Add the `IProductRepository` interface and a `ProductRepository` class that will implement the `IProductRepository` interface.
3. Again, we name the folder `Persistence` to follow the general principle for easy identification.

Chapter 2

The following code snippet provides an overview of the `IProductRepository` interface:

```
using System;
using System.Collections.Generic;
using FlixOne.BookStore.ProductService.Models;

namespace FlixOne.BookStore.ProductService.Persistence
{
  public interface IProductRepository
  {
    void Add(Product product);
    IEnumerable<Product> GetAll();
    Product GetBy(Guid id);
    void Remove(Guid id);
        void Update(Product product);
  }
}
```

Our `IProductRepository` interface has all of the required methods:

- `Add`: This method is responsible for adding a new product.
- `GetAll` fetches all the product records and returns a collection of products.
- `GetBy` fetches one product, based on the given product ID.
- `Remove` deletes a specific record.
- `Update` is responsible for updating the existing record.

The next code snippet provides an overview of the `ProductRepository` class (it is still without any implementation, and it does not have any interaction with the database yet):

```
using FlixOne.BookStore.ProductService.Contexts;
using FlixOne.BookStore.ProductService.Models;
using Microsoft.EntityFrameworkCore;

namespace FlixOne.BookStore.ProductService.Persistence
{
  public class ProductRepository : IProductRepository
  {
    public void Add(Product Product)
    {
      throw new NotImplementedException();
    }
    public IEnumerable<Product> GetAll()
    {
          throw new NotImplementedException();
       }
        public Product GetBy(Guid id)
```

```
      {
         throw new NotImplementedException();
      }
   public void Remove(Guid id)
      {
         throw new NotImplementedException();
      }
      public void Update(Product Product)
      {
         throw new NotImplementedException();
      }
   }
}
```

The preceding code implements the `IProductRepository` interface. The code example is for demo purposes, so we did not add definitions to the implemented methods.

Next, let's see how to register our repository using `ConfigureServices` of `Startup.cs`.

Registering repositories

For `ProductService`, we will use built-in dependency injection support with ASP.NET Core. To do so, follow these simple steps:

1. Open `Startup.cs`.
2. Add the repository to the `ConfigureServices` method. It should look like this:

   ```
   using FlixOne.BookStore.ProductService.Persistence;
   public void ConfigureServices(IServiceCollection services)
   {
     // Add framework services.

      services.AddSingleton<IProductRepository,
      ProductRepository>();
   }
   ```

In the preceding code, we register our repository as a singleton service for the **Inversion of Control (IoC)** provided by the .NET Core framework.

In the upcoming section, we will discuss our product controller and will see how to add a controller in our code.

Adding a product controller

Finally, we have reached the stage where we can proceed to add our controller class. This controller will be responsible for responding to the incoming HTTP requests with the applicable HTTP response. In case you are wondering what is to be done with that, you can see the `HomeController` class, as it is a default class provided by the ASP.NET Core template.

Right-click on the `controllers` folder, choose the **Add** | **New Item** option, and select **API Controller Class**. Name it `ProductController`. Here, we are going to utilize whatever code and functionality we can from the monolithic application. Go back to the legacy code, and look at the operations you're performing there; you can borrow them for our `ProductController` class. Refer to the following screenshot:

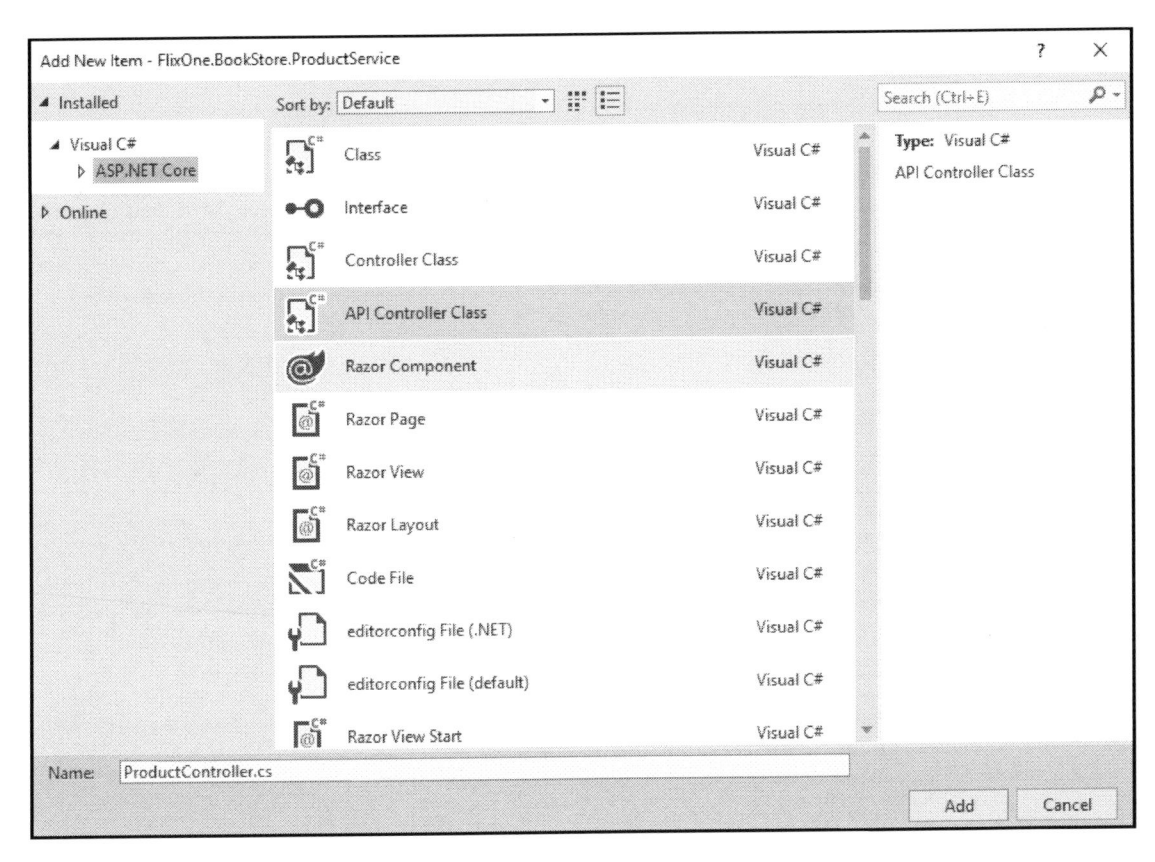

Refactoring the Monolith

After we have made the required modifications to `ProductController`, it should look something similar to this:

```
using Microsoft.AspNetCore.Mvc;
using FlixOne.BookStore.ProductService.Persistence;
namespace FlixOne.BookStore.ProductService.Controllers
{
  [Route("api/[controller]")]
  public class ProductController : Controller
  {
    private readonly IProductRepository _ProductRepository;
    public ProductController(IProductRepository ProductRepository)
    {
      _ProductRepository = ProductRepository;
    }
  }
}
```

In the previous section, we registered `ProductRepository` for IoC and in `ProductController`, we are using the repository. We used a constructor injection in the preceding code example, and we used a parameterized constructor with a parameter of the `IProductRepository` type.

The ProductService API

In our monolithic application, for the `Product` module, we are doing the following:

- Adding a new `Product` module
- Updating an existing `Product` module
- Deleting an existing `Product` module
- Retrieving a `Product` module

Now, we will create `ProductService`; we require the following APIs:

API Resource	Description
GET /api/Product	Gets a list of products
GET /api/Product/{id}	Gets a product
PUT /api/Product/{id}	Updates an existing product
DELETE /api/Product/{id}	Deletes an existing product
POST /api/Product	Adds a new product

Next, we will see how to add EF Core support to these.

Adding EF Core support

Before going further, we need to add EF Core support, so that our service can interact with the product database. So far, we have not added any methods to our repository that could interact with the database. To add EF Core support, we need to add EF Core's `sqlserver` package (we are adding the `sqlserver` package because we are using SQL Server as our DB server). Open the **NuGet Package Manager** (**Tools** | **NuGet Package Manager** | **Manage NuGet Package**).

Open the **NuGet Package** and search for `Microsoft.EntityFrameworkCore.SqlServer`:

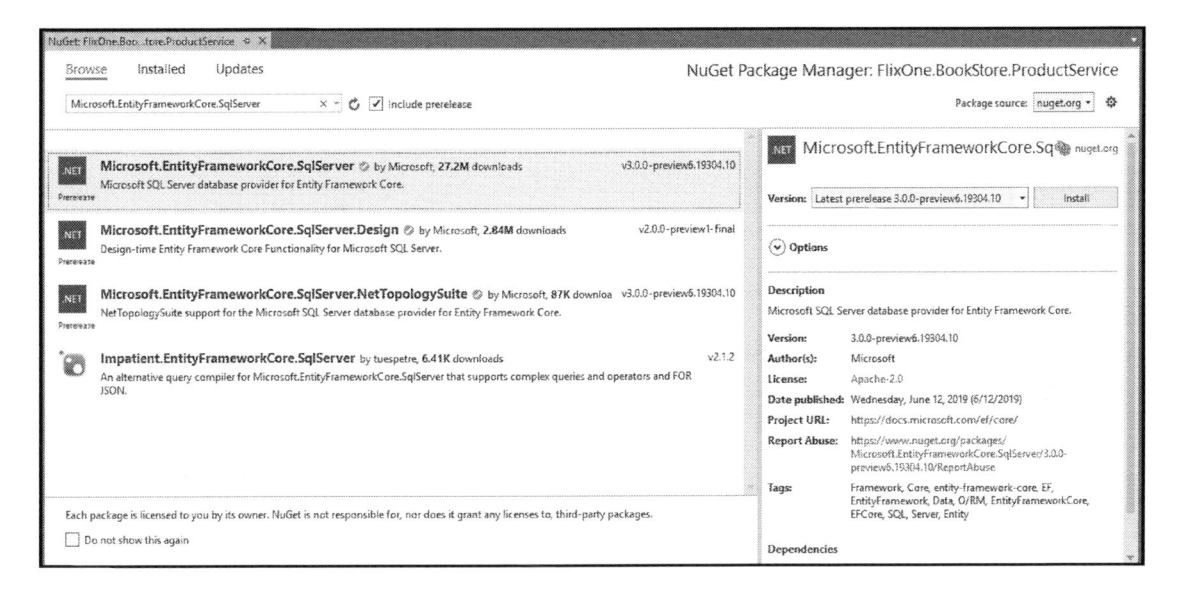

The preceding screenshot shows the search results of `Microsoft.EntityFrameworkCore.SqlServer` as an input.

EF Core DbContext

In the preceding section, we added the EF Core 3.1 package for SQL Server support; now we need to create a context so our models can interact with our product database. We have the `Product` and `Category` models, and you can refer to the following steps:

1. Add a new folder, and then name it `Contexts`—it is not compulsory to add a new folder.

Refactoring the Monolith

2. In the `Contexts` folder, add a new C# class and name it `ProductContext`. We are creating `DbContext` for `ProductDatabase`, so to make it similar here, we create `ProductContext`.
3. Make sure the `ProductContext` class inherits the `DbContext` class.
4. Make the changes, and our `ProductContext` class will look like this:

```csharp
using FlixOne.BookStore.ProductService.Models;
using Microsoft.EntityFrameworkCore;
namespace FlixOne.BookStore.ProductService.Contexts
{
  public class ProductContext : DbContext
  {
    public ProductContext(DbContextOptions<
    ProductContext>options): base(options)
    { }
    public ProductContext()
    { }
    public DbSet<Product> Products { get; set; }
    public DbSet<Category> Categories { get; set; }
  }
}
```

We have created our context, but this context is independent of the product database. We need to add a provider and connection string, so that `ProductContext` can talk with our database.

5. Once again, open the `Startup.cs` file and add the `SQL Server db` provider for our EF Core support, under the `ConfigureServcies` method. Once you add the provider's `ConfigureServcies` method, our `Startup.cs` file will look like this:

```csharp
public void ConfigureServices(IServiceCollection services)
{
  // Add framework services.
  services.AddSingleton<IProductRepository, ProductRepository>();
  services.AddDbContext<ProductContext>(o =>o.UseSqlServer
  (Configuration.GetConnectionString("ProductsConnection" )));
}
```

6. Open the `appsettings.json` file, and then add the required database connection string. In our provider, we have already set the connection key as `ProductConnection`. Now, add the following code to set the connection string with the same key (change `Data Source` to your data source):

```
{
  "ConnectionStrings":
  {
    "ProductConnection":
    "Data Source=.SQLEXPRESS;Initial Catalog=ProductsDB;
    IntegratedSecurity=True;MultipleActiveResultSets=True"
  }
}
```

The preceding code contains the connection string to connect our application with the database.

EF Core migrations

Although we have already created our product database, we should not underestimate the power of EF Core migrations. EF Core migrations will be helpful for us to perform any future modifications to the database. This modification could be in the form of a simple field addition or any other update to the database structure. We can simply rely on these EF Core migration commands every time to make the necessary changes for us. To utilize this capability, follow these simple steps:

1. Go to **Tools** | **NuGet Package Manager** | **Package Manager Console**.
2. Run the following commands from **Package Manager Console**:

   ```
   Install-Package Microsoft.EntityFrameworkCore.Tools
   Install-Package Microsoft.EntityFrameworkCore.Design
   ```

3. To initiate the migration, run this command:

   ```
   Add-Migration ProductDB
   ```

   It is important to note that this is to be done only the first time (when we do not yet have a database created by this command).

4. Now, whenever there are any changes in your model, simply execute the following command:

   ```
   Update-Database
   ```

From the preceding command, we can update the database.

At this point, we are done with our `ProductDatabase` creation. Now, it's time to migrate our existing database.

Database migration

There are many different ways to migrate from the old to the existing database. Our monolithic application, which presently has a huge database, contains a large number of records as well. It is not possible to migrate them by simply using a database SQL Script.

We need to explicitly create a script to migrate the database with all of its data. Another option is to go ahead and create a DB package as required. Depending on the complexity of your data and the records, you might need to create more than one data package to ensure that the data is migrated correctly to our newly created database, `ProductDB`.

In this section, we have learned about data migration and found the scope of data migration in our imaginary application. In general, SQL Script suffice for DB (both schema and data) migration. But if the database is large, even if we have broken it down into small databases per service, we need to take more precautions when we work on DB migrations.

In the next section, we will revisit application repositories and the controller and see how our application interacts with the database.

Revisiting repositories and the controller

We are now ready to facilitate interaction between our model and database via our newly created repositories. After making the appropriate changes to `ProductRepository`, it will look like this:

```
using Microsoft.EntityFrameworkCore;
using System.Collections.Generic;
using System.Linq;
using FlixOne.BookStore.ProductService.Contexts;
using FlixOne.BookStore.ProductService.Models;
namespace FlixOne.BookStore.ProductService.Persistence
  {
    public class ProductRepository : IProductRepository
    {
      private readonly ProductContext _context;
      public ProductRepository(ProductContext context)
      {
```

```
        _context = context;
    }
    public void Add(Product Product)
    {
        _context.Add(Product);
        _context.SaveChanges();
    }
    public IEnumerable<Product> GetAll() =>
    _context.Products.Include(c => c.Category).ToList();
    ...
  }
}
```

In the preceding code, we are using constructor injection to initialize the `_context` field. Further, the `Add` method inserts the new product into our database. Similarly, the `GetAll` method returns the collections of all available products in our database.

In this section, we have revisited the code of our imaginary application and discussed the flow using the repository to get, add, and perform other operations from the application to the database.

In our application, the model represents our table of the database and our ViewModel is one that provides an output for a View. In the next section, we will discuss this ViewModel.

Introducing ViewModel

Add a new class to the `models` folder and name it `ProductViewModel`. We do this because, in our monolithic application, whenever we search for a product, it should be displayed in its product category.

> **TIP**
> A ViewModel contains the various properties to hold/represent the data. This data is displayed on our View of the application. ViewModel doesn't need to have all read/write properties. This data is meant to be shown to the end user on the UI page. This is not a domain model; in our case, we have `ProductViewModel` as our ViewModel and `Product` as our domain model.

To support this, we need to incorporate the necessary fields into our ViewModel. Our `ProductViewModel` class will look like this:

```
using System;
namespace FlixOne.BookStore.ProductService.Models
{
  public class ProductViewModel
  {
    public Guid ProductId { get; set; }
    public string ProductName { get; set; }
    public string ProductDescription { get; set; }
    public string ProductImage { get; set; }
    public decimal ProductPrice { get; set; }
    public Guid CategoryId { get; set; }
    public string CategoryName { get; set; }
    public string CategoryDescription { get; set; }
  }
}
```

From the preceding code, we see that `ProductViewModel` consists of the following:

- `ProductId` contains the GUID of the product.
- `ProductName` contains the product name.
- `ProductImage` contains the product image.
- `ProductPrice` contains the product price.
- `CategoryId` represents the GUID of the category of the current product.
- `CategoryName` represents the category name.
- `CategoryDescription` gives the complete description of the category.

We have seen how and what our `ProductViewModel` consists of; this is one that binds with the View and produces the result onscreen for the end user.

Our `ProductViewModel` comes into the picture and fetches the values, while our controller's action method is being used. In the next section, we will discuss `ProductController`.

Revisiting ProductController

Finally, we are ready to create a RESTful API for `ProductService`. After the changes are made, here is what `ProductController` will look like:

```
using System.Linq;
using FlixOne.BookStore.ProductService.Models;
using FlixOne.BookStore.ProductService.Persistence;
using Microsoft.AspNetCore.Mvc;
namespace FlixOne.BookStore.ProductService.Controllers
{
  [Route("api/[controller]")]
  public class ProductController : Controller
  {
    private readonly IProductRepository _productRepository;
    public ProductController(IProductRepository
    productRepository) => _productRepository = productRepository;

    [HttpGet]
    [Route("productlist")]
    public IActionResult GetList() => new
    OkObjectResult(_productRepository.GetAll().
    Select(ToProductvm).ToList());

    [HttpGet]
    [Route("product/{productid}")]
    public IActionResult Get(string productId)
{
var productModel = _productRepository.GetBy(new Guid(productId));
    return new OkObjectResult(ToProductvm(productModel));
    }

    ...
  }
}
```

We have completed all of the tasks that are required for web API creation. Now, we need to tweak a few things so that the client can get information about our web APIs. So, in the upcoming section, we will add Swagger support to our web API documentation.

Refactoring the Monolith

Adding Swagger support

We are using Swagger in our API documentation. We will not dive into the details of Swagger here, as this is beyond the scope of this book. Swagger is a tool and is built on the OpenAPI Specification, which helps us to easily document our APIs. With the help of Swagger, we can easily create documentation for our various APIs/services. These documents are very useful for the end users who will be using these APIs.

> Swagger is a famous open source library that provides documentation for web APIs. Refer to the official link, `https://swagger.io/`, for more information.

It is very easy to add documentation using Swagger. Follow these steps:

1. Open **NuGet Package Manager**.
2. Search for the `Swashbuckle.AspNetCore` package.
3. Select the package and then install the package:

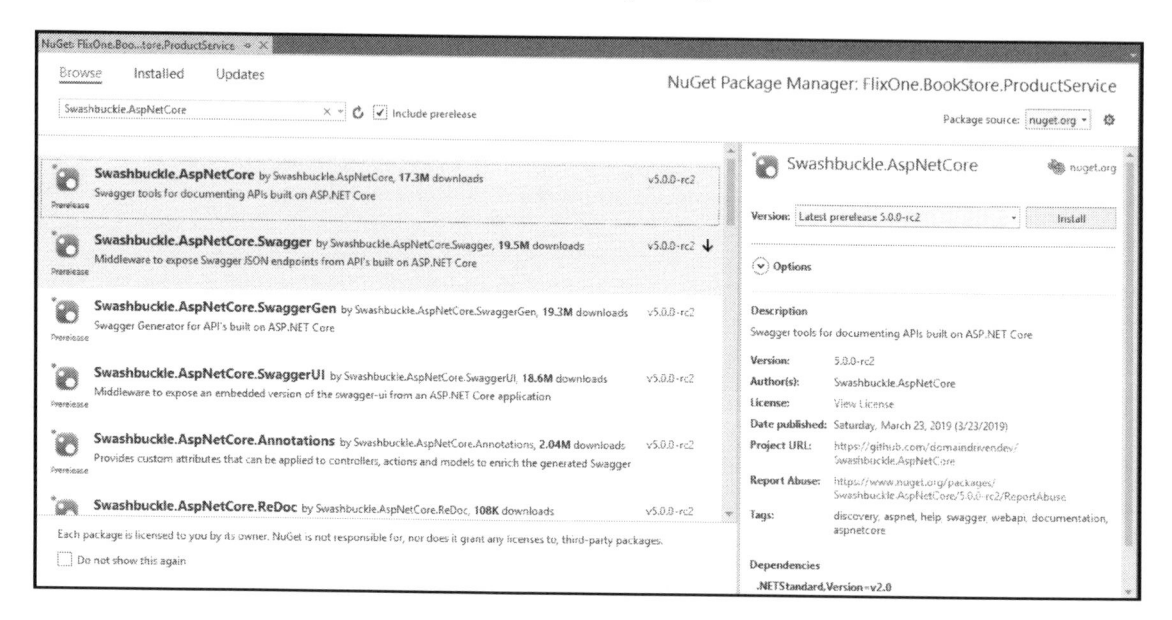

4. It will install the following:
   - **Swashbuckle.AspNetCore**
   - **Swashbuckle.AspNetCore.Swagger**
   - **Swashbuckle.AspNetCore.SwaggerGen**
   - **Swashbuckle.AspNetCore.SwaggerUI**

   This is shown in the following screenshot:

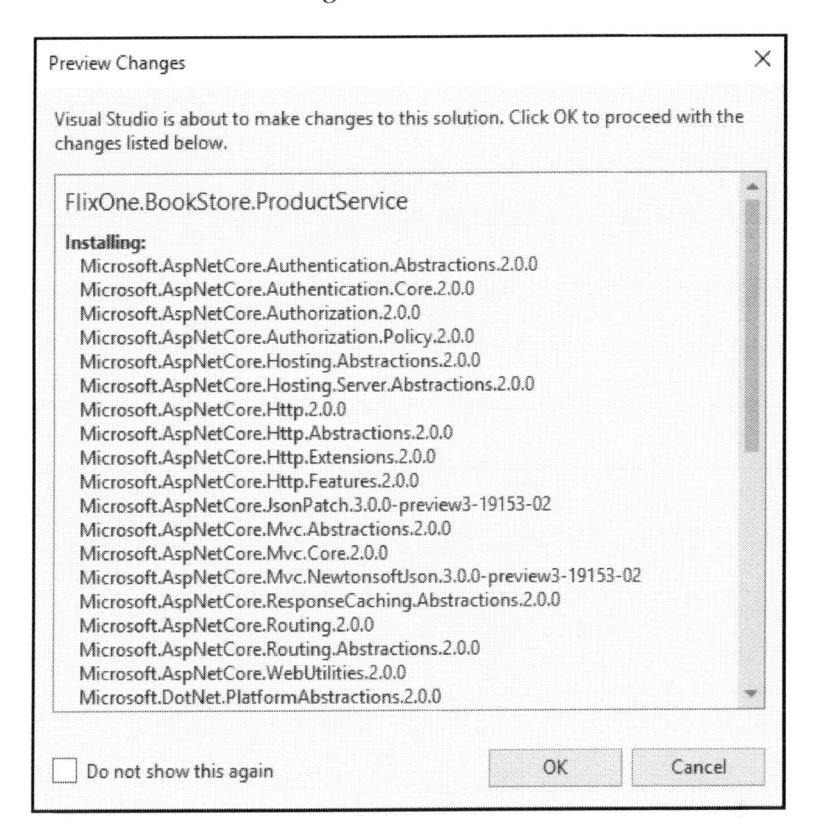

5. Open the `Startup.cs` file, move to the **ConfigureServices** method, and add the following lines to register the Swagger generator:

```
//Register Swagger
services.AddSwaggerGen(swagger =>
{
    swagger.SwaggerDoc("v1", new Info { Title = "Product APIs",
Version = "v1" });
});
```

Refactoring the Monolith

6. Next, in the **Configure** method, add the following code:

```
app.UseSwagger();

app.UseSwaggerUI(option =>
{
  option.SwaggerEndpoint("/swagger/v1/swagger.json", "Product API V1");
});
```

7. Press *F5*, and then run the application; you'll get a default page.
8. Open the Swagger documentation by adding `swagger` in the URL. So, the URL is `http://localhost:44338/swagger/`:

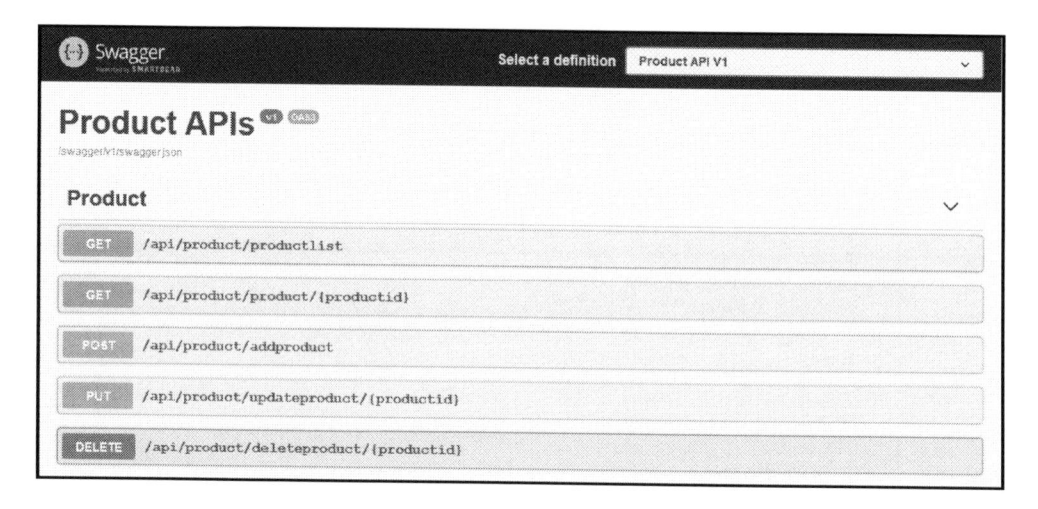

The preceding screenshot shows the **Product APIs** resources, and you can try these APIs from within the Swagger documentation page.

Finally, we have completed the transition of our monolith .NET application to microservices, and we discussed the step-by-step transition of `ProductService`. There are more steps to come for this application:

- **How microservices communicate**: This will be discussed in `Chapter 3`, *Effective Communication between Services*.
- **How to test a microservice**: This will be discussed in `Chapter 4`, *Testing Microservices with Microsoft Unit Testing Framework*.
- **Deploying microservices**: This will be discussed in `Chapter 5`, *Deploying Microservices with Docker*.

- **How we can make sure our microservices are secure, and how we can monitor our microservices**: This will be discussed in Chapter 6, *Securing Microservices Using Azure Active Directory*, and Chapter 7, *Monitoring Microservices*.
- **How microservices are scaled**: This will be discussed in Chapter 8, *Scaling Microservices with Azure*.

We laid out entire APIs of our product service, and we discussed API documentation, with the help of Swagger.

This entire section provided us with a complete working Product API, from its foundation to the documentation. With this, we have revisited the entirety of our imaginary application. We have seen how our application interacts with the database, and how our user interface provides various values. In this section, we have also created our product services. Similarly, we can now create other required services. To make our code simpler, we have taken product services as an example and elaborated on this throughout this book.

Summary

In this chapter, we discussed the different factors that can be used to identify and isolate microservices, at a high level. We also discussed the various characteristics of a good service. When talking about DDD, we learned its importance, in the context of microservices.

Furthermore, we analyzed in detail, how we can correctly achieve the vertical isolation of microservices through various parameters. We drew on our previous understanding of the challenges posed by a monolithic application and its solution in microservices, and we learned that we can use factors, such as module interdependence, technology utilization, and team structure, to identify seams and perform the transition from a monolithic architecture to microservices in an organized manner.

It became apparent that the database can pose a clear challenge in this process. However, we identified how we can still perform the process, by using a simple strategy, and we discussed the possible approaches to do this. We then established that, with the foreign keys reduced/removed, the transactions can be handled in a completely different manner.

Moving on from a monolith to bounded contexts, we further applied our knowledge to transition the FlixOne application to a microservice architecture.

In the next chapter, we will discuss communication between services, by covering integration patterns and Azure Service Fabric.

Questions

1. What are all of the factors we should consider while refactoring a monolith application?
2. What are the default interface methods of C# 8.0?
3. Why do we use Swagger?

Further reading

- *Hands-On Microservices with C#*, by Matt R. Cole, from Packt Publishing, available at: https://www.packtpub.com/in/application-development/hands-microservices-c
- *Hands-On Microservices – Monitoring and Testing* by Dinesh Rajput, from Packt Publishing, available at: https://www.packtpub.com/in/application-development/hands-on-microservices-monitoring-and-testing

3
Effective Communication between Services

In the previous chapter, we developed microservices using a .NET monolithic application. These services are independent of each other and are located on different servers. What would be a better way to have interservice communication, where one service interacts and communicates with the other? In microservices, each and every service may or may not be independent of each other. For example, the Checkout service may require the Product service, but the Product service may not require the Checkout service. In this scenario, communication between services is very important. There are certain patterns that we will discuss in detail that support communication between services.

In this chapter, we will discuss the various patterns and methods that will help us foster this communication. We will also cover integration patterns using Azure Service Fabric and Kubernetes.

In this chapter, we will cover the following topics:

- Understanding communication between services
- Learning about integration patterns
- Understanding Azure Service Fabric
- Microservices with Kubernetes
- Considering IoT when building microservices apps

Technical requirements

This chapter contains various code examples to explain some concepts. The code will be simple and is just for demonstration purposes.

To run and execute the code, you'll need the following prerequisites:

- Visual Studio 2019
- .NET Core set up and running

To run these code examples, you need to install Visual Studio 2019 or later (our preferred IDE). To do so, follow these instructions:

1. Download Visual Studio 2019 (Community is free) from https://docs.microsoft.com/en-us/visualstudio/install/install-visual-studio.
2. Follow the installation instructions for your operating system. Multiple versions are available for Visual Studio. We are using Visual Studio for Windows.

If you don't have .NET Core 3.1 installed, you can download it and set it by going to https://www.microsoft.com/net/download/windows.

> The complete source code is available here: https://github.com/PacktPublishing/Hands-On-Microservices-with-C-8-and-.NET-Core-3.0.

Let's start the first section, which is about understanding communication between the services.

Understanding communication between services

In the case of a .NET monolithic application, if there is a need to access third-party components or external services, we use the HTTP client or another client framework to access the resources. In Chapter 2, *Refactoring the Monolith*, we developed the Product service in such a way that it could work independently. But this isn't beneficial for our application; we need a few services to interact with each other.

This is a challenge—having services communicate with each other. Both the Product service and the Order service are hosted on separate servers. Both of these servers are independent of each other, are based on REST, and have their own endpoints from which they communicate with each other. (When a service interacts with another service and vice versa, we refer to it as *interservice communication*).

There are several ways in which services communicate with each other; let's discuss them briefly:

- **Synchronous**: In this case, the client makes a request to the remote service (called a **service**) for a specific functionality, and then it waits until it gets the response:

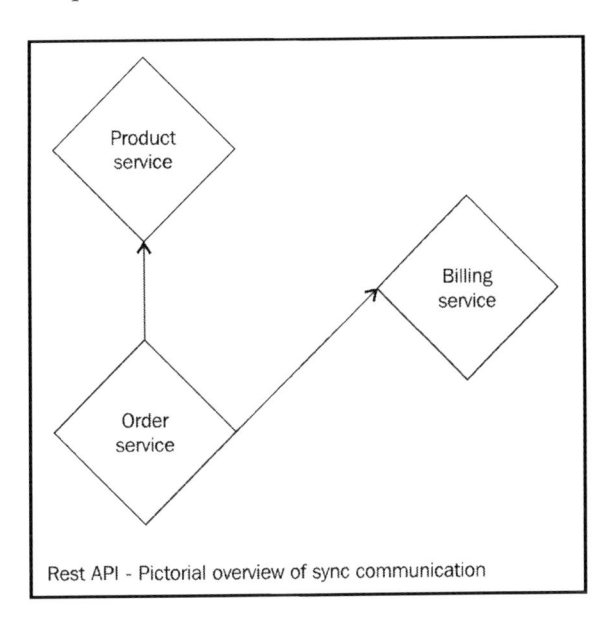

Rest API - Pictorial overview of sync communication

In the preceding diagram (pictorial view, not complete), you can see that our different microservices communicate with each other. All our services are RESTful. They are based on the ASP.NET Core Web API. In the upcoming section, we will discuss how a service is called. This is known as the synchronous method, where clients have to wait for a response from the service. In this case, the client had to wait until it got a complete response.

- **Asynchronous**: In this case, the client makes a request to the remote service (called a *service*) for a specific functionality. The client doesn't wait, but it does care about the response. Asynchronous completes the tasks as they are assigned, and it is also applicable in our routine lives. For example, if we are cooking our breakfast, then we would follow certain tasks; that is, we may prepare our tea, cook an egg, and so on. Now, let's use our imaginary application as an example. Here, we are trying to add a product. The user instructs the system to do this and passes the data values to the controller. Then, the controller calls the repository, which saves the data by using the context of the Entity Framework. We will discuss this in detail in the upcoming sections.

Styles of collaboration

In the preceding section, we discussed two different modes of how services intercommunicate. These modes are styles of collaborations. Let's take a look at them:

- **Request/response**: In this case, the client sends a request and waits for the response from the server. This is an implementation of synchronous communication. However, the request/response isn't just an implementation of synchronous communication; we can use it for asynchronous communication as well. Let's look at an example to understand this. In `Chapter 2`, *Refactoring the Monolith*, we developed `ProductService`. This service includes the `GetProduct` method, which is synchronous. The client has to wait for a response whenever it calls this method:

    ```
    [HttpGet]
    [Route("GetProduct")]
    public IActionResult Get() =>
    return new
    OkObjectResult(_productRepository.GetAll().ToViewModel());
    ```

    As per the preceding code snippet, whenever this method is called by the client (which is requesting this), they will have to wait for the response. In other words, they will have to wait until the `ToViewModel()` extension method is executed:

    ```
    [HttpGet]
    [Route("GetProductSync")]
    public IActionResult GetIsStillSynchronous()
    {
        var task = Task.Run(async() => await
        _productRepository.GetAllAsync());
        return new OkObjectResult(task.Result.ToViewModel());
    }
    ```

In the preceding code snippet, we can see that our method is implemented, in such a way, that whenever a client makes a request, they will have to wait until the `async` method is executed. In the preceding code, we used `async` as `sync`. By taking a look at `task.Result.ToViewModel()`, which is returning the response in the preceding code, we can see that `.Result` is what made our code `sync`.

To shorten our code, we added some extension methods to the already existing code that we wrote in Chapter 2, *Refactoring the Monolith*:

```
namespace FlixOne.BookStore.ProductService.Helpers
{
    public static class Transpose
    {
        public static ProductViewModel ToViewModel(
                            this Product product)
        {
            return new ProductViewModel
            {
                CategoryId = product.CategoryId,
                CategoryDescription = product.Category.Description,
                CategoryName = product.Category.Name,
                ProductDescription = product.Description,
                ProductId = product.Id,
                ProductImage = product.Image,
                ProductName = product.Name,
                ProductPrice = product.Price
            };
        }

        public static IEnumerable<ProductViewModel>
ToViewModel(this IEnumerable<Product> products) =>
products.Select(ToViewModel).ToList();
    }
}
```

In conclusion, we can say that the collaborative style of the request/response doesn't mean that it can only be implemented synchronously; we can use asynchronous calls for this as well.

Effective Communication between Services

- **Event-based**: The implementation of this collaborative style is purely asynchronous. This is a method of implementation, in which clients that emit an event don't know how to react. In the preceding section, we discussed `ProductService` in a synchronous manner. Let's look at an example of how users/customers can place an order. The following flowchart is a pictorial overview of the functionality of purchasing a book:

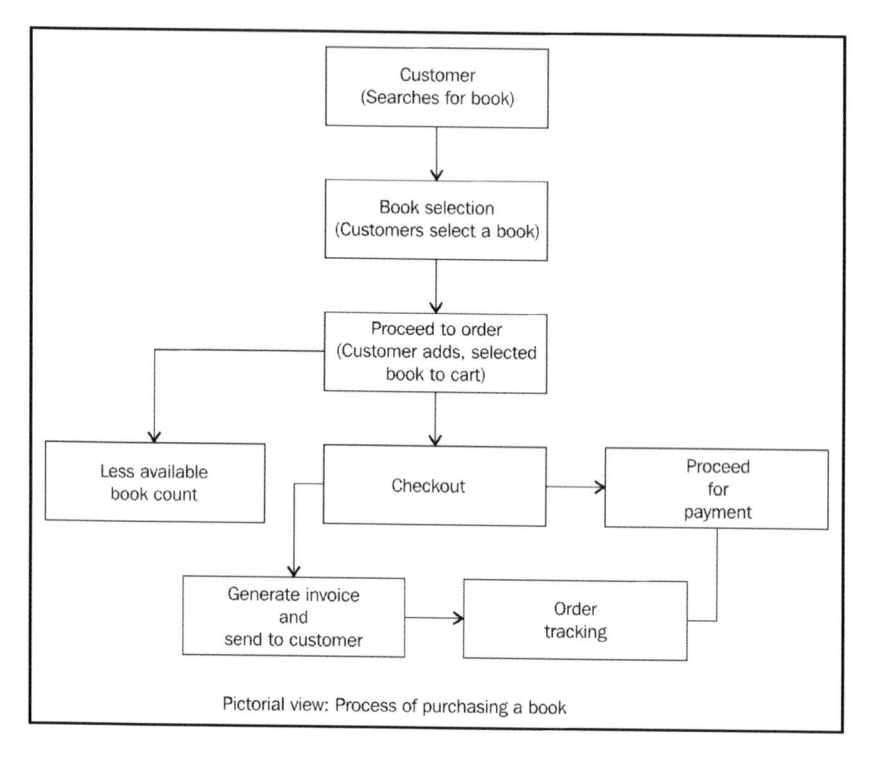

```
                    ┌──────────────────────┐
                    │      Customer        │
                    │ (Searches for book)  │
                    └──────────┬───────────┘
                               ▼
                    ┌──────────────────────┐
                    │   Book selection     │
                    │(Customers select a book)│
                    └──────────┬───────────┘
                               ▼
                    ┌──────────────────────┐
                    │  Proceed to order    │
                    │ (Customer adds, selected│
                    │    book to cart)     │
                    └──────────┬───────────┘
                               ▼
 ┌────────────────┐  ┌──────────────┐   ┌──────────┐
 │ Less available │◄─│   Checkout   │──►│ Proceed  │
 │   book count   │  │              │   │   for    │
 └────────────────┘  └──────┬───────┘   │ payment  │
                            ▼           └──────────┘
                  ┌──────────────────┐   ┌──────────┐
                  │ Generate invoice │   │  Order   │
                  │       and        │──►│ tracking │
                  │ send to customer │   │          │
                  └──────────────────┘   └──────────┘
```

Pictorial view: Process of purchasing a book

The preceding diagram shows the following:

- With the help of the search functionality, customers can find a specific book.
- After getting the results for the searched book, customers can view the details of the book.
- As soon as they proceed to the **Checkout**, our system will make sure that the display (the available books to purchase) shows the right quantity. For example, the available quantity is 10 copies of *Microservices for .NET* and the customer checks out with one book. In this case, the available quantity should now show nine copies.

[116]

- The system will generate an invoice for the purchased book and send it to the customer via their registered email address.

Conceptually, this looks easy; however, when we discuss implementing microservices, we are talking about services that are hosted separately and have their own REST API, database, and so on. This is now sounding more complex. There are many aspects involved, for example, how a service will call or invoke another service upon a successful response from one or more services. The following diagram shows what the event-driven architecture of this looks like:

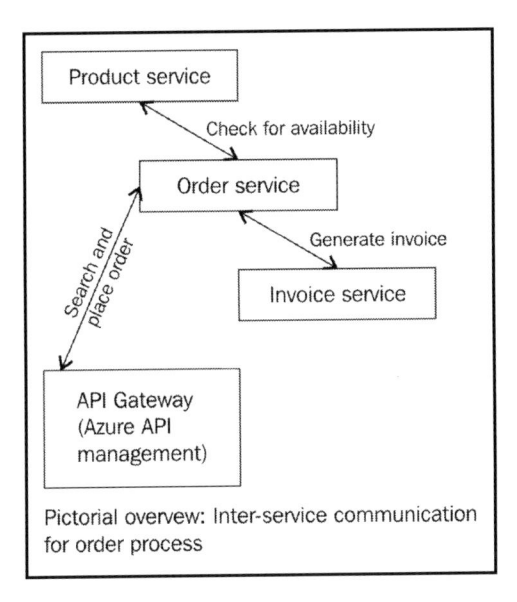

Pictorial overvew: Inter-service communication for order process

In the preceding diagram, we can see that **Invoice service** and **Product service** are triggered when the **Order service** is executed. These services call other internal asynchronous methods to complete their functionalities.

> We are using Azure API management as our API gateway. In the upcoming sections, we will discuss this in detail.

This section was all about communication between services, where we learned about the various ways of communication, followed by a discussion on collaboration.

In the next section, we will discuss how to implement various integration patterns that are required for our application.

Learning about integration patterns

So far, we've discussed interservice communication and have gone through the practical implementation of `ProductService`, with the use of synchronous and asynchronous communication. We've also implemented microservices, using different styles of collaboration. Our FlixOne bookstore (developed as per the microservice architectural style) required more interaction, which meant it required more patterns. In this section, we will help you understand them.

> The complete application of the FlixOne bookstore can be found in `Chapter 11`, *Building a Microservice Application*.

The API gateway

In the *Styles of collaboration* section, we discussed two styles we can use to foster intercommunication between microservices. Our application is split into various microservices:

- Product service
- Order service
- Invoice service
- Customer service

In our FlixOne bookstore (user interface), we need to show a few details:

- Book title, author name, price, discount, and so on
- Availability
- Book reviews
- Book ratings
- Publisher ranking and other publisher information

Before we check out the implementation, let's discuss the API gateway.

The API gateway is a single entry point for all the clients. It acts as a proxy between client applications and services. In our example, we are using **Azure API Management (APIM)** as our API gateway.

> Please refer to the *Appendix* for more details and implementation of an API gateway and the related BFF pattern.

The API gateway is responsible for the following functionalities:

- Accepting API calls and routing them to our backends
- Verifying API keys, JWT tokens, and certificates
- Supporting Auth through Azure AD and the OAuth 2.0 access token
- Enforcing usage quotas and rate limits
- Transforming our API on the fly, without code modifications
- Caching backend responses, wherever they are set up
- Logging call metadata for analytics purposes

> Refer to *Azure API Management* (https://docs.microsoft.com/en-us/azure/api-management/) to find out more about the process of setting up the API Azure portal and working with REST APIs.

The following diagram shows Azure API management working as an API gateway:

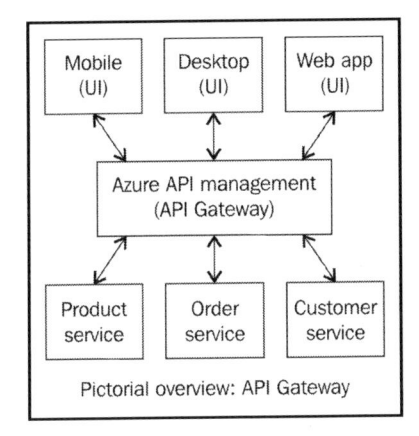

```
        Mobile      Desktop     Web app
         (UI)         (UI)        (UI)
            ↘          ↑          ↙
              Azure API management
                 (API Gateway)
            ↙          ↓          ↘
        Product       Order      Customer
        service      service     service

          Pictorial overview: API Gateway
```

Effective Communication between Services

In the preceding flowchart, we have different clients, such as a mobile application, a desktop application, and a web application, that are using microservices.

Our client doesn't know which server our services can be found on. The API gateway provides the address of its own server, and it internally authenticates the request from the client, with the use of a valid `Ocp-Apim-Subscription-Key`.

> **TIP**: Additional steps must be taken to force traffic through APIM. With the respective URL, it is possible to bypass this by going directly to the backend, if it is exposed externally.

Our `ProductService` has a REST API. It contains the following resources:

API resource	Description
GET /api/product	Gets a list of products
GET /api/product/{id}	Gets a product
PUT /api/product/{id}	Updates an existing product
DELETE /api/product/{id}	Deletes an existing product
POST /api/product	Adds a new product

We have already created `ProductClient`, which is a .NET console application. It makes a request to Azure API Management by supplying the subscription key. Here is the code snippet for this:

```
namespace FlixOne.BookStore.ProductClient
{
   class Program
   {
      private const string ApiKey = "myAPI Key";
      private const string BaseUrl = "http://localhost:3097/api";
      static void Main(string[] args)
      {
         GetProductList("/product/GetProductAsync");
         //Console.WriteLine("Hit ENTER to exit...");
         Console.ReadLine();
      }
      private static async void GetProductList(string resource)
      {
         using (var client = new HttpClient())
         {
            var queryString =
            HttpUtility.ParseQueryString(string.Empty);
```

```
            client.DefaultRequestHeaders.Add("Ocp-Apim-Subscription-
            Key", ApiKey);

            var uri = $"{BaseUrl}{resource}?{queryString}";

            //Get asynchronous response for further usage
            var response = await client.GetAsync(uri);
            Console.WriteLine(response);
        }
      }
   }
}
```

In the preceding code, our client is requesting a REST API to get all the products. Here's a brief description of the terms that appear in the code:

`BaseUrl`	This is the address of the proxy server.
`Ocp-Apim-Subscription-Key`	This is a key that's assigned by API Management to a specific product the client has opted for.
`Resource`	This is our API resource, which is configured over Azure API Management. It will be different from our actual REST API resource.
`Response`	This refers to the response to a specific request. In our case, this is the default JSON format.

Since we're using Azure API Management as an API gateway, there are certain benefits we'll receive:

- We can manage our various APIs from a single platform; for example, `ProductService`, `OrderService`, and other services can be easily managed and called by many clients.
- Because we're using API Management, it doesn't only provide us with a proxy server; it also allows us to create and maintain documentation for our APIs.
- It provides a built-in facility, so that we can define various policies for quota, output formats, and format conversions, such as XML to JSON or vice versa.

So, with the help of the API gateway, we can gain access to some great features.

The event-driven pattern

The microservice architecture uses the database-per-service pattern, which means it includes an independent database for every dependent or independent service:

- **Dependent service**: Our application will require a few external services (third-party services or components, and so on) and/or internal services (these are our own services) to work or function as expected. For instance, **CHECKOUT-SERVICE** requires **CUSTOMER-SERVICE** and also requires an external (third-party) service to verify a customer's identity (such as an Aadhaar card ID in the case of Indian customers or SSN for USA customers). Here, our **CHECKOUT-SERVICE** is a dependent service, as it requires two services (an internal service and external service) to function as expected. Dependent services don't work, if any or all the services that the service is dependent on don't work properly (there are a lot of reasons a service wouldn't work, including network failure, unhandled exceptions, and so on).
- **Independent service**: In our application, we have services that don't depend on any other service to work properly. Such services are called independent services, and they can be self-hosted. Our **CUSTOMER-SERVICE** doesn't require any other service to function properly, which means it is an independent service and doesn't need any input from other services. This doesn't mean that our other services are not dependent on **CUSTOMER-SERVICE**, though; other services may or may not depend on this service.

The main challenge is to maintain business transactions to ensure data consistency across these services. For instance, as shown in the following diagram, for **CUSTOMER-SERVICE** to know when and how **CHECKOUT-SERVICE** has functioned, it would need the functionality of **CUSTOMER-SERVICE**. There may be several services in an application (services may be self-hosted). In our case, when **CHECKOUT-SERVICE** is triggered and **CUSTOMER-SERVICE** is not invoked, then how will our application identify the customer's details?

> ASP.NET WebHooks (https://docs.microsoft.com/en-us/aspnet/webhooks/) can also be used to provide event notifications.

To overcome the related problems and challenges we've discussed (for **CHECKOUT-SERVICE** and **CUSTOMER-SERVICE**), we can use an event-driven pattern (or the eventual consistency approach) and use distributed transactions.

Chapter 3

> Distributed transactions are where data flows on more than one network. These transactions are capable of updating this data on networked computer systems. These also detect and roll back the subsequent operations, if any fail.

The following diagram describes an actual implementation of the event-driven pattern in our application, where **PRODUCT-SERVICE** subscribes to the events and **Event-Manager** manages all the events:

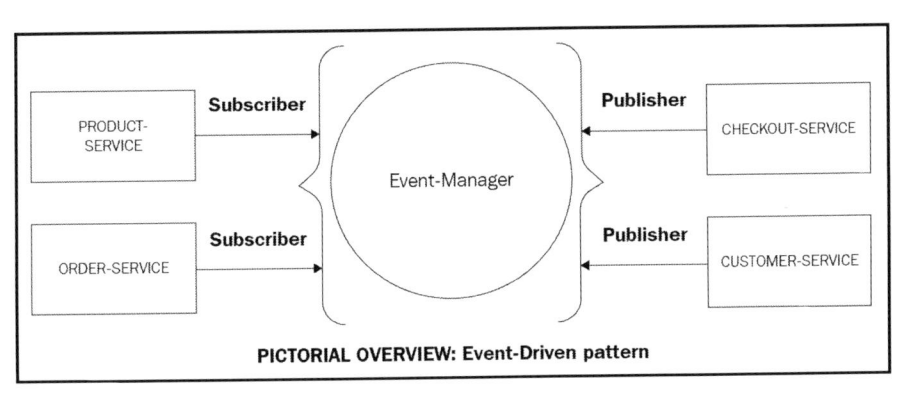

PICTORIAL OVERVIEW: Event-Driven pattern

In an event-driven pattern, we implement a service in such a way that it publishes an event whenever a service updates its data, and another service (dependent service) subscribes to this event. Now, whenever a dependent service receives an event, it updates its data. This way, our dependent services can get and update their data if required. The preceding diagram shows an overview of how services subscribe to and publish events. Here, **Event-Manager** could be a program running on a service or a mediator helping you manage all the events of the subscribers and publishers.

It registers an event of the **Publisher** and notifies a **Subscriber** whenever a specific event occurs/is triggered. It also helps you form a queue and wait for events. In our implementation, we will use Azure Service Bus queues.

Let's consider an example. In our application, this is how our services will publish and receive an event:

- **CUSTOMER-SERVICE** performs a few checks for the users, namely login check, customer details check, and so on. After these necessary checks are conducted, the service publishes an event called `CustomerVerified`.
- **CHECKOUT-SERVICE** receives this event and, after performing the necessary operations, publishes an event called `ReadyToCheckout`.

- **ORDER-SERVICE** receives this event and updates the quantity.
- As soon as the checkout is performed, **CHECKOUT-SERVICE** publishes an event. Whichever result is received from the external service (either `CheckedoutSuccess` or `CheckedoutFailed`), is used by **CHECKOUT-SERVICE**.
- When `InventoryService` receives these events, it updates the data to make sure that item is added or removed.

With the use of event-driven patterns, services can automatically update the database and publish an event.

Event-sourcing pattern

This pattern helps us ensure that the service will publish an event whenever the state changes. In this pattern, we take a business entity (product, customer, and so on) as a sequence of state-changing events. The **Event Store** persists the events, and these events are available for subscription or as other services. This pattern simplifies our tasks since we don't need to synchronize the data model and the business domain. It improves performance, scalability, and responsiveness. This simply defines an approach that indicates how we can handle the various operations on our data, by a sequence of events. These events are recorded in a store. An event represents a set of changes that are made to the data, for example, `InvoiceCreated`.

The following diagram describes how an event would work for **ORDERSERVICE**:

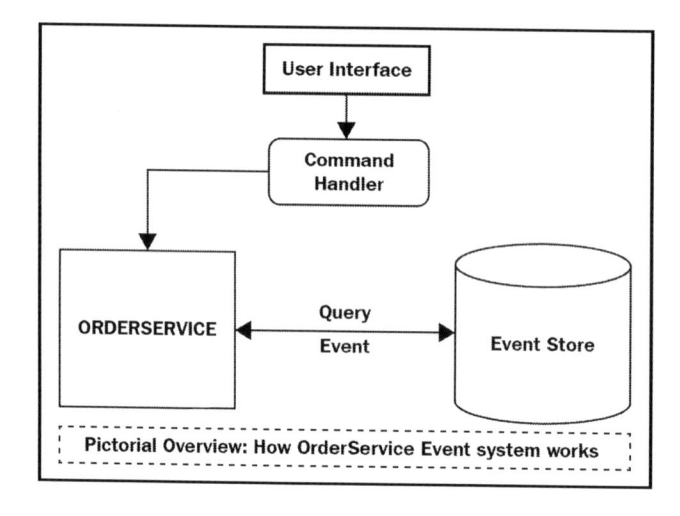

Pictorial Overview: How OrderService Event system works

The preceding diagram shows the following implementation:

1. The commands issue a book from the **User Interface** to be ordered.
2. **ORDERSERVICE** queries (from the **Event Store**) and populates the results with the `CreateOrder` event.
3. Then, the command handler raises an event to order the book.
4. Our service performs the related operations.
5. Finally, the system appends the event to the event store.

Eventual consistency pattern

Eventual consistency is an implementation of the data consistency approach. This suggests implementation, so the system would be a scalable system with high availability.

> "The distributed system needs to be specified as having eventual consistency as an explicit requirement. Eventual consistency comes from the systems that exhibit scalability and high availability."

According to this distributed data, stores are subject to the **Consistency, Availability (network), Partition tolerance (CAP)** theorem. The CAP theorem is also known as Brewer's theorem. According to this theorem, in a distributed system, we can only choose two out of the following three:

- Consistency (C)
- Availability (A)
- Partition tolerance (CA)

Consider our imaginary system as an example, which is highly available (A), highly consistent (C), and there is no partition (CA). When we require and do the partitioning (P), our system has up to n number of partitions, or we say we are continuously partitioning our system. In this case, this is a very complex scenario, and data could hardly reach or cover all the partitions. This is the reason that, when we do partitioning, we either make the system highly available (AP) or highly consistent (CP).

Compensating transactions

Compensating transactions allow us to roll back or undo all the tasks we've performed in a series of steps. Suppose one or more services have implemented operations in a series, and one or more of them have failed. What would our next step be? Would we reverse all the steps, or would we commit to a half-completed functionality?

In our case, a customer orders a book, and `ProductService` marks the ordered book as sold temporarily. After the confirmation of the order, `OrderService` calls an external service to complete the payment process. If the payment fails, we would need to undo our previous tasks, which means we will have to check `ProductService` so that it marks the specific book as unsold.

Competing consumers

Competing consumers allow us to process messages for multiple concurrent consumers, so that they receive these messages on the same channel. This application is meant for handling a large number of requests.

The following diagram shows the implementation of this:

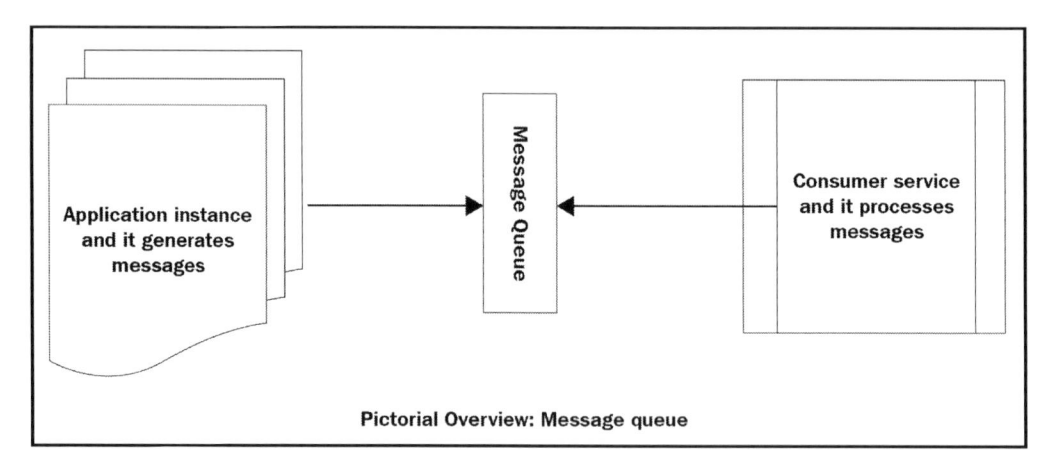

Pictorial Overview: Message queue

This message flow happens by passing a messaging system to another service (a consumer service), which can be handled asynchronously.

This scenario can be implemented with the use of Azure Service Bus queues. We will look at this in the next section.

Understanding Azure Service Fabric

Azure Service Fabric is a platform for distributed systems; it helps us easily manage scalable microservices. It overcomes various challenges for developers and infrastructure folks. Azure Service Fabric is a distributed systems platform that makes it easy for us to package, deploy, and manage scalable and reliable microservices and containers.

Service Fabric architecture

Service Fabric is a collection of services. Each collection is grouped into different subsystems. Every subsystem has its own specific responsibility and allows us to write the following types of applications:

- Scalable applications
- Manageable applications
- Testable applications

The major subsystems form the Service Fabric architecture, which can be visualized in the following diagram:

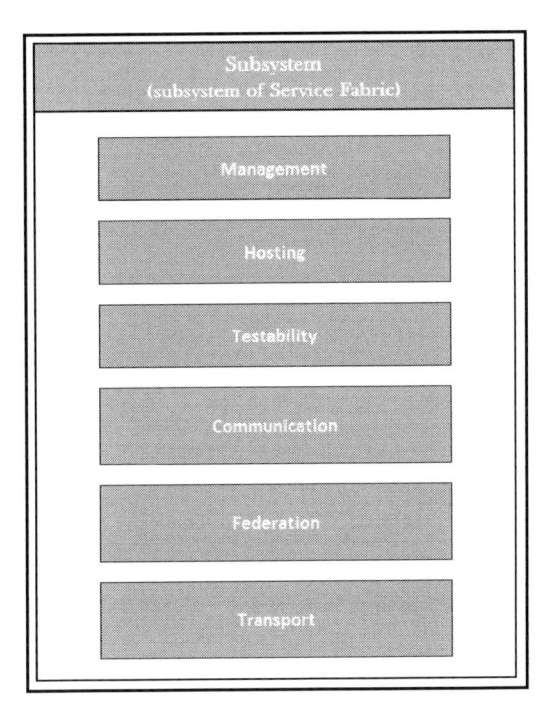

Effective Communication between Services

The first layer from the bottom, that is, the Transport subsystem, is responsible for providing secure communication channels between nodes in a Service Fabric cluster. Let's go over all of these subsystems in more detail:

- The **Transport subsystem** provides a communication channel for intra- and inter-cluster communication. The channels that are used for communication are secured by an X509 certificate or Windows security. The subsystem supports both one-way and request-response communication patterns. These channels are used by the Federation subsystem to broadcast and multicast messages. This subsystem is internal to Service Fabric and cannot be used directly by developers for application programming.
- The **Federation subsystem** is responsible for logically grouping virtual or physical machines together to form a Service Fabric cluster. This subsystem uses the communication infrastructure provided by the Transport subsystem to achieve this grouping. This helps Service Fabric manage resources more efficiently. The key responsibilities of this subsystem include failure detection, leader election, and routing. The subsystem forms a ring topology over the nodes that have been allocated for the cluster. A token-leasing mechanism, along with a heartbeat check, is implemented within the system to detect failures, perform leader election, and to achieve consistent routing.
- The **Reliability subsystem** of the service that's hosted on the platform is ensured by managing failover, replicating, and balancing resources across nodes in a cluster. The replicator logic within this subsystem is responsible for replicating the state across multiple instances of a service. The main task of this subsystem is to maintain consistency between the primary and the secondary replicas in a service deployment. It interacts with the failover unit and the reconfiguration agent, in order to understand what needs to be replicated.

- The **Management subsystem** deals with the application life cycle management of workloads that have been deployed on a Service Fabric cluster. Application developers can access the Management subsystem's functionalities, through administrative APIs or PowerShell cmdlets, to provision, deploy, upgrade, or deprovision applications. All of these operations can be performed without any downtime. The Management subsystem has three key components: the cluster manager, health manager, and image store. The cluster manager interacts with the failover manager. Meanwhile, the resource manager in the Reliability subsystem deploys the applications of the available nodes, while considering the placement constraints. It is responsible for the life cycle of the application, starting from provisioning to deprovisioning. It also integrates with the health manager to perform health checks during service upgrades. The health manager, as its name suggests, is responsible for monitoring the health of applications, services, nodes, partitions, and replicas. It is also responsible for aggregating the health status and storing it in a centralized health store. APIs are exposed out of this system to query health events so that they can perform corrective actions. The APIs can either return raw events or aggregated health data for a specific cluster resource. The image store is responsible for persisting and distributing application binaries that are deployed on a Service Fabric cluster.
- The **Hosting subsystem** takes care of managing application deployments, within the scope of a node. The cluster manager signals the Hosting subsystem, informing it about the application deployments to be managed on a particular node. Then, the Hosting subsystem manages the life cycle of the application on that node. It interacts with the Reliability subsystem and Management subsystem to ensure the health of each deployment.
- The **Communication subsystem** provides features for service discovery, and it provides intra-cluster messaging features that use a naming service. The naming service is used to locate a service within a cluster. It also lets users securely communicate with any node on a cluster, retrieve service metadata, and manage service properties. The naming service also exposes APIs, which allows users to resolve network locations for each service, despite them being dynamically placed.
- The **Testability subsystem** provides a list of tools for developers, deployment engineers, and testers, so that they can introduce controlled faults and run test scenarios to validate state transitions and the behaviors of services that have been deployed on Service Fabric. The fault analysis service is automatically started when a cluster is provisioned or when a fault action or test scenario has initiated a command.

In the upcoming sections, we will discuss Service Fabric in more detail, where we will elaborate on the orchestrator and programming models.

Discussing the orchestrator

Simply put, the orchestrator is an automated piece of software that's used to manage service deployments. This software package is meant to abstract the complexities around provisioning, deploying, fault handling, scaling, and optimizing the applications it's managing from the top user. For example, associate degree orchestration should be ready to consume a configuration that specifies the number of instances of the service, to run and perform the task of deploying the services, based on multiple advanced factors. These factors include resource availability on nodes during a cluster, placement constraints, and so on. Orchestrators can charge for fault handling and the recovery of services. If a node in a cluster fails, the arranger must graciously handle this while guaranteeing service handiness.

The Service Fabric Cluster Resource Manager can be a central service that runs within our clusters. It manages the specified state of the services within the cluster, with the relevant resource consumption and placement rules. We'll look at this in the next section.

Service Fabric programming models overview

Service Fabric offers multiple ways in which we can write and manage our services. Services can choose to use the Service Fabric APIs to get the most out of the platform's features and application frameworks. Services can also be any compiled executable program written in any language or code running in a container that's hosted on a Service Fabric cluster. Let's go over these now:

- **Guest Executable** is an existing executable that can be written in any language, and it can be run as a service in the application. Service Fabric APIs haven't been directly used by these Guest Executables. Visual Studio allows us to deploy Guest Executables on Service Fabric clusters.
- **Container** is a part of the complete filesystem and contains tools, the runtime, and system libraries.
- **Reliable services** is a lightweight framework for writing services that integrate with the Service Fabric platform and that benefit from the platform's features. Reliable services provide a minimal set of APIs that allow the Service Fabric runtime to manage the life cycle of your services, so that they can interact with the runtime. The application framework is minimal, so that you have full control over design and implementation choices. It can also be used to host any other application framework, such as ASP.NET Core.

- **ASP.NET Core** is an open source and cross-platform framework that we can use to build web apps, IoT apps, and mobile backends. Service Fabric integrates with ASP.NET Core, so that we can write both stateless and stateful ASP.NET Core applications that take advantage of Reliable Collections and Service Fabric's advanced orchestration capabilities.
- **Reliable Actors**, which is built on top of Reliable Services, is an application framework that implements the Virtual Actor pattern, based on the actor design pattern. The Reliable Actor framework uses independent units of compute and state with a single-threaded execution called actors. The Reliable Actor framework provides built-in communication for actors and preset state persistence and scale-out configurations. Because Reliable Actors is an application framework built on Reliable Services, it is fully integrated with the Service Fabric platform, and it benefits from the full set of features offered by the platform.

The aim of this section was to discuss Service Fabric and to provide an overview of its programming model. In the next section, we will learn how to implement information on competing consumers.

Implementing information on competing consumers

In the *Competing consumers* section, we discussed that competing consumers is a way to pass messages. In this section, we will discuss Azure Service Bus and implement Azure message queues.

Azure Service Bus

In the event-driven pattern, we discussed publishing and subscribing to events. We used an event manager to manage all the events. In this section, we will learn how Azure Service Bus manages events and provides the facility to work with microservices. It works like an information delivery service, and it makes communication between services flawless. In our case, whenever services need to exchange information, they will communicate using this service.

Effective Communication between Services

There are two main types of services provided by Azure Service Bus:

- **Brokered communication**: This service is also known as a **hired service**. It works similarly to the postal service in the real world. Whenever a person wants to send messages or information, he/she can send a letter to another person. With the post office, we can send various types of messages, in the form of letters, packages, gifts, and so on. When we use the brokered communication type, we don't bother with delivering messages ourselves because it ensures that our messages are delivered, even though both the sender and receiver aren't online. This is a messaging platform, with components such as queues, topics, subscriptions, and so on.
- **Non-brokered communication**: This is similar to making a phone call. In this case, the caller (sender) calls a person (receiver) without any confirmation that indicates whether he/she will answer the call or not. Here, the sender sends information and depends on the receiver to receive the communication and pass the message back to the sender. Take a look at the following diagram, which illustrates Azure Service Bus:

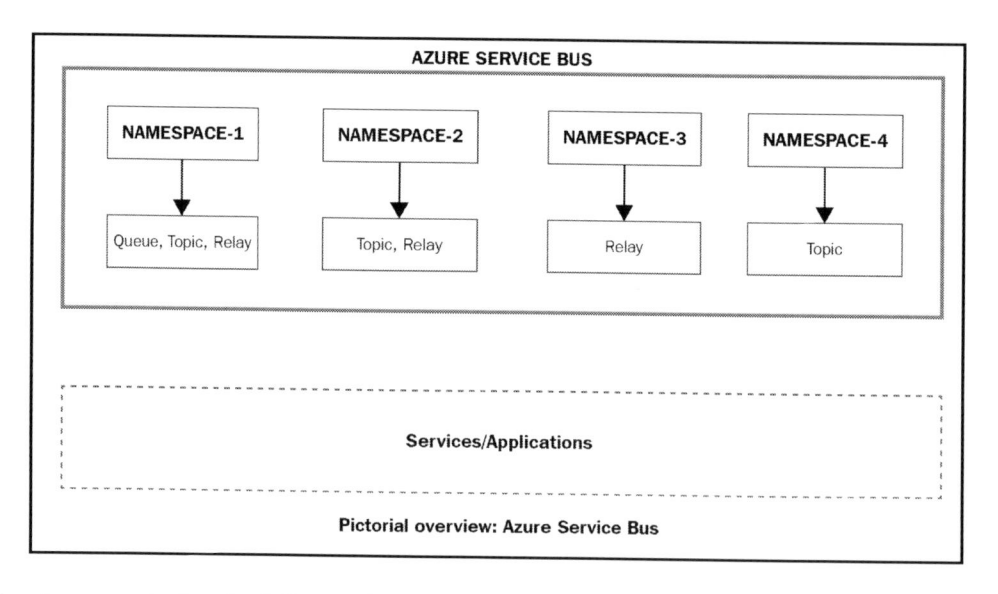

AZURE SERVICE BUS

NAMESPACE-1	NAMESPACE-2	NAMESPACE-3	NAMESPACE-4
Queue, Topic, Relay	Topic, Relay	Relay	Topic

Services/Applications

Pictorial overview: Azure Service Bus

See the documentation for Microsoft Azure Service Bus (https://docs.microsoft.com/en-us/azure/service-bus-messaging/service-bus-fundamentals-hybrid-solutions). Here is one description:

> "Service Bus is a cloud service and is shared by multiple users. To get started with it, you need to create a namespace and define the communication mechanism."

The preceding diagram is a pictorial overview of Azure Service Bus and depicts four different communication mechanisms. Everyone has their own taste in terms of which it uses to connect to the application:

- **Queues**: These act like brokers, in that they allow unidirectional communication.
- **Topics**: Similar to queues, topics provide unidirectional communication, but a single topic can have multiple subscriptions.
- **Relays**: These don't store any messages like queues and topics do. Instead, they provide bidirectional communication and pass messages to the application.
- **Notification Hubs**: This distributes messages from the server application to client devices across the platform.

Azure message queues

Azure queues are cloud storage accounts that use Azure Table. They allow us to queue a message between applications. Azure Queue Storage has a different set of features than Azure Service Bus. In the upcoming sections, we will implement message queues, which is a part of Azure Service Bus.

In this section, we have discussed Azure message queues, by following Azure Service Bus, which allows us to gather information about competing consumers. In the next section, we will implement information on Service Fabric.

Implementing information on Service Fabric

In this section, we will look at the actual implementation of an Azure Service Bus queue by creating the following:

- A Service Bus namespace
- A Service Bus messaging queue
- A console application to send a message to
- A console application to receive a message

Prerequisites

We need the following to implement this solution:

- Visual Studio 2019 or later
- A valid Azure subscription

Effective Communication between Services

> If you don't have an Azure subscription, you can get one for free by signing up at https://azure.microsoft.com/en-us/free/.

Now that you have everything, follow these steps to get started:

1. Log in to the Azure portal (https://portal.azure.com/).
2. In the left navigation bar, click **Service Bus**. If this option is unavailable, you can find it by clicking **More Services**.
3. Click **Add**. This opens the **Create namespace** dialog:

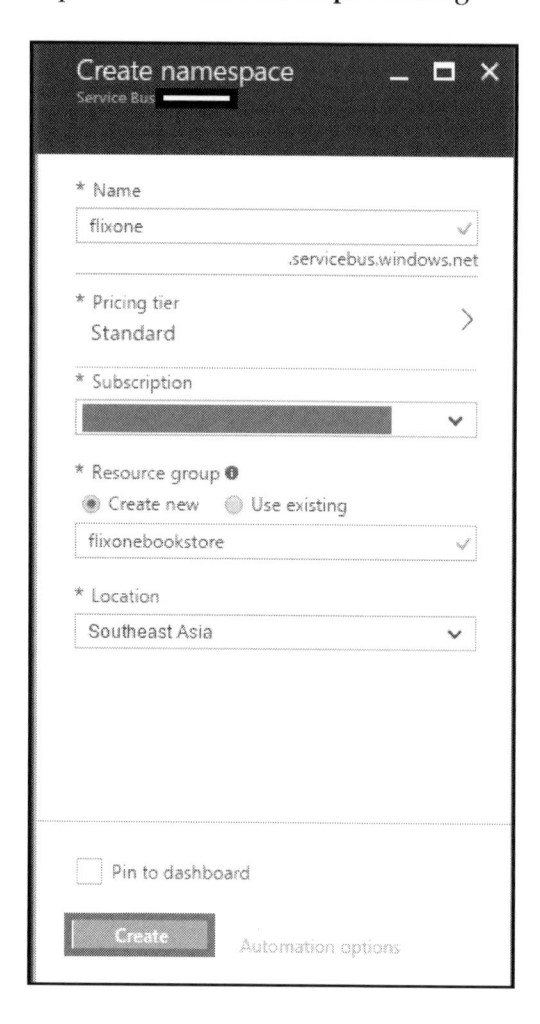

![Create namespace dialog with Name: flixone, Pricing tier: Standard, Resource group: flixonebookstore (Create new), Location: Southeast Asia]

4. In the **Create namespace** dialog, enter a namespace (the namespace should be globally unique), like `flixone`. Select the pricing tier next, that is, `Basic`, `Standard`, or `Premium`.
5. Select your **Subscription**.
6. Choose an existing resource or create a new one.
7. Select the location where you want to host the namespace. Click **Create** when you're done.
8. Open a newly created namespace (we just created `flixone`).
9. Now, click **Shared access policies**.
10. Click **RootManageSharedAccessKey**, as shown in the following screenshot:

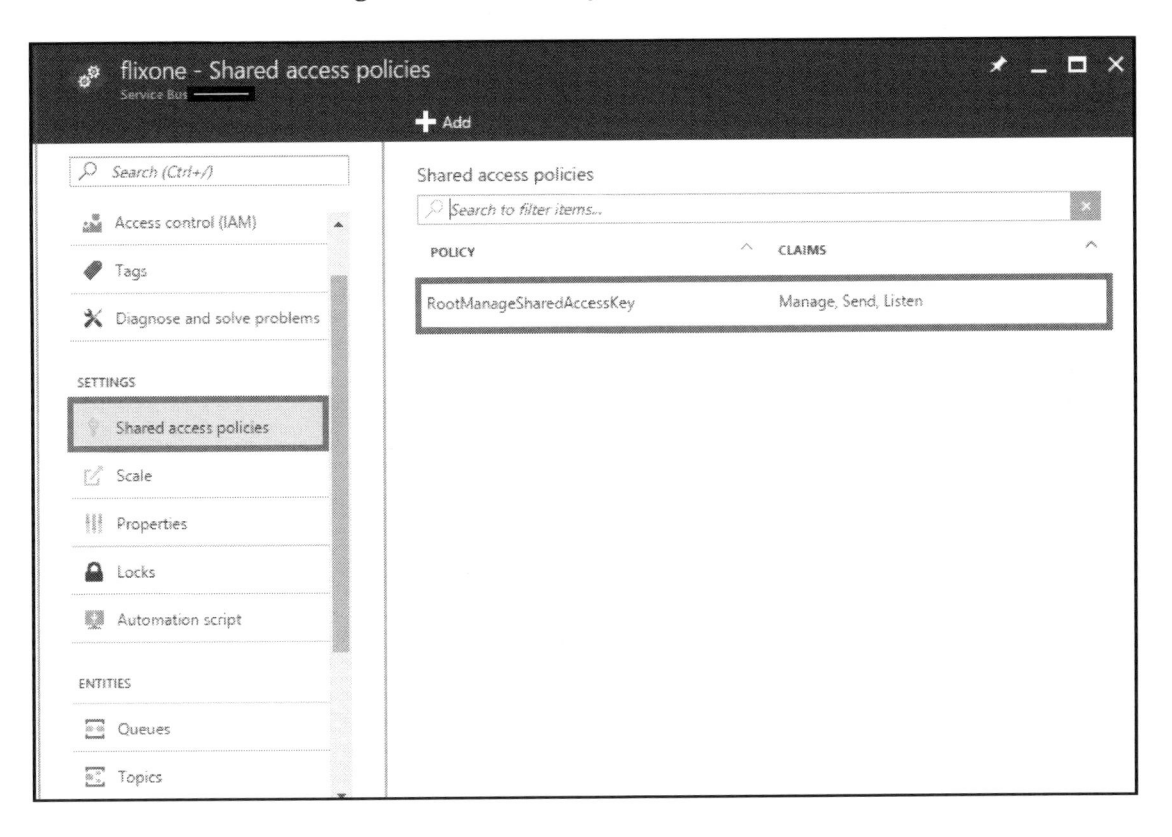

Effective Communication between Services

11. Click **Queues** in the main dialog of the `flixone` namespace, as shown in the following screenshot:

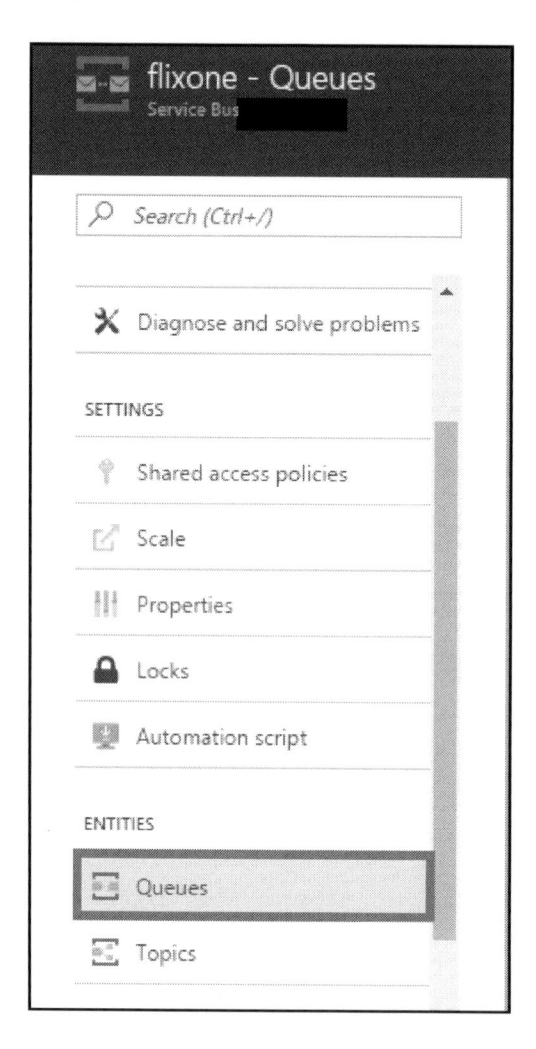

12. From the **Policy: RootManageSharedAccessKey** window, note the primary key connection string so that you can use it later.

[136]

13. Click **Name** to add a queue (say, `flixonequeue`). Then, click **Create** (we're using REST values as default values), as shown in the following screenshot:

The preceding screenshot is of the **Create Queue** dialog. In the **Create Queue** dialog, we can create a queue. For example, here, we are creating a queue called **flixonequeue**. Queues can be verified by visiting the **Queues** dialog.

Now, we are ready to create our sender and receiver applications.

Sending messages to the queue

In this section, we will create a console application that will actually send messages to the queue. To create this application, follow these steps:

1. Create a new console application, and then name it `FlixOne.BookStore.MessageSender` using Visual Studio's new project (C#) template:

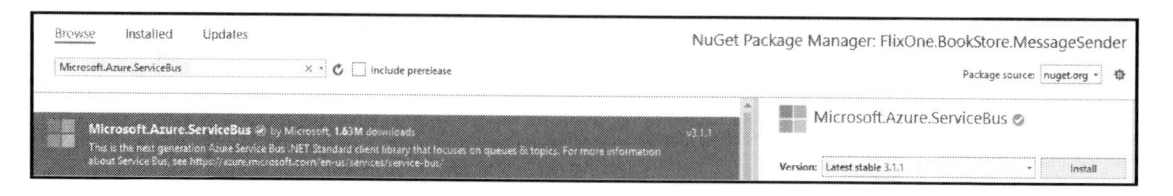

2. Add the **Microsoft Azure Service Bus** NuGet package by right-clicking the project.
3. Use the following code to send the message to the queue. Your `Program.cs` file will contain the following `MainAsync()` method:

```
private static async Task MainAsync()
{
    const int numberOfMessagesToSend = 10;
    _client = new QueueClient(_connectionString, _queuename);
    WriteLine("Starting...");
    await SendMessagesAsync(numberOfMessagesToSend);
    WriteLine("Ending...");
    WriteLine("Press any key...");
    ReadKey();
    await _client.CloseAsync();
}
```

In the preceding code, we are creating our queue client by providing the `ConnectionString` and `QueueName` that we have already set in our Azure portal. This code calls the `SendMessagesAsync()` method, which accepts a parameter that contains the count of the number of messages that need to be sent.

4. Create a `SendMessagesAsync()` method, and add the following code:

```
private static async Task SendMessagesAsync(int
numberOfMessagesToSend)
{
    try
    {
        for (var index = 0; index < numberOfMessagesToSend;
index++)
        {
            var customMessage = $"#{index}:A message from
                            FlixOne.BookStore.MessageSender.";
            var message = new Message(Encoding.UTF8.GetBytes(
                                    customMessage));
            WriteLine($"Sending message: {customMessage}");
            await _client.SendAsync(message);
        }
    }
    catch (Exception exception)
    {
        WriteLine($"Weird! It's exception with message:
                {exception.Message}");
    }
}
```

5. Run the program and wait for a while. You will get the following output:

```
Starting...
Sending message: #0:A message from FlixOne.BookStore.MessageSender.
Sending message: #1:A message from FlixOne.BookStore.MessageSender.
Sending message: #2:A message from FlixOne.BookStore.MessageSender.
Sending message: #3:A message from FlixOne.BookStore.MessageSender.
Sending message: #4:A message from FlixOne.BookStore.MessageSender.
Sending message: #5:A message from FlixOne.BookStore.MessageSender.
Sending message: #6:A message from FlixOne.BookStore.MessageSender.
Sending message: #7:A message from FlixOne.BookStore.MessageSender.
Sending message: #8:A message from FlixOne.BookStore.MessageSender.
Sending message: #9:A message from FlixOne.BookStore.MessageSender.
Ending...
Press any key...
```

Effective Communication between Services

6. Go to the Azure portal, and then go to the created queue to check whether it displays a message. In the following screenshot, we can see an overview of **flixonequeue**, where we can see the **Active Message Count** and more:

The preceding screenshot is from the Azure portal and is the **Overview** screen of **flixonequeue (Service Bus)**. Currently, we have 10 messages (the active message count).

Adding configuration settings

In the previous section, we used constant values for `ConnectionString` and `QueueName`. If we need to change these settings, we have to make changes to the code. However, why should we make code changes for such a small change? To overcome this situation, we will use the configuration settings.

In this section, we will add configurations, with the help of `IConfigurationRoot` from the `Microsoft.Extensions.Configuration` namespace.

1. First of all, right-click the project, and then click **Manage NuGet packages**. Search for the `Microsoft.Extensions.Configuration` NuGet package, as shown in the following screenshot:

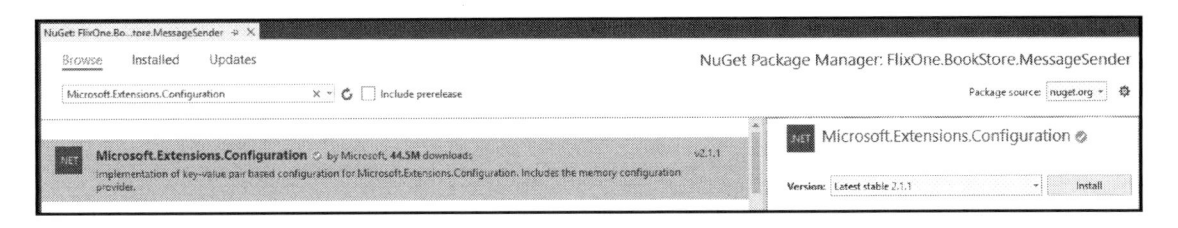

Chapter 3

[screenshot: NuGet Package Manager showing Microsoft.Extensions.Configuration]

2. Now, search for the `Microsoft.Extensions.Configuration.Json` NuGet package and select it:

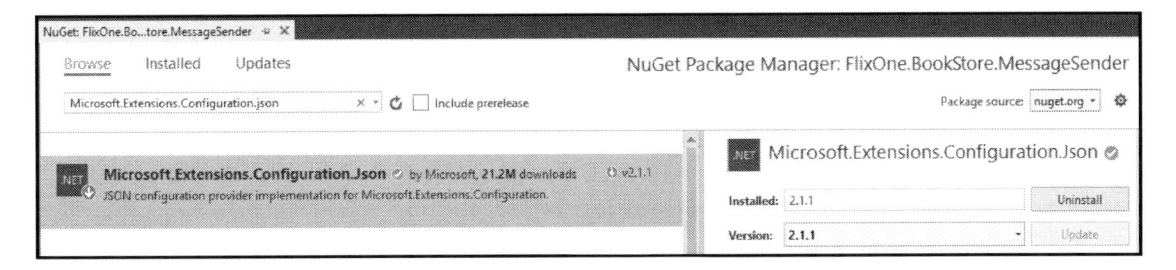

[screenshot: NuGet Package Manager showing Microsoft.Extensions.Configuration.Json]

3. Add the following `ConfigureBuilder()` method to the `Program.cs` file:

```
private static IConfigurationRoot ConfigureBuilder()
{
    return new ConfigurationBuilder()
 .SetBasePath(Directory.GetCurrentDirectory())
 .AddJsonFile("appsettings.json")
 .Build();
}
```

4. Now, add the `appsettings.json` file to the project, including the following properties:

```
{
    "connectionstring":
    "Endpoint=sb://flixone.servicebus.windows.net/;
    SharedAccessKeyName=
    RootManageSharedAccessKey;SharedAccessKey=
    BvQQcB5FhNxidcgEhhpuGmi/
    XEqvGho9GmHH4yjsTg4=",
    "QueueName": "flixonequeue"
}
```

5. Add the following code to the `main()` method:

```
var builder = ConfigureBuilder();
```

[141]

```
_connectionString = builder["connectionstring"];
_queuename = builder["queuename"];
```

By adding the preceding code, we can get the `connectionstring` and `queuename` from the `.json` file. Now, if we need to change any of these fields, we don't need to make changes to the code files.

Receiving messages from the queue

In this section, we will create a console application that will receive messages from the queue. To create this application, follow these steps:

1. Create a new console application (in C#) and name it `FlixOne.BookStore.MessageReceiver`.
2. Add the NuGet package for Azure Service Bus (which we added in the previous application), including `Microsoft.Extensions.Configuration` and `Microsoft.Extensions.Configuration.Json`.
3. Use the following code to receive messages from the Azure Bus Service queue. Here, your `program.cs` file contains the `ProcessMessagesAsync()` method:

   ```
   static async Task ProcessMessagesAsync(Message message,
   CancellationToken token)
   {
       WriteLine($"Received message: #
       {message.SystemProperties.SequenceNumber}
       Body:{Encoding.UTF8.GetString(message.Body)}");
       await _client.CompleteAsync
       (message.SystemProperties.LockToken);
   }
   ```

4. Run the application, and then look at the result:

   ```
   Starting...
   Sending message: #0:A message from FlixOne.BookStore.MessageSender.
   Sending message: #1:A message from FlixOne.BookStore.MessageSender.
   Sending message: #2:A message from FlixOne.BookStore.MessageSender.
   Sending message: #3:A message from FlixOne.BookStore.MessageSender.
   Sending message: #4:A message from FlixOne.BookStore.MessageSender.
   Sending message: #5:A message from FlixOne.BookStore.MessageSender.
   Sending message: #6:A message from FlixOne.BookStore.MessageSender.
   Sending message: #7:A message from FlixOne.BookStore.MessageSender.
   Sending message: #8:A message from FlixOne.BookStore.MessageSender.
   Sending message: #9:A message from FlixOne.BookStore.MessageSender.
   Ending...
   Press any key...
   ```

5. The console window will display the message and its ID. Now, go to the Azure portal and verify the message. It should show zero messages, as shown in the following screenshot:

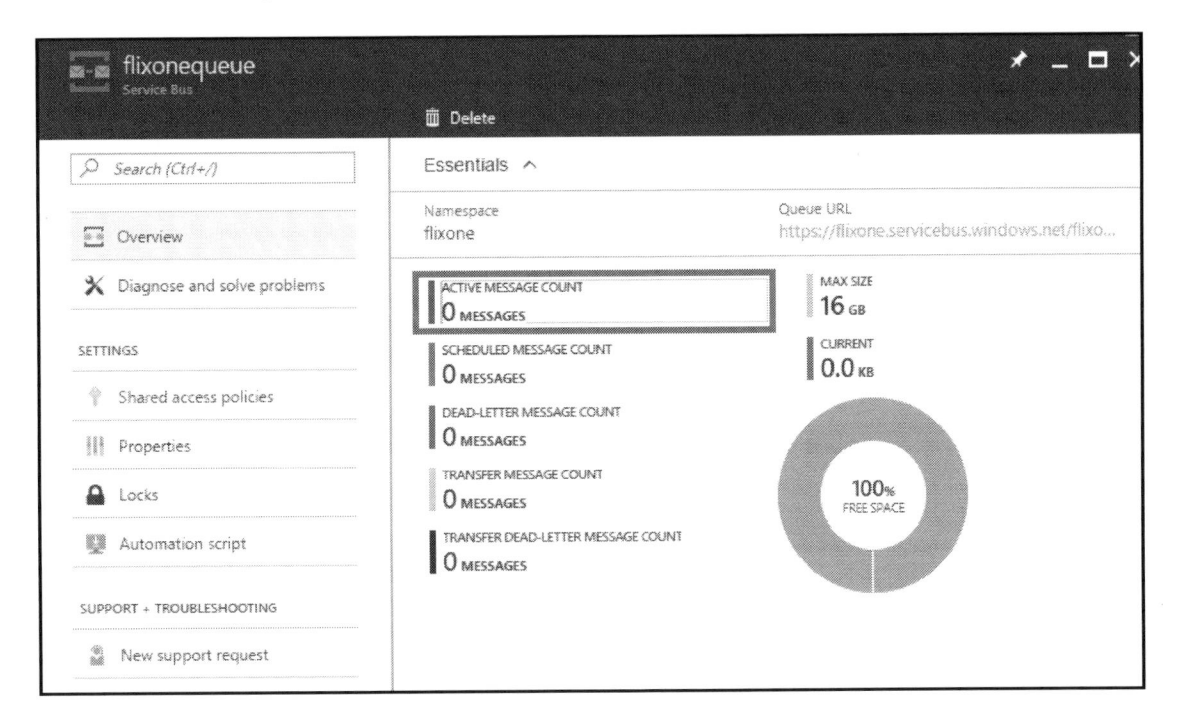

The preceding example demonstrates how we can use Azure Bus Service to send/receive messages for our microservices.

We discussed implementing information on Service Fabric by covering a small application. By doing this, we can connect services using containers. We will look at this in more detail in the next section.

Implementing information on containers

A container is a part of the complete filesystem. As its name suggests, it contains tools, the runtime, and system libraries. Containers share their host operating system and kernel with other containers on the same host. The technology around containers isn't new. It has been a part of the Linux ecosystem for a long time. Due to the recent microservice-based discussions surrounding it, the container technology came into the limelight again. Note that it can be run on Google, Amazon, and Netflix.

Effective Communication between Services

> We will discuss Docker (containers) in more detail in Chapter 5, *Deploying Microservices with Docker*.

Containers on Service Fabric

In the previous section, we learned that Service Fabric deploys services as processes. However, we can also deploy services in containers. Service Fabric supports the deployment of containers on Linux and Windows servers, and it also supports Hyper-V isolation mode.

In this section, we will discuss the prerequisites and execution plan of deploying microservices with Docker.

Prerequisites

To work with the example application, you should have the following prerequisites set up on your system:

- **Integrated Development Environment (IDE)**: Preferable Visual Studio 2019.
- **Service Fabric SDK and Tools**: You'll need to install the SDK and Tools of Service Fabric, if you don't have them installed on your system. You can download the SDK and Tools by going to https://docs.microsoft.com/en-us/azure/service-fabric/service-fabric-get-started.
- **Docker for Windows**: If Docker isn't installed on your Windows system, go to https://hub.docker.com/editions/community/docker-ce-desktop-windows?tab=description and install it.

Execution

In this section, we will briefly list the execution points. We will write a complete application in Chapter 5, *Deploying Microservices with Docker*. Here are the execution points:

- Create a new application (we will create a Product microservice)
- Create a Docker image
- Add Service Fabric to the preceding project
- Configure the communication of the Service Fabric microservice
- Deploy the Service Fabric container application

> We will discuss this implementation using code examples in Chapter 5, *Deploying Microservices with Docker*.

In this section, we understood what Service Fabric is and laid the foundations of the application by looking at the Message Queue, by discussing containers and how to deploy microservices with Docker.

The next section will help us understand microservices with Kubernetes.

Microservices with Kubernetes

In the previous section, we discussed Service Fabric and Docker containers and discussed their implementation steps for microservices. Here, we will discuss microservices with Kubernetes by looking at an overview of **Azure Kubernetes Service (AKS)**.

An overview of Azure Kubernetes Service (AKS)

AKS is based on open source Google Kubernetes. This is a service that is available on the Microsoft Azure public cloud. Since it's a managed container orchestration service, you can manage containers (Docker) and container-based applications.

> Kubernetes (K8s) is an open source container orchestration system that automates deployment for applications. Kubernetes was designed by Google and, these days, the Cloud Native Computing Foundation is maintaining this. The complete source code can be found at https://github.com/kubernetes/kubernetes.
>
> You may also be interested to know about the story of Kubernetes. A very interesting document on this was written by Matt Butcher and Karen Chu, which you can find at https://azure.microsoft.com/mediahandler/files/resourcefiles/phippy-goes-to-the-zoo/Phippy%20Goes%20To%20The%20Zoo_MSFTonline.pdf.

AKS has many features that are useful for applications that have been released on their production environment. These features include service naming and discovery, load balancing, application health checking, horizontal autoscaling, and rolling updates.

Important concepts

There are some concepts that we should know about before we start implementing AKS. These important concepts will help us to use AKS to its full potential.

Kubernetes has a basic unit called a pod. The pod can contain one or more containers and these share the same resources, which are guaranteed to be co-located on the host machine. Containers are deployed inside the pod and can be located via localhost. Since these are based on clusters, every pod has its IP address within the cluster.

These pods (collection of pods) are jointly called a service. A service is exposed inside a cluster by default, but it can also be exposed to an external IP address that could be outside of the cluster. We can expose it using any of the following available characteristics:

- `ClusterIP`
- `NodePort`
- `LoadBalancer`
- `ExternalName`

The Kubernetes controller has a specific type of controller called the **replication controller**. With the help of this, we can handle replication and scaling by running a specified number of copies of a pod across the cluster. This could also replace the pod if the underlying node crashes.

Ease of deploying and managing microservices

AKS provides various features that can help us streamline the deployment and management of microservices in terms of load balancing, application health checking, horizontal autoscaling, and rolling updates.

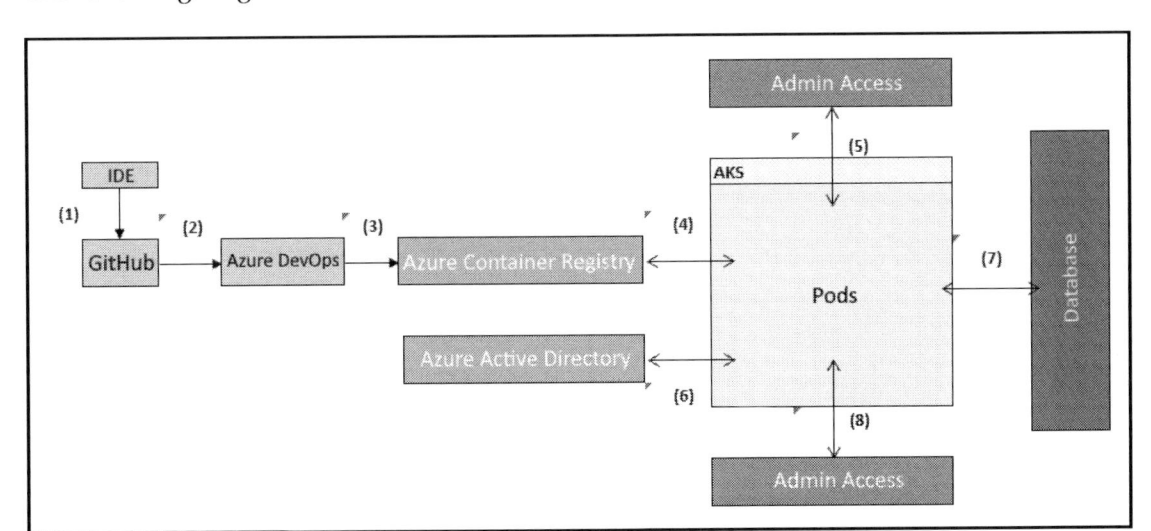

The following diagram shows the microservices contained within AKS:

![Diagram showing microservices workflow: IDE (1) → GitHub (2) → Azure DevOps (3) → Azure Container Registry (4) → AKS Pods, with Admin Access (5), Azure Active Directory (6), Database (7), and Admin Access (8)]

The preceding diagram shows the following process:

1. The developer commits the changes to GitHub using Visual Studio.
2. Changes commit and GitHub pushes/triggers the build to **Azure DevOps** (formerly known as **VSTS**).
3. In this step, DevOps packages our microservices (also known as microservices containers), which are sent to Azure Container Registry.

> Azure Container Registry is a service that manages private containers. It allows us to store images for all types of container deployments. It also includes DC/OS, Docker Swarm, Kubernetes, and Azure services such as App Service, Batch, Service Fabric, and others.

4. In this step, containers (packaged microservices) are deployed to an Azure Kubernetes Service cluster.
5. The users access these microservices with the help of apps and websites.

[147]

6. We secure against unauthorized access with the help of Azure Active Directory.
7. Databases are essential here since microservices persist and fetch data from a variety of databases, for example, **SQL Database, Azure CosmosDB**, or **Azure Database for MySQL**.
8. We have a separate admin portal that's specifically for administrators.

> **Kubernetes versus Docker**: Both Kubernetes and Docker work collectively. Docker helps us package and distribute containerized applications with open standards. With the use of Docker, we can build and run containers, as well as storing and sharing container images. On the other hand, Kubernetes helps us manage distributed and containerized applications that are created by Docker. Also, Kubernetes provides us with the necessary infrastructure so that we can deploy and run these applications on a cluster of machines.

In the forthcoming sections, we will use the sidecar and ambassador patterns to understand the deployment and logging required for our application and we will see how these patterns are helpful with containers.

The sidecar pattern

The name of this pattern refers to the sidecar of a motorcycle. You can imagine that with the help of a sidecar attached to a motorcycle, we could carry loads of things that it's not possible for us to carry directly on the motorcycle. Similarly, the sidecar application is very helpful in performing peripheral tasks that do not depend upon the main application, but that assist in monitoring, auditing, or logging the main application.

The sidecar application can be a third-party application; utility service/components; an audit, logging, or monitoring application; and so on. This pattern also gives us the option to deploy it as a separate component or service. If the main application is hampered because of an unavoidable situation, such as an exception or network failure, then our sidecar application will be needed.

Let's consider the following diagram:

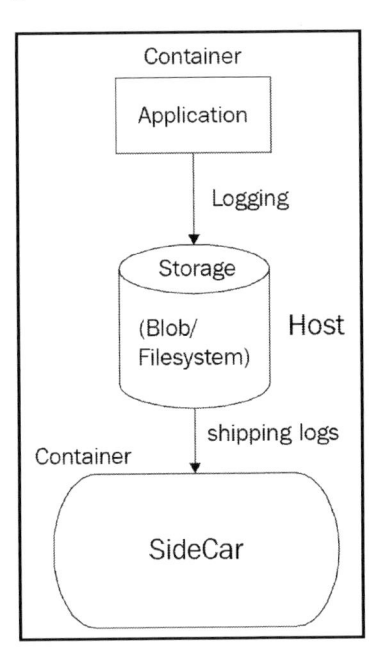

```
                Container
              ┌─────────────┐
              │ Application │
              └──────┬──────┘
                     │ Logging
                     ▼
                 ┌───────┐
                 │Storage│     Host
                 │(Blob/ │
                 │Filesys│
                 │tem)   │
                 └───┬───┘
                     │ shipping logs
     Container       ▼
              ┌─────────────┐
              │   SideCar   │
              └─────────────┘
```

The preceding diagram clearly shows the implementation of the sidecar pattern, where we are persisting logs to the blob storage (filesystem) of our main application and our sidecar application gets shipped to these logs. Here, we are extending a feature of our main application, which is simply saving the logs in the filesystem, with the help of the sidecar application, where we can apply the logic and analyze the shipped logs.

When to use the sidecar pattern

This pattern has many advantages. Both the main and sidecar applications can be written in different languages, so there is no need to think about the different languages or runtime to help to keep the sidecar intact. Resources that are available to the main application can be accessed by the sidecar. While the sidecar application is communicating with the main application, the latency is very minimal—for example, if we are using a single pod for the main and sidecar applications.

The sidecar pattern is useful in the following situations:

- When the component or sidecar application and its logic/functionalities can be consumed by applications written in different languages using different frameworks
- When a component or feature must be colocated on the same host as the application

The pattern is best avoided in the following situations:

- When you want to optimize interprocess communication.
- The deployment of multiple applications would incur a cost; if the budget is limited, do not try this pattern.
- If the main services are independent of the main application and need optimization, then this is not the pattern you need.

Best practices to be observed

Generally, this pattern is used with containers and referred to as a sidecar container. We should follow the prescribed best practices when implementing this pattern in the application. The following practices are just basic best practices and there could be more such practices that are specific to the application:

- Containers should be well suited to the sidecar pattern.
- We should keep interprocess communication in mind when designing a sidecar application/component.
- When we decide to make a sidecar application, we should make sure that we have already decided that the functionality that we need from the sidecar would not be fulfilled by a separate/independent service or a classic daemon.

In this section, we discussed the implementation of logging using the sidecar pattern. Similarly, we have the ambassador pattern, which we will discuss in the next section.

The ambassador pattern

The ambassador pattern is almost the same as the sidecar pattern that we just discussed. The only difference is that every request comes through the container, which is also called an **ambassador** (sometimes called a proxy container). In other words, we can say that the main application cannot contact the outside world (user interfaces, clients, and/or remote services) without the ambassador pattern.

Let's consider the following diagram:

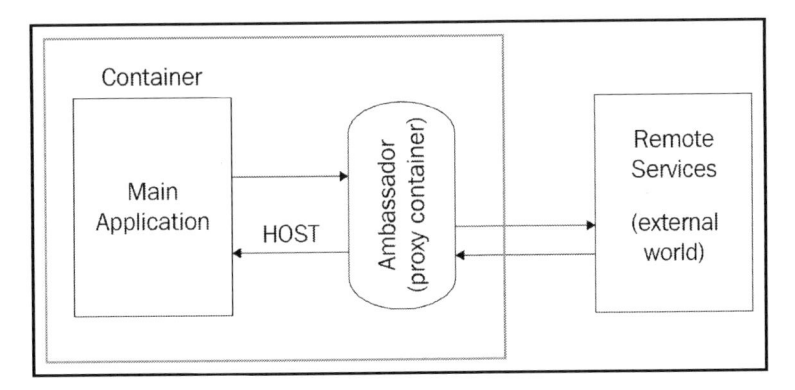

The preceding diagram clearly visualizes the implementation of the ambassador pattern, where the main application and ambassador container are deployed on the same host. Now, whenever the main application interacts with the remote services (these services may be external APIs, the user interface, and so on), it interacts via the ambassador or proxy container. Here, the ambassador works as a proxy and routes all network requests to the main application.

When to use the ambassador pattern

The ambassador pattern is useful in the following situations:

- When we have multiple services/features developed in multiple languages or frameworks and we need to build common-client connectivity
- When a legacy application or an application that is difficult to modify is being supported
- When we want to standardize and extend instrumentation

And the pattern is best avoided in the following situations:

- If having an efficient network is the priority and if latency would affect various operations and couldn't be handled.
- If the connectivity features are consumed by a single language of the client. A better option might be to have this as a client library that is distributed to the development teams as a package.
- When connectivity features cannot be generalized and require deeper integration with the client application.

Best practices to be observed

There are best practices we should follow once we have started implementing the ambassador pattern. Although the ambassador pattern is almost the same as the sidecar pattern, we should be careful when implementing it. The following are the suggested points favoring best practices for this pattern:

- Whenever we use a proxy or whenever we route network requests via any external components, it adds latency. So when we use the ambassador pattern, we should keep the latency overhead in our mind.
- With the implementation of this pattern, we should consider whether we'd implement a circuit breaker or retry the ambassador, because it might not be safe to do so unless all operations are idempotent.
- The most important consideration for this pattern is how we package and deploy the proxy.

The ambassador pattern helps us to set up a single connectivity client that routes all the network requests from external services to the main application. There are chances of latency, but we have to be careful when selecting this pattern, especially if there is no other alternative for the feature that we want to implement.

Considering IoT when building microservices apps

These days microservices are increasingly being adopted as the preferred way to create enterprise applications. Microservices are ideal for supporting a range of platforms and devices spanning web, mobile, and IoT (including wearables). In this scenario, our application FlixOne connects with IoT devices. We can use various components, like monitor, which can be used to stream the data, wearable devices can be used to capture the data, and so on.

IoT is an area with many significant use cases and lots of potential. Microsoft Azure provides managed cloud services, such as the **Internet of Things** (**IoT**), which connects, monitors, and controls billions of IoT assets. To simplify this, an IoT solution has one or more IoT devices and one or more backend services running in the cloud, which communicate with one another. When building a solution on IoT, our considerations are for large-scale enterprise solutions.

Every system contains a few essential parts that make the system reliable. The same concept is applicable in the case of any IoT solution. These main parts are as follows:

- Devices
- Backend services
- The communication between the two

However, the development of an IoT system incurs huge cost and requires significant investment in hardware, infrastructure, and apps.

Using IoT with microservices, provides a way to reduce infrastructure usage and cost. Furthermore, containerization effectively helps deploy microservices, with the best resource utilization, and it monitors this entire infrastructure through various frameworks, reducing our operational overhead. So, when building an IoT solution, the development part needs to be considered for the following reasons:

- **Architecture**: Planning and selecting your architecture, is one of the basic and important steps for building IoT applications. For instance, the IoT Architectures for a healthcare IoT application would consist of 3 stages: physical (using devices such as sensors), communication (using devices to gather and send data to the application), and applications (where data is received, and various operations like analysis can be performed).
- **Topology and protocol**: The selection of a communication protocol is very important, in respect to the implementation of your business requirements. For device-side communication, the protocols allowed by Azure IoT Hub include MQTT, AMQP, HTTPS, and so on. The hub-spoke topology is one of the preferred network topologies in Azure. Hub is the virtual network in Azure, and it acts as a central point of connectivity between on-premises devices and the Azure IoT network.
- **Scalability** : Scalability is always a top priority while developing enterprise applications, and it is even more important when we discuss IoT applications. Data and application usage tend to increase tremendously over time, so we should give considerable attention to scaling. Azure IoT Hub provides scaling features (Basic and Standard Tier) that we can select from, as per our business needs.
- **Security**: Security is always a concern, and when we work with multiple devices, we should be more careful about our security implementation. The best way to be secure, is to ensure that every connected device has its own authentication.

- **Testing and deployment**: Devices should be well tested and then deployed. We should validate that each device is connected and communicating with its IoT Hub. Performance testing (or load testing) would be the best way to analyze the IoT application.

In the upcoming sections, we will discuss IoT Hub and IoT Edge.

An overview of IoT Hub

The IoT Hub is a service (managed) is hosted on the cloud; it works like a mediator that stays in the middle of the IoT applications and the devices that the application is managing.

When we work with Azure IoT, we have the ability to communicate between IoT applications and millions of devices that are associated with them, with the help of the backend system hosted on the cloud. For example, you can send telemetry data from your device to Azure IoT Hub; and with our application in the cloud, we can perform analysis or other operations, as per the business model. We are not covering the implementation part of this example, because it is beyond the scope of this book. However, you can refer to this link for the complete implementation: https://docs.microsoft.com/en-us/azure/iot-hub/quickstart-send-telemetry-dotnet

Moreover, any device can be virtually connected with IoT Hub, and it will support two-way communication: Device to cloud, and cloud to device. IoT Hub allows us to manage scalable, full-featured IoT solutions, so that we can do the following:

- **Scale the solution**: IoT Hub provides a facility to scale numerous connected devices. The important point related to scaling the solution, is that it provides different scaling options, because it recognizes that every IoT solution is different from another. As mentioned earlier, you can choose either the basic or standard price tier, as per the requirement of your IoT solution.
- **Secure the communication**: IoT Hubs also facilitate a secure communication channel, as every connected device has its own authentication.
- **Integrate with other devices**: The best part of IoT Hub is that it can be connected with various Azure services, like Azure Event Grid, Azure Logic Apps, Azure Stream Analytics, and so on.

An overview of IoT Edge

Azure IoT Edge helps with the business logic and analysis of the device. With this, we don't need to bother with data management. We only need to concentrate on the business logic and the working solution. It also helps package business logic and helps us move into standard containers, so that we can scale out the IoT solution. Since the business logic is maintained in containers, we can deploy these containers to any device and then monitor them from within the cloud.

Azure IoT Edge is made up of three components:

- **IoT Edge Modules**: The Azure IoT Edge module is the smallest computation unit that is managed by Azure IoT Edge. It can contain different Azure services, such as Azure Stream Analytics. It can also contain the customized code, as per the business requirement.
- **IoT Edge Runtime**: This module enables customized logic and cloud logic on IoT Edge devices. It performs management and communication operations. It also helps to install and update workloads on the devices.
- **Cloud-based interface**: It provides the facility to manage and monitor IoT devices from anywhere, remotely.

To develop, deploy, and maintain any of these modules, the following four elements are required:

- *module image*: This is a package of multiple software that define a module.
- *module instance*: This is the instance that is initiated by IoT Edge Runtime; an instance is a specific code or computation that executes the module image.
- *module identity*: This is the security information (including any other required information) that is stored on IoT Hub.
- *module twin*: This comprises of the meta data and configuration information, in the form of a JSON file; it is stored on IoT Hub.

The aim of this section was to provide you with an overview of the various considerations of IoT for microservices. Here, we discussed IoT Hub and IoT Edge, and we understood that one is a managed service while the other allows us to add business logic and perform analysis for the IoT device.

Summary

Interservice communication is possible with synchronous or asynchronous communication, which are styles of collaboration. Microservices should have asynchronous APIs. The API gateway is a proxy server that allows various clients to interact with APIs. Azure API Management, as an API gateway, provides plenty of features that we can use to manage and host various RESTful APIs. There are various patterns that help us communicate with microservices.

With the use of Azure Bus Service, we can easily manage and play with interservice communication, using the Azure Bus Service message queue. (Services can easily send or receive messages between themselves using this.) Eventual consistency is all about scalable systems with high scalability, and it can be proven by the CAP theorem.

In the next chapter, we will discuss various testing strategies, so that we can test our applications and build on the microservice architectural style.

Questions

1. What are synchronous communication and asynchronous communication?
2. What is an integration pattern?
3. What is an event-driven pattern, and why is it so important for microservices?
4. What is the CAP theorem?

Further reading

- *Getting Started with Kubernetes – Third Edition, by Jonathan Baier and Jesse White, published by Packt Publishing*: https://www.packtpub.com/virtualization-and-cloud/getting-started-kubernetes-third-edition
- *DevOps with Kubernetes – Second Edition, by Hideto Saito, Hui-Chuan Chloe Lee, Et al, published by Packt Publishing*: https://www.packtpub.com/virtualization-and-cloud/devops-kubernetes-second-edition
- *Kubernetes for Developers, by Joseph Heck, published by Packt Publishing*: https://www.packtpub.com/virtualization-and-cloud/kubernetes-developers
- *Docker on Windows – Second Edition, by Elton Stoneman, published by Packt Publishing*: https://www.packtpub.com/virtualization-and-cloud/docker-windows-second-edition

4
Testing Microservices with the Microsoft Unit Testing Framework

Quality assurance, or testing, is a great way to assess a system, program, or application in a variety of ways. Sometimes, a system requires testing for it to identify erroneous code, while on other occasions, we may need it to assess our system's business compliance. Testing can vary from system to system, and it can be considerably different, depending on the architectural style of the application. Everything depends on how we strategically approach our testing plan. For example, testing a monolith .NET application is different from testing SOA or microservices.

The aim of this chapter is to understand the testing strategies and the different types of testing we can use. We will learn how to implement unit tests, with the help of the Microsoft Unit Testing Framework and with the help of Moq (an open-source, friendly mocking framework).

In this chapter, we will cover the following topics:

- Testing the microservice application
- Understanding our testing strategies
- The testing pyramid
- Types of microservice tests
- Testing the microservice application

Technical requirements

This chapter contains various code examples, to explain the concepts within. The code will be simple and is just for demonstration purposes.

To run and execute the code, you will need the following prerequisites:

- Visual Studio 2019
- .NET Core set up

Installing Visual Studio 2019:

To run these code examples, you'll need to install Visual Studio 2019 or later (preferred IDE). To do so, follow these instructions:

1. Download Visual Studio 2019 (Community is free) from https://docs.microsoft.com/en-us/visualstudio/install/install-visual-studio.
2. Follow the installation instructions for your system. Multiple versions are available for Visual Studio. We are using Visual Studio for Windows.

Setting up .NET Core 3.1:

If you don't have .NET Core 3.1 installed, you can download it from https://www.microsoft.com/net/download/windows.

> The complete source code is available at https://github.com/PacktPublishing/Hands-On-Microservices-with-CSharp-8-and-.NET-Core-3-Third-Edition/tree/master/Chapter%2004.

Testing the microservice application

Testing microservices can be a challenging job, as it is different from how we test applications that have been built using the traditional architectural style. Testing a .NET monolithic application is a bit easier than testing a microservice, which provides implementation independence and short delivery cycles.

Let's understand it in the context of our .NET monolithic application, where we didn't utilize continuous integration and deployment. It becomes more complex when testing is combined with continuous integration and deployment. For microservices, we need to understand the tests for every service and how these tests differ from each other. Also, note that automated testing doesn't mean that we will not perform any manual testing.

Here are a few things that make microservice testing a complex and challenging task:

- Microservices may have multiple services that work together or individually for an enterprise system, so they can be complex.
- Microservices are meant to target multiple clients (but not always), so they involve more complex use cases.
- Each component/service of the microservice architectural style is isolated and independent, so it is a bit complex to test them, as they need to be tested both individually and as a complete system.
- There may be independent teams working on separate components/services that may be required to interact with each other. Therefore, tests should cover not only internal services but also external services. This makes the job of testing microservices more challenging and complex.
- Each component/service in a microservice is designed to work independently, but they may have to access common/shared data, where each service is responsible for modifying its own database. So, testing microservices is going to be more complex, as services need to access data using API calls to other services, which adds further dependencies to other services. This type of testing will have to be handled using mock tests.

This section helped us understand how we can test microservices. In the next section, we will discuss the various challenges of testing and how to handle them.

Handling testing challenges with microservices

In the previous section, we discussed how testing a microservice is a complex and challenging job. In this section, we will discuss some points that will indicate how conducting various tests could help us overcome these challenges. Let's have a look at some now:

- A unit test framework, such as the Microsoft Unit Testing Framework, provides a facility that we can use to test individual operations of independent components. To ensure that all the tests pass and that any new functionality or changes don't break anything (if any functionality breaks down, then the related unit test will fail), these tests can be run on every compilation of code.

- To make sure that responses are consistent with the expectations of the clients or consumers, consumer-driven contract testing can be used.
- Services use data from an external party or from other services, and they can be tested by setting up the endpoint of the services that are responsible for handling the data. By doing this, we can use a mocking framework or library, such as `Moq`, to mock these endpoints during the integration process.

In the next section, we will look at some test strategies that can help us overcome all these challenges.

Understanding testing strategies

As we mentioned in the *Technical requirements* section of Chapter 1, *An Introduction to Microservices*, deployment and QA requirements can be very demanding. The only way to effectively handle this scenario would be through preemptive planning. I have always favored the inclusion of the QA team during the early requirement gathering and design phase. In the case of microservices, it becomes a necessity to have a close collaboration between the architecture group and the QA group. Not only will the QA team's input be helpful, but they will be able to draw up a strategy to test the microservices effectively.

Test strategies are merely a map or outlined plan that describes the complete approach of testing. Different systems require different testing approaches. It isn't possible to implement a pure testing approach, to a system that has been developed using a newer approach, rather than the earlier developed system. Testing strategies should be clear to everyone, so that the created tests can help non-technical members of the team (such as stakeholders) understand how the system is working. Such tests can be automated to simply test the business flow, or they could be manual tests, which can be performed by a user working on the User Acceptance Testing system.

Testing strategies or approaches have the following techniques:

- **Proactive**: This is an early approach, and it tries to fix defects, before the build is created from the initial test designs.
- **Reactive**: In this approach, testing is started once coding is completed.

In this section, we looked at the strategies we can use for testing, and we discussed the proactive and reactive testing approaches. In the next section, we will look at the testing pyramid and how testing approaches flow.

Testing pyramid

The testing pyramid is a strategy or a way to define what you should test in microservices. In other words, we can say it helps us define the testing scope of microservices. The concept of the testing pyramid was created by Mike Cohn (http://www.mountaingoatsoftware.com/blog/the-forgotten-layer-of-the-test-automation-pyramid) in 2009. There are various flavors of the testing pyramid; different authors have described this by indicating how they had placed or prioritized their testing scope. The following diagram depicts the concept that was defined by Mike Cohn:

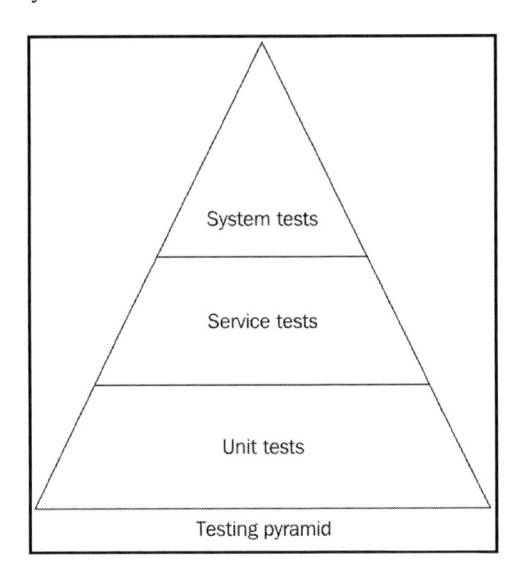

Testing pyramid

The **testing pyramid** showcases how a well-designed test strategy is structured. When we look closely at it, we can easily see how we should follow the testing approach for microservices (note that the testing pyramid is not specific to microservices). Let's start from the bottom of this pyramid. We can see that the testing scope is limited to the use of **Unit tests**. As soon as we move to the top, our testing scope is expanded into a broader scope, where we can perform the complete system testing.

Let's talk about these layers in detail (with a bottom-to-top approach):

- **Unit tests**: These are tests that test the small functionalities of an application, based on the microservice's architectural style.
- **Service tests**: These are tests that test an independent service or a service that communicates with another/external service.
- **System tests**: These are tests that help test an entire system, with an aspect of the user interface. These are end-to-end tests.

One interesting point is that the top-layered tests, that is, system tests, are slow and expensive to write and maintain. On the other hand, the bottom-layered tests, that is, unit tests, are comparatively fast and less expensive.

The testing pyramid is all about various tests that can be done on different layers of an application. In this section, we discussed unit, service, and system tests, by following the test pyramid. In the next section, we will discuss these tests in detail, and we will cover various types of microservice tests.

Types of microservice tests

In the previous section, we discussed test approaches or testing strategies. These strategies help us decide how we will proceed with testing the system. Testing strategies give us various types of tests that can help us test the entire system. In this section, we will discuss various types of microservice testing.

Unit testing

Unit tests are tests that typically test a single function call, to ensure that the smallest piece of the program is tested. These tests are meant to verify specific functionality, without considering other components.

The following are the various components that help verify specific functionality:

- Testing will be more complex, when components are broken down into small, independent pieces that are supposed to be tested independently. Here, testing strategies come in handy, and they ensure that the best quality assurance of a system will be performed. We add more power, when it comes to the **test-driven development** (TDD) approach. We will discuss this with the help of an example in the *Unit tests* section, which is a subsection of the *Tests in action* section.

> You can learn and practice TDD, with the help of Katas at `https://github.com/garora/TDD-Katas`.

- Unit tests can be of any size; there is no definite size for a unit test. Generally, these tests are written at the class level.
- Smaller unit tests are good for testing every possible functionality of a complex system.

Component (service) testing

Component testing (or service testing) is a method where we bypass the UI and directly test the API (in our case, the ASP.NET Core Web API). Using this test, we confirm that an individual service doesn't have any code bugs and that it is working fine, functionality-wise.

Testing a service doesn't mean it is an independent service. This service may be interacting with an external service. In such a scenario, we shouldn't call the actual service, but instead we use the mock and stub approach. The reason for this is in our motto: to test code and make sure it is bug-free. In our case, we will use the `moq` framework to mock our services.

There are a few things worth noting, when it comes to component or service testing:

- Since we need to verify the functionality of the services, these kinds of tests should be small and fast.
- With the help of mocking, we don't need to deal with the actual database; therefore, the test execution time is less or nominally higher.
- The scope of these tests is broader than unit tests.

Integration testing

In unit testing, we test a single unit of code. In component or service testing, we test mock services by depending on an external or third-party component. However, integration testing in microservices can be a bit challenging, since we test components that work together. Here, service calls should be made so that they integrate with external services. In this test strategy, we make sure that the system is working correctly and that the services behave as expected. In our case, we have various microservices, and some of them depend on external services.

For example, StockService depends on OrderService, in that a particular number of items is reduced from the stock, as soon as the customer successfully orders that specific item. In this scenario, when we test StockService, we should mock OrderService. Our goal should be to test StockService and not to communicate with OrderService. We don't test the database of any service directly.

Contract testing

Contract testing is an approach where each service call independently verifies the response. If any service is dependent, then dependencies are stubbed. This way, the service functions without interacting with any other service. This is an integration test that allows us to check the contract of external services. This follows a concept called the consumer-driven contract (we will discuss this in detail in the following section).

For example, `CustomerService` allows new customers to register with the FlixOne Store. We don't store new customers' data in our database. We verify customer data first, to check for blacklisting or fraud user listing, and so on. This process happens by calling an external service that is maintained by another team or entirely by a third party. Our tests will still pass, if someone changes the contract of this external service, because such a change shouldn't affect our test since we stubbed the contract of this external service.

Microservices could have several independent services that may or may not communicate with each other. To test these services, we should have some pattern or mechanism that ensures and verifies the interactions. To do this, we can use consumer-driven contracts.

Consumer-driven contracts

In microservices, we have several services that are independent, or services that need to communicate with each other. Apart from this, from the user's point of view (here, the user is a developer, who is consuming the API being referred to), they know about the service and whether it has, or doesn't have, several clients/consumers/users. These clients can have the same or different needs.

Consumer-driven contracts refer to a pattern that specifies and verifies all the interactions between clients/consumers and the API owner (application). Here, consumer-driven means that the client/consumer specifies what kind of interactions it is asking for with the defined format. On the other hand, the API owner (application services) must agree to these contracts and ensure that they are not breaking them. The following diagram is a pictorial overview of the consumer-driven contract, where **Contract** serves in-between the **Consumer** and its **Provider**:

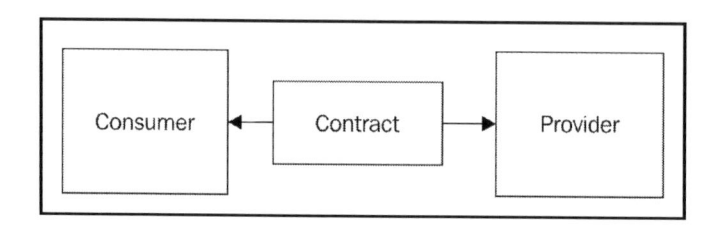

| Consumer | ← | Contract | → | Provider |

These are the contracts:

- **Provider contract**: This is merely a complete description of the service provided by the API owner (application). Swagger's documentation can be used for our REST API (web API).
- **Consumer contract**: This is a description of how the consumers/clients are going to utilize the provider contract.
- **Consumer-driven contract**: This is a description of how the API owner satisfies consumer/client contracts.

How to implement a consumer-driven test

In the case of microservices, it's a bit more challenging to implement a consumer-driven test, than it is for a .NET monolithic application. This is because, in monolithic applications, we can directly use any unit test framework, such as MS tests or NUnit, but we can't do this directly in the microservice architecture. In microservices, we would need to mock not only the method calls but also the services themselves, which get called via either HTTP or HTTPS.

To implement a consumer-driven test, we can use various tools. One famous open source tool for .NET frameworks is *PactNet* (https://github.com/SEEK-Jobs/pact-net), while another for .NET Core is *Pact.Net Core* (https://github.com/garora/pact-net-core). These are based on *Pact* (https://docs.pact.io/) standards. At the end of this chapter, we will look at consumer-driven contract testing in action.

How Pact-net-core helps us achieve our goal

In a consumer-driven test, our goal is to make sure that we are able to test all the services and internal components that depend on or communicate with other/external services.

Pact-net-core is written in a way that guarantees the contracts will be met. Here are a few points on how it helps us achieve our goal:

- The execution is very fast.
- It helps identify failure causes.
- Pact doesn't require a separate environment to manage automation test integration.

We need to follow two steps to work with Pact:

1. **Defining expectations**: Here, the consumer team has to define the contract. In the following diagram, Pact helps record the consumer contract, which will be verified when it's replayed:

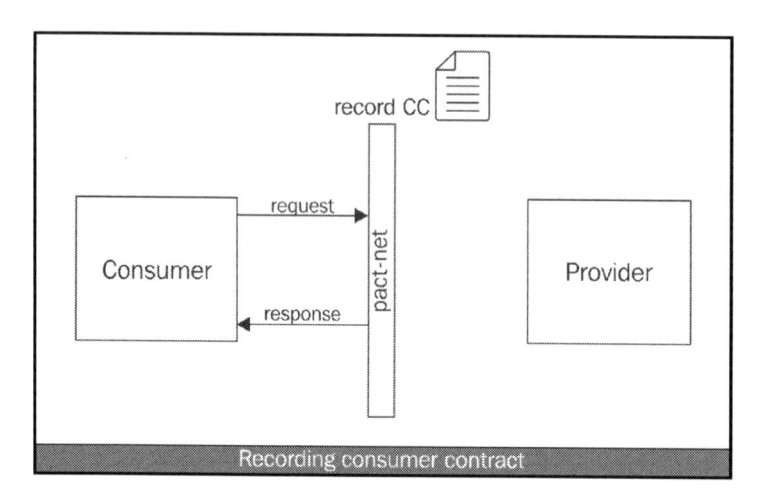

    Recording consumer contract

2. **Verifying expectations**: As part of the next step, the contract is given to the provider team, and then the provider service is implemented to fulfill the same. In the following diagram, we are showing how the contract is replayed on the provider side, to fulfill the defined contract:

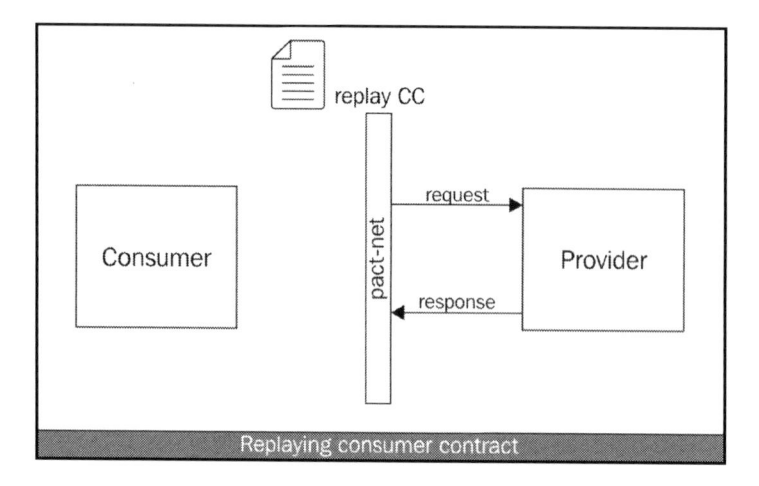

    Replaying consumer contract

In this section, we looked at consumer-driven contracts, which help us mitigate the challenges of microservice architectures, with the help of an open-source tool called Pact-net. With the help of a consumer-driven contract, we can ensure that we can work without having actual input from services. To see how it works, we will look at performance testing.

Performance testing

This is a form of non-functional testing, and its main motto is to not verify the code or test the code's health. This is meant to ensure that the system is performing well, based on the various measures, that is, scalability, reliability, and so on.

The following are the different techniques, or types of performance testing, that help us test the system on various aspects, so that we can test its performance:

- **Load testing**: This is a process where we test the behavior of the system under various circumstances of a specific load. This also covers critical transactions, database load, application servers, and so on.
- **Stress testing**: This is an approach where the system goes under regress testing and finds the upper limit capacity of the system. It also determines how a system behaves in a situation where the current load goes above the expected maximum load.
- **Soak testing**: This is also called endurance testing. In this test, the main purpose is to monitor memory utilization, memory leaks, or various factors that affect system performance.
- **Spike testing**: This is an approach where we make sure that the system is able to sustain the workload. One of the best tasks to determine performance is to suddenly increase the user load.

End-to-end (UI/functional) testing

End-to-end, UI, or functional tests, are those that are performed for the entire system, including the entire service and database. These tests increase the scope of testing. It is the highest level of testing, it includes front-end integration, and it tests the system the way an end user would use it. This testing is similar to how an end user would work on the system.

Sociable versus isolated unit tests

Sociable unit tests are those that contain concrete collaborators and cross boundaries. They are not solitary tests. Solitary tests ensure that the methods of a class are tested. Sociable testing is not new. This concept is explained in detail by Martin Fowler as a unit test (https://martinfowler.com/bliki/UnitTest.html). Let's take a look at these two in more detail:

- **Sociable tests**: This is a test that lets us know the application is working as expected. This is the environment where other applications behave correctly, run smoothly, and produce the expected results. It also tests the functionality of new functions/methods, including other software, for the same environment. Sociable tests resemble system testing, because these tests behave like system tests.
- **Isolated unit tests**: As the name suggests, you can use these tests to perform unit testing in an isolated way, by performing stubbing and mocking. We can perform unit testing with a concrete class, using stubs.

Unit testing is a way to make sure that the application code is well tested; the code is tested by writing code. Unit tests are written by developers, so that these tests ensure that the code is working. By adapting these tests, we can make sure that our application is working fine in specific environments.

This section provided an overview of the different tests that we can use to verify the functionality of a class method and an application, in certain environments. However, we need to understand the testing functionality of a flow while using data during tests, as we do not recommend you play with actual data. Because of this, we need to understand how we can make mocks. In the next section, we will discuss stubs and mocks.

Stubs and mocks

Sometimes, we need to test the flow with or without our data. In cases where we need to do tests, we can't go with the actual data, because using actual data during tests isn't recommended (one reason is that you don't want to alter data). The same goes for tests where we don't use data; in this case, we need to validate the output. To go with these tests, we need an arrangement where we can create a skeleton that has some standard output, without depending on the input of a method that's being tested. This can be done with stubs and mocks, where stubs are objects that represent the response/result or output, but any changes in input wouldn't affect the stubs. Mock objects, on the other hand, are fake objects that contain the expected output from the method that's being tested.

Stubs are canned responses to calls that are made during the test; mocks are meant to set expectations. See the following descriptions:

- **Stubs**: A stub object doesn't depend on the input that's received, which means the response or result is not hampered due to correct or incorrect input. Initially, we create stubs that are meant to be objects.
- **Mocks**: A mock object isn't real and might always be a fake object. Using this, you can test methods that can be called and tell us whether a unit test has failed or passed. In other words, we can say that a mock object is just a replica of our actual object. In the following code, we use the `moq` framework to implement a mocked object:

```
[Fact]
public void Get_Returns_ActionResults()
{
    // Arrange
    var mockRepo = new Mock<IProductRepository>();
    mockRepo.Setup(repo => repo.GetAll().
    ToViewModel()).Returns(GetProducts());
    var controller = new ProductController(mockRepo.Object);
    // Act
    var result = controller.Get();
    // Assert
    var viewResult = Assert.IsType<OkObjectResult>(result);
    var model = Assert.IsAssignableFrom<
    IEnumerable<ProductViewModel>>(viewResult.Value);
    Assert.Equal(2, model.Count());
}
```

In the preceding code example, we mocked our repository, IProductRepository, and we verified the mocked result.

The aim of this section was to cover various tests that we can use for microservice-based applications. In the next section, we will understand these terms in more detail, by using more code examples from our FlixOne bookstore application.

Testing the microservice application

So far, we have discussed test strategies and various types of microservice tests. We've also discussed how to test and what to test. In this section, we will see some tests in action. We will implement these tests, with the following minimal requirements:

- Visual Studio 2019

- .NET Core 3.1
- C# 8.0
- xUnit and MS tests
- The moq framework

Getting ready for the test project

First, we will test our microservice application, the FlixOne bookstore. With the help of some code examples, we will learn how to perform unit tests, stubbing, and mocking.

> We created the FlixOne bookstore application in `Chapter 2`, *Refactoring the Monolith*.

Before we start writing tests, we should set up a test project in our existing application. There are a few simple steps we can follow for this:

1. From the **Solution Explorer**, within Using Visual Studio, right-click on **Solution** and click **Add | New Project**, as shown in the following screenshot:

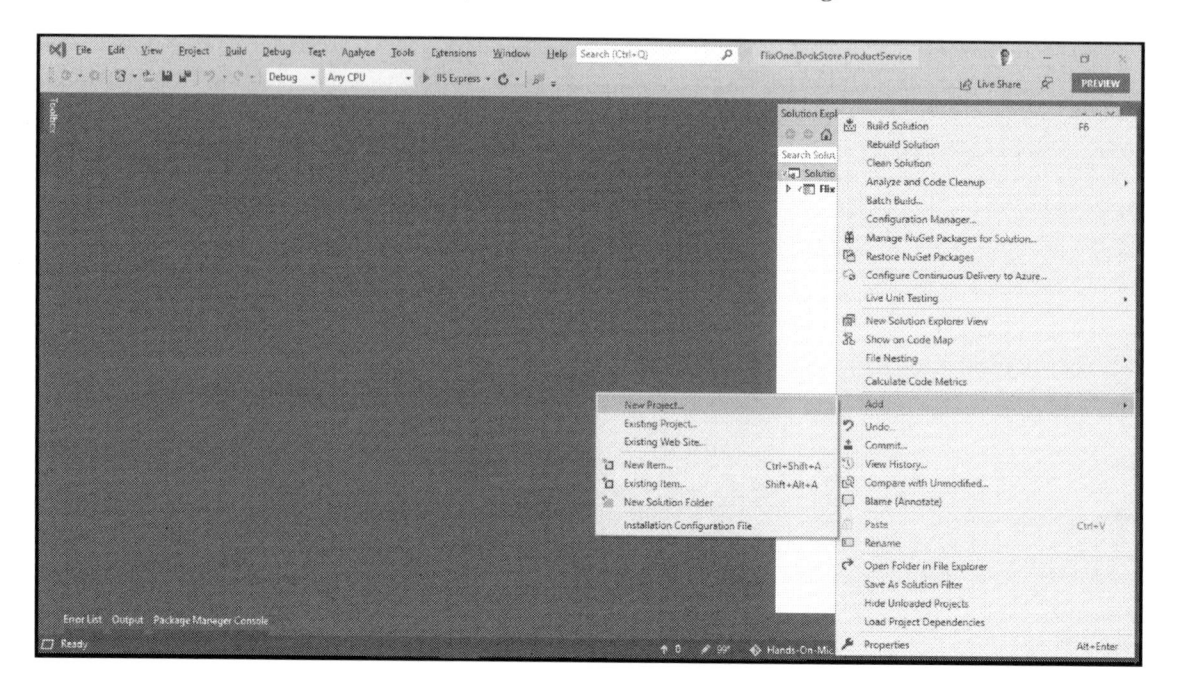

2. From the **Add a new project** template, search for **.NET Core** and select **xUnit Test Project (.NET Core)**:

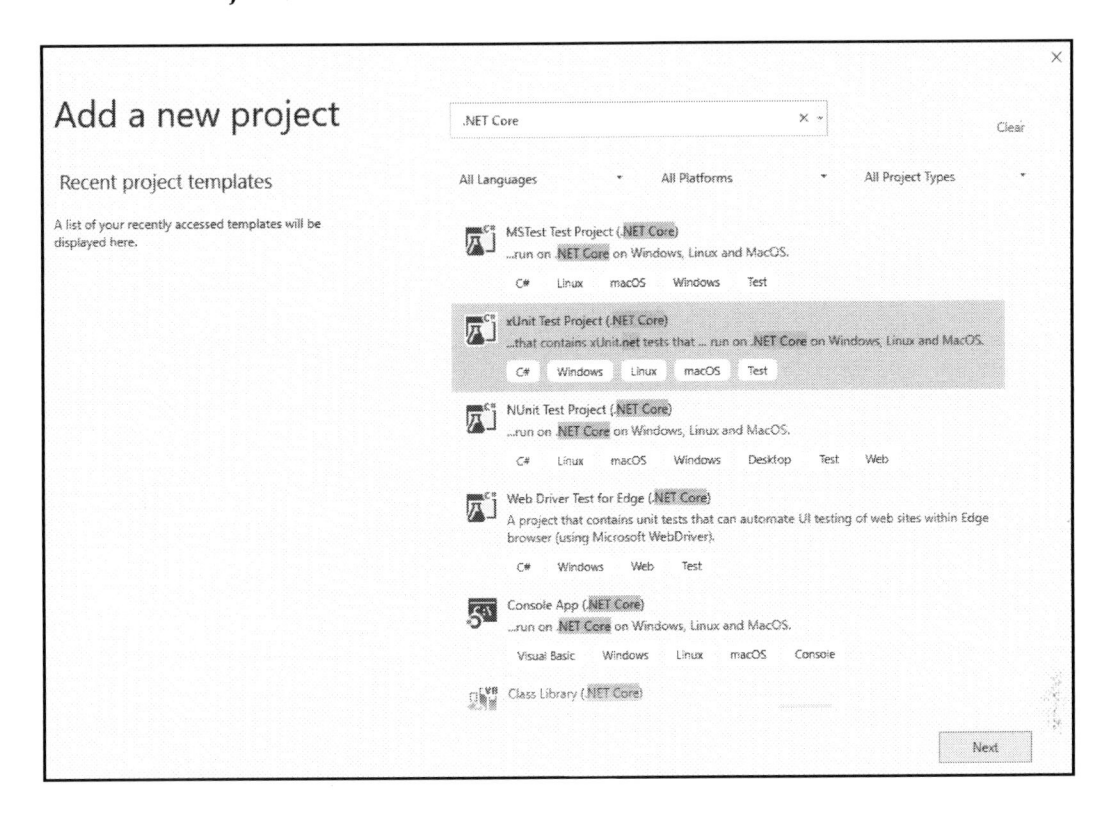

3. Provide a meaningful name, for example, `FlixOne.BookStore.ProductService.UnitTests`:

Testing Microservices with the Microsoft Unit Testing Framework

4. The default language version of our project is **C# 8.0** (refer to `Chapter 2`, *Refactoring the Monolith*, to find out more about selecting a language version).

Our project structure should look like this:

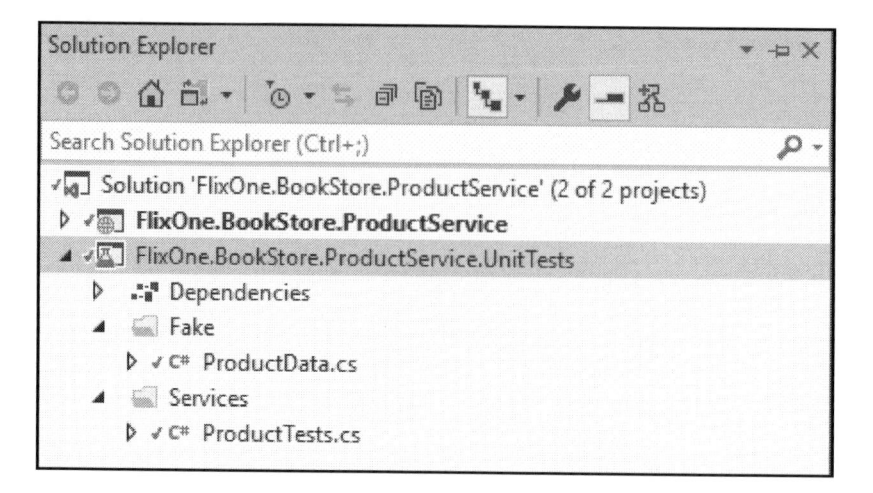

```
Solution Explorer
Search Solution Explorer (Ctrl+;)
  Solution 'FlixOne.BookStore.ProductService' (2 of 2 projects)
    FlixOne.BookStore.ProductService
    FlixOne.BookStore.ProductService.UnitTests
      Dependencies
      Fake
        C# ProductData.cs
      Services
        C# ProductTests.cs
```

The preceding screenshot shows the structure of our test project, that is, **FlixOne.BookStore.ProductService.UnitTests**. It has two folders: **Fake** and **Services**. The **ProductData.cs** file contains fake data and belongs in the **Fake** folder. On the other hand, the **ProductTest.cs** file belongs to the **Services** folder and contains unit tests.

Unit tests

Let's test `ProductService`, to make sure that our service returns product data without failure. Here, we will use fake objects. Follow these steps:

1. Delete the default `UniTest.cs` file from your test project.
2. Add a new folder, and then name it `Fake` in the `FlixOne.BookStore.ProductService.UnitTests` project.
3. Under the `Fake` folder, add the `ProductData.cs` class, and then add the following code:

```
public IEnumerable<ProductViewModel> GetProducts()
  {
    var productVm = new List<ProductViewModel>
    {
      new ProductViewModel
      {
```

```
            CategoryId = Guid.NewGuid(),
            CategoryDescription = "Category Description",
            CategoryName = "Category Name",
            ProductDescription = "Product Description",
            ProductId = Guid.NewGuid(),
            ProductImage = "Image full path",
            ProductName = "Product Name",
            ProductPrice = 112M
        },
        new ProductViewModel
        {
            CategoryId = Guid.NewGuid(),
            CategoryDescription = "Category Description-01",
            CategoryName = "Category Name-01",
            ProductDescription = "Product Description-01",
            ProductId = Guid.NewGuid(),
            ProductImage = "Image full path",
            ProductName = "Product Name-01",
            ProductPrice = 12M
        }
    };
    return productVm;
}
```

The preceding code snippet is creating fake or dummy data of the `ProductViewModel` type.

In the following code block, we create fake data by making two lists of `ProductViewModel` and `Product`:

```
public IEnumerable<Product> GetProductList()
{
    return new List<Product>
    {
        new Product
        {
            Category = new Category(),
            CategoryId = Guid.NewGuid(),
            Description = "Product Description-01",
            Id = Guid.NewGuid(),
            Image = "image full path",
            Name = "Product Name-01",
            Price = 12M
        },
        new Product
        {
            Category = new Category(),
            CategoryId = Guid.NewGuid(),
```

```
                Description = "Product Description-02",
                Id = Guid.NewGuid(),
                Image = "image full path",
                Name = "Product Name-02",
                Price = 125M
            }
        };
    }
```

The preceding code shows the two lists. These lists contain fake data to test the output of `ProductViewModel` and `Product`.

4. Add the `Services` folder to the `FlixOne.BookStore.ProductService.UnitTests` project.
5. Under the `Services` folder, add the `ProductTests.cs` class.
6. Open **NuGet Manager**, and then search for and add `moq`, as shown in the following screenshot:

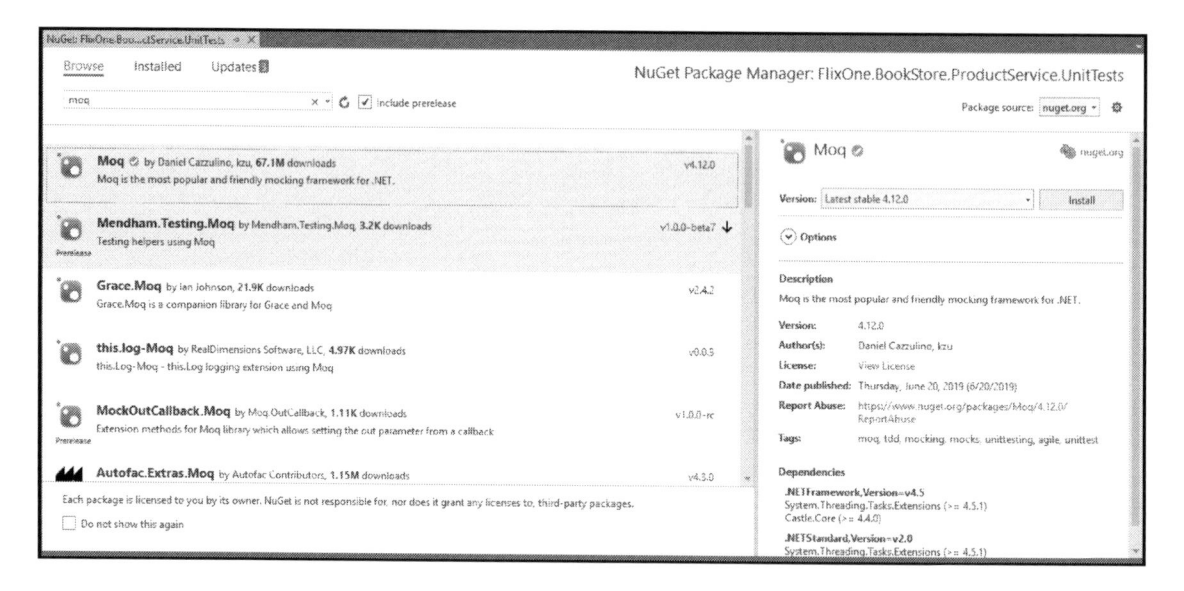

7. Add the following code to the `ProductTests.cs` class:

```
public class ProductTests
{
    [Fact]
    public void Get_Returns_ActionResults()
    {
      // Arrange
      var mockRepo = new Mock<IProductRepository>();
      mockRepo.Setup(repo => repo.GetAll()).
      Returns(new ProductData().GetProductList());
      var controller = new ProductController(mockRepo.Object);
      // Act
      var result = controller.GetList();
      // Assert
      var viewResult = Assert.IsType<OkObjectResult>(result);
      var model = Assert.IsAssignableFrom<IEnumerable<
      ProductViewModel>>(viewResult.Value);
      Assert.NotNull(model);
      Assert.Equal(2, model.Count());
    }
}
```

In the preceding code, which is a unit test example, we are mocking our repository and testing the output of our Web API controller. This test is based on the *AAA* technique; it will be passed if you meet the mocked data during setup.

In this section, we covered unit tests by performing unit testing for `ProductService`, and we validated its method output by using fake objects. Now, we need to learn how to test the methods or code blocks that integrate one or two modules/blocks. To do this, we need to learn about integration tests.

Integration tests

In `ProductService`, let's make sure that our service returns the product data without failure. Before we proceed, we have to add a new project and subsequent test classes. Follow these steps to do so:

1. Right-click on **Solution**, and then click **Add Project**.

Testing Microservices with the Microsoft Unit Testing Framework

2. From the **Add a new project** window, select **XUnit Test Project (.NET Core)**, as shown in the following screenshot:

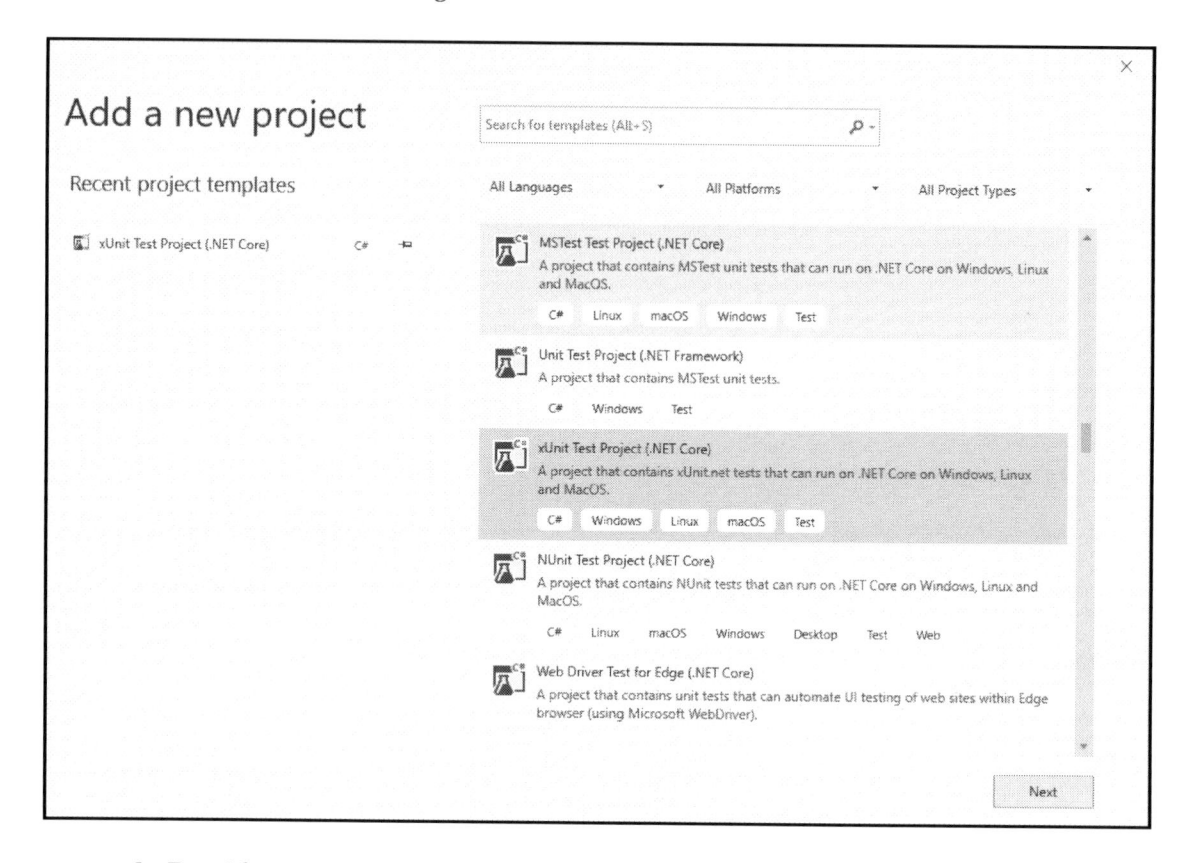

3. Provide a meaningful name; for example, `FlixOne.BookStore.ProductService.IntegrationTests`:

Configure your new project

xUnit Test Project (.NET Core)   C#   Windows   Linux   macOS   Test

Project name

FlixOne.BookStore.ProductService.IntegrationTests

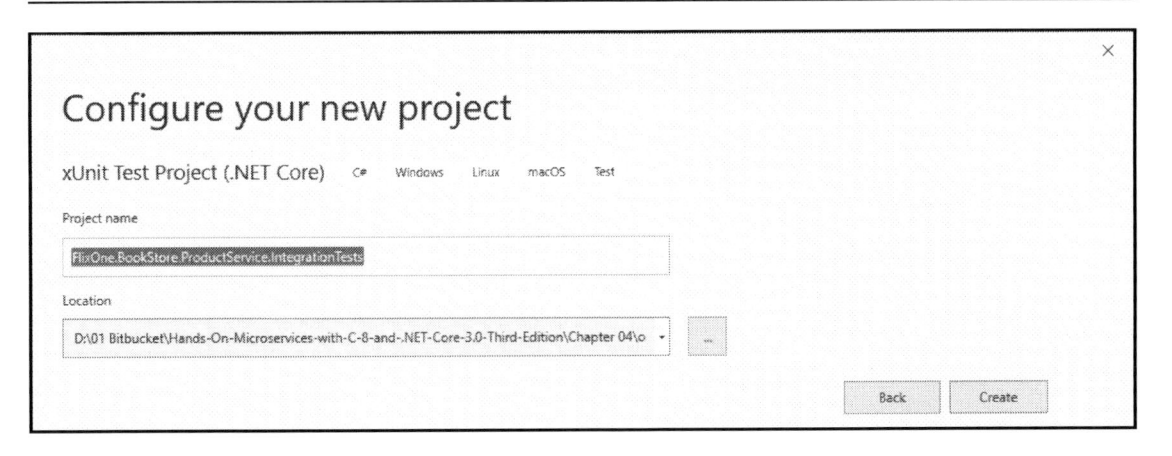

Location

D:\01 Bitbucket\Hands-On-Microservices-with-C-8-and-.NET-Core-3.0-Third-Edition\Chapter 04\o

4. Add the `appsettings.json` file, and then add the following code to it:

```
{
  "ConnectionStrings":
  {
    "ProductConnection": "Data Source=.;Initial
    Catalog=ProductsDB;Integrated
    Security=True;MultipleActiveResultSets=True"
  },
  "buildOptions":
  {
    "copyToOutput":
    {
      "include": [ "appsettings.json" ]
    }
  }
}
```

5. Open the `Startup.cs` file, of the `FlixOne.BookStore.ProductService` project.

[177]

6. Now, make the `ConfigureServices` and `Configure` methods void. We're doing this, so that we can override these methods in our `TestStartup.cs` class. These methods will look as follows:

```
public virtual void ConfigureServices(IServiceCollection services)
{
   services.AddTransient<IProductRepository,
   ProductRepository>();
   services.AddDbContext<ProductContext>(
   o => o.UseSqlServer(Configuration.
   GetConnectionString("ProductConnection")));
   services.AddMvc();
   //Code ommited
}
public virtual void Configure(IApplicationBuilder app,
IHostingEnvironment env)
{
 if (env.IsDevelopment())
 {
 app.UseDeveloperExceptionPage();
 app.UseBrowserLink();
 }
 else
 {
 app.UseExceptionHandler("/Home/Error");
 }
 app.UseStaticFiles();
 app.UseMvc(routes =>
 {
 routes.MapRoute(name: "default",
 template: "{controller=Home}/{action=
 Index}/{id?}");
 });
 app.UseSwaggerUI(op =>
 {
 op.SwaggerEndpoint("/swagger/v1/swagger.json",
 "Product API V1");
 });
}
```

7. Add a new folder called `Services`.
8. Add the `TestStartup.cs` class.
9. Open **NuGet Manager**. Search for and add the **Microsoft.AspNetCore.TestHost** package, as shown in the following screenshot:

Chapter 4

[Screenshot of NuGet Package Manager showing Microsoft.AspNetCore.TestHost package selected for installation in FlixOne.BookStore.ProductService.IntegrationTests project]

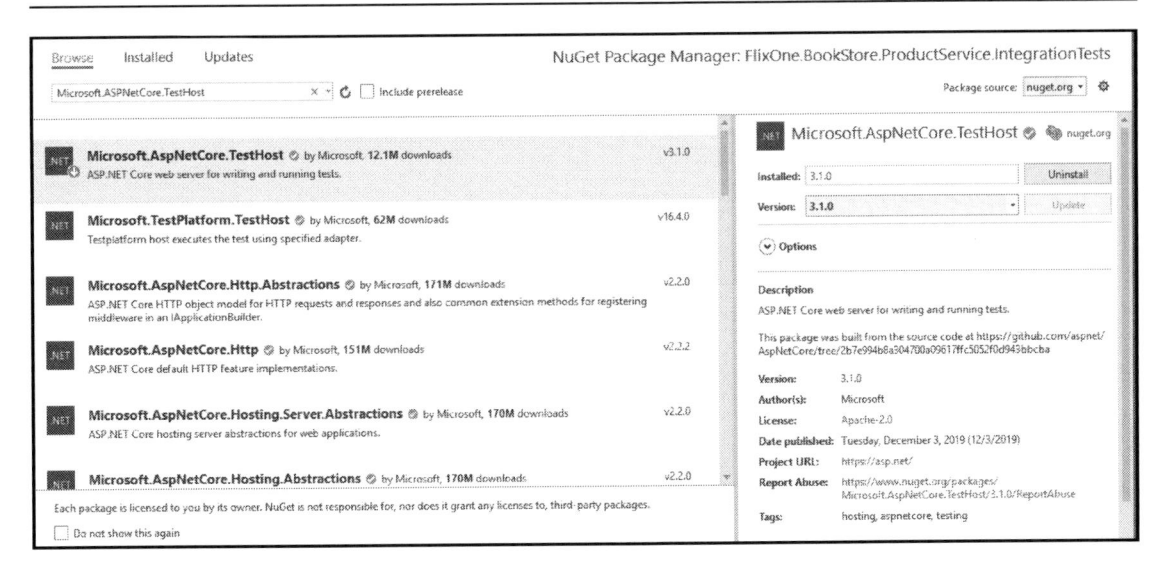

10. Add the following code to `TestStartup.cs`:

```
public class TestStartup : Startup
{
    public TestStartup(IConfiguration
    configuration) : base(configuration)
    { }
    public override void ConfigureServices
    (IServiceCollection services)
    {
    //mock context
    services.AddDbContext<ProductContext>(
    o => o.UseSqlServer(Configuration.
    GetConnectionString("ProductConnection")));
    services.AddMvc();
    }
    public override void Configure(IApplicationBuilder
    app, IHostingEnvironment env)
    { }
}
```

11. Under the `Services` folder, add a new `ProductTest.cs` class, and then add the following code to it:

```
public class ProductTest
{
    public ProductTest()
    {
        // Arrange
```

[179]

```
            var webHostBuilder = new WebHostBuilder()
              .UseStartup<TestStartup>();
            var server = new TestServer(webHostBuilder);
            _client = server.CreateClient();
        }
        private readonly HttpClient _client;
        [Fact]
        public async Task ReturnProductList()
        {
          // Act
          var response = await _client.GetAsync
          ("api/product/productlist"); //change per //setting
          response.EnsureSuccessStatusCode();
          var responseString = await response.Content.
          ReadAsStringAsync();
          // Assert
          Assert.NotEmpty(responseString);
        }
    }
```

12. To verify these tests, right-click the solution, and then select **Run tests** (if you face NuGet package errors, make sure you restore all the packages).

In the preceding code example, we are checking a simple test. We are trying to verify the response of the service, by setting up a client with the use of `HttpClient`. The test will fail if the response is empty.

Summary

Testing microservices is a bit different from testing applications that have been built in the traditional architectural style. In a .NET monolithic application, testing is a bit easier, compared to microservices, and it provides implementation independence and short delivery cycles. Microservices face challenges while testing.

With the help of the testing pyramid concept, we can strategize our testing procedures. In terms of the testing pyramid, we can easily see that unit tests allow us to test a small function of a class, and they are less time-consuming. On the other hand, the top layer of the testing pyramid has a large scope, with system or end-to-end testing, and these tests are time-consuming and very expensive. Consumer-driven contracts are a very useful way to test microservices. Pact-net is an open source tool that's used for this purpose. Finally, we went through the actual test implementation.

In the next chapter, we will learn how to deploy a microservice application, using Docker. We will discuss continuation integration and continuation deployment in detail.

Questions

1. What is unit testing?
2. Why should developers adhere to test-driven development?
3. What are stub and mock objects?
4. What is the testing pyramid?
5. What are consumer tests?
6. How can we use consumer tests in microservice-based applications?

Further reading

The following are a few references that will enhance your knowledge of testing:

- *Practical Test-Driven Development using C# 7:* https://www.packtpub.com/web-development/practical-test-driven-development-using-c-7
- *Building RESTful Web Services with .NET Core:* https://www.packtpub.com/application-development/building-restful-web-services-net-core

5
Deploying Microservices with Docker

Both monolith and microservice architectural styles come with different deployment challenges. In the case of .NET monolithic applications, deployments are often made using Xcopy. Xcopy deployments are where the required files and folders are deployed (pasted) into the server. The word *Xcopy* comes from the Xcopy command of Microsoft Disk Operating System (MS-DOS). Microservice deployments present a different set of challenges. Continuous integration and continuous deployment are key practices when delivering microservice applications. Also, container and toolchain technologies, which promise greater isolation boundaries, are essential for microservice deployment and scaling.

In this chapter, we will discuss the fundamentals of microservice deployment and the influence of emerging practices, such as CI/CD tools and containers, when it comes to microservice deployment. We will also walk through the deployment of a simple .NET Core service in a Docker container.

By the end of this chapter, you will have an understanding of the following topics:

- Monolithic application deployment challenges
- Understanding the deployment terminology
- Prerequisites for successful microservice deployments
- Isolation requirements for microservice deployments
- The need for a new deployment paradigm
- The way out—containers
- Introducing Docker
- Microservice deployment example using Docker

Technical requirements

This chapter contains various code examples, in order to explain the concepts at hand in more detail. The code is simple and is just for demonstration purposes.

To run and execute this code, you will need the following prerequisites:

- Visual Studio 2019
- .NET Core set up and running

To install and run these code examples, you'll need to install Visual Studio 2019 (our preferred IDE). To do so, follow these steps:

1. Download Visual Studio 2019 (Community is free) from https://docs.microsoft.com/en-us/visualstudio/install/install-visual-studio.
2. Follow the installation instructions that are available for your operating system. Multiple versions are available for a Visual Studio installation. We are using Visual Studio for Windows.

Setting up .NET Core 3.1:

If you don't have .NET Core 3.1 installed, you can download it from https://www.microsoft.com/net/download/windows.

> The source code is available at https://github.com/PacktPublishing/Hands-On-Microservices-with-CSharp-8-and-.NET-Core-3-Third-Edition/tree/master/Chapter%2005.

Deployment is one of the most important and critical steps in the application/software development life cycle. Deploying both monolithic and microservices-based applications has its challenges. In this chapter, we'll discuss the challenges related to application deployment.

Monolithic application deployment challenges

Monolithic applications are applications where all of the database and business logic is tied together and packaged as a single system. Since, in general, monolithic applications are deployed as a single package, deployments are somewhat simple but painful, due to the following reasons:

- **Deployment and release as a single concept**: There is no differentiation between deploying build artifacts and actually making features that are available to the end user. More often, releases are coupled to their environment. This increases the risk of deploying new features.
- **All or nothing deployment**: All or nothing deployment increases the risk of application downtime and failure. In the case of rollbacks, teams fail to deliver expected new features and hotfixes, or service packs have to be released to deliver the right kind of functionality.

> **TIP**
> A **Hotfix**, also known as a **Quickfix**, is a single or cumulative package (generally called a **patch**). It contains fixes for issues/bugs that are found in production and that must be fixed before the next major release.

- **Central databases as a single point of failure**: In monolithic applications, a big, centralized database is a single point of failure. This database is often quite large and difficult to break down. This results in an increase in the **mean time to recover** (**MTTR**) and the **mean time between failures** (**MTBF**).
- **Deployment and releases are big events**: Due to small changes in the application, the entire application could get deployed. This comes with a huge time and energy investment for developers and ops teams. The teams that are involved in this, need to collaborate in order to have a successful release. This becomes even harder when many teams are spread globally, and they are working on the development and release stages. These kinds of deployments/releases need a lot of hand-holding and manual steps. This has an impact on the end users, who have to face application downtime. If you are familiar with these kinds of deployments, then you'll also be familiar with marathon sessions in the so-called war rooms, as well as endless sessions of defect triage in conference bridges.
- **Time to market**: Making any changes to the system becomes harder. In such environments, executing any business change takes time. This makes responding to market forces difficult—the business can also lose its market share.

With the microservice architecture, we can address some of these challenges. This architecture provides greater flexibility and isolation for service deployment. It has proven to deliver a much faster turnaround time and much-needed business agility.

While we are working with monolithic applications, especially in terms of deployment, we will face new challenges. This section described, in detail, a variety of challenges we may face. In the next section, we will look at the deployment terminology that microservices use.

Understanding the deployment terminology

The microservice deployment terminology is where we code changes until the application's release. In this section, we will discuss all these steps of the deployment terminology, as follows:

- **Build**: In the build stage, the service source is compiled without any errors and passes all the corresponding unit tests. This stage produces build artifacts.
- **Continuous integration (CI)**: CI forces the entire application to build again every time a developer commits any change. The application code is compiled, and a comprehensive set of automated tests are run against it. This practice emerged from the problems of the frequent integration of code in large teams. The basic idea is to keep the delta, or changes to the software, small. This provides confidence that the software is in a workable state. Even if a check-in that's made by a developer breaks the system, it is easy to fix it.
- **Deployment**: The prerequisites for deployment include hardware provisioning and installing the base OS and the correct version of the .NET framework. The next part of this is to promote these build artifacts in production, through various stages. The combination of these two parts is referred to as the deployment stage. There is no distinction between the deployment stage and release stage, in most monolithic applications.
- **Continuous deployment (CD)**: In CD, each successful build is deployed to production. CD is more important from a technical team's perspective. Under CD, there are several other practices, such as automated unit testing, labeling, versioning of build numbers, and traceability of changes. With continuous delivery, the technical team ensures that the changes that are pushed to production, through various lower environments, work as expected in production. Usually, these are small and are deployed very quickly.

- **Continuous delivery:** Continuous delivery is different from CD. CD is typically used by technical teams, whereas continuous delivery is more focused on providing the deployed code as early as possible to the customer. To make sure that customers get the right product, in continuous delivery, every build must pass through all the quality assurance checks. Once the product passes these checks, it's up to the business stakeholders to choose when to release it.
- **Build and deployment pipelines**: The build and deployment pipeline is part of implementing continuous delivery through automation. It is a workflow of steps through which the code is committed to the source repository. At the other end of the deployment pipeline, the artifacts for release are produced. Some of the steps that may make up the build and deployment pipeline are as follows:
    - Unit tests
    - Integration tests
    - Code coverage and static analysis
    - Regression tests
    - Deploying to the staging environment
    - Load/stress tests
    - Deploying to the release repository

- **Release**: A business feature that's made available to the end user is referred to as the release of a feature. To release a feature or service, the relevant build artifacts should be deployed beforehand. Usually, the feature toggle manages the release of a feature. If the feature flag (also called the feature toggle) isn't switched on in production, it is called a dark release of the specified feature.

In this section, we have discussed the deployment terminology and learned about the various phases of deployment, such as CI/CD. To make a perfect deployment, we need a few basic things, all of which will be discussed in the next section.

Prerequisites for successful microservice deployments

Any architectural style comes with a set of associated patterns and practices to follow. The microservice architectural style is no different. Microservice implementation has more chances of being successful with the adoption of the following practices:

- **Self-sufficient teams**: Amazon, who is a pioneer of SOA and microservice architectures, follows the *Two Pizza Rule*. This means that a microservice team will have no more than 7-10 team members (*the number of people two pizzas can feed*). These team members will have all the necessary skills and roles; for example, development, operations, and business analyst. Such a service team handles the development, operations, and management of a microservice.
- **CI and CD**: Smaller self-sufficient teams, who can integrate their work frequently, are precursors to the success of microservices. This architecture isn't as simple as a monolith. However, automation and the ability to push code upgrades regularly allows teams to handle complexity. Tools, such as **Azure DevOps** (formerly **Team Foundation Online Services (TFS)** and **Visual Studio Team Services (VSTS)**), **TeamCity**, and Jenkins, are quite popular toolchains in this space.
- **Infrastructure as code**: The idea of representing hardware and infrastructure components, such as networks with code, is new. It helps us make deployment environments, such as integration, testing, and production, look identical. This means developers and test engineers will be able to easily reproduce production defects in lower environments. With tools such as CFEngine, Chef, Puppet, Ansible, and PowerShell DSC, you can write your entire infrastructure as code. With this paradigm shift, you can also put your infrastructure under a version control system and ship it as an artifact in deployment.
- **Utilization of cloud computing**: Cloud computing is a big catalyst for adopting microservices. It isn't mandatory for microservice deployment, though. Cloud computing comes with a near-infinite scale, elasticity, and rapid provisioning capability. It is a no-brainer that the cloud is a natural ally of microservices. So, having knowledge and experience with the Azure cloud will help you adopt microservices.

To make a perfect and flawless deployment, we need some basic components. In this section, we discussed all the prerequisites of deployment. In the next section, we will discuss the isolation requirements for microservice deployment.

Isolation requirements for microservice deployment

In 2012, Adam Wiggins, the co-founder of the Heroku cloud platform, presented 12 basic principles. These principles talk about defining new modern web applications from an idea to deployment. This set of principles is now known as the *12-factor app*. These principles paved the way for new architectural styles, which evolved into microservice architectures. One of the principles of the 12-factor app is as follows:

> "Execute the app as one or more stateless processes"
>
> – Adam Wiggins

Here, services will be essentially stateless (except the database, which acts as the state store). The **shared nothing** principle is also applied across the entire spectrum of patterns and practices. We don't need anything except the isolation of components, in order to achieve scale and agility.

In the microservice world, this principle of isolation is applied in the following ways:

- **Service teams**: There will be self-sufficient teams built around services. In effect, the teams will be able to make all the necessary decisions to develop and support the microservices they are responsible for.
- **Source control isolation**: The source repository of every microservice will be separate. It will not share any source code, files, and so on. It is okay to duplicate a few bits of code in the microservice world across services.
- **Build stage isolation**: The build and deploy pipelines for every microservice should be kept isolated. Build and deploy pipelines can even run in parallel, isolated, and deployed services. Due to this, CI-CD tools should be scaled to support different services and pipelines at a much faster speed.
- **Release stage isolation**: Every microservice should be released in isolation with other services. It is also possible that the same service with different versions is in the production environment.
- **Deploy stage isolation**: This is the most important part of isolation. Traditional monolith deployment is done with bare-metal servers. With more advances in virtualization occurring, virtual servers have replaced bare-metal servers.

Deploying Microservices with Docker

In general, a monolith's standard release process looks like this:

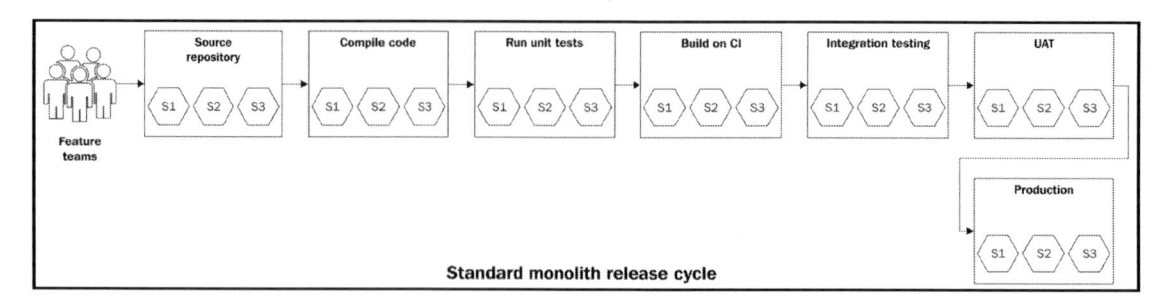

Standard monolith release cycle

Considering these isolation levels, the microservice build and deployment pipeline might look like this:

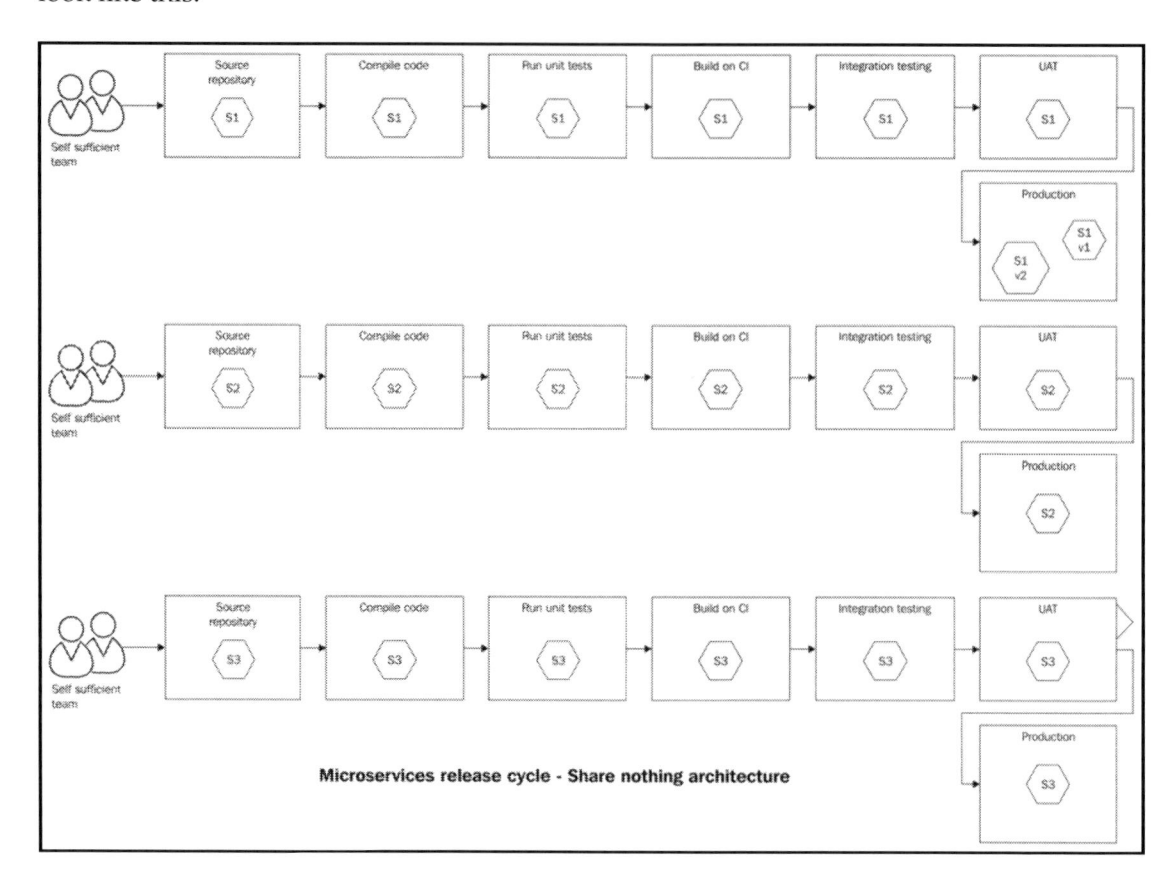

Microservices release cycle - Share nothing architecture

In this section, we discussed and understood the principles of isolation. For many microservices, a purely Xcopy deployment will not work. In the next section, we will come discuss the need for a new deployment paradigm.

The need for a new deployment paradigm

The highest level of isolation for an application can be achieved by adding a new physical machine or bare-metal server, so that there's a server with its own operating system that's managing all the system resources. This was a regular occurrence in legacy applications, but it isn't practical for modern applications. Modern applications are massive systems. Some examples of these systems include Amazon, Netflix, and Nike, or even traditional financial banks, such as ING. These systems are hosted on tens of thousands of servers. These kinds of modern applications demand ultra-scalability, so that they can serve their millions of users. For a microservice architecture, it doesn't make any sense to set up a new server, just to run a small service on top of it.

With new CPU architectural breakthroughs, one of the options that emerged was virtual machines. Virtual machines abstract out all the hardware interactions of an operating system, through the hypervisor technology. Hypervisors allow us to run many machines or servers on a single physical machine. One significant point to note is that all the virtual machines get their piece of an isolated system resource from physical host resources.

This is still a good isolated environment to run an application on. Virtualization brought the rationale of raising servers for entire applications. While doing so, it kept the components fairly isolated; this helped us utilize spare computer resources in our data centers. It improved the efficiency of our data centers, while satisfying the applications' fair isolation needs.

However, virtualization on its own isn't able to support some of a microservice's needs. Under the 12-factor principles, Adam Wiggins also talks about this:

> *"The twelve-factor app's processes are disposable, meaning they can be started or stopped at a moment's notice. This facilitates fast elastic scaling, rapid deployment of code or config changes, and robustness of production deploys."*
>
> *- Adam Wiggins*

This principle is important for the microservice architectural style. So, with microservices, we must ensure that the services start up faster. In this case, let's assume that there is one service per virtual machine. If we want to spin this service, it needs to spin the virtual machine; however, the boot time of a virtual machine is long. There will also be a lot of cluster deployments. This means that our services will definitely be distributed in clusters.

This also implies that virtual machines may need to be raised up on one of the nodes in the clusters and booted. This is also a problem with the virtual machine's boot time. This doesn't bring the kind of efficiency that we expect for microservices.

Now, the only option left is to use the operating system process model, which has a quicker boot time. The process programming model has been known for ages, but even processes come at a cost. They aren't well isolated; they share system resources, as well as the kernel of the operating system.

For microservices, we need a better isolation deployment model and a new paradigm of deployment. The answer is to innovate with the container technology. A good consideration factor is that the container technology sits well between virtualization and the operating system's process model. We'll learn about this in the next section.

The way out – containers

Container technology isn't new to the Linux world. Containers are based on Linux's LXC technology. In this section, we'll learn how containers are important in the case of microservices.

What are containers?

A container is a piece of software in a complete filesystem. It contains everything that is needed to run code, the runtime, system tools, and system libraries—anything that can be installed on a server. This guarantees that the software will always run in the same way, regardless of its environment. Containers share their host operating system and kernel with other containers on the same host. The technology around containers isn't new; it has been a part of the Linux ecosystem for a long time.

Suitability of containers over virtual machines

Let's understand the difference between containers and virtual machines. At the surface level, both are tools that can be used to achieve isolation and virtualization.

The architectural difference between virtual machines and containers can be seen in the following diagram:

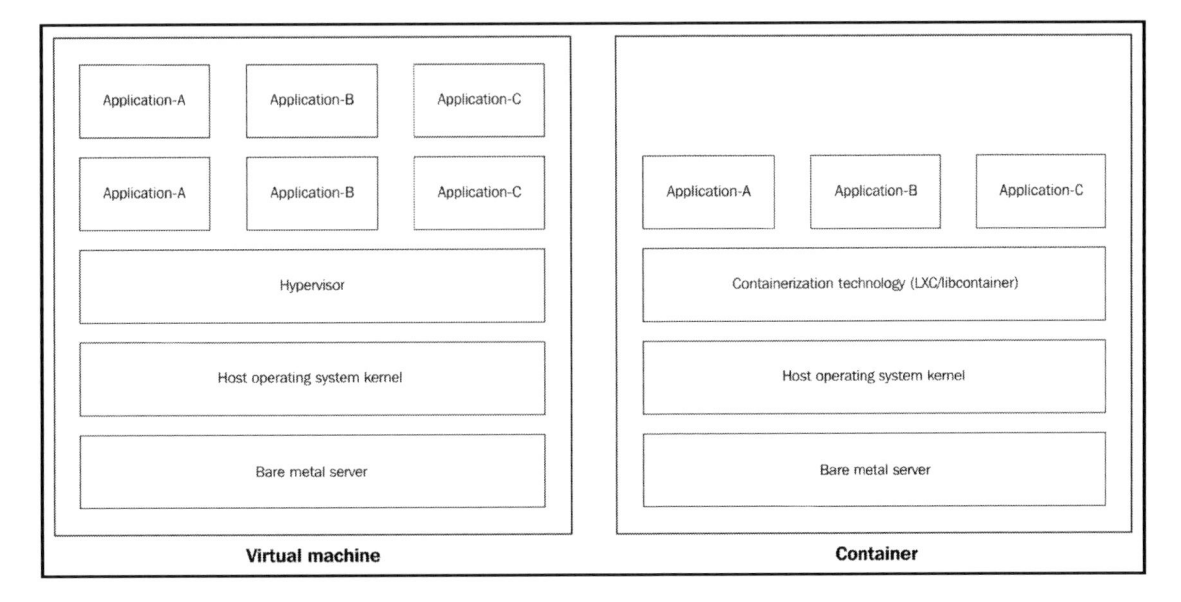

Virtual machine (left): Application-A, Application-B, Application-C (two rows) / Hypervisor / Host operating system kernel / Bare metal server

Container (right): Application-A, Application-B, Application-C / Containerization technology (LXC/libcontainer) / Host operating system kernel / Bare metal server

As we can see, in terms of the virtual machine, there is a host operating system, along with a kernel and a hypervisor layer. Hosted applications have to bring in their own operating system and environment. However, in containers, the containerization technology layer serves as a single layer, and it is shared across different applications.

> Containers don't provide the same level of isolation as VMs. For containers, if you run services for multiple customers, you shouldn't run `customer_1` and `customer_2` on the same Docker host. With VMs, this isn't an issue. Also, remember performance issues—if you don't configure resource limits on your containers, it's possible for one *bad* container to bring down the others.

This removes the need for a guest operating system. Thus, applications in a container come with a smaller footprint and strong isolation levels. Another aspect that will encourage you to use containers for microservice deployment, is that we can pack more applications on the same physical machine, compared to the same applications that are deployed on a virtual machine. This helps us achieve a greater economy of scale benefits, and it provides a comparison of the benefits of virtual machines.

One more thing to note with containers is that they can be run on virtual machines as well. This means it's okay to have a physical server with a virtual machine on it. This virtual machine serves as a host for a number of containers. This depends on the CPU of the host and its support for nested virtualization.

Transformation of the operation team's mindset

Microsoft's Bill Baker came up with an analogy of pets and cattle, and he applied it to servers in a data center. Okay; honestly, we care for our pets. We love them and show affection toward them, and we name them as well. We think of their hygiene; if they get sick, we take them to the vet. Do we take such care of our cattle? We don't; this is because we don't care as much about cattle.

The same analogy is true with respect to servers and containers. In pre-DevOps days, server admins cared about servers. They used to name those server machines and also have dedicated maintenance downtime and so on. With DevOps practices, such as infrastructure as code and containerization, containers are treated like cattle. As the operations team, we don't need to care for them, since containers are meant to have a short lifespan. They can be booted up quickly in clusters and torn down quickly as well. When you are dealing with containers, always keep this analogy in mind. As far as daily operations go, expect the spinning up and teardown of containers to be a normal practice.

This analogy changes our perspective of microservice deployment and how it supports containerization.

Containers are new binaries

There is a new reality you will face, as a .NET developer working with microservices: containers are new binaries. With Visual Studio, we compile the .NET program, and, after compilation, Visual Studio produces .NET assemblies, namely DLLs or EXEs. We take this set of associated DLLs and EXEs, which have been emitted by the compiler, and we deploy them on the servers.

> It was Steve Lasker, a Principal Program Manager at Microsoft, who first called containers the new binaries of deployment.

So, in short, our deployment unit was in the form of assemblies. Not anymore! Well, we still have the .NET program generating EXEs and DLLs, but our deployment unit has changed in the microservice world. Now, it's a container. We'll still compile programs into assemblies. These assemblies will be pushed to the container and ensured that they're ready to be shipped.

When we walk through the code for this, you will understand this concept. We, as .NET developers, have the ability (and may I say *necessity*) to ship the containers. Along with this, another advantage of container deployment is that it removes the barrier between different operating systems and even different languages and runtimes.

Does it work on your machine? Let's ship your machine!

Usually, we hear this a lot from developers: *Well, it works on my machine!* This usually happens when there is a defect that isn't reproducible in production. Since containers are immutable and composable, it's possible to eliminate the configuration impedance between the development and production environment.

Introducing Docker

Docker (`https://www.docker.com/`) has been a major force behind popularizing the containerization of applications. Docker is to containers what Google is to search engines. Sometimes, people even use containers and Docker as synonyms. Microsoft has partnered with Docker and is actively contributing to the Docker platform and tools via open source. This makes Docker important for us as .NET developers.

Docker is a very important topic and is significant enough that any serious .NET developer should learn about it. However, due to time and scope constraints, we will just scratch the surface of the ecosystem of Docker here. We strongly recommend that you read through the Docker books that have been made available by Packt Publishing.

> **TIP**
> If you want to safely try and learn about Docker without installing it on your machine, you can do so by going to `https://KataCoda.com`.

Deploying Microservices with Docker

Now, let's focus on some of the terminologies and tools of the Docker platform. This will be essential for the next section:

- **Docker image**: This is a template that contains instructions for creating a Docker container. You can only read the instructions; you can't add your own instructions to this template, since it's read-only. It consists of a separate filesystem, associated libraries, and so on. Here, an image is always read-only and can run exactly the same abstract and underlying host differences. A Docker image can be composed, so that there's one layer on top of another. This composability of the Docker image can be compared with the analogy of a layered cake. Docker images that are used across different containers can be reused. This also helps reduce the deployment footprint of applications that use the same base images.
- **Docker registry**: You can correlate this with the Windows Registry (as a hierarchical database) or a Software Product (as a library of numerous programs). Similarly, the Docker registry contains various images in such a manner that, if a set of information on images can be retrieved or used, it's called a library of images. You can have a public or private registry that can be on the same server, where the Docker daemon or Docker client is on a totally separate server.

> The Windows Registry is a database that stores information about the internal or low-level settings of the Microsoft Windows operating system.

- **Docker hub**: This is a public registry that stores images. It is located at http://hub.docker.com.
- **Dockerfile**: Dockerfile is a build or scripting file that contains instructions that we can use to build a Docker image. Multiple steps can be documented in a Dockerfile, starting with getting the base image.
- **Docker container**: An instance of a Docker image is called a Docker container.
- **Docker compose**: Docker compose allows you to define an application's components—their containers, configuration, links, and volumes—in a single file. A single command will set everything up and start your application. It is an architecture/dependency map for your application.
- **Docker swarm**: Swarm is the Docker service where container nodes work together. It runs a defined number of instances of a replica task, which is itself a Docker image.

Now, let's look into the individual components of the Docker ecosystem and understand one of the ways in which the Docker workflow makes sense in the software development life cycle.

Deploying a sample application

In order to support this workflow, we need a CI tool and a configuration management tool. For illustration purposes, we have taken the **Azure DevOps** (erstwhile **Visual Studio Team Services (VSTS)**) build service for continuous integration and the Azure DevOps release management for continuous delivery. The workflow will remain the same for any other tools or modes of deployment.

The following diagram depicts this:

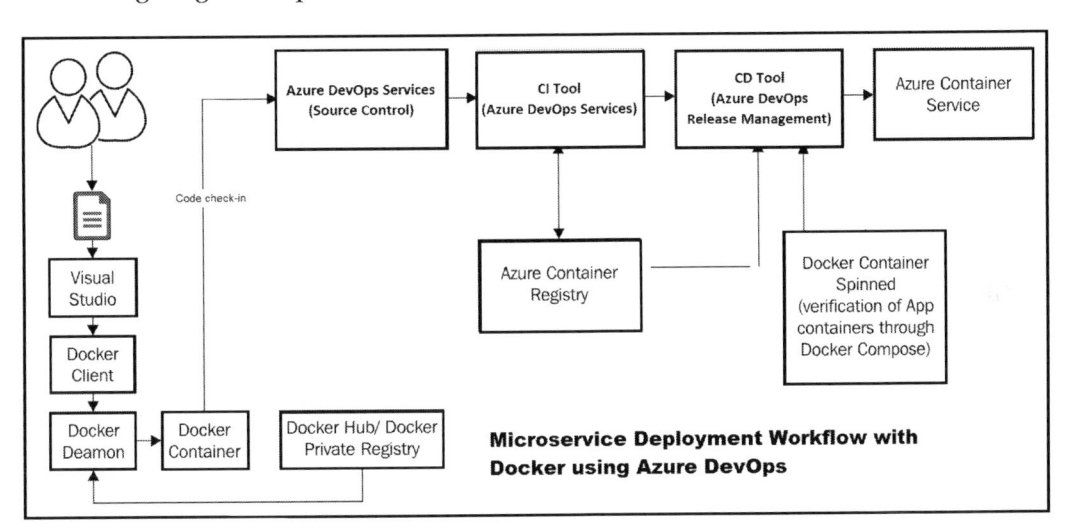

The following are requirements of a microservice deployment with Docker:

1. The code is checked into the Azure DevOps repository. If this is the project's first check-in, it is done along with the Dockerfile for the project.
2. The preceding check-in triggers Azure DevOps, so that it can build the service from the source code and run unit/integration tests.
3. If the tests are successful, Azure DevOps builds a Docker image that is pushed to a *Docker registry*. The Azure DevOps release service deploys the image to the Azure container service.
4. If the QA tests pass as well, Azure DevOps is used to promote the container, so that it can be deployed and started in production.

> The usual .NET CI-CD tools, such as TeamCity and Octopus Deploy (their capabilities are in the alpha stage), have features that can produce a Docker container as a build artifact and then deploy it to production.

In the next section, we'll learn how microservice deployment works in Docker.

Microservice deployment example using Docker

Now that we have all the essentials, we can start coding and see how things work. We have taken the product catalog service example here, which we will deploy as a Docker container. After running the accompanying source code, you should be able to successfully run the product catalog service in the Docker container.

Setting up Docker on your machine

If you've never worked with, or used Docker on your machine, or if you don't have any prior experience with Docker, then don't worry! In this section, we will walk through these steps so that you can work with Docker, within 20 or 30 minutes.

Prerequisites

To set up Docker on your machine, you will need to do the following:

1. Install Microsoft Visual Studio 2019 (https://www.visualstudio.com/downloads/download-visual-studio-vs).
2. Install .NET Core 3.1 (https://www.microsoft.com/net/download/core).
3. Install Docker for Windows so that you can run your Docker containers locally (https://www.docker.com/products/docker#/windows).

> We are using Docker Community Edition for Windows to demonstrate this example.

4. After installation, your system will need to be restarted.

5. After restarting your system, Docker for Windows will prompt you to enable the Hyper-V feature, if it's not enabled on your system. Click **OK** to enable the Hyper-V feature on your system (a system restart will be required):

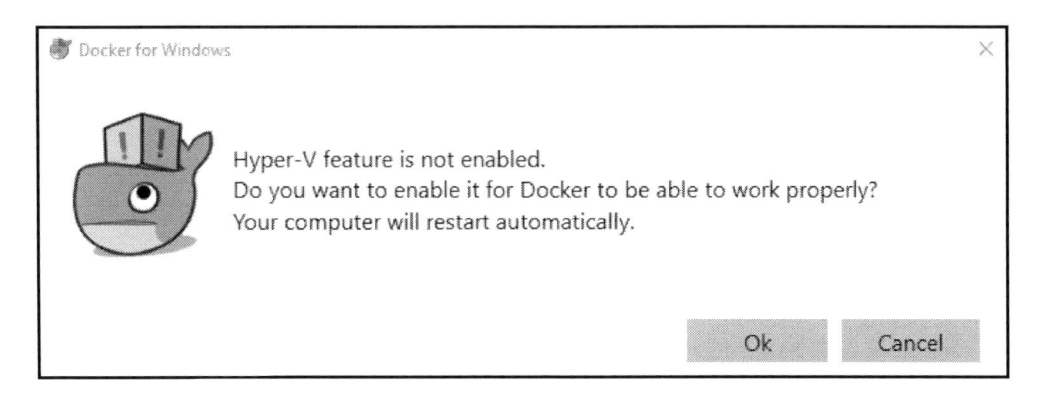

6. Once Docker for Windows has been installed, right-click the Docker icon in the system tray, and then click **Settings**. Then, select **Shared Drives**:

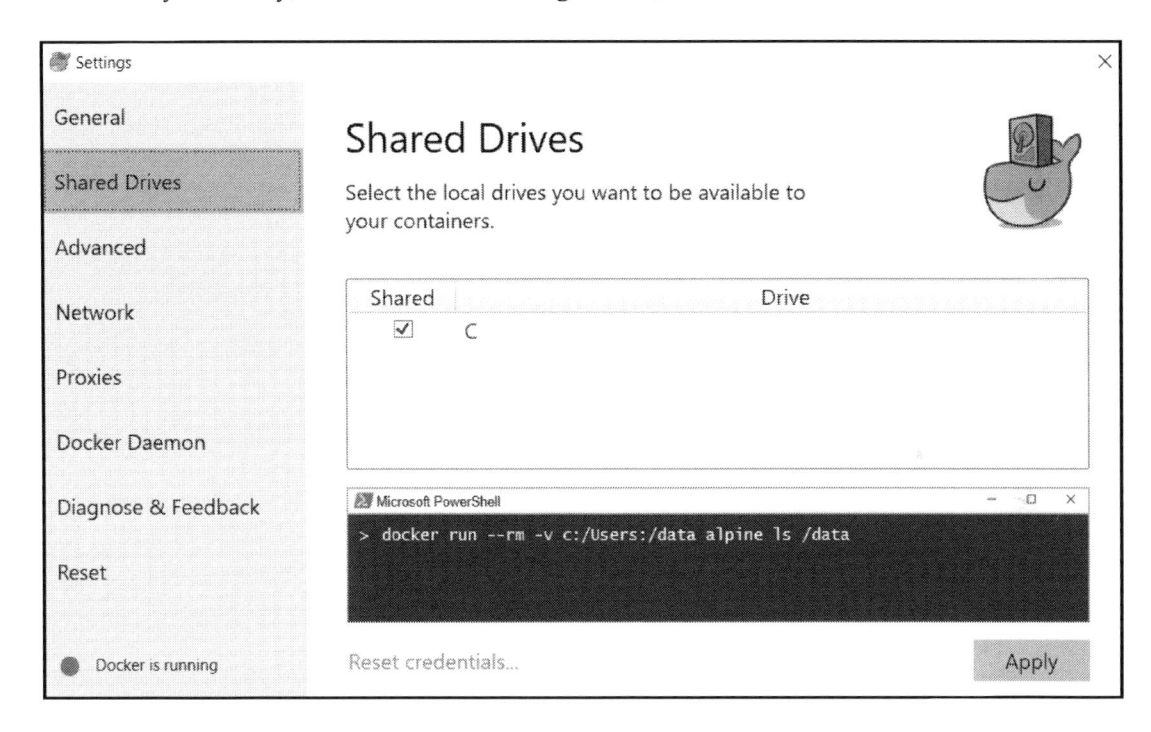

Now, we can create an application.

Creating an ASP.NET Core web application

In the previous sections, we discussed containers, setting up Docker on a machine, and deploying with Docker. Now, it's time to look at an example, so that we can implement everything we've learned about so far. To do so, follow these steps:

1. Create a new project, by navigating to **File** | **New Project** | **.NET Core** and selecting **ASP.NET Core Web Application**, as shown in the following screenshot:

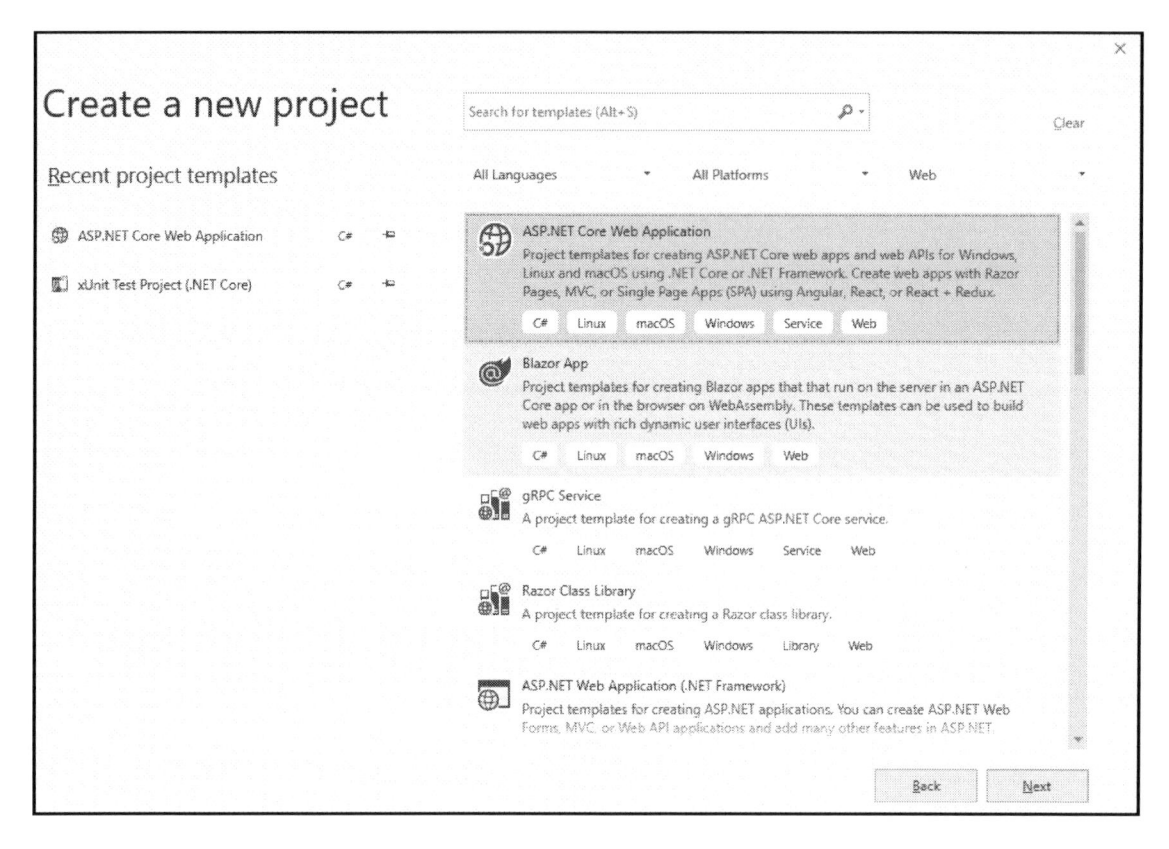

2. From the **New ASP.NET Core Web Application** window, select **.NET Core** and **ASP.NET Core 3.1**:

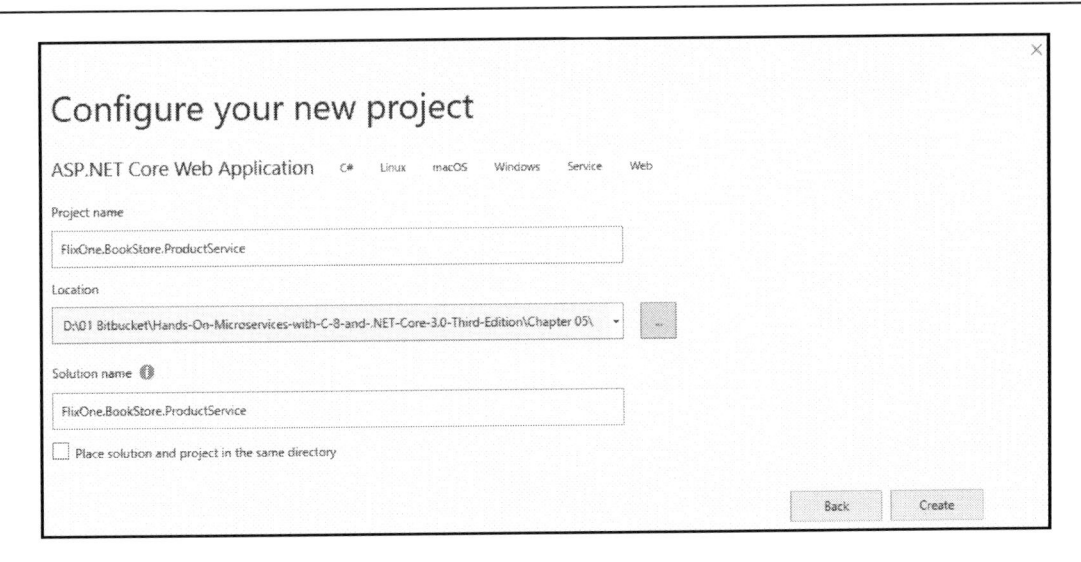

3. From the **Create a new ASP.NET Core web application** window, select **.NET Core** and **ASP.NET Core 3.1**. Select **Web Application (Model-View-Controller)** from the available templates:

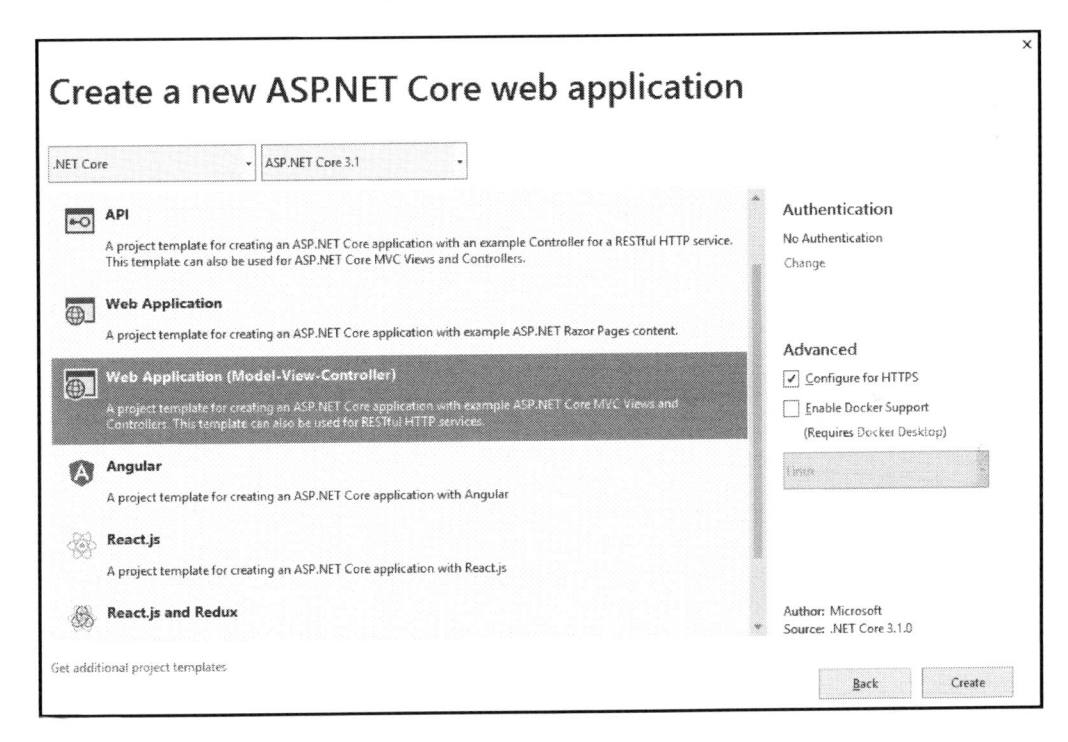

Deploying Microservices with Docker

4. Check **Enable Docker support** (on the right).
5. Since we are using Windows, select it as the OS (if you haven't installed Docker, you'll need to install Docker for Windows).
6. Click **Create** to proceed.

The preceding steps will create the `FlixOne.BookStore.ProductService` project with Docker support. The following screenshot shows our project's structure:

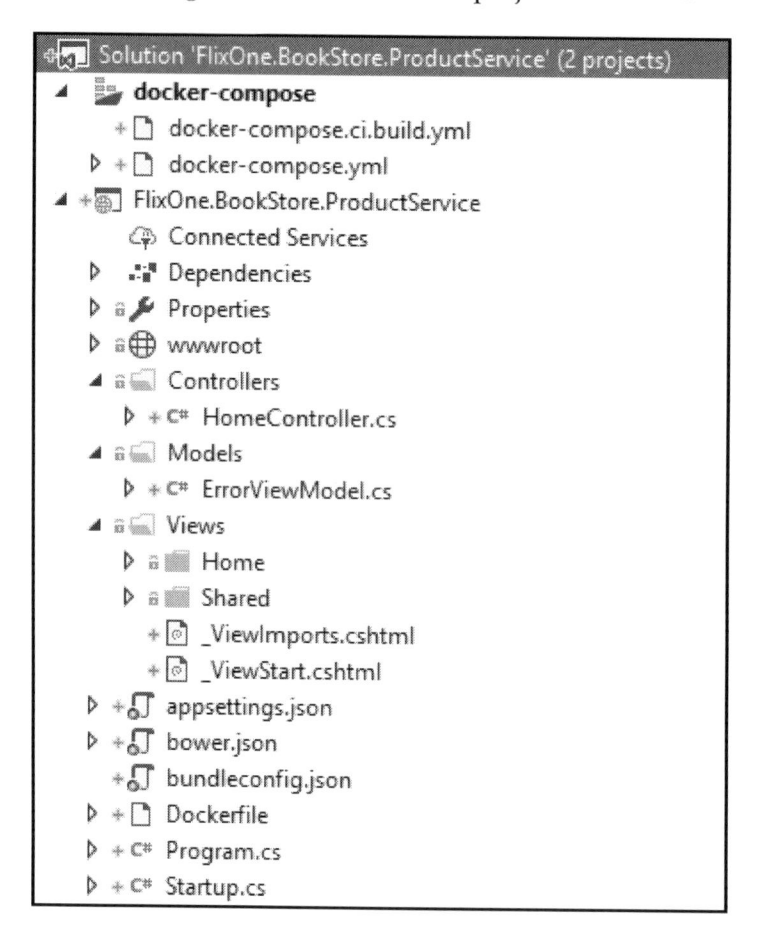

```
Solution 'FlixOne.BookStore.ProductService' (2 projects)
├── docker-compose
│   ├── docker-compose.ci.build.yml
│   └── docker-compose.yml
└── FlixOne.BookStore.ProductService
    ├── Connected Services
    ├── Dependencies
    ├── Properties
    ├── wwwroot
    ├── Controllers
    │   └── HomeController.cs
    ├── Models
    │   └── ErrorViewModel.cs
    ├── Views
    │   ├── Home
    │   ├── Shared
    │   ├── _ViewImports.cshtml
    │   └── _ViewStart.cshtml
    ├── appsettings.json
    ├── bower.json
    ├── bundleconfig.json
    ├── Dockerfile
    ├── Program.cs
    └── Startup.cs
```

The following files will be added to the project:

- **Dockerfile**: The Dockerfile for ASP.NET Core applications is based on the `microsoft/aspnetcore` image (https://hub.docker.com/r/microsoft/aspnetcore/). This image includes the ASP.NET Core NuGet packages, which have been prefitted, in order to improve startup performance. When building ASP.NET Core applications, the Dockerfile `FROM` instruction (command) points to the most recent `microsoft/dotnet` image (https://hub.docker.com/r/microsoft/dotnet/) on the Docker hub. The following is the default code snippet that's provided by the template:

    ```
    FROM mcr.microsoft.com/dotnet/core/aspnet:3.0-nanoserver-1903
    AS base WORKDIR /app
    EXPOSE 80 EXPOSE 443
    FROM mcr.microsoft.com/dotnet/core/aspnet:3.0 AS runtime
    WORKDIR /app
    COPY ${source:-obj/Docker/publish} .
    ENTRYPOINT ["dotnet", "FlixOne.BookStore.ProductService.dll"]
    ```

    The preceding code is basically a set of instructions. Let's go over some of the properties that are included in these instructions:

    - `FROM` is a message that tells Docker to pull the base image onto the existing image, called `microsoft/aspnetcore:3.0`.
    - `COPY` and `WORKDIR` will copy content to a new directory inside the `called/app` container and set it to the working directory for subsequent instructions.

To expose our `Product` service on port `80` of the container, we can use `EXPOSE ENTRYPOINT`, which specifies the command we use to execute when the container starts up. In our example, we have `ProductService` and our entry point is `["dotnet", "FlixOne.BookStore.ProductService.dll"]`.

Let's take a look at the various components/config files that are required for Docker:

- `Docker-compose.yml`: This is the base Compose file that's used to define a collection of images that can be built and run with `Docker-compose` build/run.
- `Docker-compose.dev.debug.yml`: This is an additional Compose file for iterative changes, when your configuration is set to debug mode. Visual Studio will call `-f docker-compose.yml` and `-f docker-compose.dev.debug.yml` to merge them. This Compose file is used by Visual Studio development tools.

Deploying Microservices with Docker

- `Docker-compose.dev.release.yml`: This is an additional Compose file that we can use to debug our release definition. It will load the debugger in isolation, so that it doesn't change the content of the production image.
- The `docker-compose.yml` file contains the name of the image that is created when the project is run.

Now, we have everything we need to run/launch our service in the Docker container. Before we go any further, please refer to Chapter 2, *Refactoring the Monolith*, and add the complete code (that is, the controller, repositories, and so on) so that the project's structure looks as follows:

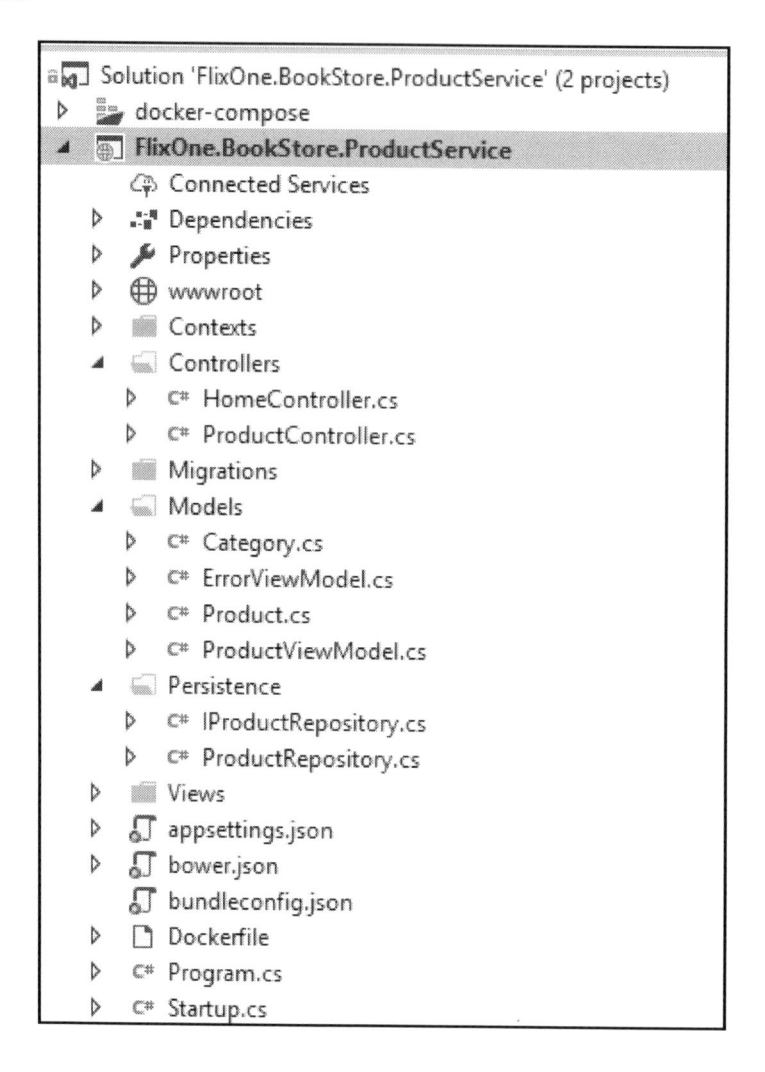

```
Solution 'FlixOne.BookStore.ProductService' (2 projects)
    docker-compose
    FlixOne.BookStore.ProductService
        Connected Services
        Dependencies
        Properties
        wwwroot
        Contexts
        Controllers
            HomeController.cs
            ProductController.cs
        Migrations
        Models
            Category.cs
            ErrorViewModel.cs
            Product.cs
            ProductViewModel.cs
        Persistence
            IProductRepository.cs
            ProductRepository.cs
        Views
        appsettings.json
        bower.json
        bundleconfig.json
        Dockerfile
        Program.cs
        Startup.cs
```

Now, all you have to do is press *F5* and launch your service in the container. This is the simplest and easiest way to put your service in the container. Once your microservice is containerized, you can use Azure DevOps (previously Visual Studio Team Services) and Azure container services to deploy your container to the Azure cloud.

In this section, we have deployed a sample application and discussed deployment using Docker as a container. We also learned how to enable Docker on a local machine.

Summary

Microservice deployment is an exciting journey for us. For a successful microservice delivery, we should follow the deployment best practices. We need to focus on implementing the isolation requirements for microservices, before we discuss deploying by using automated tools. With successful microservice deployment practices, we can deliver business changes rapidly. The different isolation requirements, from self-sufficient teams to continuous delivery, give us the agility and scalability that are fundamental for the implementation of microservices.

Containerization is by far one of the most important innovative technologies that we have, and we must take advantage of it for microservice deployment. Combining the Azure cloud with Docker will help us deliver the scale and isolation we expect from microservices. With Docker, we can easily achieve greater application density, which means reducing our cloud infrastructure costs. We also saw how easy it is to start these deployments, with Visual Studio and Docker for Windows.

In the next chapter, we will look at microservice security. We will discuss the Azure Active Directory for authentication, how to leverage OAuth 2.0, and how to secure an API gateway with Azure API Management.

Questions

1. What is a Docker image, and why it is so important?
2. What is the Docker repository?
3. What is a Docker container?
4. What is a Docker hub?
5. Can I use JSON instead of YAML in Docker files? If so, how?

6. Can you explain the following words, which are all related to containers: FROM, COPY, WORKDIR, EXPOSE, ENTRYPOINT?
7. Can you write a simple ASP.NET web application to display the Add, Delete, and Update products in a tabular view, with the help of Product Services?

Further reading

- *Building RESTful Web Services with .NET Core* (https://www.packtpub.com/in/application-development/building-restful-web-services-net-core)
- *Mastering Docker – Third Edition* (https://www.packtpub.com/virtualization-and-cloud/mastering-docker-third-edition)
- *Docker Cookbook – Second Edition* (https://www.packtpub.com/virtualization-and-cloud/docker-cookbook-second-edition)

6
Securing Microservices Using Azure Active Directory

Security is one of the most important cross-cutting concerns for web applications. Unfortunately, data breaches of well-known sites seem commonplace these days. Taking this into account, information and application security has become critical to web applications. For the same reason, secure applications should no longer be an afterthought. Security is everyone's responsibility in an organization.

Monolithic applications have a bigger surface area for attacks, compared to microservices; however, microservices are distributed systems by nature. Also, in principle, microservices are isolated from each other, so well-implemented microservices are more secure, compared to monolithic applications. A monolith has different attack vectors, compared to microservices. The microservice architecture style forces us to think differently, in the context of security. Let me tell you upfront, microservice security is a complex domain to understand and implement.

Before we dive deep into microservice security, let's understand our approach toward it. We will focus more on how **authentication** (**authn**) and **authorization** (**authz**)—collectively referred to as **auth** in this chapter—work, and we'll discuss the options that are available within the .NET ecosystem.

We will also explore the Azure API Management service and its suitability as an API gateway for .NET-based microservice environments, as well as how Azure API Management can help us protect microservices, through its security features. Then, we'll briefly touch on different peripheral aspects that have *defense in depth* mechanisms for microservice security.

In this chapter, we will discuss the following topics:

- Why won't a traditional authentication system work?
- Introducing OAuth 2.0
- Introducing Azure API Management as an API gateway
- Using Azure API Management for security
- Interservice communication security approaches
- Container security and other peripheral security aspects

Technical requirements

This chapter contains various code examples, in order to explain the concepts that it describes. The code is kept simple and is just for demonstration purposes. Most of the examples involve a .NET Core console application, which is written in C#.

> Note that there will be a difference between the actual screen you'll see and the screenshots that are in this chapter. The look and feel of Visual Studio depends on the themes you select.

To run and execute the code in this chapter, you'll need the following prerequisites:

- Visual Studio 2019 or later
- .NET Core 3.1 or later

To install and run these code examples, you'll need to install Visual Studio 2019 or later (the preferred IDE). To do so, follow these steps:

1. Download Visual Studio 2019 (Community is free) from https://docs.microsoft.com/en-us/visualstudio/install/install-visual-studio.
2. Follow the installation instructions for your operating system. Multiple versions are available for Visual Studio. We are using Visual Studio for Windows.

If you don't have .NET Core 3.1 installed, you can download and set it up, by going to https://dotnet.microsoft.com/download/dotnet-core/3.0.

> The complete source code is available at: https://github.com/PacktPublishing/Hands-On-Microservices-with-CSharp-8-and-.NET-Core-3-Third-Edition/tree/master/Chapter%2006.

Security in monolithic applications

To understand microservice security, let's step back and recall how we secured .NET monolithic applications. This will help us grasp why a microservice's auth mechanism needs to be different.

The critical mechanism that's used to secure applications has always been auth. Authentication verifies the *identity* of a user. Authorization manages what a user can or cannot access, also known as *permissions*. Encryption is the mechanism that helps you protect data, as it passes between the client and server. We're not going to discuss encryption too much, though—just to ensure that the data that goes over the wire is encrypted everywhere. This can be achieved through the use of the HTTPS protocol.

The following diagram depicts the flow of a typical auth mechanism in .NET monoliths:

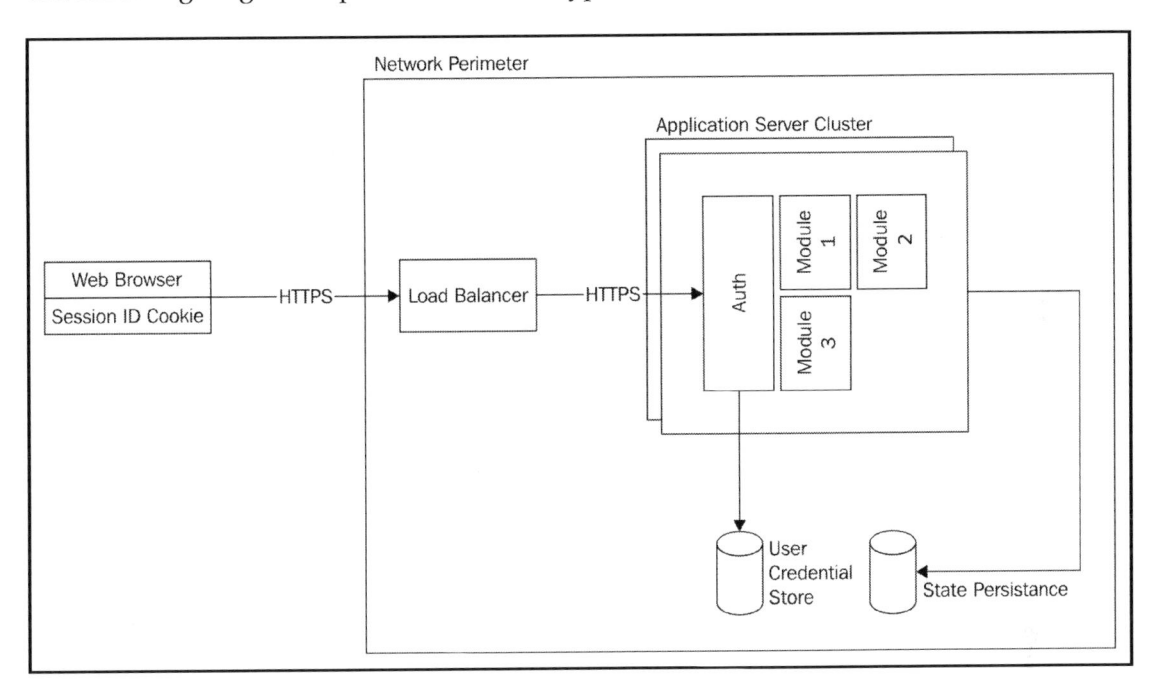

In the preceding diagram, we can see that the user enters his or her username and password, typically through a web browser. Then, this request hits a thin layer in a web application that is responsible for auth. This layer or component connects to the user credential store, which is typically an SQL server, in the case of a .NET Core application. The auth layer verifies the user-supplied credentials against the username and password that are stored in the credential store.

Once the user's credentials are verified for the session, a session cookie is created in the browser. Unless the user has a valid session cookie, they cannot access the app. Typically, a session cookie is sent with every request. Within these kinds of monolithic applications, modules can freely interact with each other, since they are in the same process and have in-memory access. This means that trust is implicit within those application modules, so they do not need separate validation and verification of requests, while talking to each other.

The focus of this section was mainly to look at security in monolithic applications, where we have learned about the flow of security by looking at a diagram. In the next section, we will discuss security in microservices and learn how distributed systems can be secured.

Security in microservices

Now, let's look at the case of microservices. By nature, microservices are distributed systems. There is never a single instance of an application; rather, there are several distinct applications that coordinate with each other, in harmony, to produce the desired output.

In microservice security, while working with ASP.NET Core, we can use different mechanisms of security, such as OAuth2.0, JWT, and Azure Active Directory (with extra implementation for authorization). In the case of microservices, it isn't mandatory for each and every service to have authentication—some services do not require any authentication to return a response. Overall, security is a big concern these days.

In the following section, we will discuss why the traditional .NET auth mechanism won't work, and then we will discuss various other authentication mechanisms.

Why won't a traditional .NET auth mechanism work?

One of the possible approaches for microservice security is as follows: we mimic the same behavior as that of the auth layer in a monolith. This can be depicted as follows:

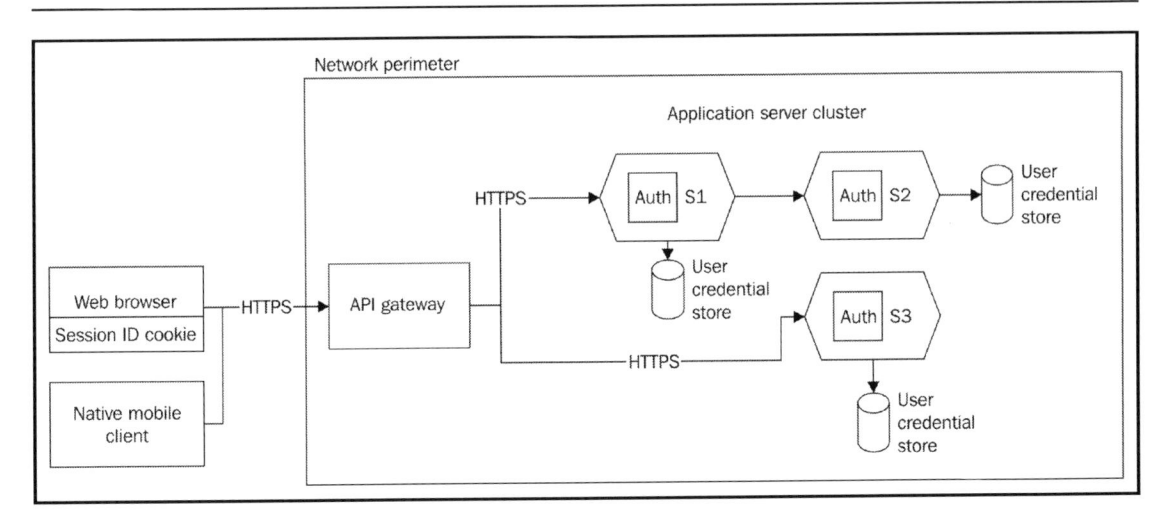

[Diagram: Network perimeter containing API gateway connecting via HTTPS to an Application server cluster with Auth S1, Auth S2, Auth S3 hexagons, each with their own User credential store. Web browser (with Session ID cookie) and Native mobile client connect via HTTPS to the API gateway.]

In this approach, we distributed the auth layer and provided it to all the microservices. Since each one is a different application, it will need its own auth mechanism. This inherently means that the user credential store is also different for every microservice. This raises so many questions, such as, how do we keep the auth in sync across all our services? How can we validate interservice communication, or do we skip it? We don't have satisfactory answers to these questions, and so this approach doesn't make sense and just increases the complexity. We can't even be sure whether this approach will work in the real world.

There is one more factor that we need to take into account for modern applications. In the microservice world, we need to support native mobile apps and other nonstandard form factor devices, as well as IoT applications. With the significant proliferation of native mobile applications, the microservice architecture also needs to support secure communication between those clients and microservices. This is different from the traditional web-browser-based user interface. On mobile platforms, a web browser is not part of any native mobile app. This means that cookie-based or session-based authentication is not possible, in most applications, unless you use special approaches or frameworks. You can, for example, use cookies and sessions on mobile, especially with **progressive web apps** (**PWAs**). Therefore, microservices need to support this kind of interoperability between client applications. This was never a concern for .NET monolithic applications.

In the case of traditional authentication, the browser is responsible for sending the cookie upon each request. But we're not using the browser for a native mobile app. In fact, we're not using ASPX pages either, nor the form's authentication module. For an iOS client or Android, it's something different altogether. What's more, we are also trying to restrict unauthorized access to our API. In the preceding example, we'd secure the client, be it an MVC app or a phone app, and not the microservice. Moreover, all of these mobile client devices are not part of the trust subsystem. For every request, we cannot trust that the mobile user is indeed the owner; the communication channel is not secured either. This means that any request coming from them cannot be trusted at all.

But apart from these problems, there's another more conceptual problem that we have. Why should the application be responsible for authenticating users and authorization? Shouldn't this be separated out?

One more solution to this is using the SAML protocol, but again, this is based on SOAP and XML, so it's not really a good fit for microservices. The complexity of the implementation of SAML is also high.

Therefore, it is evident that we need a token-based solution. The solution for microservices' auth comes in the form of OpenID Connect and OAuth 2.0. OpenID Connect is the standard for authentication, while OAuth 2.0 is the specification for the authorization; however, this authorization is delegated by nature.

We will look at this in detail in the upcoming sections. But before that, let's take a detour and look at JSON Web Tokens and see why they are significant, with respect to microservice security.

JSON Web Tokens

JSON Web Tokens (JWT) is pronounced *JOT*. It is a well-defined JSON schema or format to describe the tokens involved in a data exchange process. JSON Web Tokens is defined in detail at `https://tools.ietf.org/html/rfc7519`. JWTs can be used to authenticate the request, without using OpenID and OAuth2.0. We can get the benefit from built-in support of JWT, when working with .NET Core applications.

> OpenID Connect is an authentication layer, on top of OAuth 2.0 (which is an authorization framework).

In the implementation of JWT, we use a JWT-based security token. This token is a JSON object that contains information about the issuer and the recipient, along with the identity of the sender. Therefore, tokens should be protected over the wire, so that they cannot be tampered with. To do so, tokens are assigned symmetric or asymmetric keys. This means that when a receiver trusts the issuer of the token, it can also trust the information inside it.

> If you want to find more general information related to security, visit the **Open Web Application Security Project (OWASP)** at `http://www.owasp.org` and the Microsoft Security development life cycle at `https://www.microsoft.com/en-us/sdl/`.

Here is an example of a JWT:

```
eyJhbGciOiJIUzI1NiIsInR5cCI6IkpXVCJ9.eyJzdWIiOiIxMjM0NTY3ODkwIiwibmFtZSI6Ik
pvaG4gRG9lIiwiYWRtaW4iOnRydWV9.TJVA95OrM7E2cBab30RMHrHDcEfxjoYZgeFONFh7HgQ
```

This is the encoded form of a JWT. If we see the same token in its decoded form, it has three components: the header, payload, and signature. They are all separated by a period (.). The preceding token can be decoded as follows:

```
Header: {"alg": "HS256", "type": "JWT"}
Payload: {"sub": "1234567890","name": "John Doe","admin": true}
Signature: HMACSHA256(base64UrlEncode(header) + "." +
base64UrlEncode(payload),secret)
```

.NET Core has built-in support for generating and consuming JWTs. You can install JWT support in any .NET Core application, by using the package manager console with the following command:

```
Install-Package System.IdentityModel.Tokens.Jwt
```

> Visit `https://jwt.io/` if you want to view and decode JWTs very easily. Moreover, you can add it as part of the Chrome debugger as well, which is quite handy.

This section provided you with an overview of JWT, including how it can be used independently from OpenID Connect and OAuth2.0. In the next section, we will learn how to work with OAuth2.0.

Working with OAuth 2.0

Okay, you may not know what OAuth 2.0 is, but you have surely used it in several websites. Nowadays, many websites allow you to log in with your username and password for Facebook, Twitter, and Google accounts. Go to your favorite website—for example, the `https://stackoverflow.com/` login page. For example, there is a login button that says you can sign in with your Google account. When you click the **Google** button, it takes you to Google's login page, along with some of the permissions we mentioned previously. Here, you provide your Google username and password, and then you click the **Allow** button to grant permissions to your favorite site. Then, Google redirects you to Stack Overflow, and you are logged in with the appropriate permissions in Stack Overflow. This is merely the end user experience for OAuth 2.0 and OpenID Connect.

OAuth 2.0 handles authorization on the web, in native mobile applications, and in all headless server applications (these are nothing more than microservice instances in our context). You might be wondering why we are discussing authorization first, instead of authentication. The reason for this is that OAuth 2.0 is a delegated authorization framework. This means that, to complete the authorization flow, it relies on an authentication mechanism.

Now, let's look at some of the terminology associated with this.

OAuth 2.0 roles describe the involved parties in the authorization process, as follows:

- **Resource**: The entity that is getting protected from unintended access and usage. This is a microservice, in our case.
- **Resource owner**: As its name suggests, the resource owner can be either a person or an entity who has ownership of the resource. They're also called the end user.
- **Client**: Client is the term that's used to refer to all kinds of client applications. This refers to any application that's trying to access the protected resource. In a microservice context, the applications involved are single-page applications, web user interface clients, and native mobile applications, or even microservices that are trying to access other microservices downstream.
- **Authorization server**: Simply put, this server is called an authorization server, because it authenticates the end user by issuing a valid token. We can also call it a server that authenticates the resource owner and issues the token to the client. This token is generated by the secure token service, which is hosted on the authorization server.

Chapter 6

You may have noticed that OAuth differentiates between end users and the applications that are used by an end user. This is a bit odd, but it makes perfect sense since it is basically saying, *I am authorizing this app to perform these actions on my behalf.*

The following diagram depicts how these roles interact with each other, in the general flow of authorization in the OAuth framework:

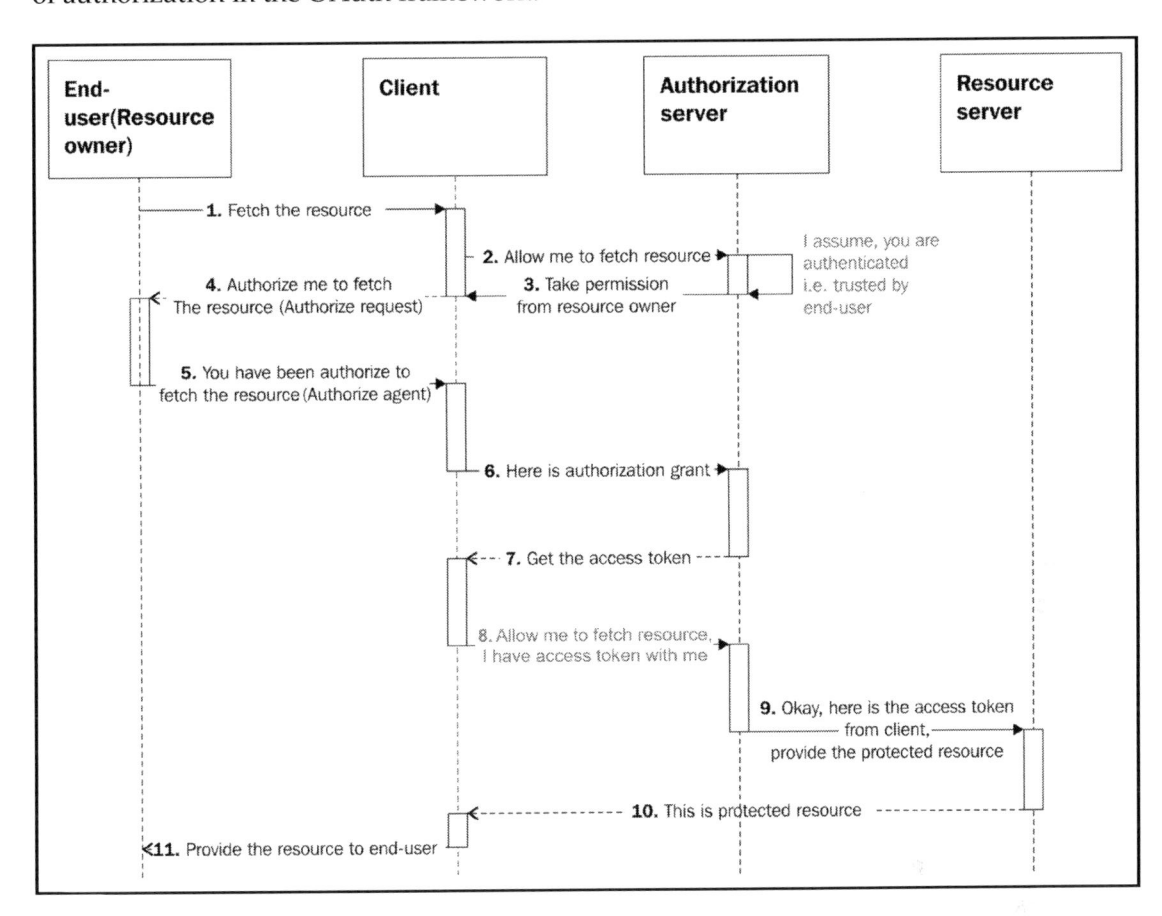

```
End-              Client           Authorization         Resource
user(Resource                      server                server
owner)

|-- 1. Fetch the resource -->|
                             |-- 2. Allow me to fetch resource -->|
                             |                                    | I assume, you are
                             |                                    | authenticated
|<- 4. Authorize me to fetch-|<-- 3. Take permission -------------| i.e. trusted by
    The resource (Authorize request)     from resource owner      | end-user
|
|-- 5. You have been authorize to -->|
    fetch the resource (Authorize agent)
                             |
                             |-- 6. Here is authorization grant -->|
                             |
                             |<-- 7. Get the access token --------|
                             |
                             |-- 8. Allow me to fetch resource, --->|
                                 I have access token with me
                                                                   |
                                                                   |-- 9. Okay, here is the access token
                                                                          from client,
                                                                          provide the protected resource -->|
                             |<------ 10. This is protected resource -----------------|
|<-11. Provide the resource to end-user -|
```

In *step 6* in the preceding diagram, the client passes the authorization grant to the authorization server. This step is not as simple as it looks. Authorization grants come in different types. The grant types represent four different possible use cases for getting access tokens in OAuth 2.0. If you choose the wrong grant type, you may be compromising security. Let's take a look at them:

- **Authorization code**: This is the typical OAuth grant that's used by server-side web applications, and it's the one you would use in your ASP.NET apps.

[215]

- **Implicit**: This is very useful for single-page applications, because communication in single-page applications is mostly public, but it can be private. The authentication is done by identifying the access token that has been returned from the server to the browser, and it can then be used to access resources.
- **Resource owner password credentials**: This requires the user to directly enter their username and password in the application. This is useful when you are developing a first-party application, to authenticate with your own servers.
- **Client credentials**: In most of the scenarios and cases you will come across, client credentials are required to access the resources that are protected. Apart from this, they are typically used when the client is acting on its own behalf (the client is also the resource owner).

The aim of this section was to highlight the security of distributed systems. Microservices are distributed systems, so we looked at why we can't go with the classic security approaches. Then, we learned about the JWT and OAuth mechanisms of security. The next section will focus on OpenID Connect, which is a layer on top of the OAuth 2.0 protocol.

Exploring OpenID Connect

OpenID Connect 1.0 is a simple identity layer on top of the OAuth 2.0 protocol. OpenID Connect is all about authentication. It allows clients to verify end users, based on the authentication that was performed by an authorization server. It is also used to obtain basic profile information about the end user, in an interoperable and REST-like manner.

OpenID Connect allows clients of all types—web-based, mobile, and JavaScript—to request and receive information about authenticated sessions and end users. We know that OAuth 2.0 defines access tokens. Well, OpenID Connect defines a standardized identity token (commonly referred to as the **ID token**). The identity token is sent to the application, so that the application can validate who the user is. It defines an endpoint to get identity information for that user, such as their name or email address. That's the user's information endpoint.

It's built on top of OAuth 2.0, so the flows are the same. It can be used with the authorization code grant and implicit grant. This isn't possible with the client credentials grant, since the client credentials grant is for server-to-server communication.

There's no end user involved in this process, so there's no end-user identity either. Likewise, it doesn't make sense for the resource owner path of usage or process. So how does this work? Well, instead of only requesting an access token, we'll request an additional ID token from the **security token service** (**STS**), which implements the OpenID Connect specification. The client receives an ID token, and usually, an access token. To gather more information for the authenticated user, the client can send a request to the user information endpoint with the access token; this user information endpoint will then return the claims about the new user. OpenID supports authorization code flow and implicit flow. It also adds some additional protocols, which are discovery and dynamic registration.

Authentication and authorization are the required and important elements of any secured application. In this section, we learned about OpenID Connect, which is an identity layer on top of the OAuth framework. In the next section, we will discuss Azure Active Directory, which is a provider that follows the specifications of both OpenID Connect and OAuth2.0.

Understanding Azure Active Directory

There are multiple providers for the OAuth 2.0 and OpenID Connect 1.0 specifications. **Azure Active Directory** (**AAD**) is one of them. AAD provides organizations with enterprise-grade identity management, for cloud applications. AAD integration will give your users a streamlined sign-in experience, and it will help your application conform to the IT policy. AAD provides advanced security features, such as multifactor authentication, and it scales really well with application growth. It is used in all Microsoft Azure Cloud products, including Office 365, and it processes more than a billion sign-ins per day.

One more interesting aspect of traditional .NET environments is that they can integrate their organizational Windows Server Active Directory with AAD really well. Here, we've used OAuth/OIDC, since we adapted **Active Directory Federation Services** (**ADFS**). But in production-based applications, we have a mixed case, where there is a different protocol set in the on-premise AD (Kerberos, LDAP, and so on).

> **Azure Active Directory** (**AAD**) is an identity and access-management service that helps organizations provide secure access to their employees, when they want to access resources. AAD is Microsoft's cloud-based service.

As an example, let's say that an employee of the organization wants to access specific resources from a specific location. Here, AAD helps validate that access. This can be done with the AAD sync tool or the new capability of pass-through authentication, so organizational IT compliance will still be managed.

> We have discussed AAD, as per the scope of this chapter. It is recommended that you read **Path-Through Authentication (PTA)** at https://docs.microsoft.com/en-us/azure/active-directory/hybrid/how-to-connect-pta and **Password Hash Synchronization (PHS)** with Azure AD at https://docs.microsoft.com/en-us/azure/active-directory/hybrid/whatis-phs, if you want to find out more.

In this section, we learned that Azure Active Directory is a provider and follows the specifications of both OpenID Connect and OAuth2.0. In the next section, we will walk through OpenID Connect, OAuth2.0, and AAD, with the help of a code example.

Microservice Auth example with OpenID Connect, OAuth 2.0, and Azure AD

Now that we are well-equipped with all the prerequisite knowledge, we can begin coding. Let's build a `ProductService` application. We are going to secure `FlixOne.BookStore.ProductService`, which represents one of our microservices. In the solution, the `FlixOne.BookStore` microservice is represented by the `FlixOne.BookStore.ProductService` project, and `FlixOne.BookStore.Web` represents the server-side web application. It will be easier to follow along if you open up the Visual Studio solution, called `OpFlixOne.BookStore.sln`, which is provided with this chapter. This example uses the client credentials grant.

Note that, because of the ever-changing nature of the Azure portal and the corresponding Azure services UI, it is advisable that you use the **Azure Resource Manager** (**ARM**) API and automate some of the registration tasks you are about to follow. However, for learning purposes, and largely to encourage developers who are new to Azure or who are trying Azure AD for the first time, we are going to follow the Azure portal user interface.

Here are the prerequisites:

- Visual Studio 2019 or later
- An Azure subscription (if you don't have this, you can use the free trial account for this demo)
- Azure AD tenant (single tenant)—you can also work with your Azure account's default directory, which should be different from that of the Microsoft organization

This section aims to get you started with the implementation of AAD. We have created two projects: service and web. In the upcoming sections, we will expand upon this example, starting with registering our application with the AAD tenant.

Registering our application with the Azure AD tenant

We need to integrate our app to the Microsoft Identity platform, which requires us to register our application using the App registrations experience in the Azure portal.

Now, let's look at how to register `FlixOne.BookStore.ProductService`.

In this step, we will add `FlixOne.BookStore.ProductService` to Azure AD tenant. To achieve this, log in to the Azure Management portal. Follow these steps:

1. Log in to the Azure portal (`https://portal.azure.com`).
2. Click **Azure Active Directory**, as shown in the following screenshot:

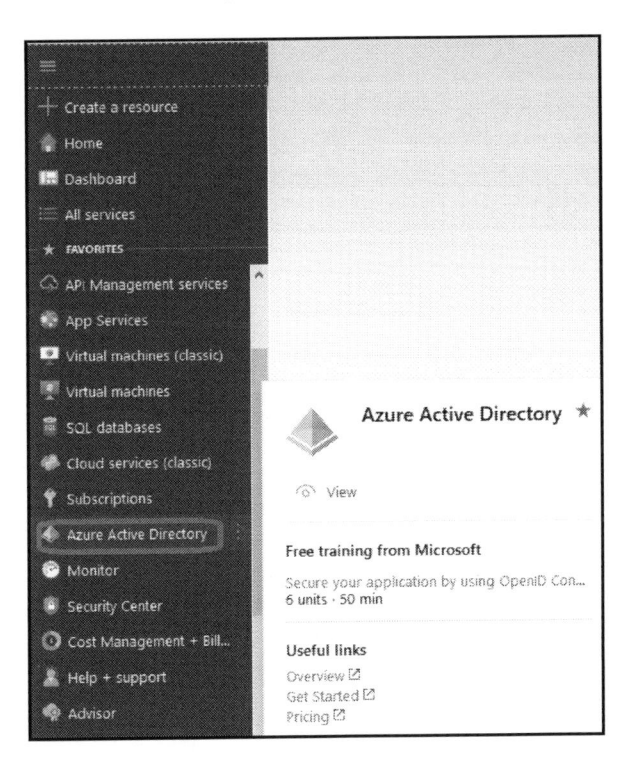

Securing Microservices Using Azure Active Directory

3. The preceding step will take you to an overview screen of **Default Directory**. Click **App registrations**, as shown here:

4. Click **New registration**. This will open the **Register an application** screen, as shown here:

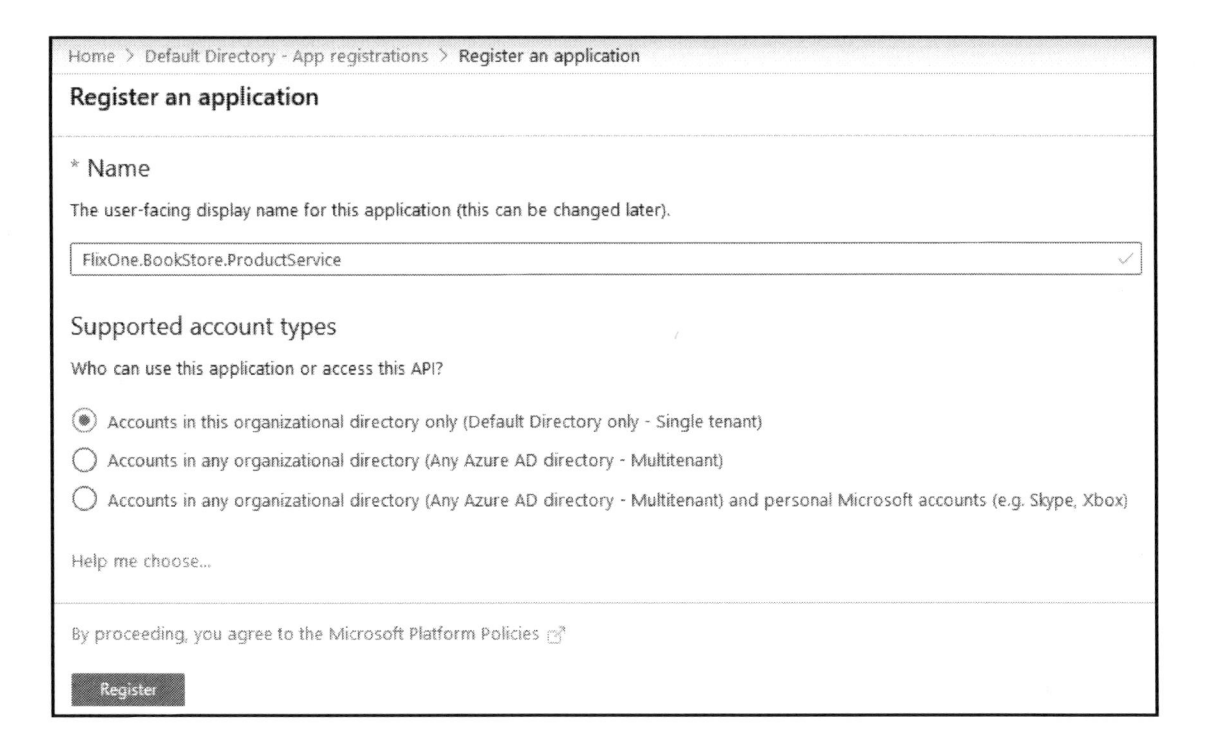

Home > Default Directory - App registrations > Register an application

Register an application

* Name

The user-facing display name for this application (this can be changed later).

FlixOne.BookStore.ProductService

Supported account types

Who can use this application or access this API?

(●) Accounts in this organizational directory only (Default Directory only - Single tenant)

( ) Accounts in any organizational directory (Any Azure AD directory - Multitenant)

( ) Accounts in any organizational directory (Any Azure AD directory - Multitenant) and personal Microsoft accounts (e.g. Skype, Xbox)

Help me choose...

By proceeding, you agree to the Microsoft Platform Policies

Register

Securing Microservices Using Azure Active Directory

Provide all the mandatory details that are displayed in the preceding screenshot, and then click the **Register** button at the bottom of the **Register an application** screen. While we are providing a sign-in URL, make sure that you are providing it for your app. In our case, `FlixOne.BookStore.ProductService` is a microservice, so we won't have a special sign-in URL. This means that we have to provide the default URL, or just the hostname of our microservice. Here, we are going to run the service from our machine, so the localhost URL will be sufficient. You can find the sign-in URL, once you right-click on the project URL under the `FlixOne.BookStore.ProductService` project, and then navigate to **Debug**, as shown in the following screenshot:

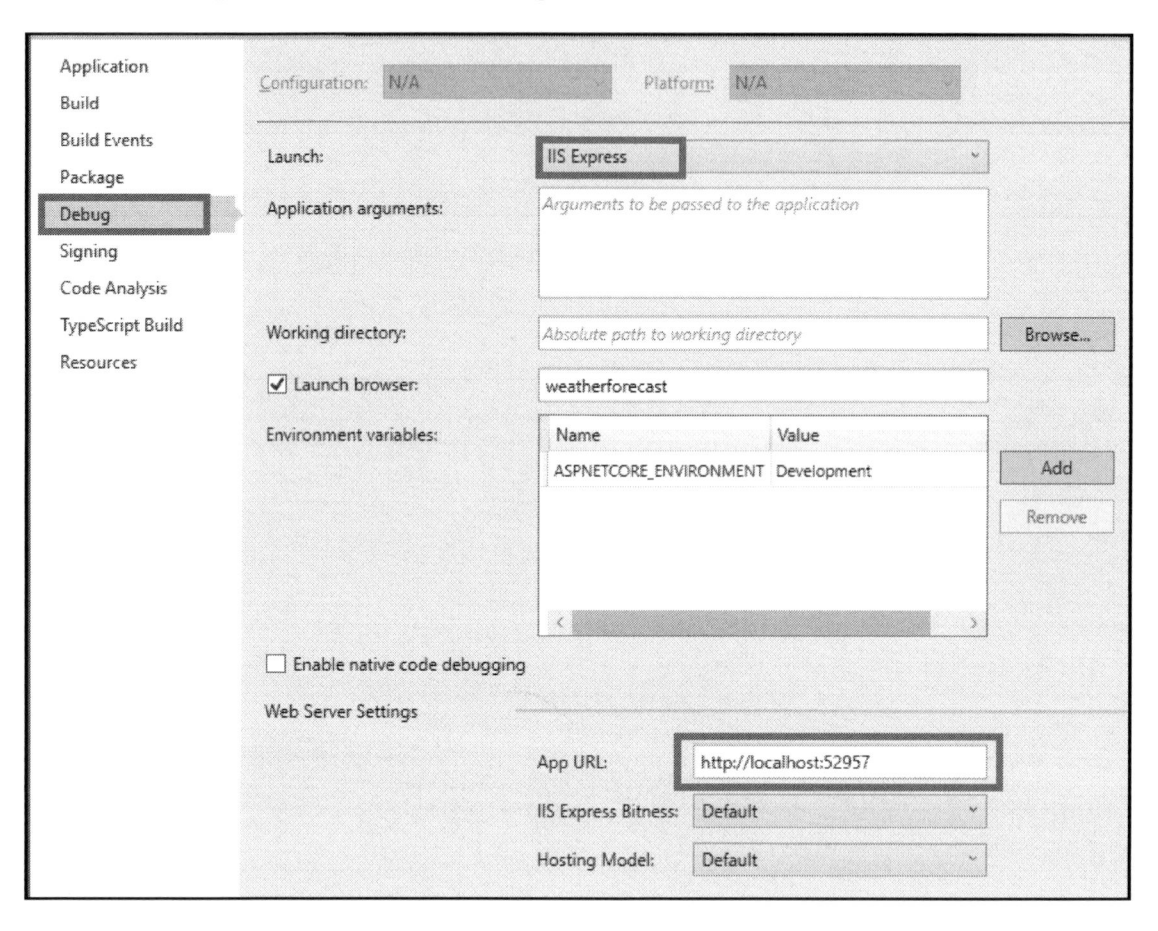

> **TIP:** A sign-in URL in the Azure portal should have the trailing /; otherwise, you may face an error, even if you execute all the steps correctly.

5. If you deploy your service with the Microsoft Azure App Service plan, you will get a URL that looks something like `https://productservice-flixone.azurewebsites.net/`. You can always change the sign-in URL, if you deploy the service on Azure.
6. Once you click the **Register** button, Azure will add the application to your Azure AD tenant. However, there are still a few more details that need to be completed, before we can finish registering `ProductService`. Navigate to **App Registration | FlixOne.BookStore.ProductService**. You will notice that there are a few more additional properties, such as **Application ID URI**, which have been provided now.
7. For the **App ID URL**, enter `https://[Your_Tenant_Name]/ProductService`, replacing `[Your_Tenant_Name]` with the name of your Azure AD tenant. Click **OK** to complete the registration process. The final configuration should look like this:

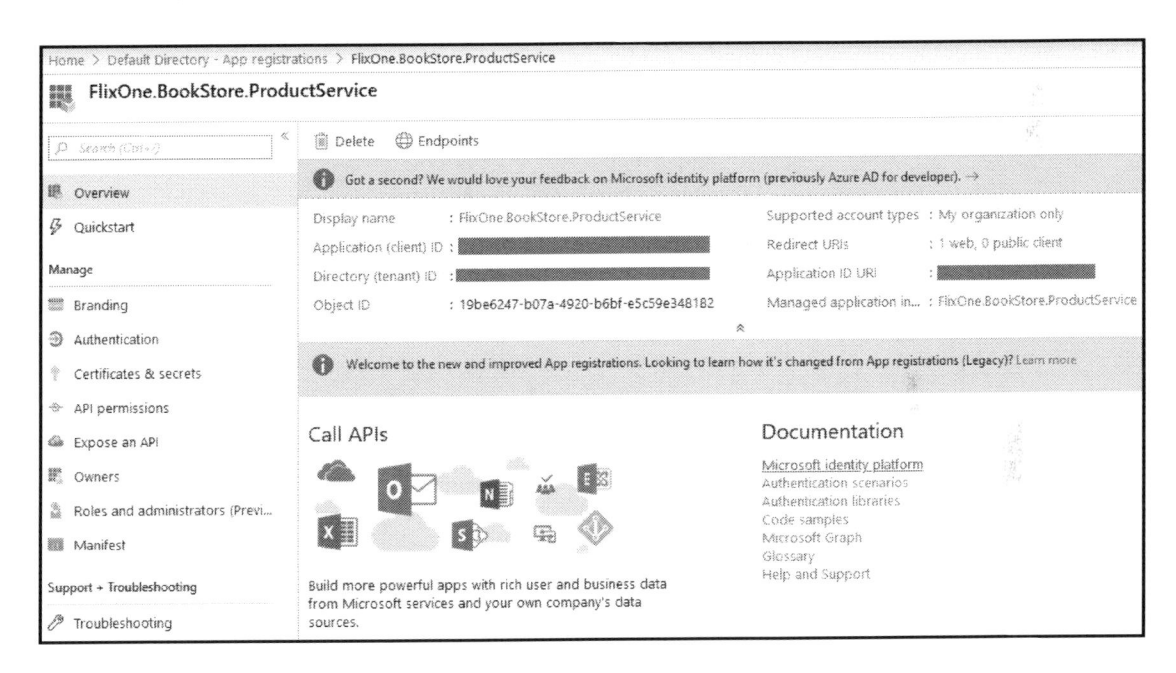

[223]

Securing Microservices Using Azure Active Directory

Now, let's move on to the registration of `FlixOne.BookStore.Web`:

1. First, we register `FlixOne.BookStore.Web`. This is necessary, since we are going to use OpenID Connect to connect to this browser-based web application. Therefore, we need to establish trust between the end user—that is, us—and `FlixOne.BookStore.Web`.

2. Click **App registrations**, then click **New Registration**. This will open the **Register an application** screen, as shown in the following screenshot. Fill in the **Name**, and then click **Register**:

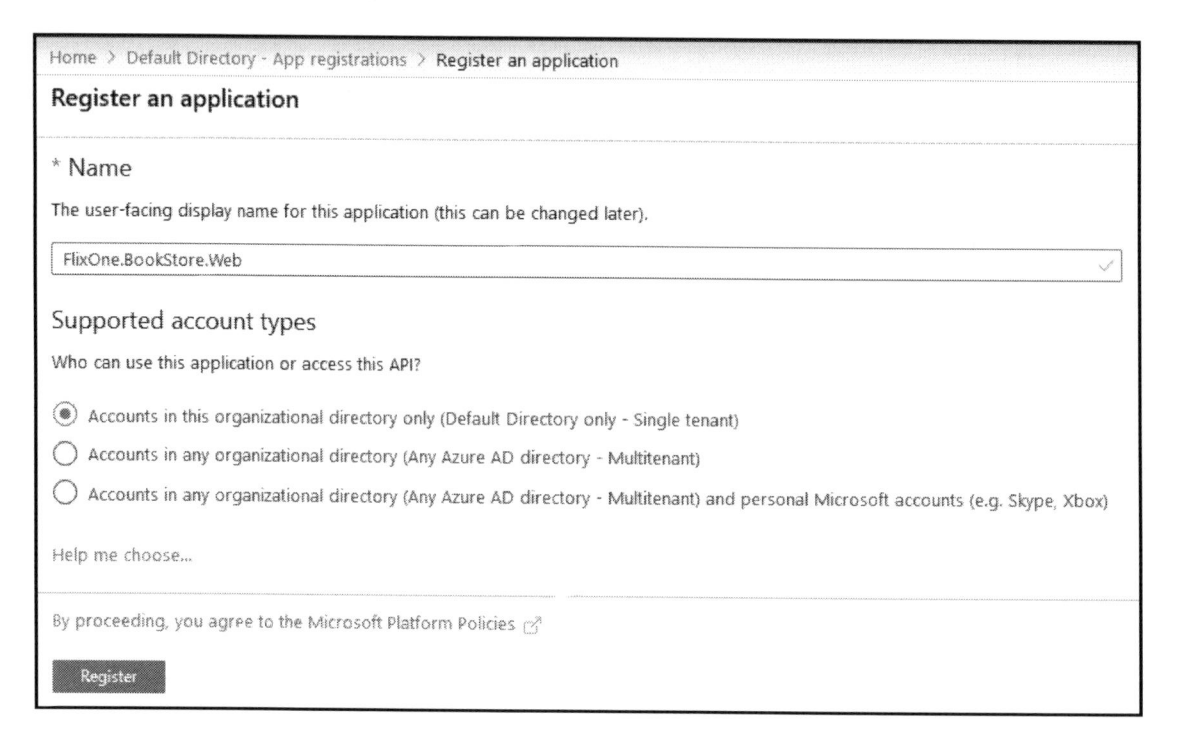

Home > Default Directory - App registrations > Register an application

Register an application

* Name

The user-facing display name for this application (this can be changed later).

FlixOne.BookStore.Web

Supported account types

Who can use this application or access this API?

(●) Accounts in this organizational directory only (Default Directory only - Single tenant)

( ) Accounts in any organizational directory (Any Azure AD directory - Multitenant)

( ) Accounts in any organizational directory (Any Azure AD directory - Multitenant) and personal Microsoft accounts (e.g. Skype, Xbox)

Help me choose...

By proceeding, you agree to the Microsoft Platform Policies

Register

3. Similar to when we registered `ProductServices`, enter some additional required information, as follows:

Chapter 6

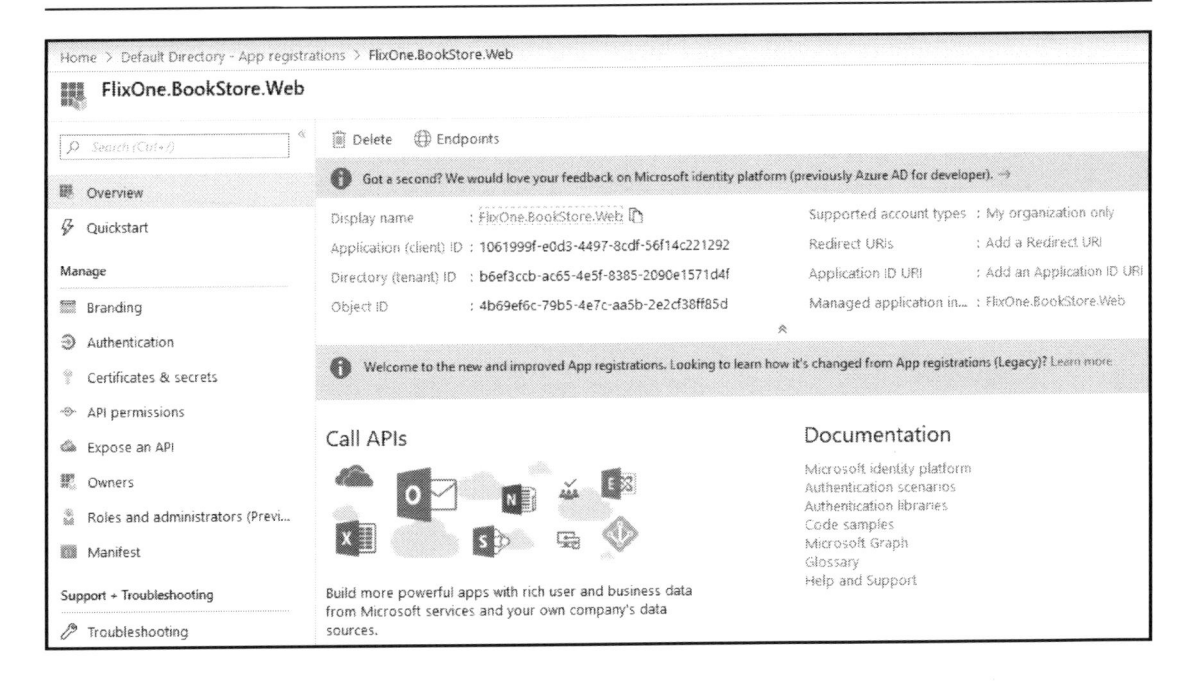

4. Note the logout URL setting: we set it as
   `https://localhost:44322/Account/EndSession`.
   This is because, after ending the session, Azure AD will redirect the user to this URL. For the **App ID URL**,
   enter `https://[Your_AD_Tenant_Name]/TodoListWebApp`,
   replacing `[Your_AD_Tenant_Name]` with the name of your Azure AD tenant. Click **OK** to complete the registration process.
5. Now, we need to set up permissions for **FlixOne.BookStore.Web**, so that it can call our microservice: **ProductServices**. Navigate to **App Registration | FlixOne.BookStore.Web | API Permissions** again, and then click **Add a permission**. This will save the permissions.

Registering an app is required, so that our services and web application can integrate with Microsoft Identity services. This section also walked us through the implementation of AAD. In the upcoming sections, we will expand on this application.

Generating AppKey for FlixOne.BookStore.Web

Another important step for registration is adding `client_secret`, which is necessary to establish trust between Azure AD and `FlixOne.BookStore.Web`. This `client_secret` is generated only once; it is configured in the web application.

[225]

Securing Microservices Using Azure Active Directory

To generate this key, follow these steps:

1. Navigate to **App Registrations | FlixOne.BookStore.Web | Certificates & secrets | New client secret**, as shown in the following screenshot:

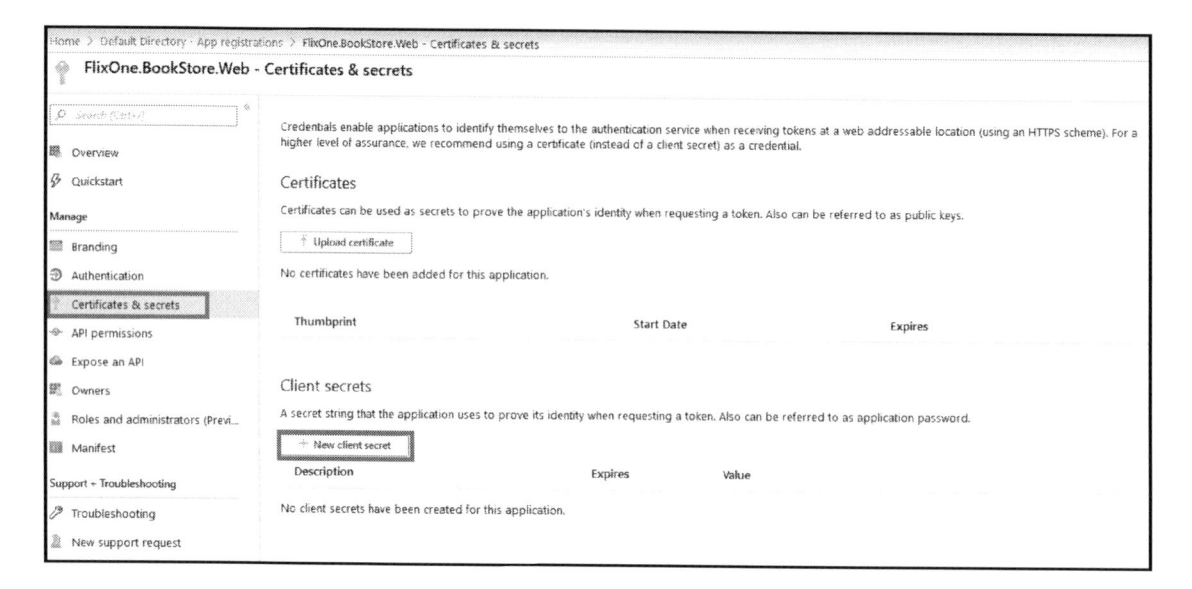

2. Then, add the description as `AppKey`, select when the key will expire (we selected **In 1 year**), and click **Add**, as shown in the following screenshot:

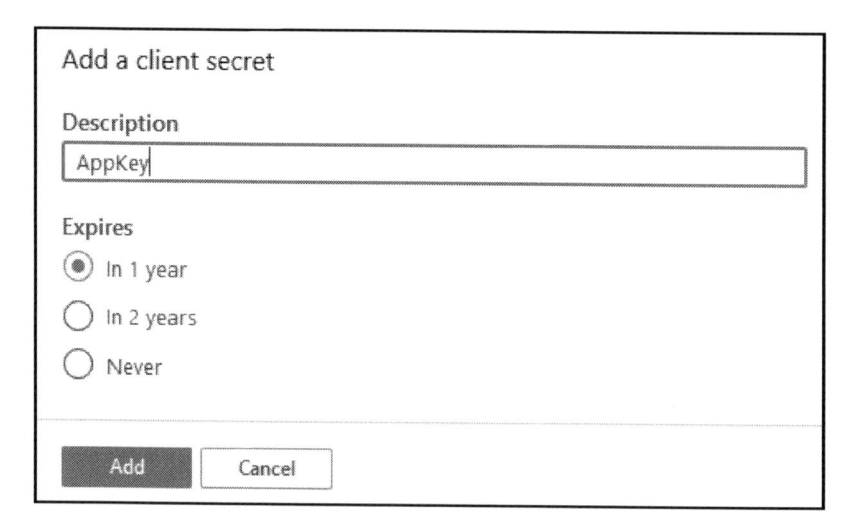

3. Once the key is saved, the value of the key will be autogenerated by Azure and will be displayed next to the description. This key is displayed only once, so you have to immediately copy it and save it for later use. We will be keeping this key in the `appsettings.json` file of `FlixOne.BookStore.Web`, in this case.

The key will be displayed on the Azure portal, as follows (the key value would be shown on the right):

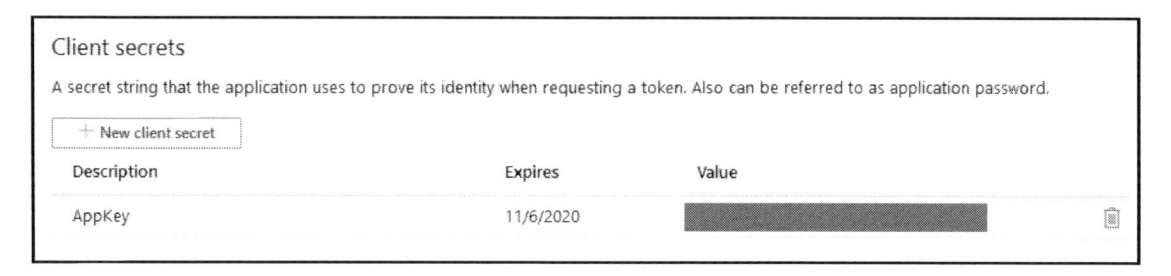

Client secrets

A secret string that the application uses to prove its identity when requesting a token. Also can be referred to as application password.

+ New client secret

Description	Expires	Value
AppKey	11/6/2020	▓▓▓▓▓▓▓▓▓▓▓▓▓▓▓▓

> For production-grade applications, it is a bad idea to keep `client_Secret` and any critical key values in the `appsettings.json` file. It is a good practice to keep them encrypted and isolated from the applications. For such purposes, in production-grade applications, you can use Azure Key Vault (https://azure.microsoft.com/en-us/services/key-vault/), to keep all your keys protected. Another advantage of a key vault is that you can manage the keys according to the environment, such as dev-test-staging and production. Another approach would be **Managed identities for Azure resources** (formerly called **MSI**—https://docs.microsoft.com/en-us/azure/active-directory/managed-identities-azure-resources/overview), which can also be used in production-grade applications.

This section helped us generate an AppKey for our imaginary application, `FlixOne.BookStore.Web`, by taking us through the steps of generating a key. Now, we need to configure this key for our application, by using the configuration settings of the project. In the next section, we will configure our solution using Visual Studio.

Configuring Visual Studio solution projects

As soon as we are done with registering the application, we need to make sure that we configure our projects, so that these projects will work as per our expectations. First of all, we will look at how to configure this with the `ProductServices` project.

Securing Microservices Using Azure Active Directory

Open the `appsettings.json` file, and then add some values for the following keys:

1. Search for the `Tenant` key. Replace its value with your AD tenant name, for example, `contoso.onmicrosoft.com`. This will also be part of any of the application's **APP ID URL**.
2. Replace the `Audience` key value with `https://[Your_AD_Tenant_Name]/FlixOneBookStoreProductService`.
Replace `[Your_AD_Tenant_Name]` with the name of your Azure AD tenant.

Now, let's learn how to configure this with `FlixOne.BookStore.Web`, so that our web project has the correct values.

Open the `appsettings.json` file. Then find and replace the following keys with the provided values:

1. Replace the value of the `WebResourceid` key with `https://[Your_Tenant_Name]/ProductService`.
2. Replace `WebBaseAddress` with `https://localhost:44321/`.
3. Replace `ClientId` with the application ID of **FlixOneBookStoreWeb**. You can get it by navigating to **App Registration | FlixOneBookStoreWeb**.
4. Replace `AppKey` with the `client_secret`, which we generated in *step 2* of the process of registering **TodoListWebApp**. If you didn't take note of this key, then you need to delete the previous key and generate a new key.
5. Replace `Tenant` with your AD tenant name—for example, `contoso.onmicrosoft.com`.
6. Replace `RedirectUri` with the URL that you want the application to redirect you to, when the user signs out of TodoListWebApp. In our case, the default is `https://localhost:44322/`, since we want the user to navigate to the home page of the application.

In this section, we learned how to take a secret key and how to handle the project. In the next section, we will see why it is crucial to manage it.

Generating client certificates on IIS Express

So far, we have registered our applications to take advantage of Microsoft Server. Now, `FlixOne.BookStore.ProductService` and `FlixOne.BookStore.Web` will talk over a secure channel. To establish a secure channel, `FlixOne.BookStore.Web` needs to trust the client certificate. Both services are hosted on the same machine, and they run on IIS Express.

To configure your computer to trust the IIS Express SSL certificate, go through the following steps:

1. Open the PowerShell command window as an administrator.
2. Query your personal certificate store to find the thumbprint of the certificate for `CN=localhost`. The following code snippet shows the PowerShell script for this. Here, we add a certificate to the IIS Express web server, by storing the thumbprint on the certificate store of our local machine:

   ```
   PS C:windowssystem32> dir Cert:LocalMachine\My
   Directory: Microsoft.PowerShell.SecurityCertificate::LocalMachineMy
   Thumbprint Subject
   ---------- -------
   C24798908DA71693C1053F42A462327543B38042 CN=localhost
   ```

3. Next, add the certificate to the trusted root store. The following code is adding the certificate to our certificate store, on our local computer:

   ```
   PS C:windowssystem32> $cert = (get-item cert:LocalMachineMyC24798908DA71693C1053F42A462327543B38042)
   PS C:windowssystem32> $store = (get-item cert:LocalmachineRoot)
   PS C:windowssystem32> $store.Open("ReadWrite")
   PS C:windowssystem32> $store.Add($cert)
   PS C:windowssystem32> $store.Close()
   ```

The preceding set of instructions will add a client certificate to the local machine's certificate store.

To use HTTPS, we should install the SSL certificate. To showcase and test this, we generated and added a certificate on our local machine. In the next section, we will run the demo application.

Running both applications

We are done with all those tedious configuration screens and key replacements. But before you press *F5*, set `ProductService` and `FlixOne.BookStore.Web` as startup projects. Once you've done this, you can safely run our application, and you'll be greeted with the landing page of our application. If you click the **Sign-in** button, you will be redirected to `login.microsoftonline.com`; this represents the Azure AD login. Once you are able to log in, you will see the landing page, as follows:

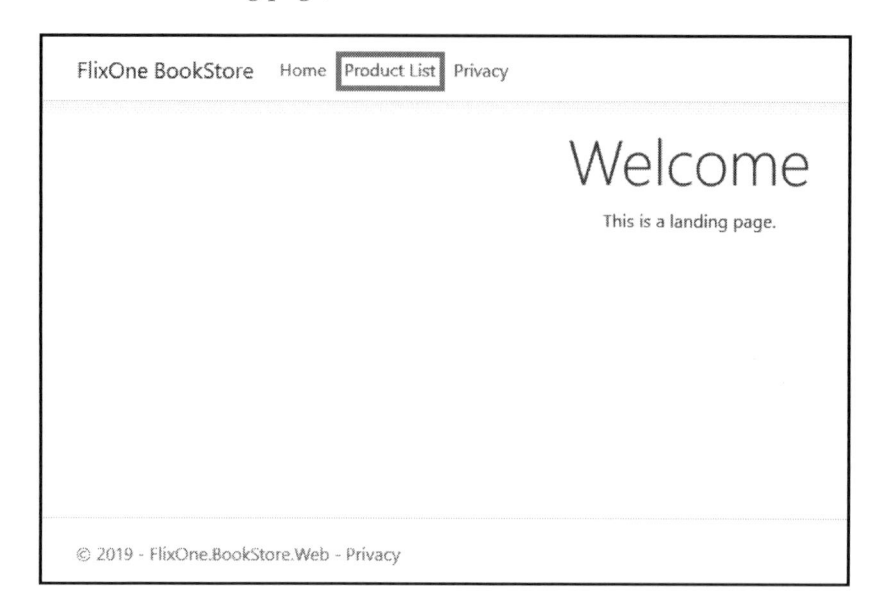

You will observe network traffic and URL redirection, when you log in to the application. So, study the detailed exchange of ID tokens, and get an access token. If you explore the application through the **Product List** menu, you will be able to access the **Product List** screen, as well as add items to the **Product List**. This is where our `ProductService` microservice is called from, as well as where it gets authorization permissions, from the `FlixOne.BookStore.Web` web application. If you explore the profile menu, you will see the ID token being returned, along with your first name, last name, and email ID, which shows OpenID Connect in action.

In this example, we used OAuth and OpenID Connect to secure a browser-based user interface, a web application, and a microservice. Things may be different, if we have an API gateway between the user interface web app and the microservice.

To validate our functionality, open `ProductController`, and then comment the `[Authorize]` attribute, as shown in the following screenshot:

```
namespace FlixOne.BookStore.Web.Controllers
{
    //[Authorize]
    public class ProductController : Controller
    {
        0 references
        public async Task<IActionResult> Index()
        {
            AuthenticationResult result = null;
            List<Product> productList = new List<Product>();
```

From the **Home** screen, click **Product List**. You will see a message saying that you should be logged in first before accessing the **Product Listing**:

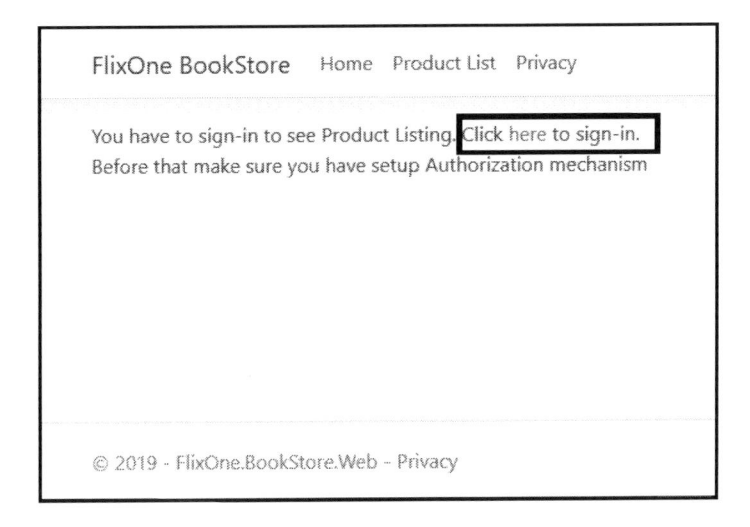

FlixOne BookStore   Home   Product List   Privacy

You have to sign-in to see Product Listing. Click here to sign-in.
Before that make sure you have setup Authorization mechanism

© 2019 - FlixOne.BookStore.Web - Privacy

This shows that we cannot access our **Product Listing**, until we are logged in or have the specific access rights.

In this case, we need to establish trust between the web app and the API gateway. We also have to pass the ID token and access token from the web app to the API gateway. This, in turn, passes the tokens to the microservice; however, it isn't feasible to discuss this and implement it in this chapter.

To take advantage of the Microsoft Identity Framework on Microsoft Azure, by using Azure Active Services and OpenID Connect, we can create secure applications. This section highlighted and implemented Azure Active Directory, using a dummy project. Next, we will learn how to manage it as an API gateway.

Managing Azure API Management as an API gateway

Another important pattern in a microservice's implementation is **backends for frontends (BFF)**. This pattern was introduced and made popular by Sam Newman. The actual implementation of the BFF pattern is done by introducing an API gateway between various types of clients and microservices.

This is depicted in the following diagram:

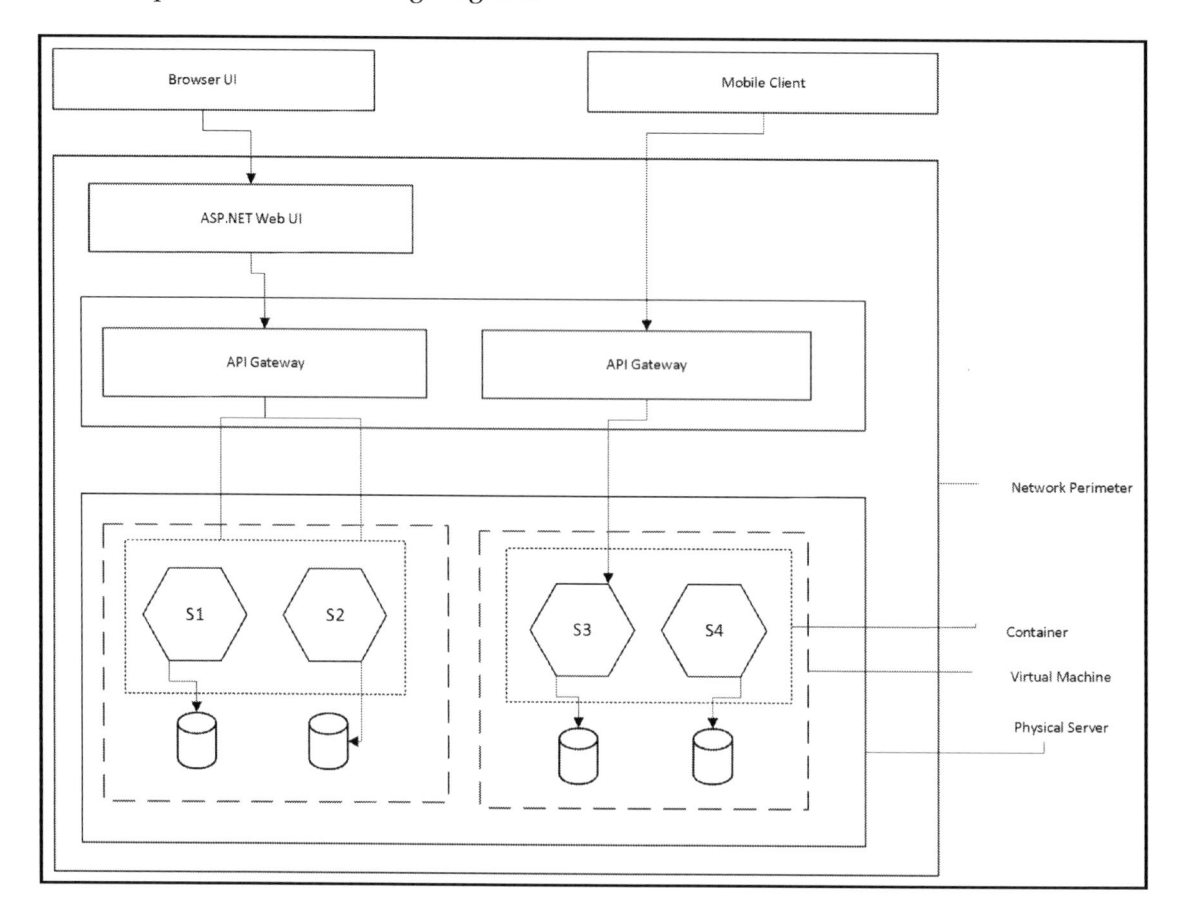

Azure API Management (henceforth referred to as **Azure APIM** or just **APIM**) is just the right fit. It can act as an API gateway in .NET-based microservice implementations. Since Azure APIM is one of the cloud services, it is ultra-scalable and can be integrated well within the Azure ecosystem. In this chapter, we will focus on showing you the features of Azure APIM.

Azure APIM is logically divided into three parts:

- **API gateway**: The API gateway is basically a proxy between client applications and services. It is responsible for the following functionalities, which are mainly used by various applications to talk to microservices:
    - Accepts API calls and routes them to your backends
    - Verifies API keys, JWTs, and certificates
    - Supports auth through Azure AD and OAuth 2.0 access tokens
    - Enforces usage quotas and rate limits
    - Transforms your API on the fly, without code modifications
    - Caches backend responses where they were set up
    - Logs call metadata for analytics purposes
- **Publisher portal**: This is the administrative interface that's used to organize and publish an API program. It is mainly used by microservice developers to make microservices/APIs available to API consumers or client applications. Through this, API developers can do the following:
    - Define or import API schemas
    - Package APIs into products
    - Set up policies, such as quotas or transformations on the APIs
    - Get insights from analytics
    - Manage users
- **Developer portal**: This serves as the main web presence for API consumers, where they can do the following:
    - Read the API documentation
    - Try out an API, via the interactive console
    - Create an account and subscribe to it to get API keys
    - Access analytics for their own usage

Azure APIM comes with an easy-to-follow user interface and good documentation. Azure API Management also comes with its own REST API, so all the capabilities of the Azure APIM portal can be programmatically achieved by the Azure REST API endpoint, which is available for Azure APIM.

Now, let's quickly look at some security-related concepts in Azure APIM and how they can be used in microservices:

- **Products**: Products are merely a collection of APIs. They also contain usage quotas and terms of use.
- **Policies**: Policies are dynamic security features of API management. They allow the publisher to change the behavior of the API through configuration. Policies are a collection of statements that are executed sequentially upon the request or response of an API. API Management is fundamentally a proxy that is sitting between our microservices, which are hosted in Azure and client applications. By virtue of the fact that it is an intermediate layer, it is able to provide additional services. These additional services are defined in a declarative XML-based syntax called **policies**. Azure APIM allows various policies. In fact, you can compose your own custom policies by combining the existing ones.
  A few of the important restriction policies are as follows:
    - **Check the HTTP header**: This policy checks whether a specific HTTP header or its value exists in every request that's received by Azure APIM.
    - **Limit call rate by subscription:** This policy provides allow or deny access to the microservice, based on the number of times the specific service has been called, on a per-subscription basis.
    - **Restrict caller IPs**: This policy refers to white-boxing IP addresses, so that only known IPs can access the services.
    - **Set usage quota by subscription**: This policy allows a number of calls. It allows you to enforce a renewable or lifetime call volume and/or bandwidth quota, on a per-subscription basis.
    - **Validate JWT**: This policy validates the JWT parameter that is used for auth in applications.

- A few of the authentication policies are as follows:
    - **Authenticate with basic**: This policy helps us apply basic authentication over the incoming request.
    - **Authenticate with client certificate**: This policy helps us carry out the authentication of a service that's behind the API gateway, using client certificates.

- A few of the cross-domain policies are as follows:
    - **Allow cross-domain calls**: This policy allows us to make CORS requests through Azure APIM.
    - **CORS**: This adds CORS support to an endpoint or a microservice, to allow cross-domain calls from browser-based web applications.
    - **JSONP**: The JSONP policy adds **JSON padding (JSONP)** support to an endpoint or to an entire microservice, to allow cross-domain calls from JavaScript web applications.
- A few of the transformation policies are as follows:
    - **Mask URLs in content**: This policy masks URLs in responses; it does so via Azure APIM.
    - **Set backend service**: This policy alters the behavior of the backend service of an incoming request.

This section highlighted the Azure API Management services that work as API gateways for our application. We also discussed policies and how they can be applied for inbound and outbound requests. Next, we will discuss the rate limit and quota policy.

An example of a rate limit and quota policy

In the preceding section, we learned what a policy is. Now, let's look at an example. The following is one of the quota policies that's been applied for an endpoint:

```
<policies>
  <inbound>
    <!-- Change the quota to immediately see the effect-->
    <rate-limit calls="100" renewal-period="60">
    </rate-limit>
    <quota calls="200" renewal-period="604800">
    </quota>
    <base />
  </inbound>
  <outbound>
    <base/>
  </outbound>
</policies>
```

In this example, we are limiting the incoming requests (`inbound`) from a single user. This means that an API user can only make 100 calls within 60 seconds. If they try to make more calls within that duration, the user will get an error with the status code 429, which basically states *the rate limit is exceeded*. We are also assigning the quota limit of 200 calls in a year, for the same user. This kind of throttling behavior is a great way to protect microservices from unwanted requests, and even DOS attacks.

Azure APIM also supports Auth with OAuth 2.0 and OpenID Connect. Inside the publisher portal, you can see OAuth and OpenID Connect tabs, so that you can configure the providers.

This section highlighted OAuth 2.0, OpenID Connect, Azure API Management services, and their policies. Next, we will discuss container security.

Understanding container security

Container security is a very important consideration, when we work with containers. We're using Docker containers for our applications. Docker is a big part of the containerization of applications in the industry. With the widespread usage of containers, it is evident that we need to have effective security measures around containers. If we take a look at the internal architecture of containers, they are quite close to the host operating system kernel.

Docker adheres to the principle of least privilege, in terms of isolation, and it reduces the attack surface. Despite the advances in this area, the following best practices will help you understand the security measures you can take for containers:

- Ensure that all the container images, that are used for microservices, are signed and originate from a trusted registry.
- Harden the host environment, the daemon process, and the images.
- To access devices, follow the principle of least privilege, and do not elevate access.
- Use control groups in Linux to keep tabs on resources, such as memory, I/O, and CPU.
- Even though containers live for a very short duration, logging all of the container activity is advisable and important to understand for post-analysis.
- If possible, integrate the container process tools, such as Aqua (http://www.aquasec.com) or Twistlock (https://www.twistlock.com).

Security is the aspect we should consider the most, while we work with any web application. This section discussed the security considerations that we should take into account, when we work with containers. Apart from container security, we should consider other security practices, to make sure our application is secure. In the next section, we will look at other security best practices.

Other security best practices

The microservice architectural style is new, although some of the security practices around the infrastructure and writing secure code are still applicable. In this section, we'll discuss some of these practices:

- **Standardization of libraries and frameworks**: There should be a process to introduce new libraries and frameworks or tools, into the development process. This will ease out patching in case a vulnerability is found; it will also minimize the risks that are introduced by the ad hoc implementation of libraries or tools around development.
- **Regular vulnerability identification and mitigation**: Using the industry-standard vulnerability scanner, to scan the source code and binaries, should be a regular part of development. These findings and observations should be addressed as functional defects.
- **Third-party audits and pen testing**: External audits and penetration testing exercises are immensely valuable. Conducting such exercises should be a regular practice. This is quite essential in applications where mission-critical or sensitive data is handled.
- **Logging and monitoring**: Logging is quite a useful technique for detecting and recovering from attacks. Having the capability of aggregating logs from different systems, is essential in the case of microservices. Some tools, such as Riverbed Azure, AppDynamics (a performance monitoring tool for Azure), and Splunk Azure, are quite useful in this space.
- **Firewalls**: Having one or more firewalls at network boundaries, is always beneficial. Firewall rules should be properly configured.
- **Network segregation**: Network partitioning is constrained and limited, in the case of monoliths. However, with microservices, we need to logically create different network segments and subnets. Segmentation, based on a microservice's interaction patterns, can be very effective, when it comes to keeping and developing additional security measures.

This section described some other security best practices. In addition to container security, we should consider all security practices to make sure our application is secure.

Summary

The microservice architectural style, being distributed by design, gives us better options when it comes to protecting valuable business-critical systems. Traditional .NET-based authentication and authorization techniques are not sufficient, and they cannot be applied to the microservices world. We also saw why secure token-based approaches, such as OAuth 2.0 and OpenID Connect 1.0, are becoming concrete standards for microservice authorization and authentication.

Azure AD can support OAuth 2.0 and OpenID Connect 1.0 very well. Azure API Management can also act as an API gateway in microservice implementation, and it provides nifty security features, such as policies.

Azure AD and Azure API Management provide quite a few powerful features so that we can monitor and log the requests that are received. This is quite useful, not only for security, but also for tracing and troubleshooting scenarios.

In the next chapter, we will look at logging, monitoring, and the overall instrumentation around troubleshooting microservices.

Questions

1. What is software security?
2. What are the security challenges of monolithic applications?
3. What is OAuth, and how would you use it?
4. What is an authorization server, and how does it work?
5. What is Azure API Management, and why do we need an API gateway for microservices?

Further reading

- *Azure for Architects – Second Edition* (https://www.packtpub.com/virtualization-and-cloud/azure-architects-second-edition)
- *Learn Microsoft Azure* (https://www.packtpub.com/virtualization-and-cloud/learn-microsoft-azure)

7
Monitoring Microservices

When something goes wrong in a system, stakeholders will want to know what has happened, why it has happened, any hint or clue you can give for how it might be fixed, and how to prevent the same problem from occurring again in the future. This is one of the primary uses of monitoring; however, monitoring can also do much more.

In .NET monoliths, there are multiple monitoring solutions available to choose from. The monitoring target is always centralized, and monitoring is certainly easy to set up and configure. If something breaks down, we know what to look for and where to look for it, since only a finite number of components participate in a system, and they have a fairly long lifespan.

However, microservices are distributed systems, and by nature, they are more complex than monoliths, so resource utilization and health and performance monitoring are quite essential in a microservice production environment. We can use this diagnostic piece of information to detect and correct issues, as well as to spot potential problems and then prevent them from occurring. Monitoring microservices presents different challenges.

In this chapter, we will discuss the following topics:

- The need for monitoring
- Monitoring and logging challenges in microservices
- Monitoring strategies
- Available tools and strategies for microservices in the .NET monitoring space
- Use of Azure Diagnostics and Application Insights
- A brief overview of the ELK stack and Splunk

What does monitoring really mean? There is no formal definition of monitoring; however, the following is appropriate:

> "Monitoring provides information around the behavior of an entire system, or different parts of a system in their operational environment. This information can be used for diagnosing and gaining insight into the different characteristics of a system."

Technical requirements

This chapter contains various code examples to explain the concepts that it describes. The code is kept simple and is just for demonstration purposes.

To run and execute the code, you'll need the following prerequisites:

- Visual Studio 2019
- .NET Core 3.1
- A valid Azure account

To install and run these code examples, you'll need to install Visual Studio 2019 (the preferred IDE). To do so, follow these steps:

1. Download Visual Studio 2019 (Community is free) from `https://docs.microsoft.com/en-us/visualstudio/install/install-visual-studio`.
2. Multiple versions of Visual Studio are available. Follow the installation instructions for your operating system. We are using Visual Studio for Windows.
3. Don't forget to install the Azure SDK (select **Azure development** from the **Workloads** tab):

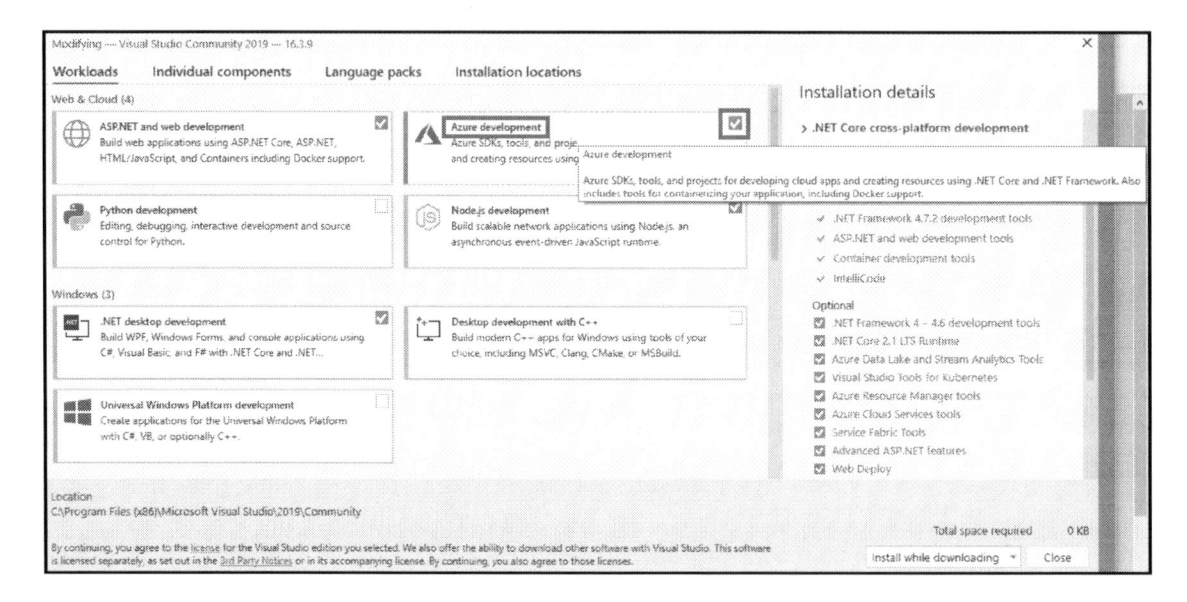

Setting up .NET Core 3.1

If you don't have .NET Core 3.1 installed, you can download it from https://dotnet.microsoft.com/download/dotnet-core/3.1.

A valid Azure account

You will need login credentials for the Azure portal. If you don't have an Azure account, you can create one for free at https://azure.microsoft.com/free/.

> The complete source code is available at https://github.com/PacktPublishing/Hands-On-Microservices-with-CSharp-8-and-.NET-Core-3-Third-Edition/tree/master/Chapter%2007.

Beginning with instrumentation and telemetry

A monitoring solution is dependent on instrumentation and telemetry. Therefore, it is only natural that, when we speak about monitoring microservices, we also discuss instrumentation and telemetry data. Application logs are nothing more than an instrumentation mechanism.

> There are two things related to monitoring that we may need to consider, while implementing this in a production-based application:
>
> **Information overload**: It is easy to go all-out and collect a lot of information, but you should make sure that the most important information is the most accessible information. One example is a Grafana-type (https://grafana.com/docs/features/panels/graph/) dashboard to verify things. It provides a value for operations, whereas detailed logging may help with forensics and advanced troubleshooting.
>
> **Alerting fatigue**: Don't set up alerts for everything—this just means that people will start ignoring the alerts. This is why, sometimes, too much information would be overkill.

Monitoring Microservices

These logs can only help us see the steps of the tasks at hand, but we can only capture the details, about every resource and action happening in the application, by the complete monitoring system.

We'll take a look at instrumentation and telemetry in more detail in the upcoming sections.

Instrumentation

Now, let's look at what instrumentation is. Instrumentation is one of the ways through which we can add diagnostic features to applications. It can be formally defined as follows:

> *"Most applications will include diagnostic features that generate custom monitoring and debugging information, especially when an error occurs. This is referred to as instrumentation and is usually implemented by adding event and error handling code to the application."*

> *– MSDN*

Under normal conditions, data from informational events may not be required, thereby reducing the cost of storage and the transactions that are required to collect it. However, when there is an issue with the application, you have to update the application configuration, so that the diagnostic and instrumentation systems can collect the event data. This event data may be informational, error messages, and/or warning messages that help fix the faults of the system.

Telemetry

Telemetry, in its most basic form, is the process of gathering information that's generated by instrumentation and logging systems. Typically, it is performed using asynchronous mechanisms that support massive scaling and the wide distribution of application services. It can be defined as follows:

> *"The process of gathering remote information that is collected by instrumentation is usually referred to as telemetry."*

> *– MSDN*

Usually, the information of highly complex systems is stored in such a way that it would be easily available, when it needs to be analyzed. The use of this information could be to understand the performance of the system, change detection, or any fault detection.

There is no built-in support/system available in the Azure cloud that can provide telemetry and reporting systems. However, we can get such systems with the help of Azure Diagnostics and Application Insights. Azure Application Insights permits us to collect telemetry data and monitoring mechanisms.

Telemetry provides data so that we can analyze the information at hand and correct the fault, or analyze the changes, in the system.

This section was all about telemetry. We can also use monitoring to detect changes in our system. We will discuss this in the next section.

The need for monitoring

Microservices are complex, distributed systems. Microservice implementation is the backbone of any modern IT business. Understanding the internals of the services, along with their interactions and behaviors, will help you make the overall business more flexible and agile. The performance, availability, scale, and security of microservices can directly affect businesses, as well as their revenue, and so monitoring microservices is vital. It helps us observe and manage the quality of the service attributes.

Let's discuss the scenarios in which it is required.

Health monitoring

With health monitoring, we monitor the health of a system and its various components at a certain frequency—typically, this is a few seconds. This ensures that the system and its components behave as expected. With the help of an exhaustive health monitoring system, we can keep tabs on the overall system health, including the CPU, memory utilization, and so on. This may be in the form of pings or extensive health monitoring endpoints, which emit the health status of services, along with some useful metadata from a particular point in time.

The metrics for health monitoring are based on the threshold values of success or failure rates. If the parameter value goes beyond the configured threshold, an alert is triggered. It is quite possible that some preventive action to maintain the health of the system will be triggered because of this failure. For example, this action could be restarting the service in the failure state, or provisioning a server resource.

Availability monitoring

Availability monitoring is quite similar to health status monitoring. However, the subtle difference is that, in availability monitoring, the focus is on the availability of systems, rather than a snapshot of the health at that point in time.

The availability of systems is dependent on various factors, such as the overall nature and domain of the application, services, and service dependencies, as well as the infrastructure or environment. The availability monitoring system captures low-level data points that are related to these factors, and the system represents them, so as to make a business-level feature available. Often, availability monitoring parameters are used to track business metrics and **service-level agreements (SLAs)**.

SLA monitoring

Systems with SLAs basically guarantee certain characteristics, such as performance and availability. For cloud-based services, this is a pretty common scenario. Essentially, SLA monitoring is all about monitoring those guaranteed SLAs for the system. SLA monitoring is enforced as a contractual obligation, between a service provider and a consumer.

It is often defined on the basis of availability, response time, and throughput. The data points that are required for SLA monitoring can come from performance endpoint monitoring or logging, and the availability of monitoring parameters. For internal applications, many organizations track the number of incidences that have been raised because of server downtime. The action that's taken on the basis of these incidences' **root cause analysis (RCA)** mitigates the risk of repeating those issues, and it helps meet the SLAs.

For internal purposes, an organization may also track the number and nature of incidents that had caused the service to fail. Learning how to resolve these issues quickly, or how to eliminate them completely, helps reduce downtime and meet SLAs.

Performance monitoring

The performance of a system is often measured by key performance indicators. Some of the key performance indicators, of a large web-based system, are as follows:

- The number of requests served per hour
- The number of concurrent users served per hour
- The average processing time required by users to perform business transactions—for example, placing an order

Additionally, performance is also gauged by system-level parameters, such as the following:

- CPU utilization
- Memory utilization
- I/O rates
- Number of queued messages

If any of these key performance indicators are not met by the system, an alert is raised.

Often, while analyzing performance issues, historical data from benchmarks, which had been captured by the monitoring system previously, are used to troubleshoot the issues.

Security monitoring

Monitoring systems can detect unusual data pattern requests, unusual resource consumption patterns, and attacks on the system. Specifically in the case of DoS, attacks or injection attacks can be identified beforehand, and teams can be alerted. Security monitoring also keeps audit trails of authenticated users, and it keeps a history of users who have checked in and out of the system. It also comes in handy for satisfying compliance requirements.

Security is a cross-cutting concern of distributed systems, including microservices, so there are multiple ways of generating this data in the system. Security monitoring can get data from various tools that are not part of the system, but they may be part of the infrastructure or environment in which the system is hosted. Different types of logs and database entries can serve as data sources; however, this really depends on the nature of the system.

Auditing sensitive data and critical business transactions

For legal obligations or compliance reasons, the system may need to keep audit trails of user activities in the system, and it may need to record all their data accesses and modifications. Since audit information is highly sensitive in nature, it may be disclosed only to a few privileged and trusted individuals in the system. Audit trails can be part of a security subsystem or separately logged.

> Azure is certified for many regulatory specs. Sometimes, it still requires you to do additional work, and you should understand what you are trying to be compliant with. However, this becomes easier when Azure has something to build it on, than if you were to build your solution from scratch.

You may need to transfer and store audit trails in a specific format, as stated by the regulation or compliance specifications.

End user monitoring

In end user monitoring, the usage of the features of the system, and/or the overall system usage by end users, is tracked and logged. Usage monitoring can be done using various user-tracking parameters, such as the features used, the time required to complete a critical transaction for the specified user, or even enforced quotas. Enforced quotas are constraints or limits put on an end user, in regard to system usage. In general, various pay-as-you-go services use enforced quotas—for example, a free trial where you can upload files that are up to 25 MB in size. The data source for this type of monitoring is typically collected in terms of logs and of tracking user behavior.

Troubleshooting system failures

The end users of a system may experience system failures. This can be in the form of either a system failure or a situation where users are unable to perform a certain activity. These kinds of issues are monitored using system logs; if not, the end user will need to provide a detailed information report. Also, sometimes, server crash dumps or memory dumps can be immensely helpful. However, in the case of distributed systems, it will be a bit difficult to understand the exact root cause of the failures.

In many monitoring scenarios, using only one monitoring technique is not effective. It is better to use multiple monitoring techniques and tools for diagnostics. In particular, monitoring a distributed system is quite challenging, and it requires data from various sources. In addition to analyzing the situation properly and deciding on the action points, we must consider a holistic view of monitoring, rather than looking into only one type of system perspective.

Now that we have a better idea about what needs to be done for general-purpose monitoring, let's revisit the microservice perspective. In the next section, we will discuss the different monitoring challenges that are presented by the microservice architectural style.

Understanding the monitoring challenges

Microservice monitoring presents different challenges. There will be scenarios where one service could depend upon another service, or a client sends a request to one service, and the response comes from another service that would make the operation complex. Scaling a microservice would be a challenging task here. Similarly, process implementation, let's say, DevOps, would be a challenging job, while implementing a huge enterprise microservice application. We'll discuss these challenges in this section.

Scaling issues

One service could be dependent on the functionality that's provided by various other microservices. This causes complexity, which isn't typical in the case of .NET monolith systems. Instrumenting all these dependencies is quite difficult. Another problem that comes along with scale, is the rate of change. With the advancement of continuous deployment and container-based microservices, the code is always in a deployable state. Containers only live for minutes, if not seconds.

> It is worth noting that containers can indeed be short-lived, so this issue doesn't always apply in the case of **virtual machines** (**VMs**). Apart from the fact that it usually takes a couple of minutes just to spin up a VM, it is generally longer lived than containers.

The same is true for virtual machines (but not always). Virtual machines have a life of around a couple of minutes to a couple of hours.

In such a case, measuring regular signals, such as CPU usage and memory consumption usage per minute, doesn't make sense. Sometimes, container instances may not even be alive for a minute; within a minute, the container instance may have already been disposed of. This is one of the challenges of microservice monitoring.

DevOps mindset

Traditionally, services or systems, once deployed, are owned and cared for by the operational teams. However, DevOps breaks down the silos between developers and operations teams. It comes with lots of practices, such as continuous integration and continuous delivery, as well as continuous monitoring. Along with these new practices, come new toolsets.

However, DevOps is not just a set of practices or tools; more importantly, it's a mindset. It is always a difficult and slow process to change the mindset of people. Microservice monitoring requires such a shift in mindset.

With the emergence of the autonomy of services, developer teams now have to own services. This also means that they have to work through and fix development issues, as well as to keep an eye on all the operational parameters and SLAs of the services. Development teams will not be transformed overnight just by using state-of-the-art monitoring tools. This is true for operational teams as well. They won't suddenly become *core platform teams* (or whatever fancy name you prefer) overnight.

To make microservices successful and meaningful for organizations, developers, and operations, teams need to help each other understand their own pain points and also think in the same direction—that is, how they can deliver value to the business together. Monitoring cannot happen without the instrumentation of services, which is where developer teams can help. Likewise, alerting and the setting up of operational metrics, won't happen without the operational team's help. This is one of the challenges in delivering microservice monitoring solutions.

Data flow visualization

There are a number of tools present on the market for data flow visualization. Some of them are AppDynamics, New Relic, and so on. These tools are capable of handling visualizations of tens to, maybe, hundreds of microservices. However, in larger settings, where there are thousands of microservices, these tools are unable to handle visualizations. This is one of the challenges in microservice monitoring.

Testing monitoring tools

We trust monitoring tools, with the understanding that they depict a factual representation of the big picture of our microservice implementation. However, to make sure that they remain true to this understanding, we will have to test the monitoring tools. This is never a challenge in monolith implementations; however, when it comes to microservices, the visualization of microservices is required for monitoring purposes. This means that we must spend time generating fake/synthetic transactions, and then we utilize the entire infrastructure, rather than just serving the customer.

Hence, testing monitoring tools is a costly affair, and it presents a significant challenge in microservice monitoring. In the next section, we will discuss monitoring strategies.

Working on monitoring strategies

In this section, we will take a look at the monitoring strategies that make microservices observable. It is common to implement the following (as well as other) strategies to create a well-defined and holistic monitoring solution, so that we can monitor the system, fix the various faults, and more.

Application/system monitoring

Application/system monitoring is also called a **framework-based strategy**. Here, the application, or in our case, the microservice, itself generates the monitoring information, within the given context of execution. The application can be dynamically configured, based on the thresholds or trigger points in the application data, which can generate tracing statements. It is also possible to have a probe-based framework (such as .NET CLR, which provides hooks to gather more information), to generate the monitoring data. So, effective instrumentation points can be embedded into the application, in order to facilitate this kind of monitoring. On top of this, the underlying infrastructure, where microservices are hosted, can also raise critical events. These events can be listened to and recorded by the monitoring agents, which are present on the same host as that of the application.

Real user monitoring

Real user monitoring is based on a real end user's transactional flow across the system. While the end user is using the system in real time, this strategy can be used to capture the parameters related to response time and latency, as well as the number of errors experienced by the user.

This is useful for specific troubleshooting and issue resolution. With this strategy, the system's hotspots and bottlenecks for service interactions can be captured as well. It is possible to record the entire end-to-end user flow or transactions, so that we can replay it at a later time. The benefits of this are that these kinds of recorded plays can be used for troubleshooting issues, as well as for various types of testing purposes.

Semantic monitoring and synthetic transactions

The semantic monitoring strategy focuses on business transactions; however, it is implemented through the use of synthetic transactions. In semantic monitoring, as the name suggests, we try to emulate end user flows. However, this is done in a controlled fashion and with dummy data, so that we can differentiate the output of the flow from the actual end user flow data. This strategy is typically used for service dependency, health checking, and diagnosing problems that are occurring across the system. To implement synthetic transactions, we need to be careful while planning the flow. We also need to be careful enough not to stress the system out—for example, creating fake orders for fake product catalogs and observing the response time and output, across the whole transaction that's propagating in the system.

Profiling

The profiling approach is specifically focused on solving performance bottlenecks across the system. This approach is different from the preceding approaches. Real and semantic monitoring focus on business transactions, or functional aspects of the system, and it collects the relevant data. Profiling is all about system-level or low-level information capture. A few of these parameters are response time, memory, and threads.

This approach uses a probing technique in the application code or framework, and it collects data. By utilizing the data points that are captured during profiling, the relevant DevOps team can identify the cause of the performance problem. Profiling using probing should be avoided in production environments. However, it is perfectly fine for generating call times and so on, without overloading the system at runtime. A good example of profiling, in general, is an ASP.NET MVC application profiled with an ASP.NET MiniProfiler, or even with Glimpse.

Endpoint monitoring

With this approach, we expose one or more endpoints of a service to emit diagnostic information related to the service itself, as well as the infrastructure parameters. Generally, different endpoints focus on providing different information. For example, one endpoint can give the health status of the service, while the other could provide the HTTP 500 error information that occurred in that service execution. This is a very helpful technique for microservices, since it inherently changes the monitoring from being a push model to a pull model, and it reduces the overhead of service monitoring. We can scrap/discard data from these endpoints at a certain time interval, and then build a dashboard and collect data for operational metrics.

> An important point about endpoint monitoring is to test where your users are. If most of the end users are in Asia, there is less value in testing from North America than testing a bit closer to home. This, of course, brings in the fact that endpoint monitoring can be both for general "everything works" checks, and also things such as latency and response times.

Working on the various monitoring strategies allows us to monitor a system in such a way that we can fix any fault, analyze the various informational data, and more. Logging will add more value when we analyze the system. In the next section, we will explain the concept of logging.

Understanding logging

Logging is a type of instrumentation that's made available by the system, its various components, or the infrastructure layer. Logging is a way to gather certain or relevant data that pertains to the system. This data is also known as logs. Logs can be of any type or as per the requirements—for example, information logs, error logs, and warning logs. Sometimes, logs may be custom logs. With the help of these logs, we can analyze the faults, crashes, or processes of any task that is performed by our system. This analysis helps us fix the problems in the system.

In this section, we will look at the challenges of logging and then discuss some strategies to reach a solution for these challenges.

Logging challenges

First, we will try to understand the problems with log management in microservices. A couple of these are as follows:

- To log the information related to a system event and parameter, as well as the infrastructure state, we will need to persist log files. In traditional .NET monoliths, log files are kept on the same machine that the application is deployed on. In the case of microservices, they are hosted either on virtual machines or containers. However, virtual machines and containers are both ephemeral, which means they do not persist states. In this situation, if we persist log files with virtual machines or containers, we will lose them. This is one of the challenges of log management in microservices.
- In the microservice architecture, there are a number of services that constitute a transaction. Let's say that we have an order placement transaction where service A, service B, and service C take part in the transaction. If, say, service B fails during the transaction, how are we going to understand and capture this failure in the logs? Not only that, but more importantly, how are we going to understand that a specific instance of service B has failed, and it was taking part in the transaction? This scenario presents another challenge for microservices.

Now that we know about the challenges, let's move on and learn about a few strategies when it comes to logging.

Logging strategies

So far in this section, we have discussed logging, its challenges, and why we should implement logging. Multiple calls at the same time are possible, so when we implement logging, we should implement it in such a way that we know the exact source of the logged transaction. We would go with the correlation ID for logging.

> **TIP**: Logging is not only used in microservices specifically; it is also important for monolithic applications.

To implement logging in microservices, we can use the logging strategies that we'll discuss in the following sections.

Centralized logging

There is a difference between centralized logging and centralized monitoring. In centralized logging, we log all the details about the events that occur in our system—they may be errors or warnings or just for informational purposes—whereas in centralized monitoring, we monitor critical parameters—that is, specific information.

With logs, we can understand what has actually happened in the system or with a specific transaction. We will have all the details about the specific transaction, such as why it started, who triggered it, what kind of data or resources it recorded, and so on. In a complex distributed system, such as microservices, this is really the key piece of information that we can use to solve the entire puzzle of the information flow or errors. We also need to treat timeouts, exceptions, and errors as events that we need to log.

The information we record, regarding a specific event, should also be structured, and this structure should be consistent across our system. Here, we would have the following:

- Our structured log entry could contain level-based information to state whether the log entry is for information, an error, or whether it's debugged information or statistics that have been recorded as log entry events.
- The structured log entry must also have a date and time, so that we know when the event happened. We should also include the hostname within our structured log, so that we know where exactly the log entry came from.

- We should also include the service name and the service instance, so that we know exactly which microservice made the log entry.
- Finally, we should also include a message in our structured logging format, which is the key piece of information associated with the event.

For example, for an error, this might be the call stack or details regarding the exception. The key thing is that we keep our structured logging format consistent. A consistent format will allow us to query the logging information. Then, we can basically search for specific patterns and issues, by using our centralized logging tool. Another key aspect of centralized logging, within a microservice architecture, is to make distributed transactions more traceable.

Using a correlation ID in logging

A correlation ID is a unique ID that is assigned to every transaction. So when a transaction becomes distributed across multiple services, we can follow that transaction across different services, by using the logging information. The correlation ID is basically passed from service to service. All the services, that process that specific transaction, will receive the correlation ID and pass it to the next service, and so on, so that they can log any events associated with that transaction to our centralized logs. This helps us hugely, when we have to visualize and understand what has happened with this transaction across different microservices.

Semantic logging

Event Tracing for Windows (**ETW**) is a structural logging mechanism, where you can store a structured payload with the log entry. This information is generated by event listeners, and it may include typed metadata about the event. This is merely an example of semantic logging. Semantic logging passes additional data, along with the log entry, so that the processing system can get the context structured around the event. This is why semantic logging is also referred to as structured logging or typed logging.

As an example, an event that indicates that an order was placed, can generate a log entry that contains the number of items as an integer value, the total value as a decimal number, the customer identifier as a long value, and the city that the delivery will take place in as a string value. An order monitoring system can read the payload and can easily extract the individual values. ETW is a standard, shipped feature with Windows.

In the Azure cloud, it is possible to get your log data source from ETW. The Semantic Logging Application Block is one of the best frameworks and makes comprehensive logging easier. It allows you to write the event to destinations of your choice, such as the disk file, databases, email messages, and so on. The Semantic Logging Application Block can also be used in Azure applications.

This section focused on understanding logging, as well as the challenges of logging and logging strategies. We also highlighted the importance of semantic logging.

Monitoring is important, when it comes to logging. In the next section, we will discuss monitoring in the Azure cloud.

Monitoring on Azure

There is no single, off-the-shelf solution or offering in Azure—or for that matter, any cloud provider—to the monitoring challenges presented by microservices. Interestingly enough, there are not too many open source tools available that can work with .NET-based microservices.

We are utilizing Microsoft Azure Cloud and cloud services to build our microservices, so it is useful to look for the monitoring capabilities it comes with. If you are looking to manage approximately a couple of hundred microservices, you can utilize a custom monitoring solution (mostly interweaving PowerShell scripts), based on a Microsoft Azure-based solution.

We will be primarily focusing on the following logging and monitoring solutions:

- **Microsoft Azure Diagnostics**: This helps in collecting and analyzing resources through resource and activity logs.
- **Application Insights**: This helps in collecting all of the telemetry data about our microservices, and it helps analyze the data. This is a framework-based approach for monitoring.
- **Log Analytics**: Log Analytics analyzes and displays data, and it provides a scalable querying capability over the collected logs.

Let's look at these solutions from a different perspective. This perspective will help us visualize our Azure-based microservice monitoring solution. A microservice is composed of the following:

- **Infrastructure layer**: A virtual machine or an application container (for example, a Docker container)
- **Application stack layer**: Consists of the operating system, .NET CLR, and the microservice application code

Each of these layer components can be monitored as follows:

- **Virtual machine**: Using Azure Diagnostics Logs
- **Docker container**: Using container logs and Application Insights, or a third-party container monitoring solution, such as cAdvisor, Prometheus, or Sensu
- **Windows operating system**: Using Azure Diagnostics Logs and Activity Logs
- **A microservice application**: Using Application Insights
- **Data visualization and metric monitoring**: Using Log Analytics or third-party solutions, such as Splunk or ELK stack

Various Azure services come with an activity ID in their log entries. This activity ID is a unique GUID that's assigned for each request, which can be utilized as a correlation ID during log analysis.

Let's move on and learn about Azure Diagnostics.

Microsoft Azure Diagnostics

Azure Diagnostics logs give us the ability to collect diagnostic data for a deployed microservice. We can also use a diagnostic extension to collect data from various sources. Azure Diagnostics is supported by web and worker roles, Azure Virtual Machines, and the Azure app service. Other Azure services have their own separate diagnostics tools.

Enabling Azure Diagnostics logs and exploring the various settings is easy, and it's available as a toggle switch.

Azure Diagnostics can collect data from the following sources:

- Performance counters
- Application logs
- Windows event logs
- .NET event sources
- IIS logs
- Manifest-based ETWs
- Crash dumps
- Custom error logs
- Azure diagnostic infrastructure logs

Let's move on and look at Azure storage.

Storing diagnostic data using Azure storage

Azure Diagnostics logs are not stored permanently. They are rollover logs—that is, they are overwritten by newer ones. So, if we want to use them for any analysis work, we have to store them. Azure Diagnostics logs can be either stored in a filesystem or transferred via FTP; better still, they can be stored in an Azure storage container.

There are different ways to specify an Azure storage container for diagnostics data, for the specified Azure resource (in our case, microservices hosted on the Azure app service). These are as follows:

- CLI tools
- PowerShell
- Azure Resource Manager
- Visual Studio 2019
- Azure portal – we can directly create the Azure storage container from the Azure portal

In the next section, we will learn how to use and create an Azure storage container from the Azure portal.

Monitoring Microservices

Using the Azure portal

The following screenshot depicts the Azure storage container that we've provisioned through the Azure portal:

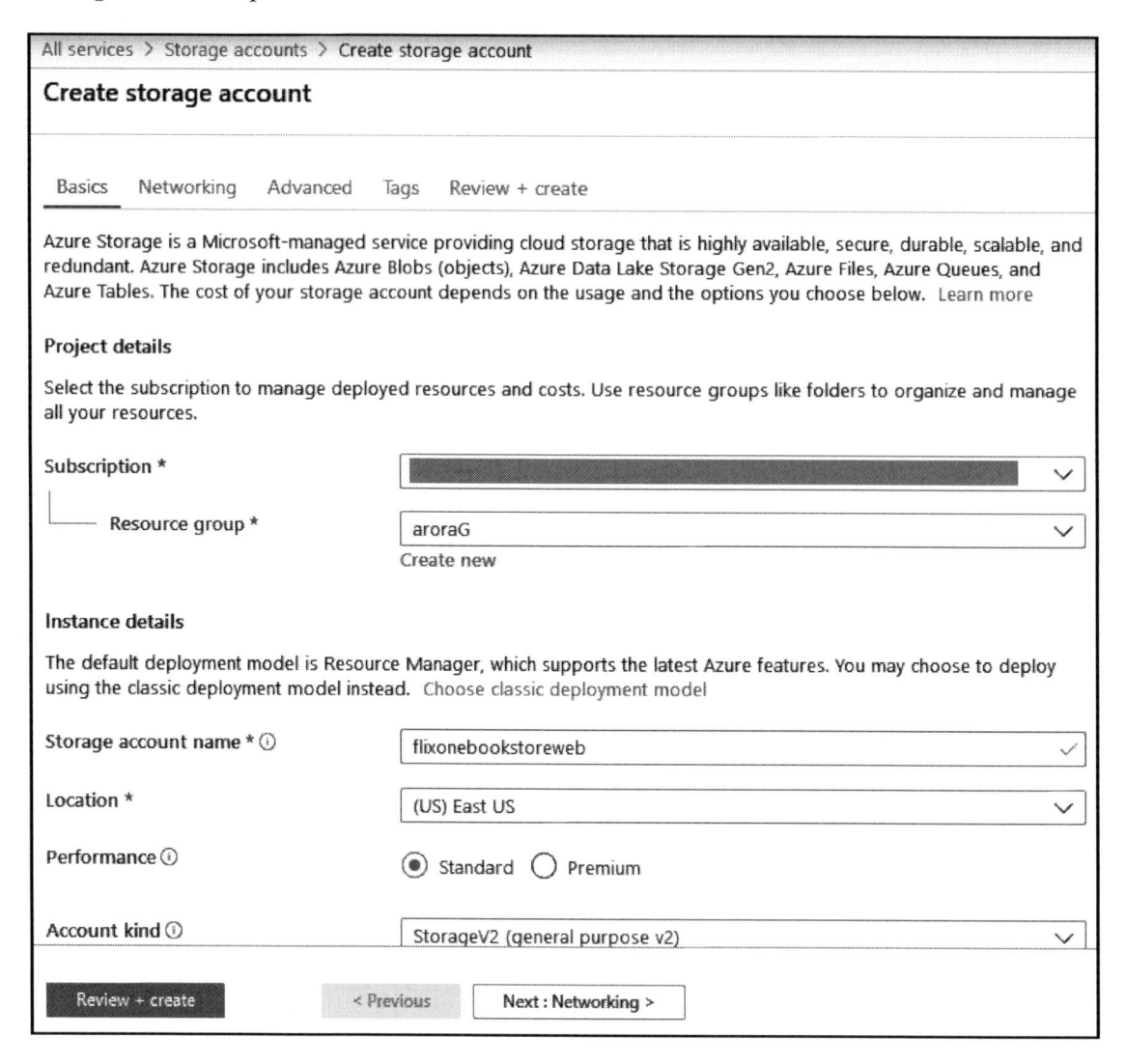

All services > Storage accounts > Create storage account

Create storage account

Basics   Networking   Advanced   Tags   Review + create

Azure Storage is a Microsoft-managed service providing cloud storage that is highly available, secure, durable, scalable, and redundant. Azure Storage includes Azure Blobs (objects), Azure Data Lake Storage Gen2, Azure Files, Azure Queues, and Azure Tables. The cost of your storage account depends on the usage and the options you choose below. Learn more

Project details

Select the subscription to manage deployed resources and costs. Use resource groups like folders to organize and manage all your resources.

Subscription *   [   ]

　　Resource group *   aroraG
　　　　　　　　　　　Create new

Instance details

The default deployment model is Resource Manager, which supports the latest Azure features. You may choose to deploy using the classic deployment model instead. Choose classic deployment model

Storage account name *   flixonebookstoreweb

Location *   (US) East US

Performance   ● Standard   ○ Premium

Account kind   StorageV2 (general purpose v2)

Review + create   < Previous   Next : Networking >

[258]

Defining an Azure storage account

We can also store diagnostic data, using an Azure storage account. To do so, we need to define a storage account, by using the Azure portal (http://portal.azure.com/), and we can also define the storage account in the ServiceConfiguration.cscfg file. This is convenient since, during development time, you can specify the storage account. It is also possible to specify different storage accounts during development and during production.

> **TIP**
> The Azure storage account can also be configured as one of the dynamic environment variables during the deployment process.

The information in the Azure storage account can be added as a configuration setting that can be used by fetching the information from the configuration settings. For our example, we are using Visual Studio. The following code shows the default connection string of a new microservice project:

```
<ConfigurationSettings>
   <Setting name="Microsoft.WindowsAzure.Plugins.
   Diagnostics.ConnectionString" value="UseDevelopmentStorage=true" />
</span></ConfigurationSettings>
```

The preceding connection string may be different for you or may need to be changed to match the information of your Azure storage account.

Now, let's learn how Azure storage stores the diagnostic data. All the log entries are stored in either a blob or table storage container. The storage you want to use can be specified while you create and associate the Azure storage container.

Azure storage schema for diagnostic data

The structure of Azure table storage for storing diagnostic data is as follows, for data stored in tables:

- **WadLogsTable**: This table stores the log statements that are written during code execution, by using the trace listener.
- **WADDiagnosticInfrastructureLogsTable**: This table specifies the diagnostic monitor and configuration changes.

Monitoring Microservices

- `WADDirectoriesTable`: This table contains the folders that are being monitored, and it includes various relevant pieces of information—for example, IIS logs, IIS-failed request logs, and so on.

> To get the location of this blob log file, you need to check the container field, the `RelativePath` field, or the `AbsolutePath` field, where the `RelativePath` field contains the name of the blob, and the `AbsolutePath` field contains both the location and the name.

- `WADPerformanceCountersTable`: This table contains data related to the configured performance counters.
- `WADWindowsEventLogsTable`: This table contains the Windows event tracing log entries.

For a blob storage container, the diagnostic storage schema is as follows:

- `wad-control-container`: If you are still using legacy code or a previous version, such as SDK 2.4 and previous versions, then this one is for you. It controls diagnostics, by using XML configuration files.
- `wad-iis-failedreqlogfiles`: This contains information from the IIS-failed request logs.
- `wad-iis-logfiles`: This contains information about IIS logs.
- `custom`: Sometimes, we need a custom Azure storage container. These containers are configured for directories that are being monitored. `WADDirectoriesTable` contains the name of this custom container.

An interesting fact to note here is that the WAD suffix, which can be seen on these container tables or blobs, comes from Microsoft Azure Diagnostics' previous product name, which is Windows Azure Diagnostics.

> **TIP**: A quick way to view the diagnostic data is with the help of Cloud Explorer. Cloud Explorer is available from Visual Studio (if you have installed the SDK).

This section described how your choice of storage can be specified while you create and associate the Azure storage container. We learned how to create a storage account, and how to capture the data. In the next section, we will discuss Application Insights.

Introduction to Application Insights

Application Insights is an **application performance management** (**APM**) offering from Microsoft. It is a feature set of the Azure Monitor service. It is a useful service offering for monitoring the performance of .NET-based microservices. It is useful for understanding the internal, operational behavior of individual microservices. Instead of just focusing on detecting and diagnosing issues, it will tune the service performance and understand the performance characteristics of your microservice.

It is an example of the framework-based approach to monitoring. What this means is that, during the development of a microservice, we will add the Application Insights package to the Visual Studio solution of our microservice. This is how Application Insights instruments your microservice for telemetry data. This may not always be an ideal approach for every microservice. However, it comes in handy if you haven't given any good, thorough thought to monitoring your microservices. This way, monitoring comes out of the box with your service.

With the help of Application Insights, you can collect and analyze the following types of telemetry data:

- HTTP request rates, response times, and success rates
- Dependency (HTTP and SQL) call rates, response times, and success rates
- Exception traces from both the server and client
- Diagnostic log traces
- Page view counts, user and session counts, browser load times, and exceptions
- AJAX call rates, response times, and success rates
- Server performance counters
- Custom client and server telemetry
- Segmentation by client location, browser version, OS version, server instance, custom dimensions, and more
- Availability tests

Along with the preceding types, there are associated diagnostic and analytics tools, which are available for alerting and monitoring with various different customizable metrics. With its own query language and customizable dashboards, Application Insights forms a good monitoring solution for microservices.

Next, we will implement Application Insights to our existing FlixOne application.

Monitoring our FlixOne application

In the previous section, we discussed monitoring telemetry, which provides us with data that we can analyze. It helps us monitor the health of the solution. In this section, we will add Application Insights to our FlixOne application.

> For this code example, you'll need to have a valid Azure account. Refer to the previous *Technical requirements* section for a list of prerequisites.

To implement Application Insights for our application, we need a valid instrumentation key. To get this key, we need to set up the Application Insights resource. Follow these steps to create the resource:

1. Log in to the Azure portal, using your credentials.
2. Search for **Application Insights**, and then click **Application Insights** from the search results list:

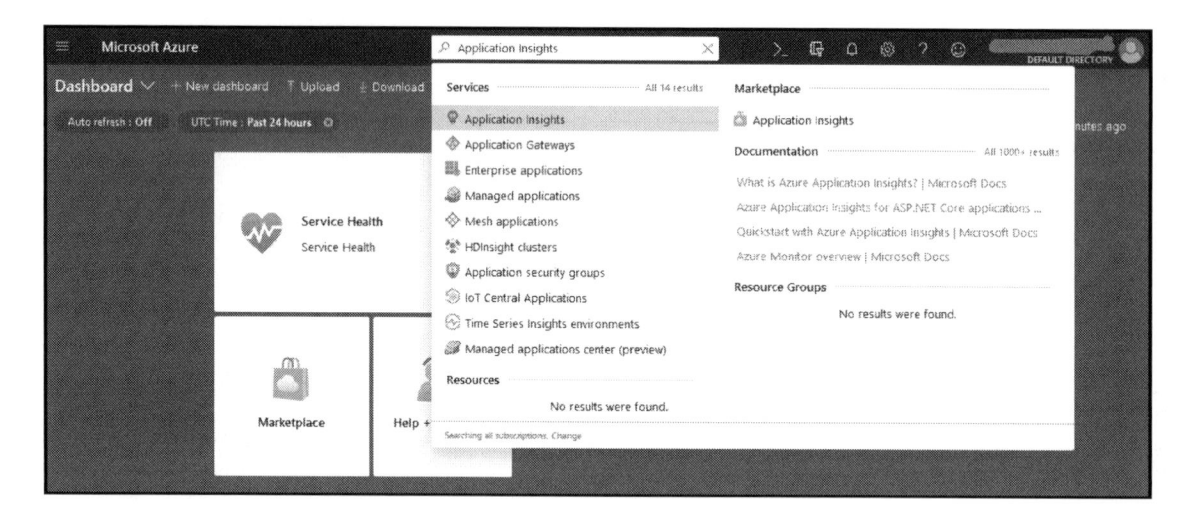

Chapter 7

3. From the **Application Insights** screens, click **Create Application Insights apps**, as shown in the following screenshot:

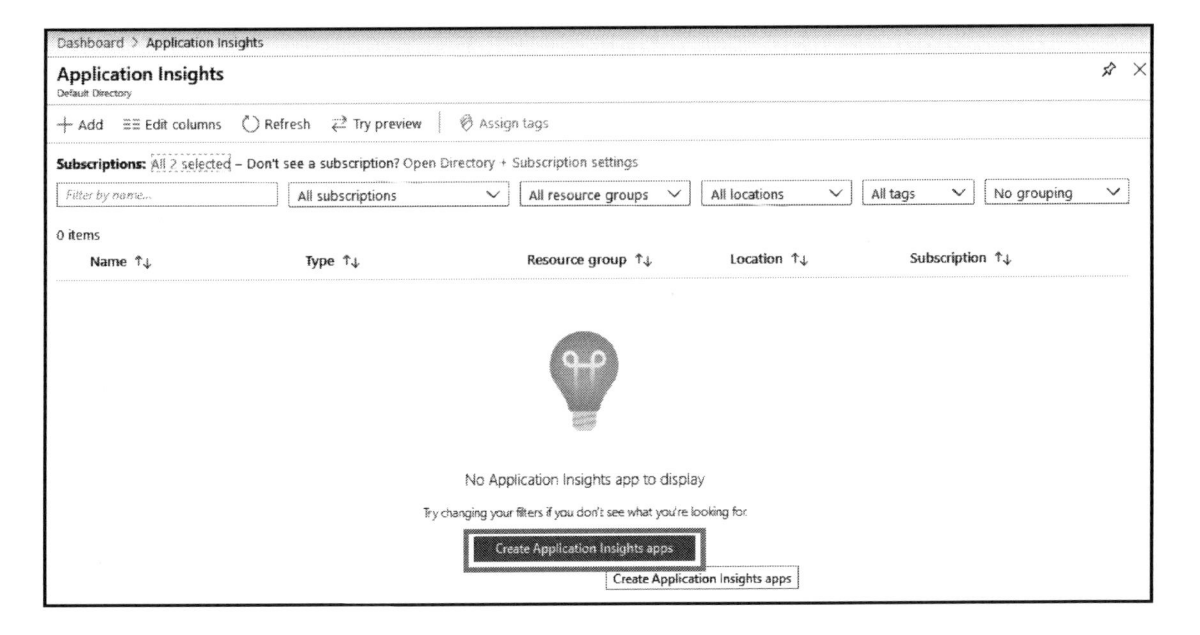

Monitoring Microservices

4. Now, provide all the required values, and then click **Review + create**, as follows:

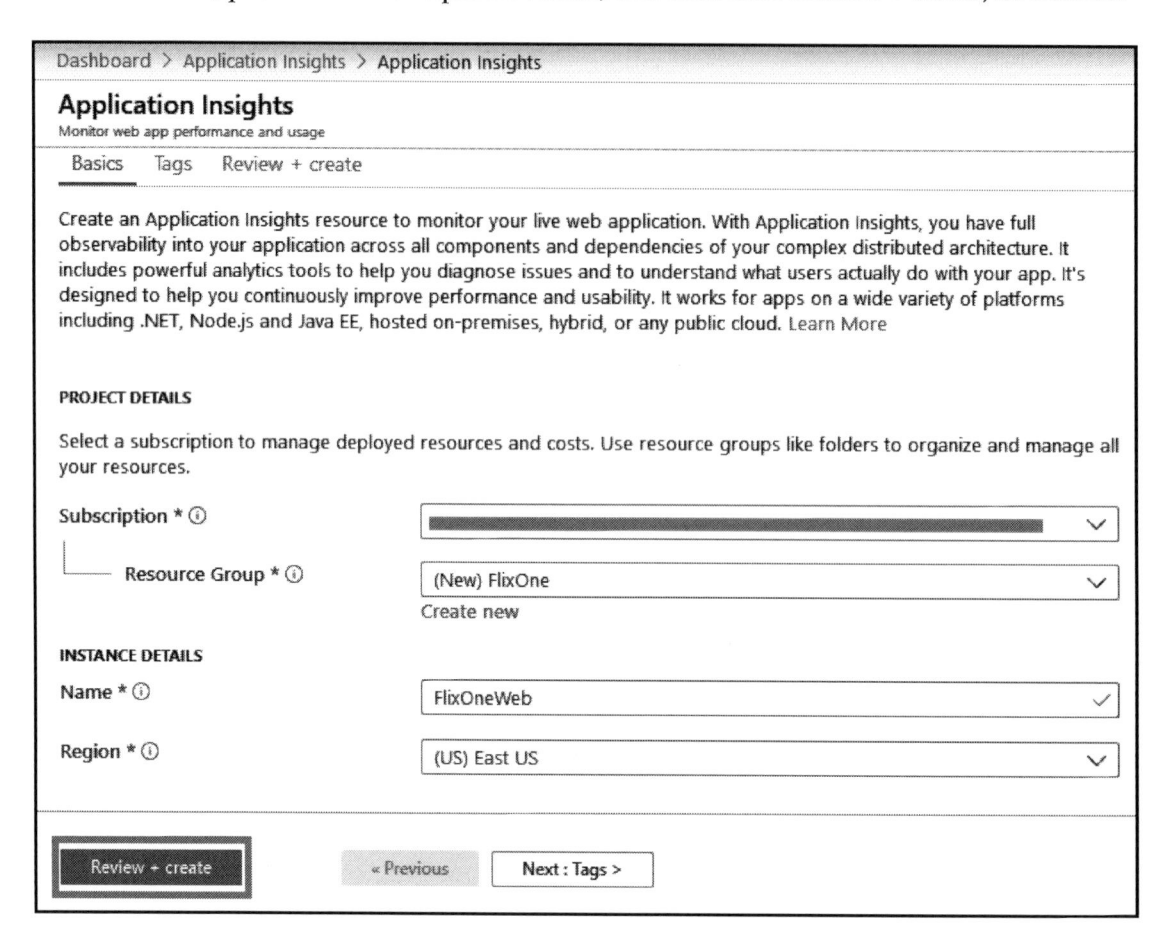

> Dashboard > Application Insights > Application Insights
>
> **Application Insights**
> Monitor web app performance and usage
>
> Basics   Tags   Review + create
>
> Create an Application Insights resource to monitor your live web application. With Application Insights, you have full observability into your application across all components and dependencies of your complex distributed architecture. It includes powerful analytics tools to help you diagnose issues and to understand what users actually do with your app. It's designed to help you continuously improve performance and usability. It works for apps on a wide variety of platforms including .NET, Node.js and Java EE, hosted on-premises, hybrid, or any public cloud. Learn More
>
> **PROJECT DETAILS**
>
> Select a subscription to manage deployed resources and costs. Use resource groups like folders to organize and manage all your resources.
>
> Subscription *
>
>   Resource Group *   (New) FlixOne
>   Create new
>
> **INSTANCE DETAILS**
>
> Name *   FlixOneWeb
>
> Region *   (US) East US
>
> [Review + create]   « Previous   Next : Tags >

Here, we have created a new resource group, called **FlixOne**, and we provided an instance name—namely, **FlixOneWeb**—for the **(US) East US** region.

5. On the next screen, review your inputs, and then click **Create**, as shown in the following screenshot:

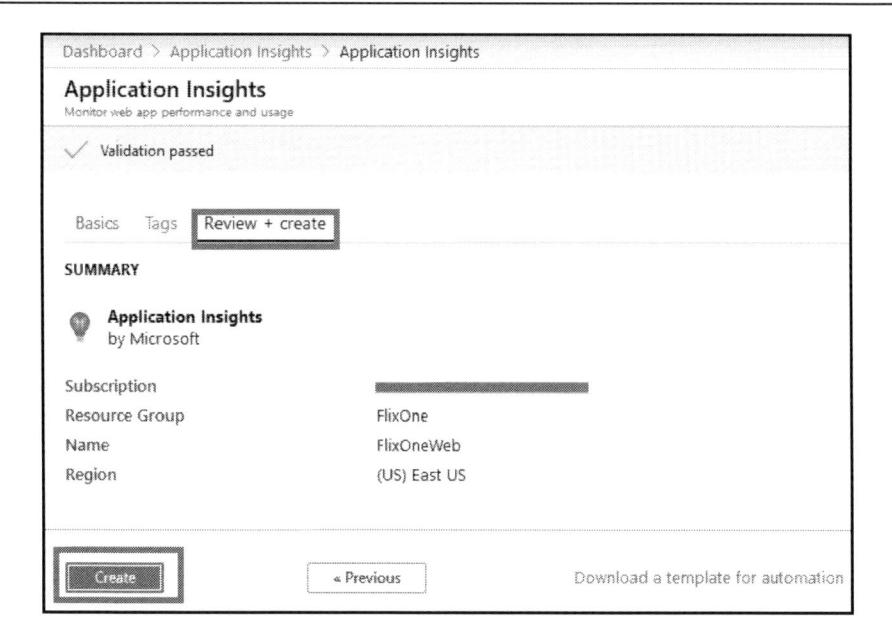

[Screenshot: Application Insights Review + create page showing Validation passed, Summary with Subscription, Resource Group: FlixOne, Name: FlixOneWeb, Region: (US) East US, and a Create button.]

> **TIP**
> For automation purposes, you can also download a template of your Application Insights. We've created a template already (`template.zip`). It can be found in the `Chapter07` folder of this book's code repository.

6. Upon the successful creation of your Application Insights instance, you will need to click **Go To Resource**. Afterward, you should see the following screen:

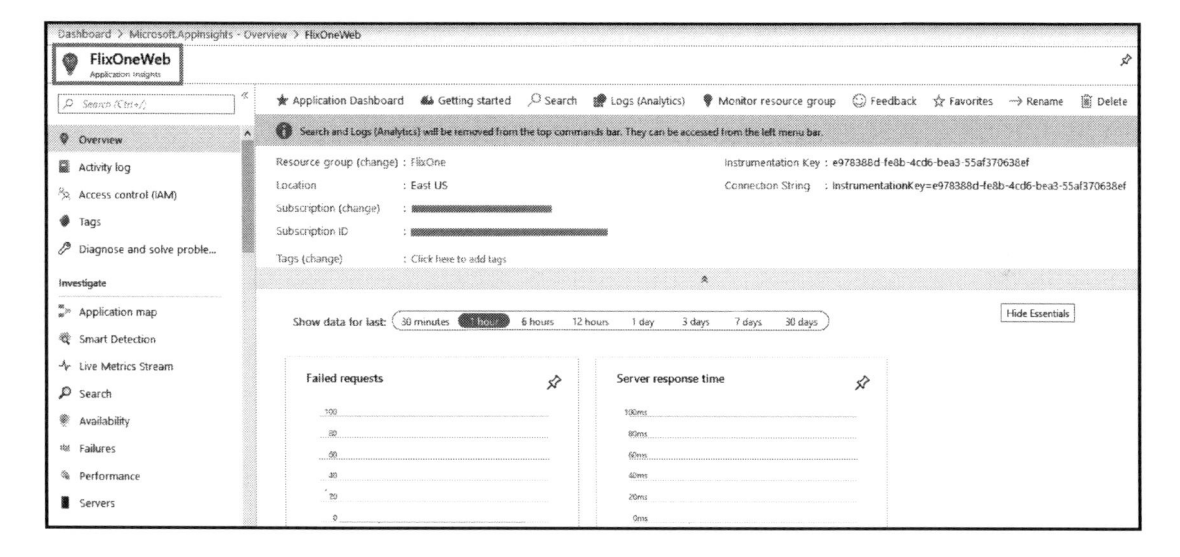

[Screenshot: FlixOneWeb Application Insights Overview page showing resource group FlixOne, Location East US, Instrumentation Key e978388d-fe8b-4cd6-bea3-55af370638ef, and left-side menu with Overview, Activity log, Access control (IAM), Tags, Diagnose and solve problems, Application map, Smart Detection, Live Metrics Stream, Search, Availability, Failures, Performance, Servers. Charts show Failed requests and Server response time.]

Monitoring Microservices

7. To get started with our code example, we've created an ASP.NET Core web application, using Visual Studio 2019. We are skipping the steps for creating the application, because we discussed these steps in the previous chapter.
8. Add the Application Insights SDK to your project from **Project | Add Application Insights Telemetry**, and then add the telemetry to the **FlixOne.BookStore.Web** project:

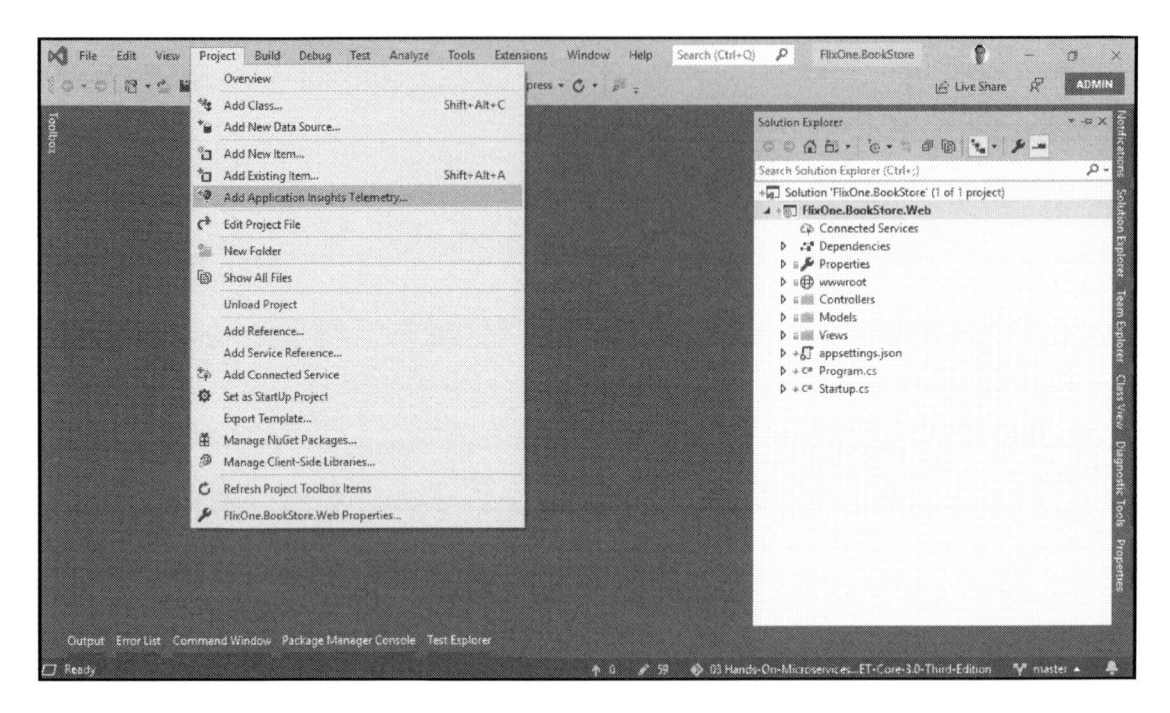

9. Now, you will see the **Get Started** page; click **Get Started**:

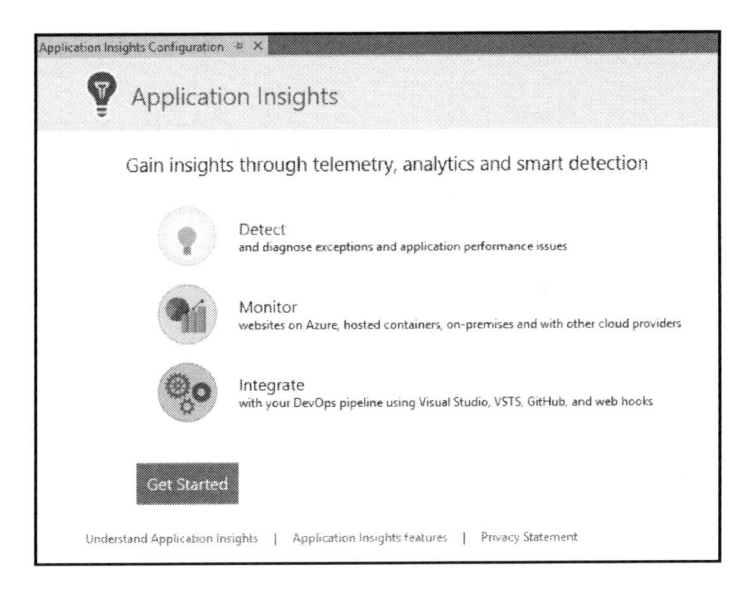

10. Register your app with **Application Insights**, by providing the correct values and clicking **Register**:

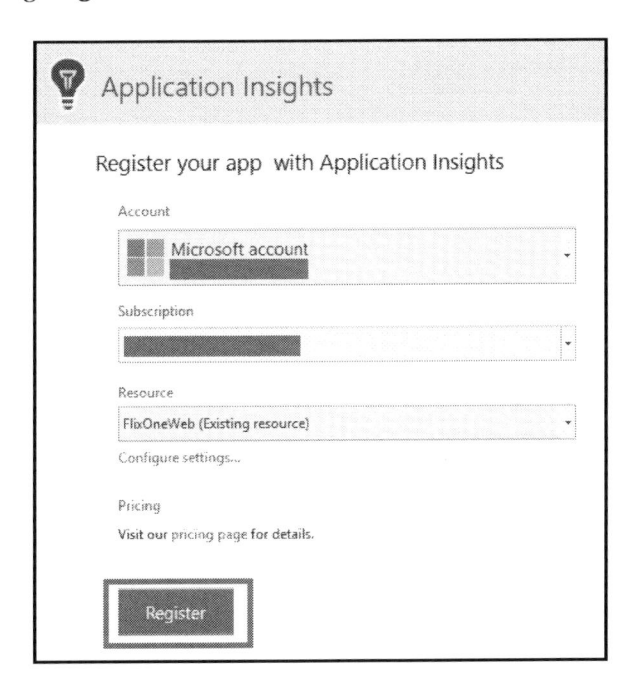

Monitoring Microservices

11. You should see the following progress screen:

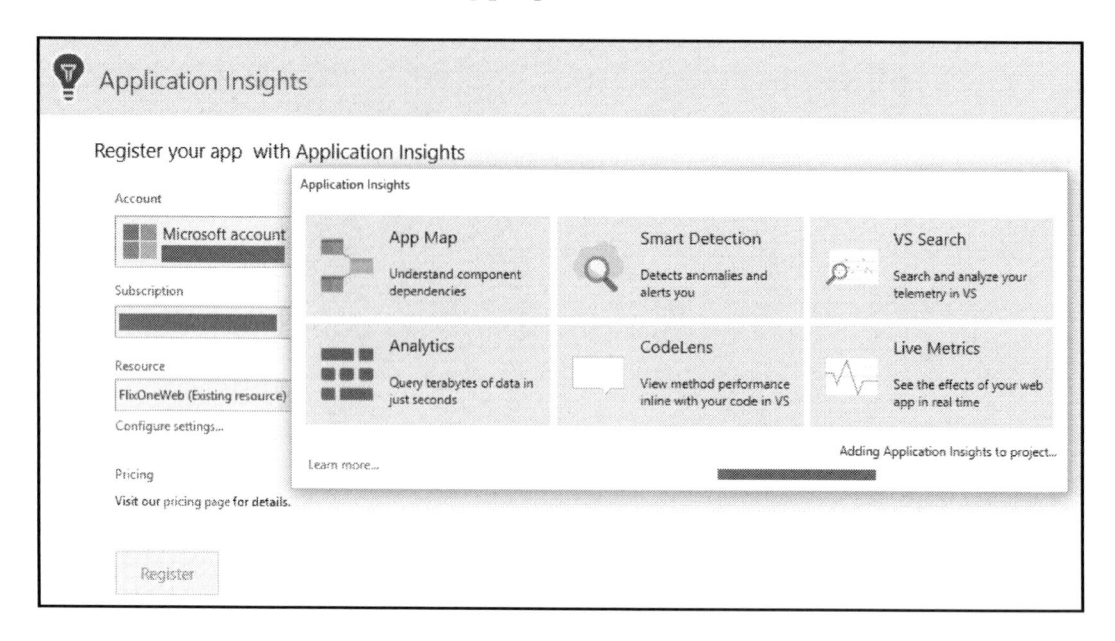

12. The following is the final screen, after completing the configuration process:

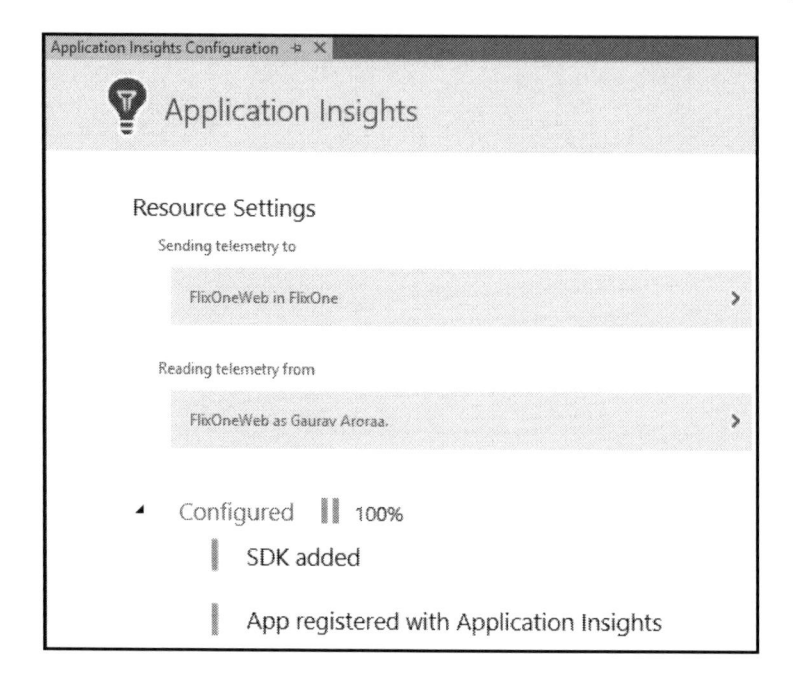

[268]

Chapter 7

13. Now, open Solution Explorer from Visual Studio. You will notice that a new package and some connected services have been added to the project:

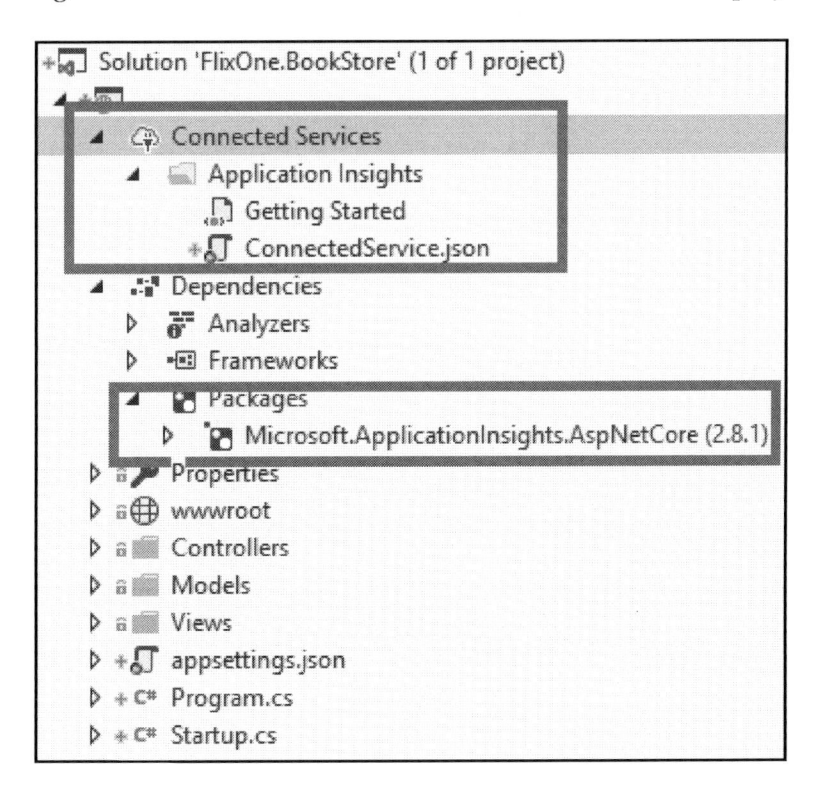

Monitoring Microservices

14. Now, run the application, and then click on the default pages (note that all the pages from the ASP.NET Core web application template are default pages). Here is the **Diagnostics Tools** window from Visual Studio:

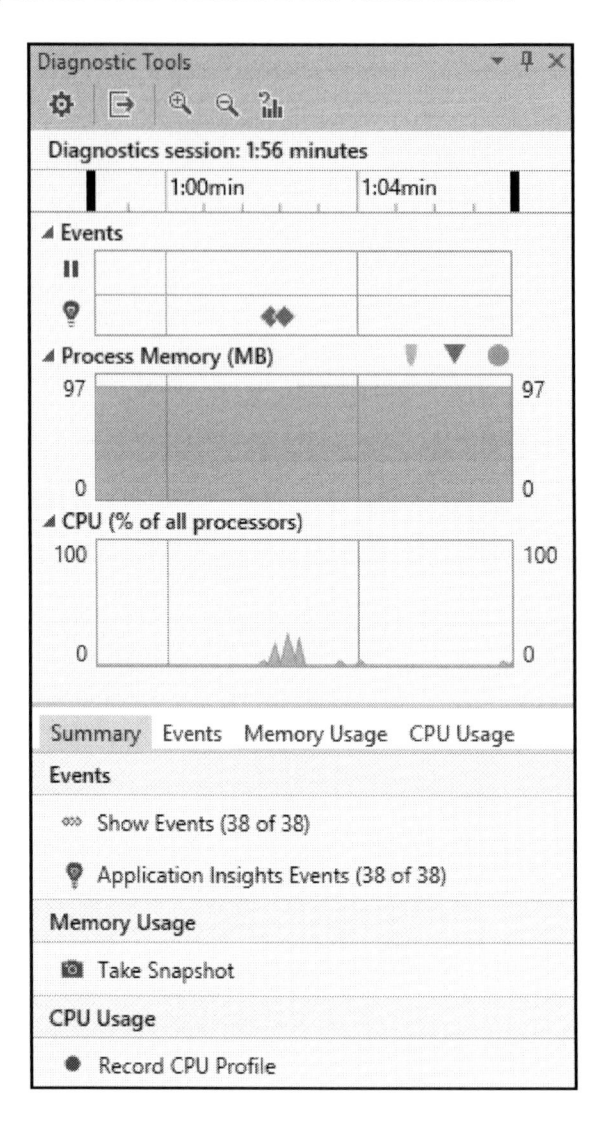

Here, you'll see the **Events** triggers from the web application, when we interacted with the application. To view the telemetry data from within Visual Studio, open the Solution Explorer, right-click **Application Insights** under **Connected Services**, and click **Search Live Telemetry**, as shown in the following screenshot:

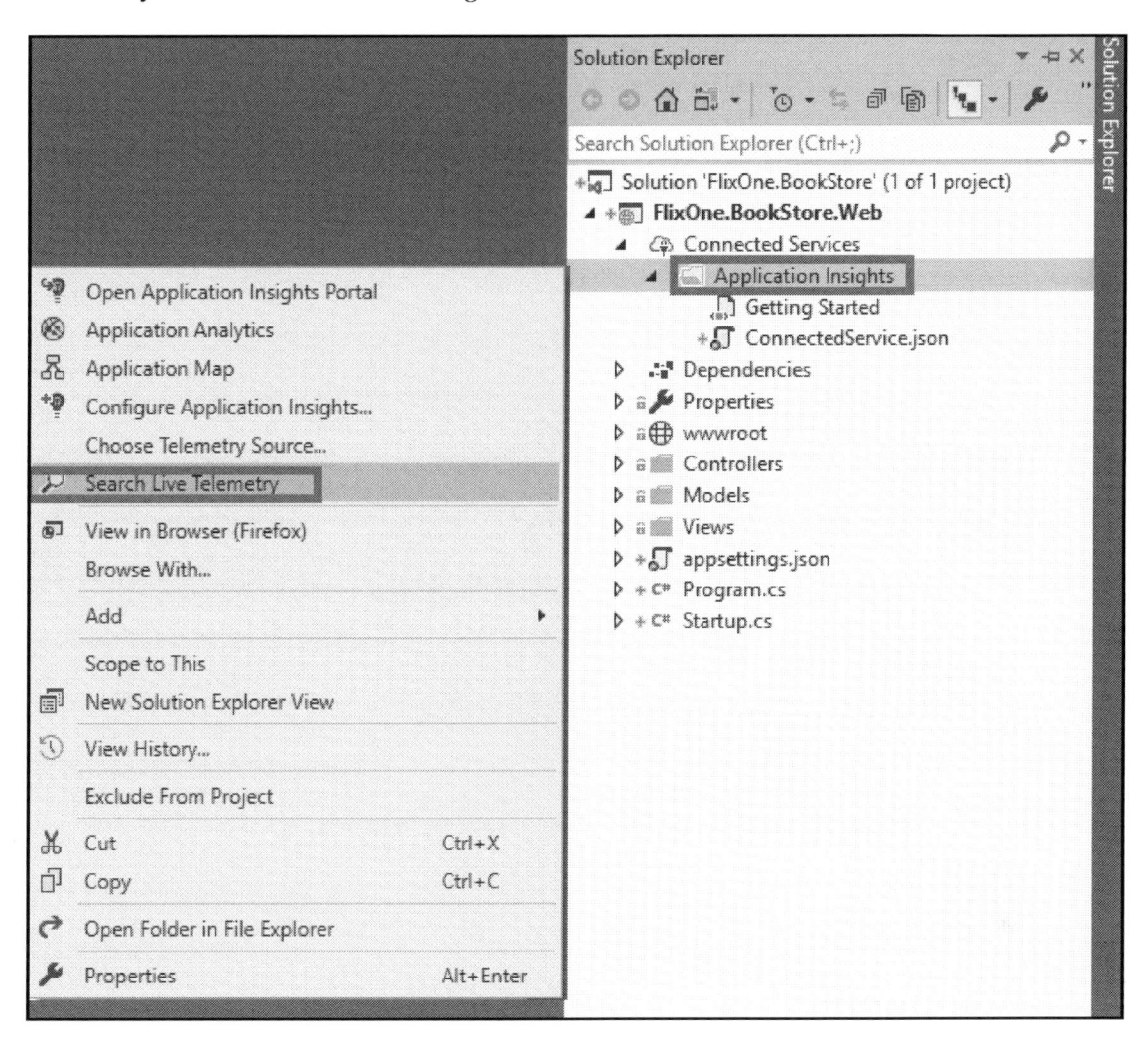

Monitoring Microservices

From here, you can view the telemetry data and perform analytic tasks on it:

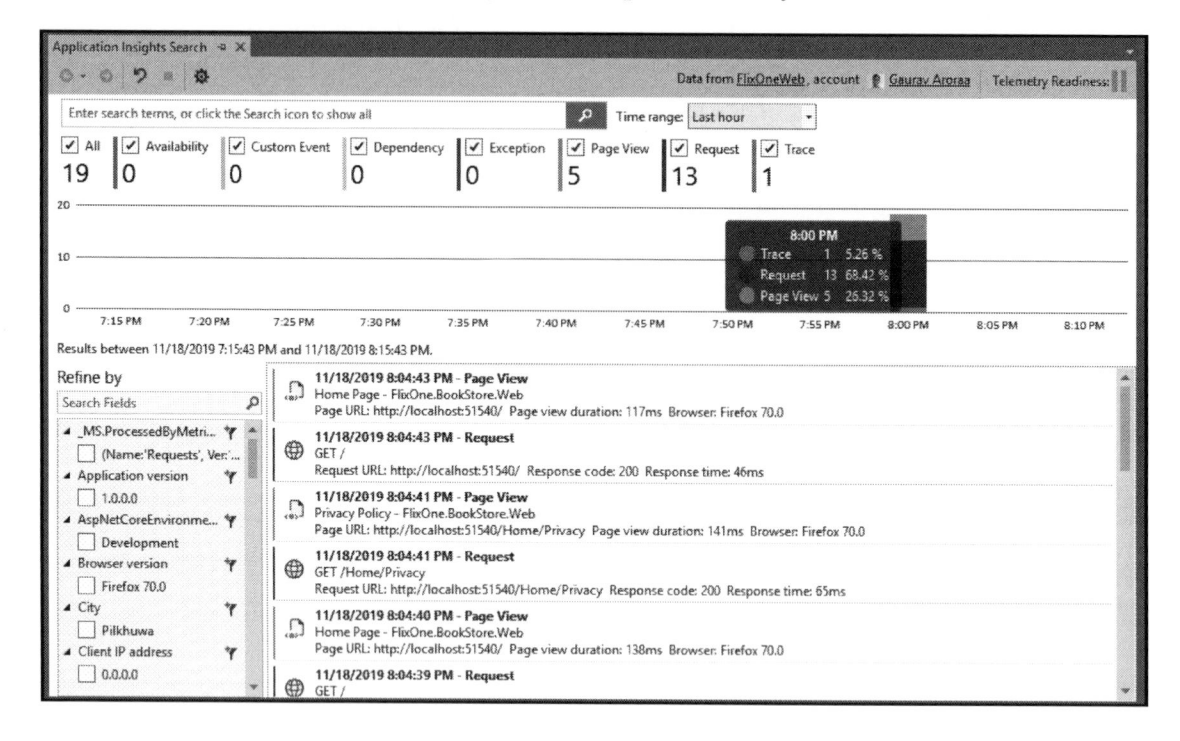

Chapter 7

To view the telemetry data in the Azure portal, click **Open Application Insights Portal** from **Solution Explorer**, under **Connected Services** (the same as we did in the previous step). This will open the Azure portal and Application Insights for our `FlixOneWeb`. You will see the graphical data from the last hour, as shown in the following screenshot:

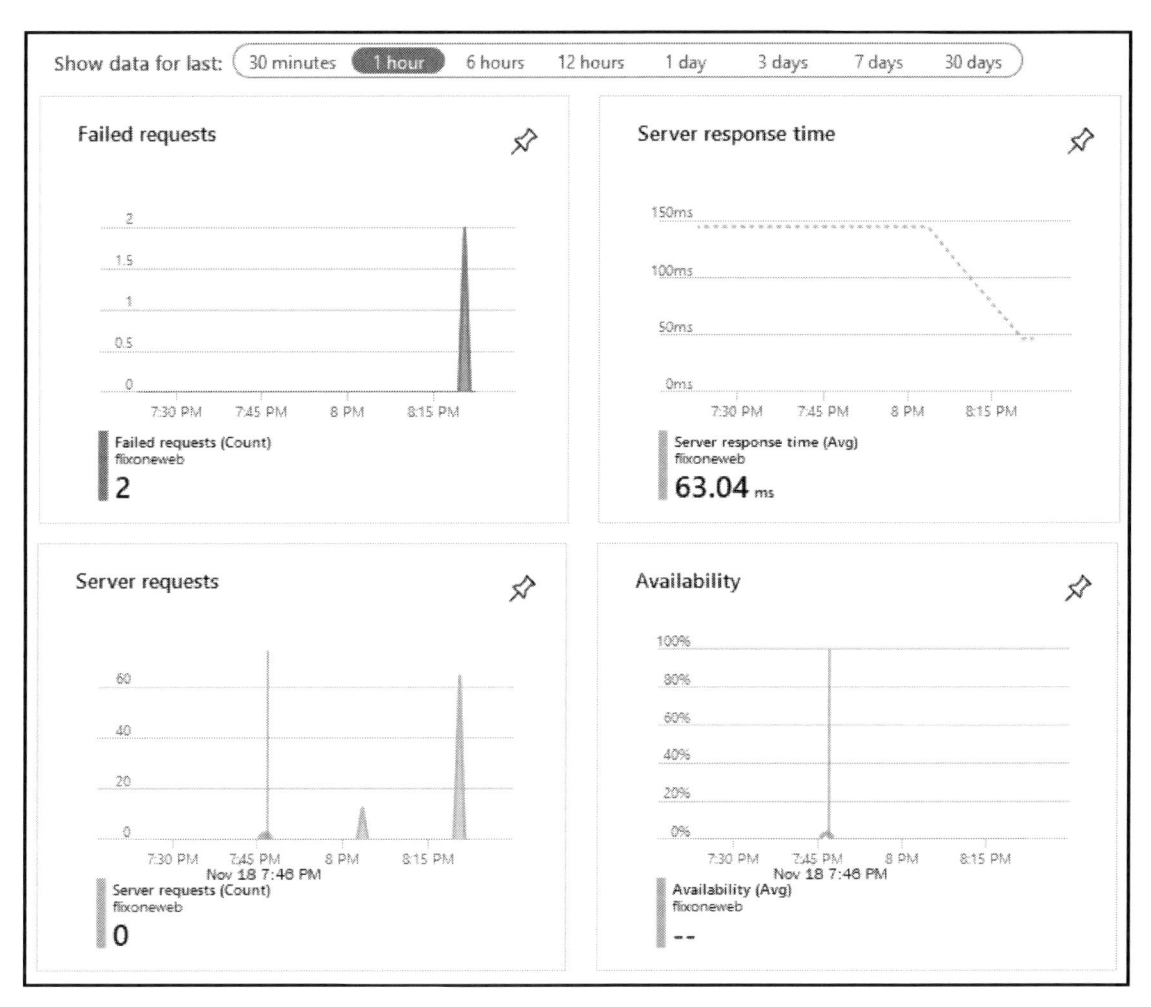

Monitoring Microservices

It's important to note that Visual Studio adds things to your web application (such as packages and connected services). An instrumentation key is also added to the `appsettings.json` file. If you open this file, you will see a new entry in Application Insights:

```json
{
    "Logging": {
        "LogLevel": {
            "Default": "Information",
            "Microsoft": "Warning",
            "Microsoft.Hosting.Lifetime": "Information"
        }
    },
    "AllowedHosts": "*",
    "ApplicationInsights": {
        "InstrumentationKey": "e978388d-fe8b-4cd6-bea3-55af370638ef"
    }
}
```

You will also see a new entry in the `Startup.cs` file, as shown in the following screenshot:

```csharp
public class Startup
{
    public Startup(IConfiguration configuration)
    {
        Configuration = configuration;
    }

    public IConfiguration Configuration { get; }

    // This method gets called by the runtime. Use this method to add services to the container.
    public void ConfigureServices(IServiceCollection services)
    {
        services.AddControllersWithViews();
        services.AddApplicationInsightsTelemetry();
    }
}
```

> It is recommended that you should store a production-based application instrumentation key in an environment variable.

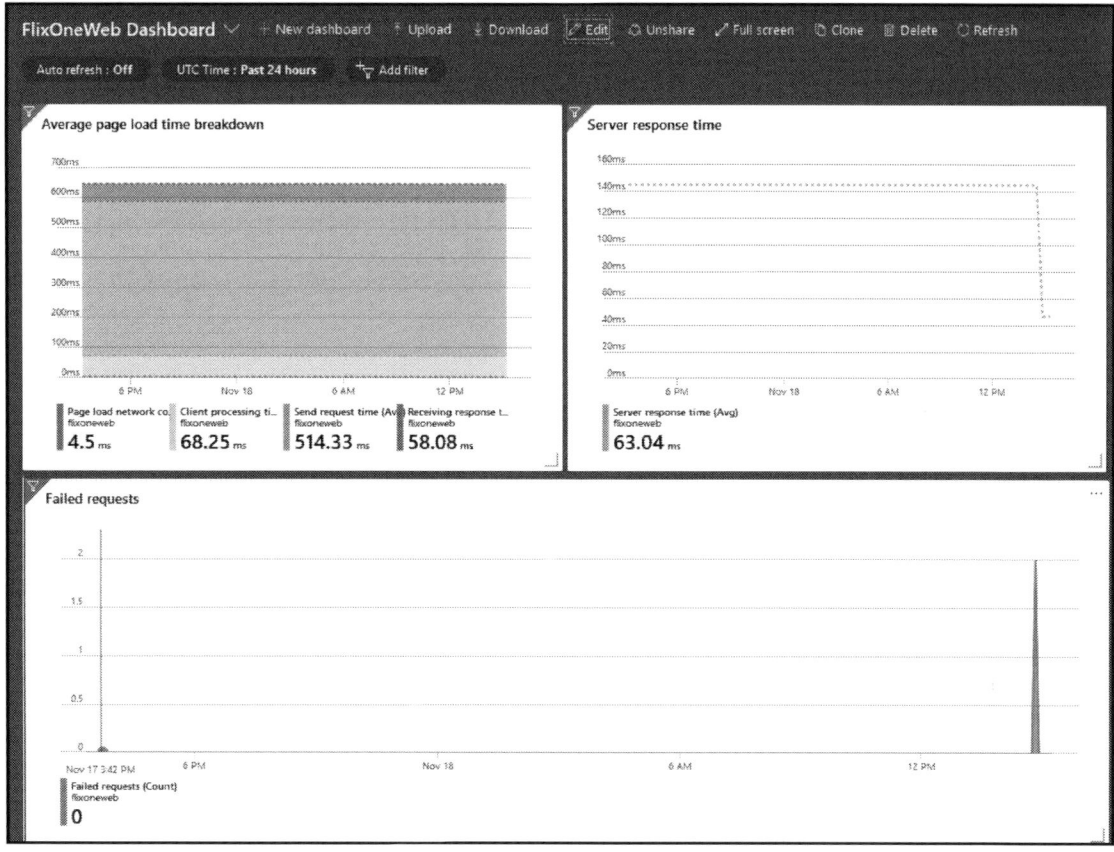

You can also create a custom dashboard on the Azure portal. Here's the one we created:

From the Azure portal (using Query Explorer), we can query our Insights data, in order to get data for analytic purposes.

> Query Explorer uses the Kusto query language to retrieve the log data. A Kusto query is a read-only request that's used to process data and return results. You can find out more by reading the official documentation at: https://docs.microsoft.com/en-us/azure/kusto/query/.

By using the following query, we can check the requests on our `FlixOne.BookStore.Web` application:

```
requests
| limit 5
```

Monitoring Microservices

The preceding query provides the following output:

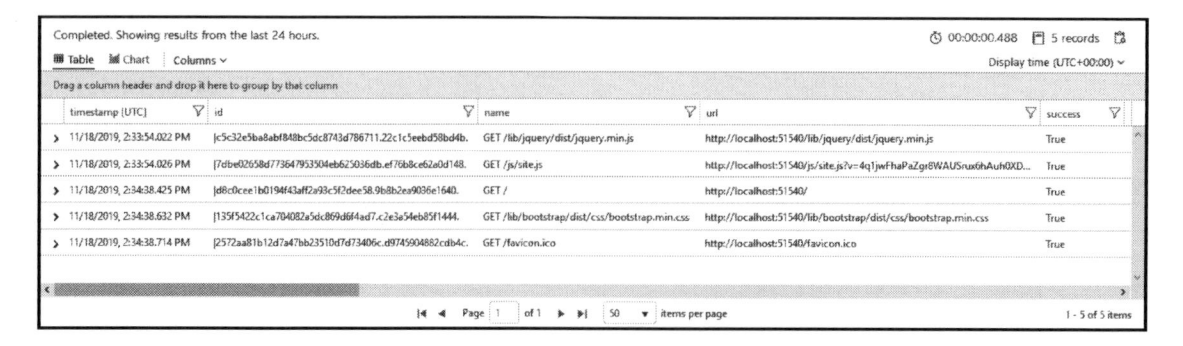

timestamp [UTC]	id	name	url	success
11/18/2019, 2:33:54.022 PM	|c5c32e5ba8abf848bc5dc8743d786711.22c1c5eebd58bd4b.	GET /lib/jquery/dist/jquery.min.js	http://localhost:51540/lib/jquery/dist/jquery.min.js	True
11/18/2019, 2:33:54.026 PM	|7dbe02658d773647953504eb625036db.ef76b8ce62a0d148.	GET /js/site.js	http://localhost:51540/js/site.js?v=4q1jwFhaPaZgr8WAUSrux6hAuh0XD...	True
11/18/2019, 2:34:38.425 PM	|d8c0cee1b0194f43aff2a93c5f2dee58.9b8b2ea9036e1640.	GET /	http://localhost:51540/	True
11/18/2019, 2:34:38.632 PM	|135f5422c1ca704082a5dc869d6f4ad7.c2e3a54eb85f1444.	GET /lib/bootstrap/dist/css/bootstrap.min.css	http://localhost:51540/lib/bootstrap/dist/css/bootstrap.min.css	True
11/18/2019, 2:34:38.714 PM	|2572aa81b12d7a47bb23510d7d73406c.d9745904882cdb4c.	GET /favicon.ico	http://localhost:51540/favicon.ico	True

Furthermore, we can visualize the data results, by using various charts. Here, we've created a pie chart from the preceding data:

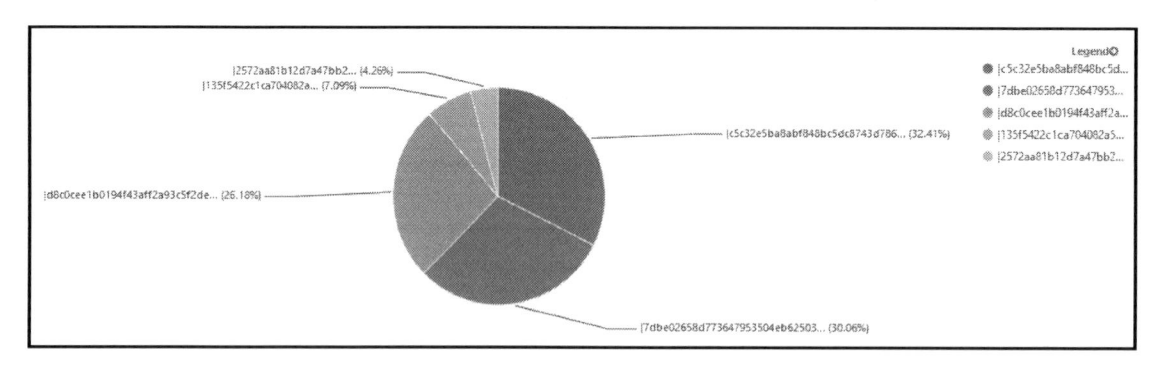

We can do further analysis and create reports from the data. To make this example simpler, we can make small queries to fetch the data. Application Insights helps us collect telemetry data and use it for analysis and reporting.

This section highlighted the features of Application Insights. Apart from the solution for monitoring applications, we also saw that there are more monitoring solutions, which we will discuss in the next section. Please write down the instrumentation key, since we will be using it in our application.

Other microservice monitoring solutions

Now, let's look at some of the popular monitoring solutions that we can use to build a custom microservice monitoring solution, to monitor the application. Obviously, these solutions do not come out of the box; however, they are definitely time-tested by the open source community, and they can easily be integrated with .NET-based environments.

In the following sections, we will discuss these monitoring tools in detail.

A brief overview of the ELK stack

The ELK stack (also referred to as the Elastic Stack) is the most popular log management platform. As we already know, one of the fundamental tools for monitoring is logging. For microservices, an astounding number of logs will be generated that are sometimes not even comprehensible to humans. ELK stack is also a good candidate for microservice monitoring, because of its ability to aggregate, analyze, visualize, and monitor. The ELK stack is a toolchain that includes three distinct tools, namely Elasticsearch, Logstash, and Kibana. Let's look at them one by one, in order to understand their role in the ELK stack.

Elasticsearch

Elasticsearch is a full-text search engine, based on the Apache Lucene library. The project is open source and developed in Java. Elasticsearch supports horizontal scaling, multitenancy, and clustering approaches. The fundamental element of Elasticsearch is its search index. This index is stored in JSON forms internally. A single Elasticsearch server stores multiple indexes (each index represents a database), and a single query can search data with multiple indexes.

Elasticsearch can really provide near real-time searches and can scale with very low latency. The search and results of the programming model are exposed through the Elasticsearch API and are available over HTTP.

Logstash

Logstash plays the role of a log aggregator in the ELK stack. It is a log aggregation engine that collects, parses, processes, and persists the log entries in its persistent store. Logstash is extensive because of its data pipeline-based architecture pattern. It is deployed as an agent, and it sends the output to Elasticsearch.

Kibana

Kibana is an open source data visualization solution. It is designed to work with Elasticsearch. You use Kibana to search, view, and interact with the data stored in the Elasticsearch indices.

It is a browser-based web application that lets you perform advanced data analysis and visualize your data in a variety of charts, tables, and maps. Moreover, it is a zero-configuration application. Therefore, it neither needs any coding nor additional infrastructure, after its installation.

This section provided an overview of Kibana, which is a data visualization solution. We can analyze the data that's captured through Kibana, using a web page so that we can visualize the data with various charts. In addition to this tool for monitoring and reporting, we need a log management solution. Splunk is one of the most favorable tools these days. In the next section, we will discuss Splunk.

Splunk

Splunk is one of the best commercial log management solutions. It can handle terabytes of log data very easily. Over time, it has added many additional capabilities and is now recognized as a full-fledged leading platform for operational intelligence. Splunk is used to monitor numerous applications and environments.

It plays a vital role in monitoring any infrastructure and application in real time, and it is essential for identifying issues, problems, and attacks before they impact customers, services, and profitability. Splunk's monitoring abilities, specific patterns, trends and thresholds, and so on, can be established as events for Splunk to look out for. This is so that specific individuals don't have to do this manually.

Splunk has an alerting capability included in its platform. It can trigger alert notifications in real time, so that the appropriate action can be taken, in order to avoid application or infrastructure downtime.

When triggering an alert and configuring an action, Splunk can do the following:

- Send an email
- Execute a script or trigger a runbook
- Create organizational support or an action ticket

Typically, Splunk monitoring marks may include the following:

- Application logs
- Active Directory changes to event data
- Windows event logs
- Windows performance logs
- WMI-based data
- Windows registry information
- Data from specific files and directories
- Performance monitoring data
- Scripted input to get data from the APIs and other remote data interfaces and message queues

The aim of this section was to provide an overview of Splunk, a log management tool. For monitoring solutions, we need alerting/notifications. In the next section, we will discuss the alerting functionality of Splunk.

Alerting

Splunk is not only a monitoring solution; it also has alert functionalities. It can be configured to set an alert, based on any real-time or historical search patterns. These alert queries can be run periodically and automatically, and alerts can be triggered by the results of these real-time or historical queries.

You can base your Splunk alerts on a wide range of threshold and trend-based situations, such as conditions, critical server or application errors, and threshold amounts for resource utilization.

Reporting

Splunk can also report on alerts that have been triggered and executed, if they meet certain conditions. Splunk's alert manager can be used to create a report, based on the preceding alert data.

Reporting and monitoring are very helpful, especially when we are working with enterprise-level applications. The reporting and monitoring solutions/tools we've discussed in this section are very helpful, if we wish to generate various reports to monitor these applications.

This section also discussed a few custom solutions for monitoring and reporting, by using tools other than the facilities provided by Microsoft Azure Cloud. Here, we discussed Splunk, a log management tool, and **Elastic Stack (ELK)**, which contains different tools, such as Elasticsearch, Logtash, and Kibana. Finally, we learned how to monitor and get various reports, by using data analysis.

Summary

Debugging and monitoring microservices isn't simple; it's a challenging problem. We have used the word *challenging* here on purpose: there is no silver bullet for this. There is no single tool that you can install that works like magic. However, with Azure Diagnostics and Application Insights, or with the ELK stack or Splunk, you can come up with solutions that will help you solve microservice monitoring challenges.

Implementing microservice monitoring strategies, is a helpful way to monitor microservice implementations. The monitoring strategies include application/system monitoring, real-time user monitoring, synthetic transactions, centralized logging, semantic logging block, and the implementation of a correlation ID throughout transactional HTTP requests. We saw how to create a report to monitor an application, with the help of various tools. With the help of the ELK stack, we can create a complete reporting and monitoring system.

In the next chapter, we will learn how we can scale microservices, and we will look at the solutions and strategies for scaling microservice solutions.

Questions

1. What is monitoring?
2. What is the need for monitoring?
3. What is health monitoring?
4. What are the challenges of monitoring?
5. What are the main logging and monitoring solutions from Microsoft Azure?

Further reading

- *Elasticsearch 7.0 Cookbook – Fourth Edition* (`https://www.packtpub.com/big-data-and-business-intelligence/elasticsearch-70-cookbook-fourth-edition`)
- *Hands-On Microservices – Monitoring and Testing* (`https://www.packtpub.com/application-development/hands-on-microservices-monitoring-and-testing`)

8
Scaling Microservices with Azure

Imagine you are part of a development and support team that is responsible for developing the company's flagship product—TaxCloud. TaxCloud helps taxpayers to file their own taxes, and then it charges them a small fee upon the successful filing of taxes. Imagine you had developed this application using microservices. Now, say the product gets popular and gains traction, and suddenly, on the last day of tax filing, you get a rush of consumers wanting to use your product and file their taxes. However, the payment service of your system is slow, which has almost brought the system down, and all of the new customers are moving to your competitor's product. This is a lost opportunity for your business.

Even though this is a fictitious scenario, it can very well happen to any business. In e-commerce, we have always experienced these kinds of things in real life, especially on special occasions, such as Christmas and Black Friday. All in all, they point toward one major significant characteristic—the scalability of the system. Scalability is one of the most important non-functional requirements of any mission-critical system. Serving a couple of users with hundreds of transactions, is not the same as serving millions of users with several million transactions. We'll also discuss how to scale microservices individually, what to consider when we design them, and how to avoid cascading failure using different patterns. In this chapter, we will discuss scalability in general.

By the end of this chapter, you will have learned about the following:

- Getting an overview of scalability
- Scaling infrastructure
- Understanding microservice scalability
- Implementing scaling infrastructure
- Scaling service design

As a developer, we can walk through various techniques of scaling, followed by scaling service design, and this will be very helpful when writing production-ready systems.

Technical requirements

This chapter contains no code examples, so there are no technical prerequisites for this chapter.

Getting an overview of scalability

Design decisions impact the scalability of a single microservice. As with other application capabilities, decisions that are made during the design and early coding phases, will largely influence the scalability of services.

Microservice scalability requires a balanced approach between services and their supporting infrastructures. Services and their infrastructures also need to be scaled in harmony.

Scalability is one of the most important non-functional characteristics of a system, as it can handle more payload. It is often felt that scalability is usually a concern for large-scale distributed systems. Performance and scalability are two different characteristics of a system. Performance deals with the throughput of the system, whereas scalability deals with serving the desired throughput, for a larger number of users or a larger number of transactions.

This section laid out the overview of scaling. In the coming section, we will discuss scaling our infrastructure.

Scaling infrastructure

Microservices are modern applications that usually take advantage of the cloud. Therefore, when it comes to scalability, the cloud provides certain advantages. However, it is also about automation and managing costs. So, even in the cloud, we need to understand how to provision infrastructure, such as virtual machines or containers, to successfully serve our microservices-based application, even in the case of sudden traffic spikes.

Now, we will visit each component of our infrastructure and see how we can scale it. The initial scaling up and scaling out methods are applied more to hardware scaling. With the autoscaling feature, you will understand Azure virtual manager scale sets. Finally, you will learn about scaling with containers in Docker Swarm mode.

Vertical scaling (scaling up)

Scaling up is a term used for achieving scalability, by adding more resources to the same machine. It includes the addition of more memory or processors with higher speed, or it could simply be the migration of applications to a more powerful machine.

With upgrades in hardware, there is a limit as to how you can scale the machine. It is more likely that you are just shifting the bottleneck, rather than solving the real problem of improving scalability. If you add more processors to the machine, you might shift the bottleneck to memory. Processing power does not linearly increase the performance of your system. At a certain point, the performance of a system stabilizes, even if you add more processing capacity. Another aspect of scaling up is that, since only one machine is serving all of the requests, it becomes a single point of failure as well.

In summary, scaling vertically is easy, since it involves no code changes; however, it is quite an expensive technique. Stack Overflow is one of those rare examples of a .NET-based system that is scaled vertically.

Horizontal scaling (scaling out)

If you do not want to scale vertically, you can always scale your system horizontally. Often, it is also referred to as **scaling out**. Google has really made this approach quite popular. The Google search engine is running out of inexpensive hardware boxes. So, despite being a distributed system, scaling out helped Google in its early days to expand its search process in a short amount of time, while still being inexpensive. Most of the time, common tasks are assigned to worker machines, and their output is collected by several machines that are doing the same task. This kind of arrangement also survives through failures. To scale out, load balancing techniques are useful. In this arrangement, a load balancer is usually added in front of all of the clusters of the nodes. So, from a consumer perspective, it does not matter which machine/box you are hitting. This makes it easy to add capacity by adding more servers. Adding servers to clusters improves scalability linearly.

Scaling out is a successful strategy, when the application code does not depend on the server that it is running on. If the request needs to be executed on a specific server, that is, if the application code has server affinity, it will be difficult to scale out. However, in the case of stateless code, it is easier to get that code executed on any server. Hence, scalability is improved when a stateless code is run on horizontally scaled machines or clusters.

Due to the nature of horizontal scaling, it is a commonly used approach across the industry. You can see many examples of large scalable systems managed this way, for example, Google, Amazon, and Microsoft. We recommend that you horizontally scale microservices as well.

> Session stickiness can be configured, where you either want sessions going to a specific node or not. In some scenarios, it might also be an option to sync the sessions in the load balancer, if that is supported.

This section aimed to specify the infrastructure of scaling; we have gone through horizontal and vertical scaling. In the next section, we will see scalability with microservices.

Understanding microservice scalability

In this section, we will review the scaling strategies that are available for microservices. We will look at the Scale Cube model of scalability, and we'll see how to scale the infrastructure layer for microservices, and how to embed scalability in microservice design.

The Scale Cube model of scalability

One way to look at scalability is by understanding the Scale Cube. Martin L. Abbott and Michael T. Fisher explained scaling and defined the Scale Cube as viewing and understanding system scalability. The Scale Cube applies to microservice architectures as well.

The following diagram is a visualization of the Scale Cube:

[Scale Cube diagram showing three axes: X-Axis (Scale by cloning Application/System), Y-Axis (Functional decomposition split application into services / Microservices: Scaling on Y-Axis), and Z-Axis (Scaling by dividing load based on the requestor or customer of the transaction).

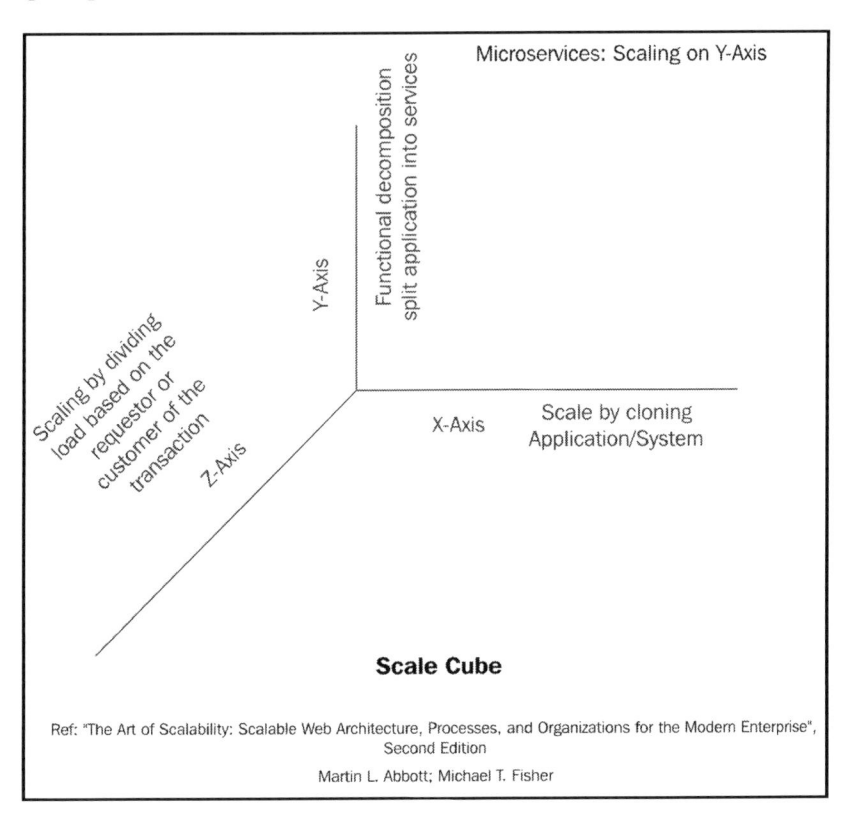

Ref: "The Art of Scalability: Scalable Web Architecture, Processes, and Organizations for the Modern Enterprise", Second Edition
Martin L. Abbott; Michael T. Fisher]

In this three-dimensional model of scalability, the origin point (0,0,0) represents the least scalable system. It assumes that the system is a monolith that's deployed on a single server instance. As shown, a system can be scaled by putting the right amount of effort into three dimensions. To move a system toward the right scalable direction, we need the right trade-offs. These trade-offs will help you to gain the highest scalability for your system. This will help your system to cater to increasing customer demand, and it is signified by the **Scale Cube** model. Let's look into every axis of this model and discuss what they signify, in terms of microservice scalability.

Scaling of the x axis

Scaling over the *x* axis means running multiple instances of an application behind a load balancer. This is a very common approach that's used in monolithic applications. One of the drawbacks of this approach is that any instance of an application can utilize all of the data available for the application. It also fails to address our application's complexity.

Microservices should not share a global state or a kind of data store that can be accessed by all of the services. This will create a bottleneck and a single point of failure. Hence, approaching microservice scaling merely over the x axis of the Scale Cube would not be the right approach.

Now, let's look at z-axis scaling. We have skipped over y-axis scaling for a reason. We'll come back to it.

Scaling of the z axis

Scaling of the z axis is based on a split, which is based on the customer or requestor of a transaction. The z-axis splits may or may not address the monolithic nature of instructions, processes, or code. However, they very often do address the monolithic nature of the data that's necessary to perform these instructions, processes, or code. Naturally, in z-axis scaling, there is one dedicated component that's responsible for applying the bias factor. The bias factor might be a country, request origin, customer segment, or any form of subscription plan that's associated with the requestor or request. Note that z-axis scaling has many benefits, such as improved isolation and caching for requests. However, it also suffers from the following drawbacks:

- It has increased application complexity.
- It needs a partitioning scheme, which can be tricky, especially if we ever need to repartition data.
- It doesn't solve the problems of increasing development and application complexity. To solve these problems, we need to apply y-axis scaling.

Due to the preceding nature of z axis scaling, it is not suitable for use in the case of microservices.

Scaling of the y axis

Scaling of the y axis refers to the decomposition of an application into different components. It also represents the separation of responsibility, by the role or type of data or work that's performed by a certain component in a transaction. To split the responsibility, we need to split the components of the system, as per their actions or roles performed. These roles might be based on large portions of a transaction or a very small one. Based on the size of the roles, we can scale these components. This splitting scheme is referred to as service- or resource-oriented splits.

This very much resembles what we see in microservices. We split the entire application, based on its roles or actions, and we scale an individual microservice, as per its role in the system. This resemblance is not accidental; it is the product of the design. So, we can say, fairly easily, that *y*-axis scaling is quite suitable for microservices.

Understanding *y*-axis scaling is very significant for scaling a microservices-based architectural system. So, effectively, we are saying that microservices can be scaled by splitting them, as per their roles and actions. Consider an order management system that is designed to, say, meet certain initial customer demand. For this, it works fine to split the application into separate services, such as a customer service, an order service, and a payment service. However, if demand increases, you would need to review the existing system closely. You might discover the sub-components of an already existing service, which can very well be separated again since they are performing a very specific role in that service, and in the application as a whole. This revisit to design, for an increased demand and load, may trigger the re-splitting of the order service into a quote service, order processing service, order fulfillment service, and so on. Now, a quote service might need more computing power, so we might push more instances (identical copies behind it), when compared to other services.

This is a near real-world example of how we should scale microservices on the AFK Scale Cube's three-dimensional model (`https://akfpartners.com/growth-blog/scale-cube`). You can observe this kind of three-dimensional scalability and *y*-axis scaling of services in some well-known microservice architectures that belong to the industry, such as Amazon, Netflix, and Spotify.

Characteristics of a scalable microservice

In the Scale Cube section, we largely focused on scaling the characteristics of an entire system or application. In this section, we will focus on scaling the characteristics of an individual microservice. A microservice is said to be scalable and performant, when it exhibits the following major characteristics:

- **Known growth curve**: For example, in the case of an order management system, we need to know how many orders are supported by the current services, and we need to know how they are proportionate to the order fulfillment service metric (measured in *requests per seconds*). The currently measured metrics are called **baseline figures**.

- **Well-studied usage metrics**: The traffic pattern generally reveals customer demand and, based on customer demand, many parameters mentioned in the previous sections regarding microservices can be calculated. Hence, microservices are instrumented, and monitoring tools are the necessary companions of microservices.
- **Effective use of infrastructure resources**: Based on qualitative and quantitative parameters, the anticipation of resource utilization can be done. This will help the team to predict the cost of infrastructure and plan for it.
- **Ability to measure, monitor, and increase the capacity, using an automated infrastructure**: Based on the operational and growth pattern of the resource consumption of microservices, it is very easy to plan for future capacity. Nowadays, with cloud elasticity, it is even more important to be able to plan and automate capacity. Essentially, cloud-based architecture is cost-driven architecture.
- **Getting an overview of scalability**: Resource requirements include the specific resources (compute, memory, storage, and I/O) that each microservice needs. Identifying these is essential for a smoother operational and scalable service. If we identify resource bottlenecks, they can be worked on and eliminated.
- **Has dependency scaling in the same ratio**: This is self-explanatory. However, you cannot just focus on a microservice, leaving its dependencies as bottlenecks. A microservice is as scalable as its least scaling dependency.
- **Fault-tolerant and highly available**: Failure is inevitable in distributed systems. If you encounter a microservice instance failure, it should be automatically rerouted to a healthy instance of the microservice. Just putting load balancers in front of microservice clusters won't be sufficient, in this case. Service discovery tools are quite helpful for satisfying this characteristic of scalable microservices.
- **Has a scalable data persistence mechanism**: Individual data store choices and design should be scalable and fault-tolerant, for scalable microservices. Caching and separating read and write storage will help in this case.

Now, while we are discussing microservices and scalability, the natural arrangement of scaling comes into the picture, which is as follows:

- **Scaling the infrastructure**: Microservices operate well over dynamic and software-defined infrastructure. So, scaling the infrastructure is an essential component of scaling microservices.
- **Scaling around service design**: Microservice design comprises an HTTP-based API, as well as a data store in which the local state for the services is stored.

This section provided an overview of scaling and its characteristics. We discussed an overview of scaling infrastructure. Next, we will discuss scaling the infrastructure in more detail.

Implementing scaling infrastructure

In this section, we will visit all of the layers of the microservice infrastructure, and we'll see them in relation to each other, that is, how each individual infrastructure layer can be scaled. In our microservice implementation, there are two major components:

- Virtual machines
- Containers hosted on the virtual or physical machine

The following diagram shows a logical view of the microservice infrastructure:

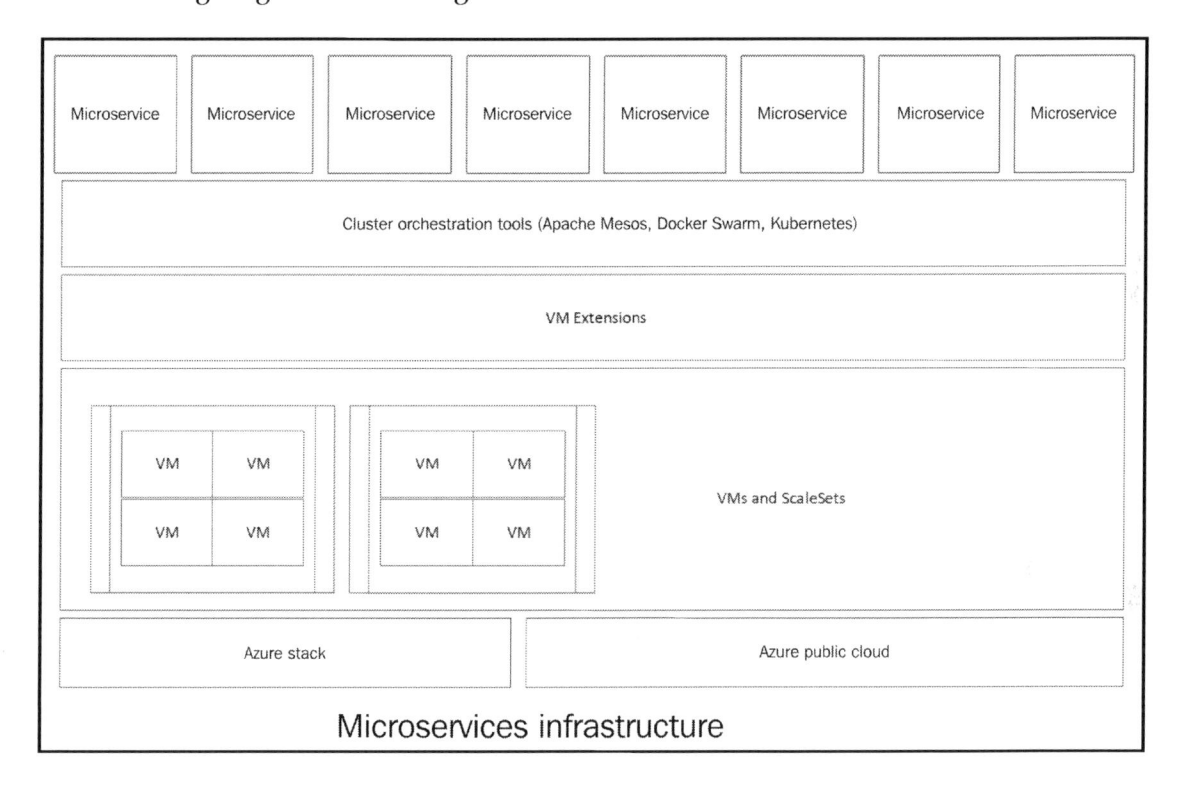

Microservices infrastructure

The preceding diagram visualizes the microservices infrastructure that uses the Azure public cloud.

Scaling virtual machines using scale sets

Scaling virtual machines is quite simple and easy in the Azure cloud. This is where microservices shine through. With scale sets, you can raise the instances of the same virtual machine images in a short amount of time, and automatically too, based on the ruleset. Scale sets are integrated with Azure Autoscale.

Azure virtual machines can be created in such a way that, as a group, they always serve the requests, even if the volume of the requests increases. In specific situations, they can also be deleted automatically, if those virtual machines are not needed to perform the workload. This is taken care of by the virtual machine scale set.

Scale sets also integrate well with load balancers in Azure. Since they are represented as compute resources, they can be used with Azure's Resource Manager. Scale sets can be configured so that virtual machines can be created or deleted on demand. This helps to manage virtual machines with the mindset of pets versus cattle, which we saw earlier in this chapter, in terms of deployment.

For applications that need to scale compute resources in and out, scale operations are implicitly balanced across the fault and update domains.

With scale sets, you don't need to correlate loops of independent resources, such as NICs, storage accounts, and virtual machines. Even while scaling out, how are we going to take care of the availability of these virtual machines? All such concerns and challenges have already been addressed with virtual machine scale sets.

A scale set allows you to automatically grow and shrink an application, based on demand. Let's say there's a threshold of 40% utilization. So, maybe once we reach 40% utilization, we'll begin to experience performance degradation. And at 40% utilization, new web servers get added. A scale set allows you to set a rule, as mentioned in the previous sections. An input to a scale set is a virtual machine. The rules on a scale set say that the average utilization of the CPU is 40%, for five minutes, so Azure will add another virtual machine to the scale set. After doing this, it calibrates the rule again. If the performance is still above 40%, it adds a third virtual machine, until it reaches the acceptable threshold. Once the performance drops below 40%, it will start deleting these virtual machines, based on traffic inactivity and so on, in order to reduce the cost of operation.

So, by implementing a scale set, you can construct a rule for the performance and make your application bigger to handle the greater load, by simply automatically adding and removing virtual machines. You, as the administrator, will be left with nothing to do, once these rules are established.

Azure Autoscale measures performance and determines when to scale up and down. It is also integrated with the load balancer and NAT. Now, the reason they're integrated with the load balancer and with NAT is because, as we add these additional virtual machines, we're going to have a load balancer and a NAT device. As requests keep coming in, in addition to deploying the virtual machine, we've got to add a rule that allows traffic to be redirected to the new instances. The great thing about scale sets is that they not only add virtual machines, but they also work with all of the other components of the infrastructure, including things such as network load balancers.

In the Azure portal, a scale set can be viewed as a single entry, even though it has multiple virtual machines included in it. To look at the configuration and specification details of virtual machines in a scale set, you will have to use the Azure Resource Explorer tool. It's a web-based tool available at https://resources.azure.com. Here, you can view all of the objects in your subscription. You can view scale sets in the Microsoft.Compute section.

Building a scale set is very easy, by using the Azure templates repository. Once you create your own **Azure Resource Manager** (**ARM**) template, you can also create custom templates based on scale sets. There are detailed discussions and instructions on how to build a scale set, by utilizing the ARM templates. You can get a quick start with these templates here: https://github.com/Azure/azure-quickstart-templates.

> An availability set is an older technology, and this feature has limited support. Microsoft recommends that you migrate to virtual machine scale sets, for faster and more reliable autoscale support.

This section provided an overview of scaling virtual machines, which is quite simple and easy in Microsoft Azure Cloud. The section discussed scaling virtual machines. Next, we will discuss autoscaling.

Autoscaling

With the help of monitoring solutions, we can measure the performance parameters of an infrastructure. This is usually in the form of performance service-level agreements (SLAs). Autoscaling gives us the ability to increase or decrease the resources that are available to the system, based on our performance thresholds.

The autoscaling feature adds additional resources to cater to increased the load. It works in reverse, as well. If the load is reduced, then autoscaling reduces the number of resources that are available to perform the task. Autoscaling does it all without pre-provisioning the resources, and it does this in an automated way.

Autoscaling can scale in both ways—vertically (adding more resources to the existing resource type) or horizontally (adding resources by creating another instance of that type of resource).

The autoscaling feature makes a decision, regarding adding or removing resources, based on two strategies. One is based on the available metrics of the resource, or on meeting some system threshold value. The other type of strategy is based on time, for example, between 9 a.m. and 5 p.m. (instead of 3 web servers, the system needs 30 web servers).

Azure monitoring instruments every resource; all of the metric-related data is collected and monitored. Based on the data collected, autoscaling makes decisions.

Azure Monitor autoscale applies only to virtual machine scale sets, cloud services, and app services (for example, web apps).

Container scaling using Docker Swarm

Earlier, in the chapter on deployment, we looked at how to package a microservice into a Docker container. We also discussed in detail why containerization is useful in the microservice world. In this section, we will advance our skills with Docker, and we'll see how easily we can scale our microservices with Docker Swarm.

Inherently, microservices are distributed systems and need to be distributed and isolated resources. Docker Swarm provides container orchestration clustering capabilities, so that multiple Docker engines can work as single virtual engines. This is similar to load balancer capabilities. Besides, it also creates new instances of containers or deletes containers, if the need arises.

You can use any of the available service discovery mechanisms, such as DNS, consul, or Zookeeper tools, with Docker Swarm.

A swarm is a cluster of Docker engines or nodes where you can deploy your microservices as *services*. Now, do not confuse these services with microservices. Services are a different concept in a Docker implementation. With Docker, a **service** is the definition of the tasks to execute on the worker nodes. You may want to understand the node that we are referring to in the last sentence. The node, in the Docker Swarm context, is used for the Docker engine participating in a cluster. A complete Swarm demo is possible, and ASP.NET Core images are available in the ASP.NET-Docker project on GitHub (`https://github.com/dotnet/dotnet-docker`).

> To date, Azure Container Service is a good solution for scaling and orchestrating Linux or Windows containers using DC/OS, Docker Swarm, or Google Kubernetes. Recently, Microsoft announced that Azure Containers will no longer be available from January 31, 2020. Instead, Microsoft is investing in Azure Kubernetes Service (AKS). To learn more about AKS, visit: `https://docs.microsoft.com/en-us/azure/aks/`.

Now that we have seen how to scale a microservice infrastructure, let's revisit the scalability aspects of microservice design in the following sections.

Scaling service design

In these sections, we will look at the components/concerns that need to be taken care of while designing or implementing a microservice. With infrastructure scaling taking care of service design, we can truly unleash the power of the microservices architecture, and we can get a lot of business value, in terms of making a microservice a true success story. So, what are the components of service design? Let's have a look.

Data persistence model design

In traditional applications, we have always relied on relational databases to persist user data. Relational databases are not new to us. They emerged in the 70s as a way of storing persistent information in a structured way, which would allow you to make queries and perform data maintenance.

In today's world of microservices, modern applications need to be scaled at the hyperscale stage. We are not recommending here, in any sense, that you abandon the use of relational databases. They still have their valid use cases. However, when we mix read and write operations in a single database, complications arise where we need to have increased scalability. Relational databases enforce relationships and ensure the consistency of data. Relational databases work on the well-known ACID model. So, in relational databases, we use the same data model for both read and write operations.

In most cases, read operations usually have to be quicker than write operations. Read operations can also be done, using different filter criteria, returning a single row or a result set. In most write operations, there is a single row or column involved, and usually, write operations take a bit longer when compared to read operations. So, we can either optimize and serve reads, or we can optimize and serve writes in the same data model.

How about we split the fundamental data model into two halves: one for all of the read operations and the other for all of the write operations? If we do that, things become far simpler, and it is easy to optimize both the data models with different strategies. The impact of this on our microservices is that they, in turn, become highly scalable for both kinds of operations.

This particular architecture is known as **Common Query Responsibility Segregation (CQRS)**. As a natural consequence, CQRS also gets extended, in terms of our programming model. Now, the database-object relationship between our programming models has become much simpler and more scalable.

With this comes the next fundamental element in scaling a microservice implementation: the caching of data.

Caching mechanism

Caching is the simplest way to increase the application's throughput. The principle is very easy. Once the data is read from data storage, it is kept as close as possible to the processing server. In future requests, the data is served directly from the data storage or cache. The essence of caching is to minimize the amount of work that a server has to do. HTTP has a built-in cache mechanism, which is embedded in the protocol itself. This is the reason it scales so well.

With respect to microservices, we can cache at three levels, namely client-side, proxy, and server-side. Let's look at each of them:

- First, we have client-side caching. With client-side caching, clients store cached results. So, the client is responsible for doing the cache invalidation.

  > During cache invalidation, which is a process in a computer system, the cache entries are replaced or removed. This requires manual intervention (using code), so that it can be done explicitly.

  Usually, the server provides guidance, using mechanisms, such as cache control and expiry headers, about how long it can keep the data and when it can request fresh data. With browsers supporting HTML5 standards, there are more mechanisms available, such as local storage, an application cache, or a web SQL database, in which the client can store more data.

- Next, we move on to the proxy side. Many reverse proxy solutions, such as Squid, HAProxy, and NGINX, can act as cache servers as well.
- Now, let's discuss server-side caching in detail. In server-side caching, we have the following two types:
    - **Response caching**: This is an important kind of caching mechanism for a web application UI, and honestly, it is simple and easy to implement as well. In response to caching, cache-related headers get added to the responses that are served from microservices. This can drastically improve the performance of your microservice. In ASP.NET Core, you can implement response caching using the `Microsoft.AspNetCore.ResponseCaching` package.
    - **Distributed caching for persisted data**: A distributed cache enhances microservice throughput, because the cache will not require an I/O trip to an external resource. This has the following advantages:
        - Microservice clients get the exact same results.
        - The distributed cache is backed up by a persistence store and runs as a different remote process. So, even if the app server restarts or has any problems, it in no way affects the cache.
        - The source's data store has fewer requests made to it.

You can use distributed providers, such as CacheCow, Redis (for our book, *Azure Cache for Redis*), or memcache, in a clustered mode for scaling your microservice implementation.

In the following section, we will provide an overview of CacheCow and Azure Cache for Redis.

CacheCow

CacheCow comes into the picture, when you want to implement HTTP caching on both the client and server. This is a lightweight library, and currently, ASP.NET Web API support is available. CacheCow is open source and comes with an MIT license that is available on GitHub (https://github.com/aliostad/CacheCow).

To get started with CacheCow, you need to get ready for both the server and client. The important steps are as follows:

- Install the `Install-Package CacheCow.Server` NuGet package within your ASP.NET Web API project; this will be your server.
- Install the `Install-Package CacheCow.Client` NuGet package within your client project; the client application will be WPF, Windows Form, Console, or any other web application.
- Create a cache store at the server side, which requires a database for storing cache metadata (https://github.com/aliostad/CacheCow/wiki/Getting-started#cache-store).

> If you want to use memcache, you can refer to https://github.com/aliostad/CacheCow/wiki/Getting-started for more information.

Azure Cache for Redis

Azure Cache for Redis is a wrapper of an open source project called **Redis** (https://github.com/antirez/redis), which is an in-memory database, and it persists on a disk. For more information about Azure Cache for Redis, see https://azure.microsoft.com/en-in/services/cache/. Here is my summary:

> "Azure Cache for Redis gives you access to a secure, dedicated Redis cache, managed by Microsoft and accessible from any application within Azure."

Getting started with Azure Cache for Redis is very simple, with the help of these steps:

1. Create a web API project—refer to our code example in Chapter 2, *Refactoring the Monolith*.
2. Implement Redis—for a referral point use https://github.com/StackExchange/StackExchange.Redis, and then install the `Install-Package StackExchange.Redis` NuGet package.
3. Update your config file for `CacheConnection` (https://docs.microsoft.com/en-us/azure/azure-cache-for-redis/cache-web-app-howto#update-the-mvc-application).

4. Then, publish on Azure (`https://docs.microsoft.com/en-us/azure/azure-cache-for-redis/cache-web-app-howto#publish-and-run-in-azure`).

> **TIP**
> You can also use this template to create Azure Cache for Redis: `https://github.com/Azure/azure-quickstart-templates/tree/master/201-web-app-redis-cache-sql-database`.
> For complete details on Azure Cache for Redis, refer to this URL: `https://docs.microsoft.com/en-us/azure/azure-cache-for-redis/`.

In this section, we discussed Azure Cache for Redis and the steps to implement it in a project. Next, we will discuss fault tolerance in scalable systems.

Redundancy and fault tolerance

We understand that a system's ability to deal with failure, and to recover from failure, is not the same as that offered by scalability. However, we cannot deny that they are closely related abilities, in terms of the system. Unless we address the concerns of availability and fault tolerance, it will be challenging to build highly scalable systems. In a general sense, we achieve availability by making redundant copies available to different parts or components of the system. So, in the upcoming section, we will touch upon two such concepts.

Circuit breakers

A circuit breaker is a safety feature in an electronic device that, in the event of a short circuit, breaks the electricity flow and protects the device, or it prevents any further damage to the surroundings. This idea can be applied to software design. When a dependent service is not available or not in a healthy state, a circuit breaker prevents calls from going to that dependent service, and it redirects the flow to an alternate path, for a configured period of time.

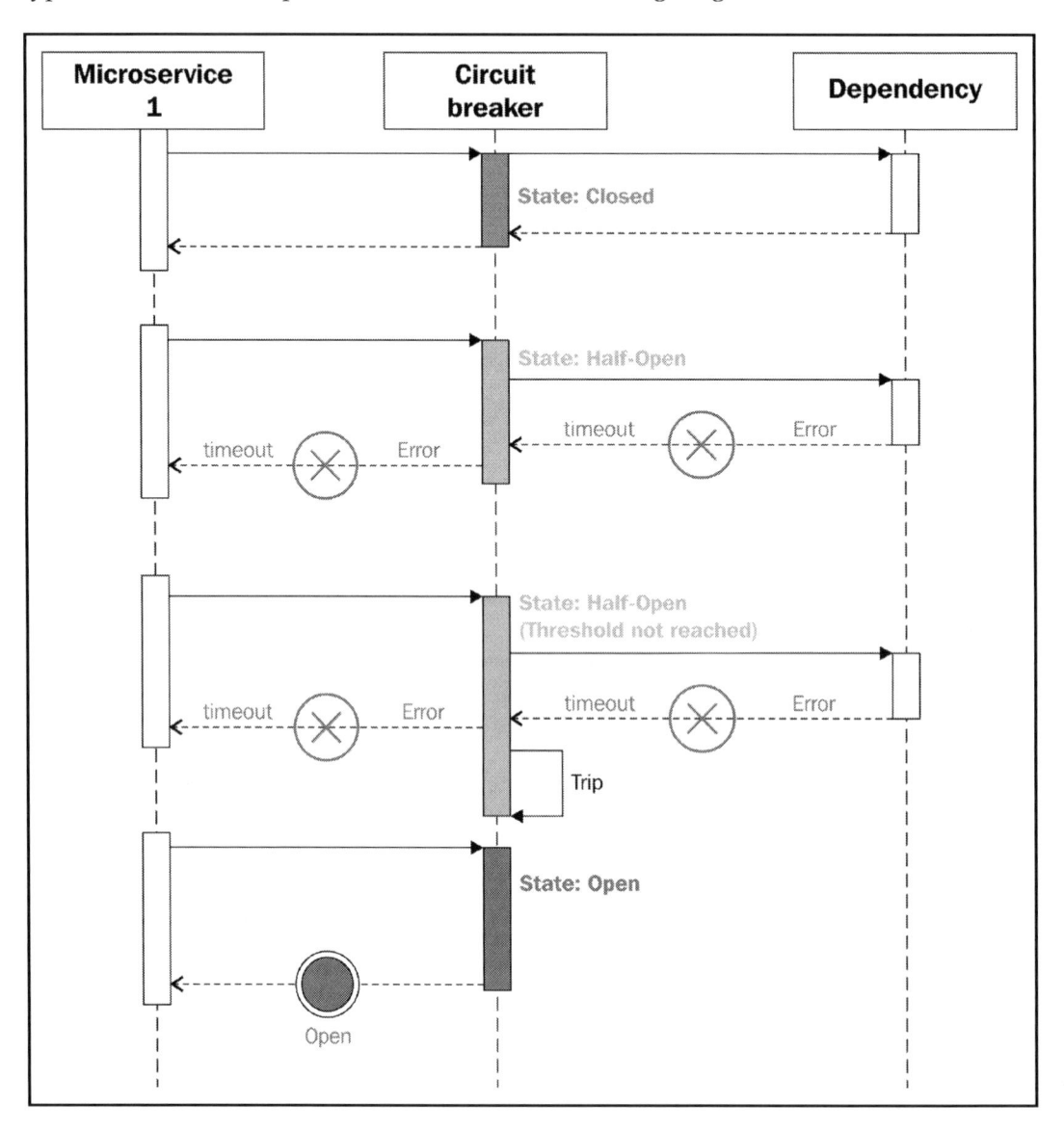

A typical circuit breaker pattern is shown in the following diagram:

As shown in the diagram, the circuit breaker acts as a state machine with three states, namely **Closed**, **Open**, and **Half-Open**.

Let's understand more about them in the following sections.

Closed state

This is the initial state of the circuit, which depicts a normal flow of control. In this state, there is a failure counter. If `OperationFailedException` occurs in this flow, the failure counter is increased by 1. If the failure counter keeps increasing, meaning the circuit encounters more exceptions, and it reaches the failure threshold set, the circuit breaker transitions to an **Open** state. But if the calls succeed without any exception or failure, the failure count is reset.

Open state

In the **Open** state, a circuit has already tripped, and a timeout counter has started. If a timeout is reached and a circuit still keeps on failing, the flow of code enters into the **Half-Open** state. This tells us that the request from the application fails immediately, and an exception is returned to the application.

Half-Open state

In the **Half-Open** state, the state machine/circuit breaker component resets the timeout counter, and again it tries to open the circuit, re-initiating the state change to the **Open** state. However, before doing so, it tries to perform regular operations, such as a call to the dependency. If it succeeds, then instead of the **Open** state, the circuit breaker component changes the state to **Closed**. This is so that the normal flow of the operation can happen, and the circuit is closed again.

> For .NET-based microservices, if you want to implement the circuit breaker and a couple of fault-tolerant patterns, there is a good library named *Polly* available, in the form of a NuGet package. It comes with extensive documentation and code samples, and it has a fluent interface. You can add *Polly* from http://www.thepollyproject.org/ or by just issuing the `install--Package Polly` command from the package manager console in Visual Studio.

Service discovery

For a small implementation, how can you determine the address of a microservice? For any .NET developer, the answer is that we simply put the IP address and port of service in the configuration file, and we are good. However, when you deal with hundreds or thousands of them dynamically, configured at runtime, you have a service location problem.

Now, if you look a bit deeper, you can see that we are trying to solve two parts of the problem:

- **Service registration**: This is the process of registration within the central registry of some kind, where all of the service-level metadata, host lists, ports, and secrets are stored.
- **Service discovery**: This is the process of establishing communication at runtime, with a dependency, through a centralized registry component.

Any service registration and discovery solution need to have the following characteristics, in order to be considered as a solution for the microservice service-discovery problem:

- The centralized registry itself should be highly available.
- Once a specific microservice is up, it should receive the requests automatically.
- Intelligent and dynamic load balancing capabilities should exist in the solution.
- The solution should be able to monitor the capability of the service health status and the load that it is subjected to.
- The service discovery mechanism should be capable of diverting the traffic to other nodes or services from unhealthy nodes, without any downtime or impact on its consumers.
- If there is a change in the service location or metadata, the service discovery solution should be able to apply the changes without impacting the existing traffic or service instances.

Some of the service discovery mechanisms, such as Zookeeper (http://zookeeper.apache.org/) and Consul, are available within the open source community.

This section helped us to understand the scaling service design and how data and circuits work around them, hence providing better caching, which reduces fault tolerance.

Summary

In this chapter, we discussed the critical advantages of pursuing the microservice architecture style, and we also took a look at the characteristics of microservice scalability. We saw how microservices can scale on the y axis, via the functional decomposition of the system. We learned the high capacity of the Azure cloud to scale, hence helping to utilize Azure scale sets and container orchestration solutions, such as Docker Swarm, DC/OS, and Kubernetes.

We then focused on scaling with service design and discussed how our data model should be designed. We also saw certain considerations, such as having a split CQRS style model, while designing the data model for high scalability. We also briefly touched on caching, especially distributed caching, and how it improves the throughput of the system. In the last section, to make our microservices highly scalable, we discussed the circuit breaker pattern and service discovery mechanism, which are essential for the scalability of microservice architecture.

In the next chapter, we will look at the reactive nature of microservices and the characteristics of reactive microservices.

Questions

1. What is caching, and what is the importance of caching in microservices applications?
2. What is a service discovery, and how does it play an important role in a microservices application?
3. Can you define Azure Cache for Redis, and describe an implementation of it, in a small program?
4. What is a circuit breaker?

Further reading

You just finished reading this chapter, but this is not the end of our learning curve. Here are a few references that could enhance your knowledge for the topic:

- *Microservices with Azure*: https://www.packtpub.com/virtualization-and-cloud/microservices-azure
- *Microservice Patterns and Best Practices*: https://www.packtpub.com/application-development/microservice-patterns-and-best-practices

9
Introduction to Reactive Microservices

We have now gained a clear understanding of microservices-based architecture and how to harness its power. Up until now, we've discussed various aspects of this architecture, such as communication, deployment, and security, in detail. We also looked at how microservices collaborate, when required. This chapter aims to combine reactive programming with our microservice-based architecture.

Reactive microservices take the concept of microservices to the next level. As the number of microservices grows, so does the need for communication between them. It won't be very long before the challenges of tracking a list of a dozen other services, orchestrating a cascading transaction between them, or just generating a notification across a set of services. In the scope of this chapter, the concept of cascading is more important than the transaction itself. Instead of the transaction, it could very well be just the need to notify some external system, based on some filtering criteria.

The challenge arises as an enterprise-level microservice-based system would always extend far beyond a handful of microservices. The sheer size and complexity of this cannot be pictured fully here in a chapter. In such a scenario, the need to track a set of microservices, and to communicate with them, can quickly become nightmarish.

What if we could take away the responsibility of communicating an event to other microservices from individual microservices? The other aspect of this could very well be freedom for the services, from being tracked in the ecosystem. To do this, you will have to keep track of their whereabouts. Add authentication to this, and you could very easily be tangled in a mess that you never signed up for.

The solution lies in a design change, where the responsibility, of tracking microservices for an event or communicating an event to others, is taken away from individual microservices. Let's take the effectiveness of microservices to the next level, by introducing the reactive programming aspect within them.

We will cover the following topics in this chapter:

- Understanding reactive microservices
- Making code reactive
- Understanding event communication
- Managing data
- Trying out the coding of reactive microservices

Technical requirements

This chapter contains various code examples to explain the concepts. The code is kept simple, and it is just for demo purposes.

To run and execute the code, the prerequisites are as follows:

- Visual Studio 2019
- .NET Core

Installing Visual Studio 2019

To run these code examples, you need to install Visual Studio 2019 or later (our preferred IDE). To do so, follow these instructions:

1. Download Visual Studio 2019 (Community is free) from the download link, which is mentioned with the installation instructions: https://docs.microsoft.com/en-us/visualstudio/install/install-visual-studio.
2. Follow the installation instructions for your operating system. Multiple versions are available for a Visual Studio installation. We are using Visual Studio for Windows.

If you do not have .NET Core 3.1 installed, you can download it from the link here: https://dotnet.microsoft.com/download/dotnet-core/3.1.

> The complete source code is available here: https://github.com/PacktPublishing/Hands-On-Microservices-with-CSharp-8-and-.NET-Core-3-Third-Edition/tree/master/Chapter%2009.

Understanding reactive microservices

Before we dive into reactive microservices, let's see what the word *reactive* means. There are certain fundamental attributes that a piece of software must possess, in order to be considered reactive. These attributes are responsiveness, resilience, elasticity, autonomy, and, above all, being message-driven. We'll discuss these attributes in detail, and we'll look at how they can make microservices stronger candidates, for most enterprise requirements.

Responsiveness

It wasn't long ago when one of the key requirements of business sponsors, discussed in requirement gathering sessions, was a guaranteed response time of a few seconds. For example, I remember when we first saw those custom t-shirt print e-shops, where you could upload an image and then have it rendered onto the chosen piece of apparel. Let's fast forward a few years and—I can vouch for this myself—now, we will close the browser window if any web page takes longer than a couple of seconds to load.

Users today expect near-instantaneous responses. But this is not possible, unless the code that you write follows certain standards to deliver the expected performance. There will always be many different components cooperating and coordinating to solve our business problems. The time in which each component is expected to return the results has, therefore, been reduced to milliseconds today. Also, the system has to exhibit consistency, along with performance, when it comes to response time. If you have a service that exhibits variable response times over a defined period, then it is a sign of an impending problem in your system. You will have to, sooner or later, deal with this baggage. And there is no doubt that, in most cases, you will manage to solve it.

However, the challenge is much bigger than what is visible on the surface. Any such trait needs to be probed for the possibility of an issue in the design. It could be some kind of dependency on another service, too many functions performing at the same time within the service, or synchronous communication blocking the workflow.

Resilience

With all of the buzz around distributed computing, what does a user expect from such a system, in the event of the failure of one or more components? Does a single failure result in a catastrophic domino effect, thereby resulting in the failure of the entire system? Or does the system bounce back from such an event, with grace and within the expected timelines? The end user shouldn't be affected at all in such scenarios, or the system should at least minimize the impact to an extent, ensuring that the user experience is not affected.

A resilient microservices-based application will follow the interservice communication. In such a resilient application, two or more services can continue to communicate with each other, without impacting the system, even if there is a communication failure in any other service. This means there should be a mechanism to handle fault, error, or failure of services, to ensure resilience.

Autonomy

All along, we have been strongly advocating the correct isolation of microservices. We touched on the topic of seam identification in the *Understanding the concept of seam* section of Chapter 2, *Refactoring the Monolith*. There were numerous benefits that we derived, while successfully implementing our microservice-style architecture. We can safely state that isolation is one of the fundamental requirements here. However, the benefits of a successful implementation of isolation go far beyond that.

Microservices need to be autonomous, or else our work will be incomplete. Even after implementing the microservice architecture, if one microservice failure results in a delay for other services, or if a domino effect takes place, it means we missed something in our design. However, if microservice isolation is done right, along with the right breakdown of the functionality to be performed by this particular microservice, it would mean that the rest of the design would fall into place itself, to handle any kind of resolution conflict, communication, or coordination.

The information, which is required to perform such an orchestration, would depend primarily on the well-defined behavior of the service itself. So, the consumer of a microservice that is well defined doesn't need to worry about the microservice failing or throwing an exception. If there is no response within the stipulated period of time, just try again.

Message-driven – a core of reactive microservices

Being message-driven is the core of reactive microservices. All reactive microservices define, as part of their behavior, any event that they might be generating. These events may or may not have additional information payloads within them, depending on the design of the individual event. The microservice that is the generator of this event would not be bothered, whether the event generated was acted upon or not. Within the scope of this specific service, there is no behavioral definition for the action, beyond the generation of this event. The scope ends there. Any service of the overall system will act within their scope, and none of these services are bothered, whether it's event-triggered or not.

The difference here is that all of these events being generated could be captured asynchronously, by listening to them. No other service is waiting in blocking mode, for any of these services. Anyone listening to these events is called a subscriber, and the action of listening for the events is called subscribing. The services that subscribe to these events are called **observers**, and the source service of the events generated is called an **observable**. This pattern is known as the **Observer Design Pattern**.

However, the very exercise of a concrete implementation, on each of the observers, is somewhat inconsistent with our goal of designing loosely coupled microservices. If this is what you are thinking, then you have the right thinking cap on, and we are on the right track. In a short while, when mapping our processes as reactive microservices, we will see how we can achieve this purpose in the world of reactive microservices.

Before we go on with mapping our processes, it is important that we briefly discuss the pattern, with respect to our topic here. To act upon a message, you first need to show your intent to watch the message of that type. At the same time, the originator of the message must have an intent to publish their message to the interested observers. So, there would be at least one observable to be observed by one or more observers. To add some spice to it, the observable can publish more than one type of message, and the observers can observe one or more of the messages that they intend to act upon.

The pattern doesn't restrict observers from unsubscribing, when they want to stop listening for these messages. So, it appears pretty, but is it as easily implemented? Let's move ahead and make our code reactive.

Introduction to Reactive Microservices

Making code reactive

Let's examine our application, and let's see how it would look with the reactive style of programming. The following diagram depicts the flow of an application that is reactive in nature and that is completely event-driven:

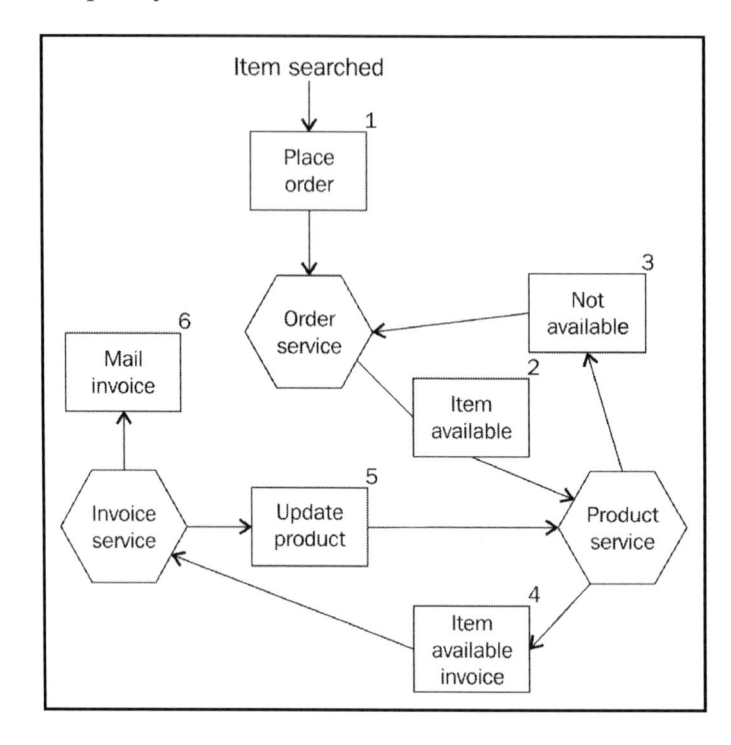

In this diagram, the services are depicted by hexagons, and the events are represented by square boxes.

The flow depicted in the diagram describes the scenario of a customer who is placing an order, after having searched for the items that he/she is looking for. This is how the process goes:

1. The **Place order** event is raised to **Order service**.
2. In response to this event, our service analyzes the arguments, such as the order item and quantity, and it raises the **Item** available event to **Product service**.
3. From here on, there are two possible outcomes: either the requested product is available and has the required quantity (it goes on to *step 4*), or it is not available or doesn't have the required quantity.

4. If the items are available, **Product service** raises an event called **generate invoice** (Item available invoice) to **Invoice service**. Since raising the invoice means we're confirming the order, the items on the invoice would no longer be available in stock; we need to take care of this and update the stock accordingly.
5. To handle this, our invoice service further raises an event called **Update product quantity** to **Product service**, and it takes care of this requirement. For the sake of simplicity, we will not go into the details of who will handle the event of **Mail invoice** (*step 6*).

This section aimed to examine our existing microservices-based application, and then we gathered the information to make it a reactive microservice app. To do so, we have gone through a couple of the steps, with the help of a diagram. Event communication is one of the most important parts of microservice-based applications, because communication between services is required when a service needs input from another service. Let's move ahead and take a look at event communication.

Understanding event communication

The preceding discussion may have left you thinking about how the event being raised, will map the call of the respective microservice perfectly; let's discuss this in further detail. Think of all of the events being raised, as being stored in an event store. The event stored has an associated delegate function, which is called to cater to the respective event. Consider the following diagram:

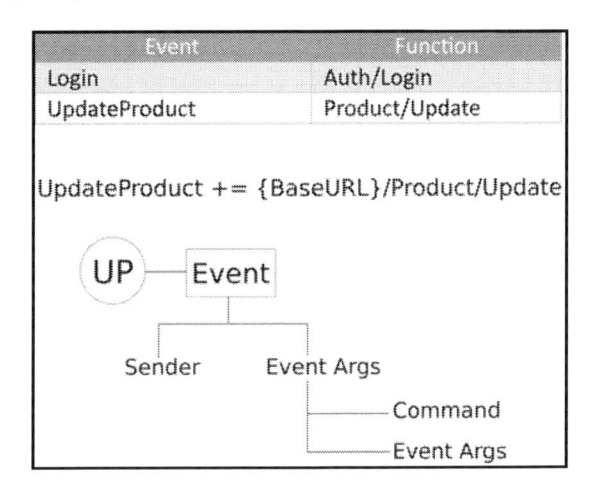

Event	Function
Login	Auth/Login
UpdateProduct	Product/Update

UpdateProduct += {BaseURL}/Product/Update

```
        UP ──── Event
                  │
       ┌──────────┴──────────┐
     Sender              Event Args
                              ├──── Command
                              └──── Event Args
```

Although we're showing that the store has just two columns of **Event** and **Function** (at the top of the diagram), it stores much more information, such as the details of the publisher and subscriber. Each event contains the complete information that is required to trigger the corresponding service. So, event delegation might be a service to be called or a function within the application itself. It doesn't matter to this architecture.

In other words, with the adaption of event communication, and with the implementation of the pub/sub model, we as developers would not worry about the lengthy code. You see, once an event has been subscribed and published, it will be automatically triggered to provide the expected output of a successful operation. One thing should be important here, and that is security. There must be some mechanism to take care of secure communication, which we will discuss in the next section.

Security

There are numerous ways in which security can be handled, while implementing reactive microservices. However, given the limited scope that we have here, we will restrict our discussion to one type only. Let's go on and discuss message-level security here and see how it is done.

Message-level security

Message-level security is the most fundamental method that's available to secure your individual request messages. After the initial authentication is performed, the request message itself may contain the OAuth bearer token or the JWTs, based on the implementation. This way, each and every request is authenticated, and the information related to the user can be embedded within these tokens. The information could be as simple as a username, along with an expiration timestamp that indicates the token's validity. After all, we don't want to allow a token to be utilized beyond a certain time frame.

The implementation would be progressive, and we should add some logic so that the token should be expired in a stipulated time frame. This can be easily achievable, with the help of the `System.IdentityModel.Tokens.Jwt` namespace. In addition to the time expiration, you can implement `jwt` by adding more information that would be required for the application.

Secure communication makes sure that the requests and/or response is secured and could not be tampered with. Message-level security specifically deals with authenticated requests. Let's move on and discuss how scalability is affected.

Scalability

There is another aspect you need to consider for reactive microservices, and that is scalability. Within this token (discussed in the previous section), we could also embed authorization information, apart from authentication information. Note that having all of this information, within a token that is being passed around frequently, could soon become an overhead. We can make the necessary changes to ensure that the information about the authorization is a one-time activity, and we can ensure it is later persisted with the services, as required.

When we decide to persist authorization-related information with individual services, in a way, we make them elastic. The task, of persisting authorization information with individual services, does away with the requirement of reaching out to the authentication service, each time for authorization-related data. This means we can scale our services quite easily.

The approach to scaling an application also depends upon the implementation of the code (for business logic). In this section, we understood that the token (probably `jwt`, as discussed in the previous section) could be an overload for the services, if it's loaded with plenty of information (even if this information is required for the application). So, we found a way to pass this information and to scale the services. When communication is secure, it should also be resilient, and this is what we will discuss next.

Communication resilience

What would happen if the authentication service, which contains all of the user authentication data and authorization data, suddenly became unavailable? Does this mean that the entire microservice ecosystem would come down to its knees, as all of the actions—or a big percentage of them—would need to be authorized for the user attempting the action? This does not fit in the domain of the microservice architecture. Let's see how we could deal with this.

One way would be to replicate the user authorization data, within each service that requires it. When the authorization data is already available with the respective services, it will reduce the data that's being transferred through the JWTs being moved around. What this would achieve is that, in the event our auth service becomes unavailable, the users who are authenticated, and who have accessed the system, would not be affected. With all of the authorization data already available within the individual services that need to verify it, the business can continue as usual without any hindrances.

Introduction to Reactive Microservices

However, this approach comes with a price of its own. It will become a challenge to maintain this data, as it is updated all of the time, with all of the services. The replication required for each service would be an exercise in itself. There is a way out of this specific challenge as well, though.

Instead of making this data available in all of the microservices, we could simply store it in a central store and have the services validate/access authorization-related data from this central store. This would enable us to build resilience beyond the authentication service.

Communication between services should be secure, and resilient and code should be written in such a way that the application can be scaled. Secure communication ensures that requests are coming from the authenticated source. Services should not be overloaded in such a way (such as when the token is overloaded with information, in our example) that would create problems to scale the application. Data management is also an important part of the application, which is what we will discuss next!

Managing data

Tracking a single order that's being placed is easy. However, multiply that number with the million orders that are being placed and canceled every hour; it could quickly become a challenge in the reactive microservices domain. The challenge is how you would perform a transaction across multiple services. Not only is it difficult to track such a transaction, but it poses other challenges, such as persisting a transaction that spans the database and message broker. For example, a user ordered a single item, added it to the cart, and checks out for payment.

In this activity, our code flow would be as follows:

1. The system checks the availability of the ordered item.
2. The system reserves the item, if it's available.
3. On checkout, the system will adjust the inventory for the item.
4. Finally, on payment, there will be a confirmation of the order, and the system will proceed with showing the progress of the delivery status of the item.

In this example, each step needs to persist the data, either in the database, in the cache, or in any other form. In a real scenario, if persistence fails at any step, then the rest of the steps should not be executed, and the steps that have already been performed, should be rolled back. In this case, we are talking about a single item from a single user. But think about a scenario where thousands of requests are performing these steps, and if something failed, how complex it would be to track all of the transactions. The task of reversing such an operation may likely break the transaction somewhere, due to a service failure, which could be even more daunting.

In such a scenario, we can utilize the event-sourcing pattern. This is a strong candidate, especially since we are not looking for a two-phase commit (generally referred to as a *2PC*). Instead of storing a transaction, we persist all of the state-changing events of our entities. In other words, we store all of the events that change their states, in the form of entities, such as the order and product. Under regular circumstances, when a client places an order, we would persist the order to the order table as a row. However, here we will persist the entire sequence of events, up to the final stage of the order being accepted or rejected.

Refer to the preceding diagram (in the *Understanding event communication* section), where we analyzed the sequence of events that are generated while creating an order. Look at how those events will be stored in the event sourcing pattern, and note how a transaction would be deduced from that set of events. First, let's think about how the data will be stored. As seen in the following diagram, individual records are saved as rows. Data consistency is confirmed after the transaction:

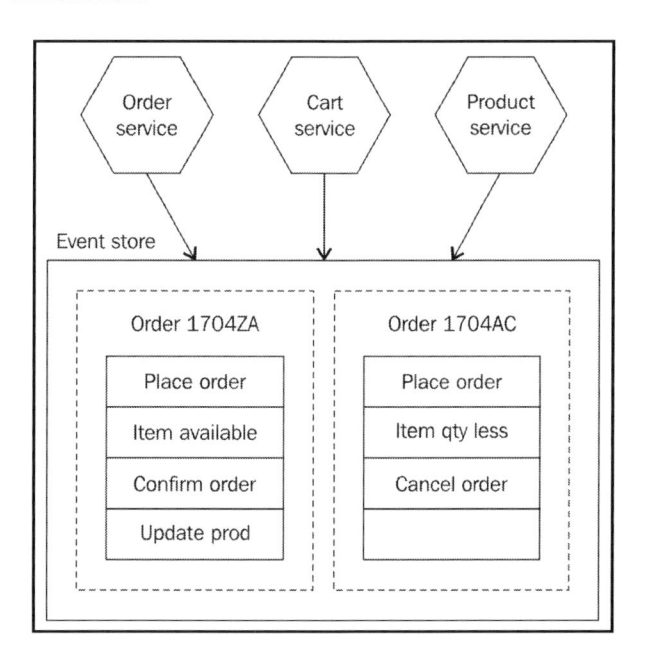

As seen in the preceding diagram, **Product service** can subscribe to the order events and update itself accordingly. The event store consists of all of the events, such as **Place order**, **Item available**, **Confirm order**, and finally, **Update prod**. These events are stored per **Order**. The whole process flow is as follows:

1. **Order service** places the order, after checking the availability of the item.
2. **Cart service** adds items into the cart, and it checks out items from the cart.
3. **Product service** will update items for a specific product. There are numerous benefits to be derived from this approach:
    - Since the events are being persisted, the challenge of recognizing a transaction is separated from the task of maintaining the database integrity.
    - It is possible to find the exact state of the system, at any given point in time.
    - It is easier to migrate a monolith with this approach.
    - It is possible to move back in time to a specific set of events, and then identify all the possible problems.

The following diagram depicts our **Order** and the **Order Details** table(s), from the perspective of **Order service**:

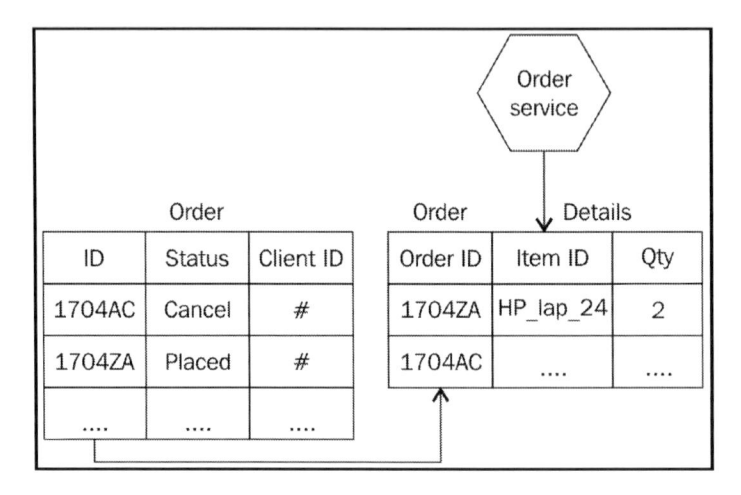

ID	Status	Client ID
1704AC	Cancel	#
1704ZA	Placed	#
....	....	....

Order

Order ID	Item ID	Qty
1704ZA	HP_lap_24	2
1704AC	....	....

Order Details

Apart from all of the benefits, it has some drawbacks as well. The most important one is how to query the event store. To reconstruct the state of a given business entity, at a given point in time, would require some complex queries. Apart from this, there would be a learning curve involved, to grasp the concept of an event store replacing the database, and then deducing the state of an entity. Query complexity can be easily handled with the help of the CQRS pattern. However, this will be outside the scope of this chapter (for more information on CQRS, refer to `https://docs.microsoft.com/en-us/azure/architecture/patterns/cqrs`). It is worth noting that the event sourcing pattern and CQRS are important patterns, in the wake of reactive microservices.

Data management is an important and integral part of the microservice application, especially when we are discussing an e-commerce application. This overall section aimed to discuss data management: the logical separation of databases, transaction data, and so on. Let's move forward to understand the microservice ecosystem.

Trying out the coding of reactive microservices

As discussed in the initial chapters, we need to get ready for big changes, when embracing microservices. The discussions we've presented on deployment, security, and testing, so far, would have had you thinking by now about accepting this fact. Unlike monoliths, the adoption of microservices requires you to prepare beforehand, so that you start building the infrastructure along with it, and not after it's done.

In a way, microservices thrive in a complete ecosystem where everything is worked out, from deployment to testing, security, and monitoring. The returns associated with embracing such a change are huge. There is definitely a cost involved in making all of these changes. However, instead of having a product that doesn't make it to the market, it is better to incur some costs, and then to design and develop something that thrives and does not die out, after the first few rollouts.

After giving you an overview of the microservices ecosystem, we now know about the system/application that is going through deployment, to testing, security, and monitoring. Next, we will write the code to implement reactive microservices, as discussed until now.

Now, let's try to sum up everything and see how it actually looks in the code. We will use Visual Studio 2019 for this. The first step is to create a reactive microservice, and then we will move on, to create a client for consuming the service that was created by us. Let's try these steps, in the following sections.

Creating the project

We will now go ahead and create our reactive microservice example. To do this, we need to create a project, of the ASP.NET web application type. Just follow these steps, and you should be able to see your first reactive microservice in action:

1. Start Visual Studio.
2. Create a new project, by navigating to **File** | **New** | **Project**, or press *Ctrl + Shift + N*, as shown in the following screenshot:

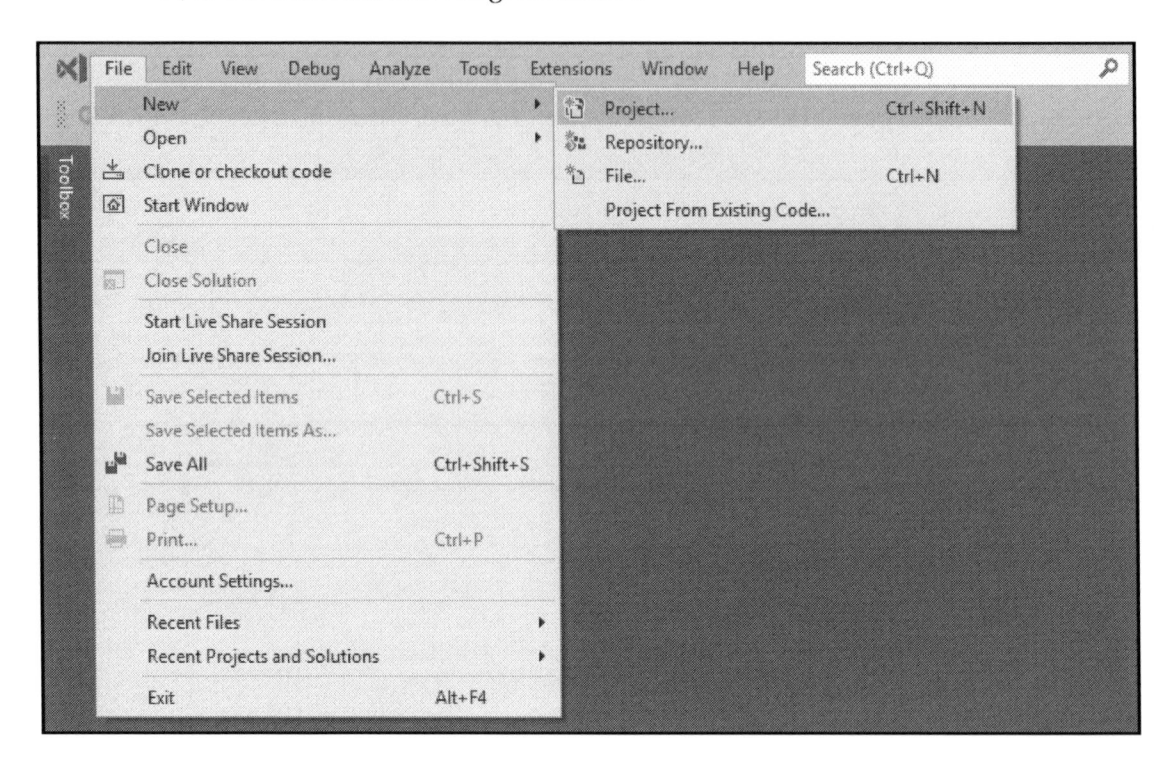

3. From the **Create a new project** screen, select **ASP.NET Core Web Application**, and then click **Next**:

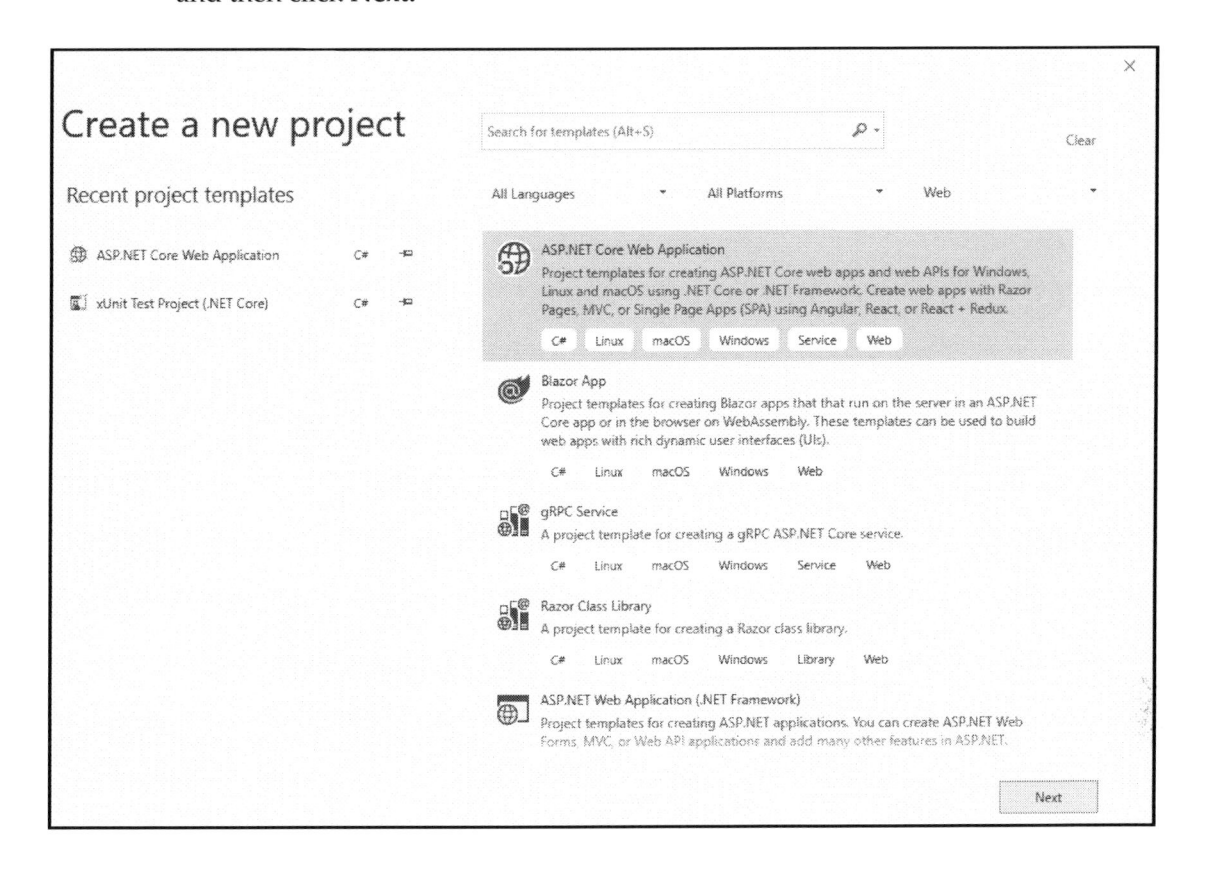

4. From the **Configure your new project** screen, go to **Project name** and add one in. I named it `FlixOne.BookStore.ProductService`, and then choose the **Location** path and the **Solution name**. When you're done, click **Create**:

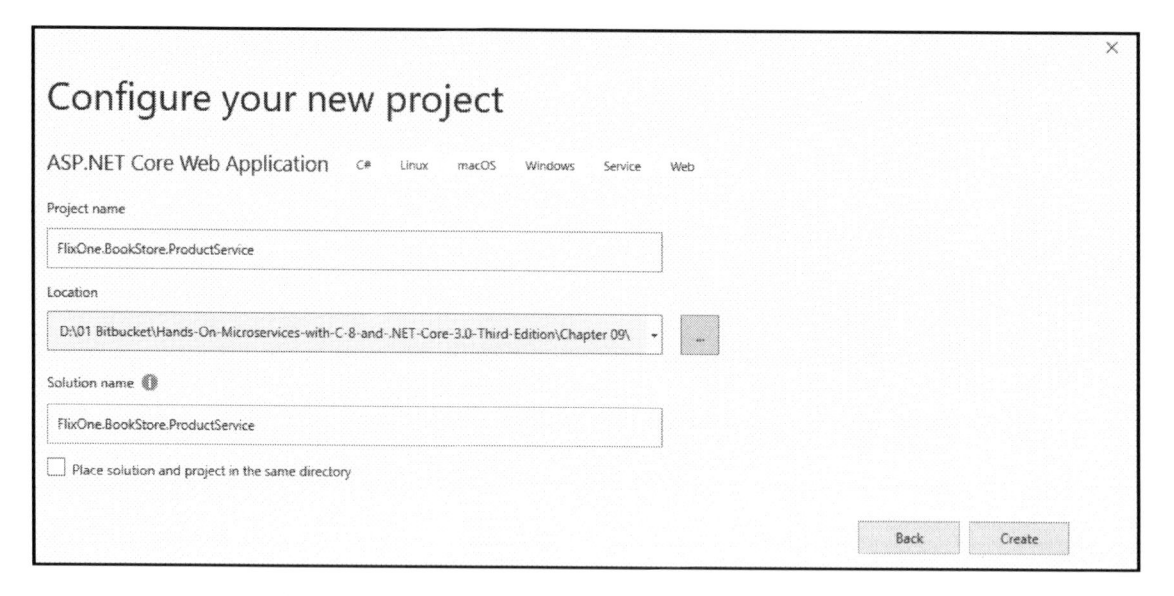

5. On the **Create a new ASP.NET Core web application** screen, make sure **.NET Core** and **ASP.NET Core 3.1** are selected, and then choose **Web Application (Model-View-Controller)**. When you're done, click **Create**:

Create a new ASP.NET Core web application

.NET Core | ASP.NET Core 3.1

API
A project template for creating an ASP.NET Core application with an example Controller for a RESTful HTTP service. This template can also be used for ASP.NET Core MVC Views and Controllers.

Web Application
A project template for creating an ASP.NET Core application with example ASP.NET Razor Pages content.

Web Application (Model-View-Controller)
A project template for creating an ASP.NET Core application with example ASP.NET Core MVC Views and Controllers. This template can also be used for RESTful HTTP services.

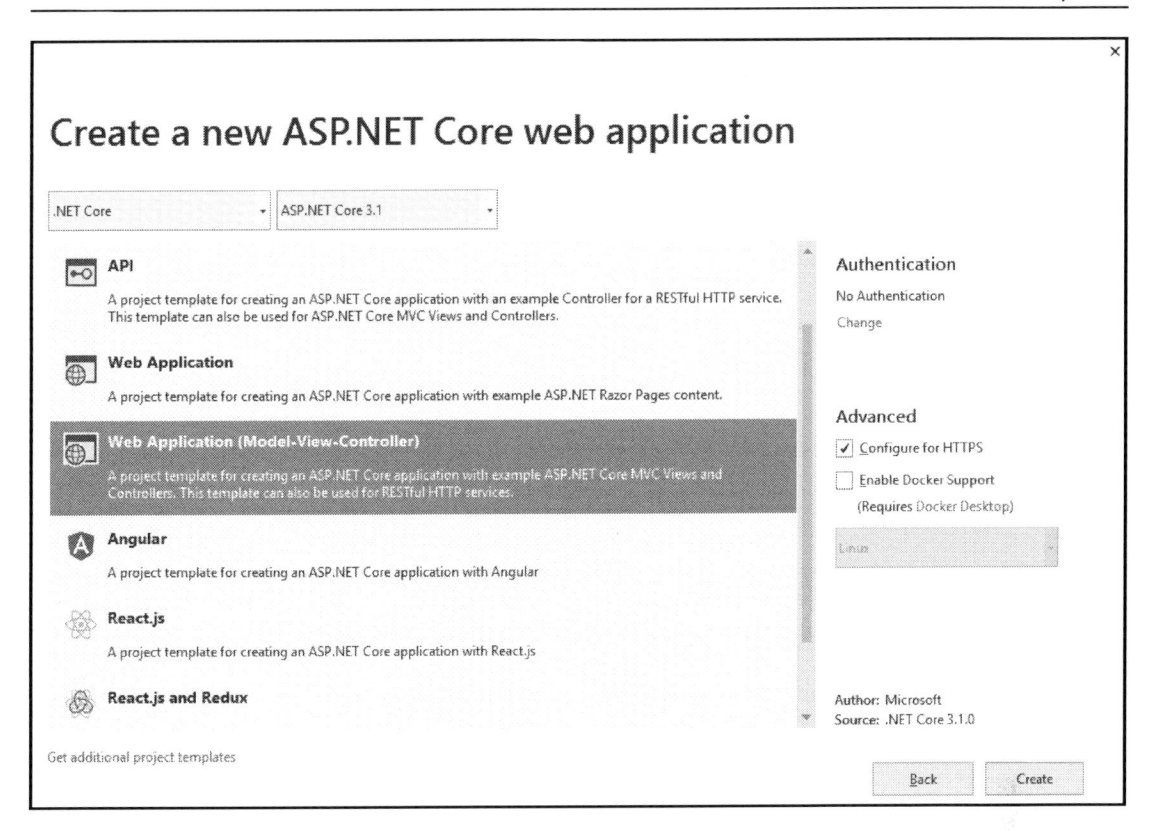

Angular
A project template for creating an ASP.NET Core application with Angular

React.js
A project template for creating an ASP.NET Core application with React.js

React.js and Redux

Get additional project templates

Authentication
No Authentication
Change

Advanced
☑ Configure for HTTPS
☐ Enable Docker Support
(Requires Docker Desktop)

Linux

Author: Microsoft
Source: .NET Core 3.1.0

Back | Create

> You can enable Docker support for Windows, if you want to enable the container. Select **Enable Docker Support**, from the **Advanced** section on the right.

Introduction to Reactive Microservices

6. Right-click the project from **Solution Explorer**, and then click **NuGet Manager** and add the **System.Reactive.Core** NuGet package to the project:

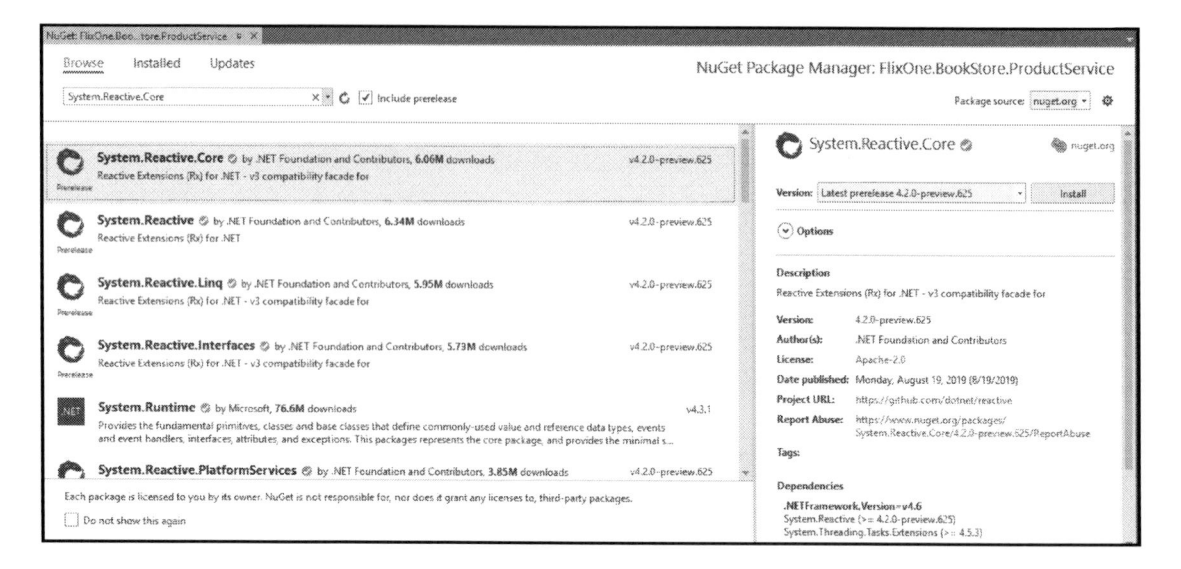

> **TIP**
> You are also required to add a package for EF Core; to do so, refer to Chapter 2, *Refactoring the Monolith*.

7. Add the `Product.cs` model to the `Models` folder, with the following code:

```
namespace FlixOne.BookStore.ProductService.Models
{
  public class Product
  {
    public Guid Id { get; set; }
    public string Name { get; set; }
    public string Description { get; set; }
    public string Image { get; set; }
    public decimal Price { get; set; }
    public Guid CategoryId { get; set; }
    public virtual Category Category { get; set; }
  }
}
```

8. Add the Category.cs model to the Models folder, with the following code:

```
namespace FlixOne.BookStore.ProductService.Models
{
  public class Category
  {
    public Category() => Products = new List<Product>();
    public Guid Id { get; set; }
    public string Name { get; set; }
    public string Description { get; set; }
    public IEnumerable<Product> Products { get; set; }
  }
}
```

9. Add the context and persistence folders to the project. Add ProductContext to the context folder, and add the IProductRepository interface and the ProductRepository class to the persistence folder.

Consider the following code snippet, showing our context and persistence classes:

```
public class ProductContext : DbContext
  {
    public ProductContext(DbContextOptions<ProductContext> options)
    : base(options)
    { }
    public ProductContext()
    { }
    public DbSet<Product> Products { get; set; }
    public DbSet<Category> Categories { get; set; }
  }
}
```

The preceding code declared ProductContext, which inherits DbContext and has DbSet Products and Categories.

Introduction to Reactive Microservices

For persistence or repositories, the following is the interface code:

```
namespace FlixOne.BookStore.ProductService.Persistence
{
  public interface IProductRepository
  {
    IObservable<IEnumerable<Product>> GetAll();
    IObservable<IEnumerable<Product>> GetAll(IScheduler scheduler);
    IObservable<Unit> Remove(Guid productId);
    IObservable<Unit> Remove(Guid productId, IScheduler scheduler);
  }
}
```

In the preceding code, we created `IProductRepository` to fetch and remove the product.

The following is the code for the `ProductRepository` class, which implements the `IProductRepository` interface:

```
namespace FlixOne.BookStore.ProductService.Persistence
{
  public class ProductRepository : IProductRepository
  {
    private readonly ProductContext _context;
    public ProductRepository(ProductContext context)
    => _context = context;
    public IObservable<IEnumerable<Product>>
    GetAll() => Observable.Return(GetProducts());
    public IObservable<IEnumerable<Product>>
    GetAll(IScheduler scheduler) =>
    Observable.Return(GetProducts(), scheduler);
    public IObservable<Unit> Remove(Guid productId) =>
    Remove(productId, null);
    public IObservable<Unit> Remove(Guid productId,
    IScheduler scheduler)
    {
      DeleteProduct(productId);
      return scheduler != null
      ? Observable.Return(new Unit(), scheduler)
      : Observable.Return(new Unit());
    }
    ...
  }
}
```

We have created our models. Our next step is to add the code for interacting with the database. These models help us to project data, from a data source, into our models.

For database interaction, we have already created a context, namely, `ProductContext`, deriving it from `DbContext`. In one of the preceding steps, we created a folder named `Context`.

The Entity Framework Core context helps to query the database. Also, it helps us to collate all of the changes that we perform on our data, and then we execute them on the database in one go. We will not go into detail about Entity Framework Core or the contexts here, because they are not part of the scope of this chapter.

The context picks the connection string from the `appsettings.json` file in the `connectionStrings` section—a key named `ProductConnectionString`.

You could name it anything, as shown in the following code snippet:

```
"ConnectionStrings":
{
  "ProductConnection": "Data Source=.;Initial
  Catalog=ProductsDB;Integrated
  Security=True;MultipleActiveResultSets=True"
}
```

You are required to update the `startup.cs` file to make sure that you're using a correct database. We have already discussed modifying the `appsettings.json` and `Statrup.cs` files in Chapter 2, *Refactoring the Monolith*. You need to add the `Swashbuckle.AspNetCore` NuGet package for Swagger support, in the project, while updating the `Startup.cs` class.

Communicating between the application and the database

With our context in place, and taking care of the communication between our application and the database, let's go ahead and add a repository for facilitating interaction between our data models and our database. Please refer to the code for our repository, as discussed in *step 10* of the *Creating the project* section.

By marking our result from `GetAll` as `IObservable`, we add the reactive functionality that we are looking for. Also, pay special attention to the return statement:

```
return Observable.Return(GetProducts());
```

With this observable model, it becomes possible for us to handle streams of asynchronous events, with the same ease we are used to when handling other, simpler collections.

Introduction to Reactive Microservices

We are now ready to expose the functionality through our controllers. Right-click the folder controller, click **Add New Item,** and then select **ASP.NET Core** and then **API Controller Class**. Name it `ProductController`. Click **Add** when you're done:

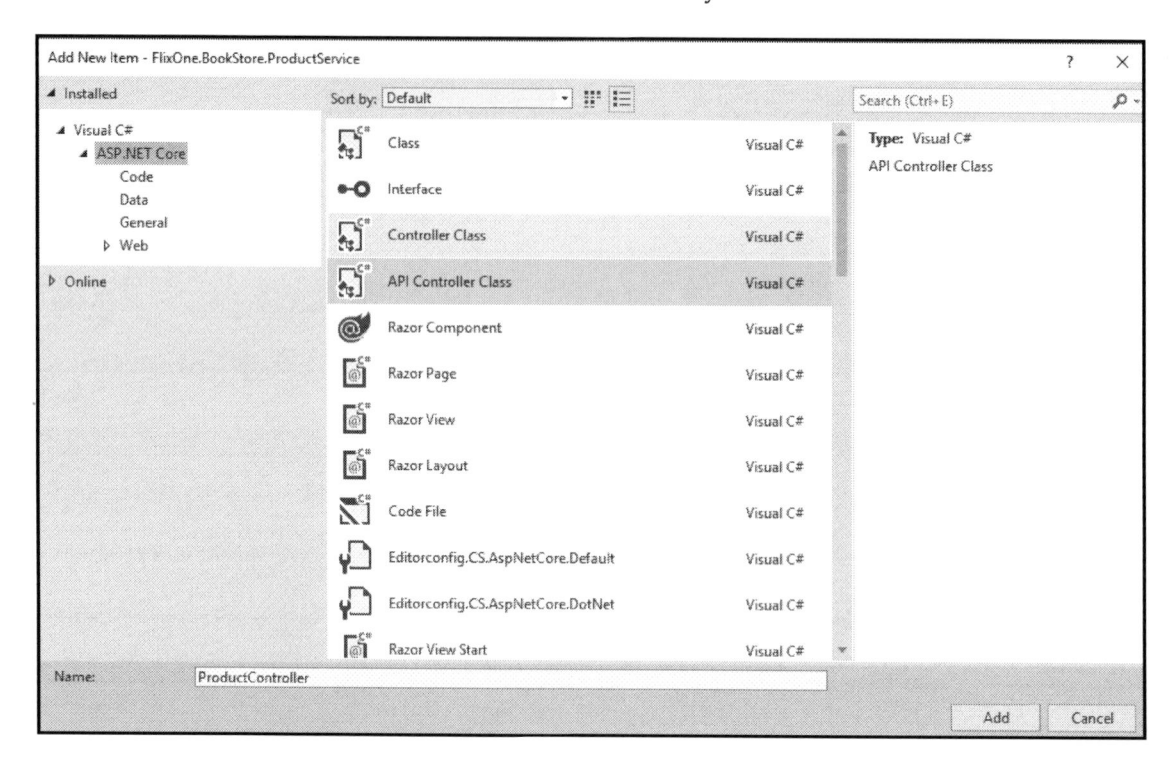

Here is what our controller looks like:

```
namespace FlixOne.BookStore.ProductService.Controllers
{
  [Route("api/[controller]")]
  public class ProductController : Controller
  {
    private readonly IProductRepository _productRepository;
    public ProductController() => _productRepository =
    new ProductRepository(new ProductContext());
    public ProductController(IProductRepository
    productRepository) => _productRepository =
    productRepository;
    [HttpGet]
    public async Task<IEnumerable<Product>> Get() =>
    await _productRepository.GetAll().SelectMany(p => p).ToArray();
  }
}
```

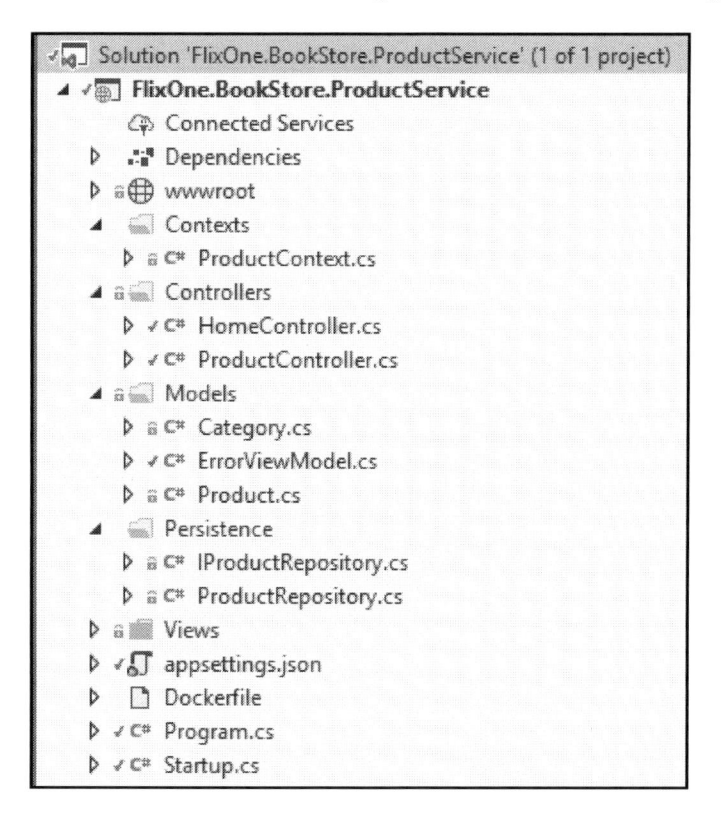

The final structure looks similar to the following screenshot of **Solution Explorer**:

```
Solution 'FlixOne.BookStore.ProductService' (1 of 1 project)
    FlixOne.BookStore.ProductService
        Connected Services
        Dependencies
        wwwroot
        Contexts
            C# ProductContext.cs
        Controllers
            C# HomeController.cs
            C# ProductController.cs
        Models
            C# Category.cs
            C# ErrorViewModel.cs
            C# Product.cs
        Persistence
            C# IProductRepository.cs
            C# ProductRepository.cs
        Views
        appsettings.json
        Dockerfile
        C# Program.cs
        C# Startup.cs
```

To create the database, you can refer to the *EF Core migrations* section in `Chapter 2`, *Refactoring the Monolith*, or simply call the Get API of our newly deployed service. When the service finds out that the database doesn't exist, the Entity Framework Core code-first approach, in this case, will ensure that the database is created.

We can now go ahead and deploy this service to our client. With our reactive microservice deployed, we now need a client to call it.

This section helped to provide an idea about reactive microservices. We have created a RESTful API in this section (that does not mean that we're done with microservices). To make it simple, we took an example of a single service. These services would be consumed by a client directly or via an API gateway.

Next, we will discuss the client who will consume this service.

Introduction to Reactive Microservices

Client – coding it down

With the help of AutoRest, we will create a web client for consuming our newly deployed reactive microservice.

> **TIP**
> **AutoRest** is a tool that helps us to generate client libraries, so that we can access RESTful web services. AutoRest fetches the API definition from the OpenAPI Specification (Swagger).

Let's create a console application for it, and let's add these NuGet packages: `System.Reactive.Core`, `Microsoft.AspNet.WebApi.Client`, `Microsoft.Rest.ClientRuntime`, and `Newtonsoft.Json`:

1. AutoRest will add a folder named `Models` to the main project and create copies of the model's product and category, a the service that we just created. It will have the necessary deserialization support built into it.
2. `ProductOperations.cs` and `ProductServiceClient.cs` contain the main plumbing that's required for the calling.
3. In the `Main` function of the `Program.cs` file, change the `Main` function as follows:

```
static void Main(string[] args)
{
  var client = new ProductServiceClient {BaseUri =
  new Uri("http://localhost:22651/") };
  var products = client.Product.Get();
  Console.WriteLine($"Total count {products.Count}");
  foreach (var product in products)
  {
    Console.WriteLine($"ProductId:{product.Id},Name:
    {product.Name}");
  }
  Console.Write("Press any key to continue ....");
  Console.ReadLine();
}
```

At this point, if the database is not created, then it will be created as required by Entity Framework.

We need to know how this list, which is returned from our microservice, differs from the regular list. The answer is that if this were a non-reactive scenario, and if you were to make any changes to the list, then it would not be reflected in the server. In the case of reactive microservices, changes that are made to such a list would be persisted to the server, without having to go through the process of tracking and updating the changes manually.

> You can use any other client to make the Web API call (for example, `RestSharp` or `HttpClient`).

You may have noticed that we had to do very little or no work at all, when it came to messy callbacks. This helps to keep our code clean and easier to maintain. With an observable, it is the producer that pushes the values, when they are available. Also, there is a difference here that the client is not aware of: whether your implementation is blocking or non-blocking. To the client, it all seems asynchronous.

You can now focus on important tasks, rather than figuring out what calls to make next or which ones you missed altogether.

Writing or creating services does not complete the task. These services should be consumed, or, if created purposely to work as business logic, without requesting anything from the client, then they should be used for intercommunication, which means the services call each other. In most of the scenarios, the services would be consumed by the client application, like **Product service**, in our example. To show you how to make the code simple, and to demonstrate the subject, we created a console application.

Summary

In this chapter, we added the aspect of reactive programming to our microservice-based architecture. There are trade-offs with this message-driven approach of microservices communicating with each other. However, at the same time, this approach tends to solve some of the fundamental problems, when we advance our microservice architecture further. The event-sourcing pattern comes to our rescue and lets us get past the limitation of an ACID transaction or a 2PC option. This topic could be greatly expanded on. We used our sample application to understand how to restructure our initial microservice in a reactive way.

In the next chapter, we will have the entire application ready for us to explore, and we will put together everything that we have discussed so far in this book.

Questions

1. What are reactive microservices?
2. What is message-level security?
3. What is AutoRest?

Further reading

You just finished reading this chapter, but this is not the end of our learning curve. Here are a few references that could enhance your knowledge about topics related to testing:

- *Hands-On Reactive Microservices in .NET Core*: `https://www.packtpub.com/application-development/hands-reactive-microservices-net-core-3-video`
- *Reactive Programming for .NET Developers*: `https://www.packtpub.com/web-development/reactive-programming-net-developers`

10
Design Patterns and Best Practices

In any programming language, the implementation of patterns and best practices is always recommended. For such implementations, design patterns are very commonly used because they help to make code reusable, allowing the code pieces to fit well with other sections and components. These are very important techniques, and a game-changer in the microservices ecosystem. In this chapter, we will cover some of the high-level design patterns and best practices that will help us to design real-world microservices applications.

The following topics will be covered in this chapter:

- The Aggregator pattern
- The Shared Data microservices pattern
- The Anti-Corruption Layer pattern

We have already covered the implementation of design patterns in the preceding chapters in the book, except for the Aggregator pattern, the Shared Data microservices pattern, and the Anti-Corruption Layer pattern, which we will cover here in depth with code examples.

Technical requirements

This chapter contains a few code examples to explain the concepts of the patterns that we will be looking at. The code is kept simple and is just for demo purposes. The examples involve a .NET Core console application written in C#.

The following are the prerequisites to run and execute the code:

- Visual Studio 2019
- Setting up .NET Core

Installing Visual Studio 2019

To install and run these code examples, you need to install Visual Studio 2019 or later (the preferred IDE). To do so, follow these instructions:

1. Download Visual Studio 2019 (the Community edition is free) from `https://docs.microsoft.com/en-us/visualstudio/install/install-visual-studio`, following the installation instructions.
2. Follow the installation instructions for your operating system. Multiple versions are available for Visual Studio installation. We are using Visual Studio for Windows.

If you do not have .NET Core 3.1 installed, you can download it and set it up from `https://www.microsoft.com/net/download/windows`.

> The complete source code is available at `https://github.com/PacktPublishing/Hands-On-Microservices-with-CSharp-8-and-.NET-Core-3-Third-Edition/tree/master/Chapter%2010`.

To begin the journey of the design patterns in this chapter, we will learn about the Aggregator pattern first, and then we will check the context of the solution to our problem.

The Aggregator pattern

In microservices, we have a tendency to break our business features into tiny items as separate services, and these services are hosted on completely different servers. Each service has its own information (sometimes services share one database), and the incoming data to these services contains this information. Sometimes, it's necessary to mix the details of the data that is coming from the services. This data requires the patron and this job/task to be done at the service level only. Data collaboration is the responsibility of the system and not of the patron.

To handle such cases, we can use the Aggregator pattern. As its name suggests, it aggregates or combines the information and returns the final response. With the assistance of the Aggregator pattern, we will mix the responses of two or more services, apply any business logic (if required,) and then return a combined response.

We can implement the Aggregator pattern with the help of composite microservices. Composite services play an important role when we need to aggregate the data from multiple microservices and then return the response to the consumer, after applying various business rules.

> Composite microservices may also be called UI composite services. These services take the output of two or more microservices, apply the business logic, and provide the combined result as a final response for the consumers. These consumers might be internet applications, mobile devices, or other consumers of the response.

In more common scenarios, if we do not need to apply any business logic to the data, then we can simply use the API gateway to aggregate the data and return it to the consumer.

Pros and cons

You should use the Aggregator pattern in the following circumstances:

- Multiple backend services are required to process or perform a client request.
- The client has an unstable network—for example, they are sending requests using a mobile device that has significant latency in the network.

The following are the situations where this pattern may not be suitable:

- When we need to make a single call so that multiple calls can be reduced. This occurs when the client makes a call to a single service but for multiple operations. In this scenario/situation, it is best to implement a batch operation for the service being called.
- When there is much low network latency. In this situation, the Aggregator pattern should not be used, because it would not add any benefit to the operation.

Best practices to be observed

We should use the following best practices if we want to implement this pattern:

- Data segregation is one of the best practices to follow when we start the implementation of this pattern. This is very important in view of our imaginary application, FlixOne, which we have discussed throughout the book (as we transitioned our monolithic application to microservices). However, this point may already be taken care of while implementing this pattern, with the help of composite microservices (because each microservice has its own database), but there may still be a need to segregate the database per service.
- Another best practice, which we will adapt in our example, is to manage services as a client-faced service and internal service. We will implement this with the help of the offer Service (a client-faced service) and the product and vendor service (an internal service).

Let's see how the implementation of these best practices would look in our FlixOne application.

The problem and its solution – example in FlixOne

In our imaginary application, we have two different services: one is the product service and the other is the vendor service. Both of these services are fine-grained and use their database. For this purpose, we need data from both of the services for our client (the consumer). The business logic for this handles the following two criteria, which we need to meet before sending the response back to the consumer:

- The response should contain complete information about the vendor.
- The product price should be specified.

To meet these criteria, we need to create a composite microservice, which will aggregate the response of the product service and the vendor service. This aggregated data will be returned to the consumer, after applying business logic:

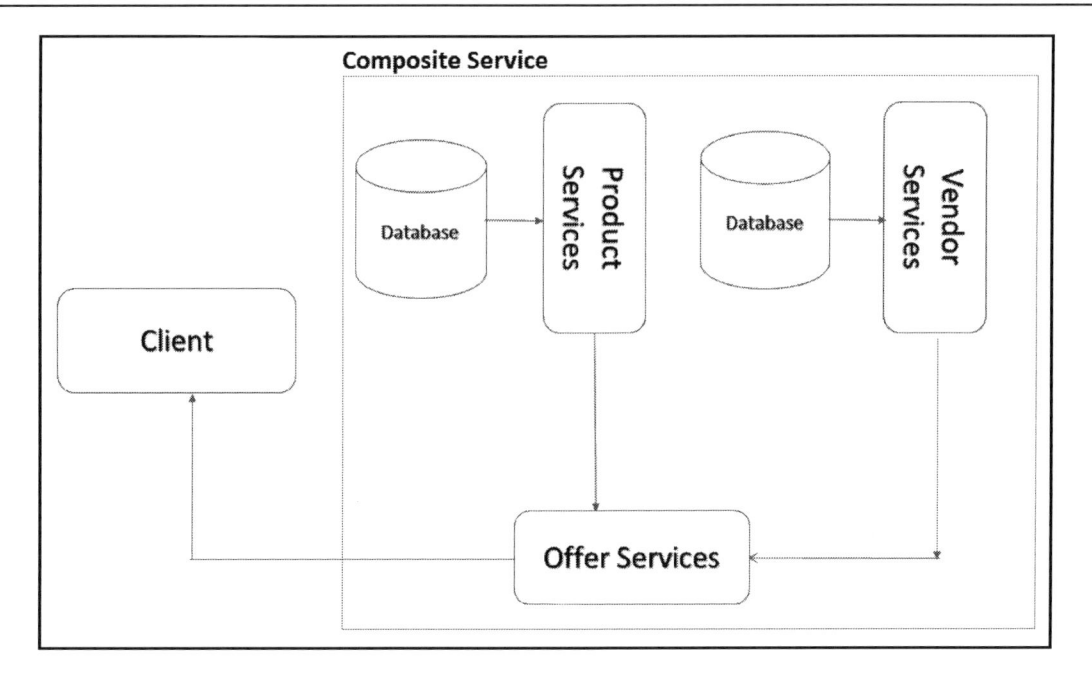

The preceding diagram is a pictorial representation of the composite service. **Product Services** and **Vendor Services** use their own databases, and **Offer Services** depend upon the information and data of these two services. Finally, **Offer Services** combine this data/information and send it back to the **Client**. Here, our **Offer Services** act as an aggregator.

Now that we know the problem, we will look at the solution and implement it using code examples.

Implementing the solution

In this section, we will create a composite microservice and implement the Aggregator pattern. Please revisit the *Technical Requirements* section to check the prerequisites for this application. Follow these steps to create our services:

1. Open Visual Studio.
2. Go to **Get Started** | **Create a new Project**. You can also click the **Continue without code** link from this screen; in this case, you need to click **File** | **New Project** to create a new project.
3. Select **ASP.NET Core Web Application**, and then click **Next**.

4. Enter the **Project** name, select the path, and then click **Create**.
5. On the next screen, select an **API** and click **Create**; make sure that you have selected **.NET Core** and **ASP.NET Core 3.1**.
6. To make a sample project simple to demonstrate, I have added the folders and files, as shown in the following screenshot:

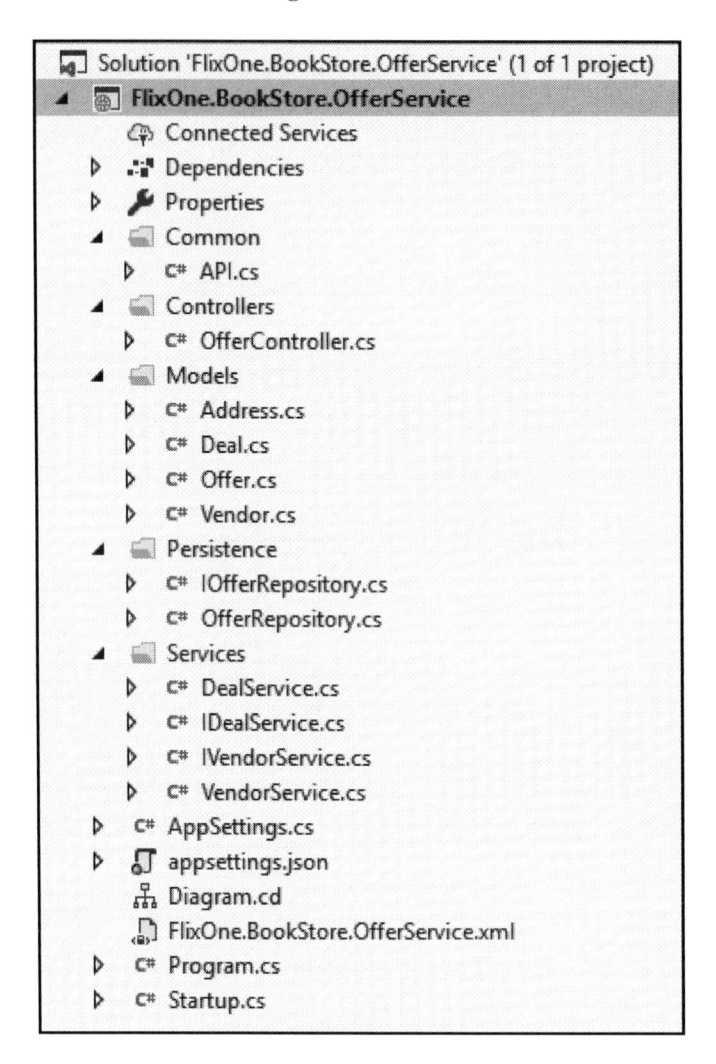

```
Solution 'FlixOne.BookStore.OfferService' (1 of 1 project)
▲ ⊕ FlixOne.BookStore.OfferService
      ⚙ Connected Services
    ▷ ⋮ Dependencies
    ▷ 🔧 Properties
    ▲ 📁 Common
       ▷ C# API.cs
    ▲ 📁 Controllers
       ▷ C# OfferController.cs
    ▲ 📁 Models
       ▷ C# Address.cs
       ▷ C# Deal.cs
       ▷ C# Offer.cs
       ▷ C# Vendor.cs
    ▲ 📁 Persistence
       ▷ C# IOfferRepository.cs
       ▷ C# OfferRepository.cs
    ▲ 📁 Services
       ▷ C# DealService.cs
       ▷ C# IDealService.cs
       ▷ C# IVendorService.cs
       ▷ C# VendorService.cs
    ▷ C# AppSettings.cs
    ▷ 🗋 appsettings.json
       🗋 Diagram.cd
       🗋 FlixOne.BookStore.OfferService.xml
    ▷ C# Program.cs
    ▷ C# Startup.cs
```

The preceding screenshot shows our **FlixOne.BookStore.OfferService** solution. This contains a few folders that we will now study in detail, namely `Common`, `Controller`, `Models`, `Persistence`, and `Services`.

[336]

The Common folder

This folder contains all our common operations. In our application, we added an `API.cs` file that contains methods to create service endpoints for the `Deal` and `Vendor` microservices.

The following code is used to gather the services endpoints:

```
public static class Deal
{
    public static string GetAllDeals(string baseUri) =>
$"{baseUri}";
    public static string GetDeal(string baseUri, string id) =>
$"{baseUri}/{id}";
}
```

In the preceding code, we created a static class called `Deal`. This class has static methods, namely `GetAllDeals` and `GetDeal`. These methods concatenate the various parameters with `baseUri`, generate the service endpoint, and return it as a `string` of a complete `baseUri`.

> The code aims to demonstrate the Aggregator pattern (using composite microservices). It does not focus on covering complete CRUD operations, but instead, it focuses on explaining the pattern, using the `Get` operation.

The following code is of the `Vendor` class:

```
public static class Vendor
{
    public static string GetList(string baseUri) => $"{baseUri}";
    public static string GetVendor(string baseUri, string id) =>
$"{baseUri}/{id}";
}
```

The preceding code generates the service endpoints to get the `Vendor` list and to fetch a vendor record, based on the `Vendor ID`.

The `Deal` and `Vendor` classes are simple to understand. These classes only form a string of service endpoints. To make our code simple, we used this method to form the string of service endpoints, but you can achieve this by putting endpoints in config files, environments, or databases. In the coming sections, we will see how to use these methods.

Design Patterns and Best Practices

The Controllers folder

This folder contains our API controllers which expose as a service. The following code explains this:

```
[HttpGet("{dealId}/{vendorId}")]
[ProducesResponseType(typeof(Models.Offer), 200)]
public async Task<Models.Offer> GetOffer(string dealId, string vendorId)
{
    var res = await _repository.Get(dealId, vendorId);
    return res;
}
```

We added a GET resource to our OfferController that fetches a record of an Offer object. The Offer object is meant to aggregate the data from the Vendor and Deal models.

The following code shows how to aggregate the data from the Deal and Vendor models:

```
public Offer Get()
{
    Offer offer = new Offer();
    if (_deal != null && _deal.StartOn.HasValue)
    {
        offer.OfferCode = _deal.Id.ToString();
        offer.OfferDetails = $"Offer:{_deal.Name}, {_deal.Description}";
        offer.OfferBanner = _deal.Image;
        offer.Discount = _deal.OfferPrice;
        offer.OfferValidTill = _deal.EndOn;
    }
    else
    {
        offer.OfferDetails = "Deal is not available.";
    }
    if (_vendor != null)
    {
        offer.VendorCode = _vendor.Code;
        offer.VendroName = _vendor.Name;
        offer.AccessURL = _vendor.URL;
        offer.VendorLogo = _vendor.Logo;

        if (_vendor.Address != null)
        {
            var address = _vendor.Address;
            offer.VendorAddress = $"{address.AddressLine1}
```

```
                {address.AddressLine2}, {address.City}, {address.State},
{address.PIN}";
            }

        }

        return offer;
    }
```

In the preceding code, as per our business needs, we have implemented the logic and clubbed the data, so that it will be available as an object, with the following properties:

```
public string OfferCode { get; set; }
public string OfferDetails { get; set; }
public string OfferBanner { get; set; }
public decimal Discount { get; set; }
public DateTime OfferValidTill { get; set; }
public string VendorCode { get; set; }
public string VendorName { get; set; }
public string AccessURL { get; set; }
public string VendorLogo { get; set; }
public string VendorAddress { get; set; }
```

The preceding properties are explained in the following list:

- OfferCode: Contains a unique ID, representing a record ID of the Deal model.
- OfferDetails: Contains the name and description of the Deal model.
- Offerbanner: Contains the Base64 string of the image of the deal.
- Discount: Contains the discount that's offered by the vendor on the deal.
- OfferValidTill: Contains the date and time of the validity of a Deal.
- VendorCode: Contains the code of the vendor who offered the deal.
- VendorName: Contains the name of the vendor who offered the deal.
- AccessURL: Contains the URL of the offered deal. This represents the URL *provided* by the vendor for the offer.
- VendorLogo: Contains the Base64 string of the Vendor logo.

The Models folder

This folder contains the model classes that will help us hold and transpose our model object data. Let's look at the following code:

```
public class Address
{
    public Guid Id { get; set; }
    public string AddressLine1 { get; set; }
    public string AddressLine2 { get; set; }
    public string City { get; set; }
    public string State { get; set; }
    public string Country { get; set; }
    public string PIN { get; set; }
    public Guid VendorId { get; set; }
}
```

The preceding code contains the `Address` class and its properties to maintain the address of the user (`Vendor`). These properties are explained as follows:

- `Id`: Contains a unique ID, representing the record ID of the `Address` model
- `AddressLine1`: Contains the address details of the `Vendor`
- `AddressLine2`: Contains the address details of the `Vendor`
- `City`: Contains the city name of the `Vendor`
- `State`: Contains the state name of the `Vendor`
- `Country`: Contains the country name of the `Vendor`
- `PIN`: Contains the **postal index number** (**PIN**)
- `VendorId`: Contains a unique ID, representing the record ID of the `Vendor` model

Let's consider the following code:

```
public class Deal
{
    public Guid Id { get; set; }
    public string Name { get; set; }
    public string Description { get; set; }
    public string Image { get; set; }
    public decimal OfferPrice { get; set; }
    public DateTime CreatedOn { get; set; }
    public DateTime? StartOn { get; set; }
    public DateTime? EndOn { get; set; }
}
```

The preceding code contains the `Deal` class and its properties to maintain the available deals for our users. These properties are explained as follows:

- `Id`: Contains a unique ID, representing the record ID of the `Deal` model.
- `Name`: Contains the name of the deal.
- `Description`: Contains the description of the deal.
- `Image`: Contains the `Base64` string of the deal's image.
- `OfferPrice`: Contains the deal price.
- `CreatedOn`: Contains the date on which the deal is created.
- `StartOn`: Contains the date that the deal starts on. This is a nullable property: if it is `null`, that means that the deal has yet to be started.
- `EndOn`: Contains the date that the deal is concluded. This is a nullable property: if it is `null`, then the deal will never expire.

Let's consider the following code:

```
public class Vendor
{
    public Guid Id { get; set; }
    public string Code { get; set; }
    public string Name { get; set; }
    public string Description { get; set; }
    public string URL { get; set; }
    public string Logo { get; set; }
    public DateTime AddedOn { get; set; } = DateTime.UtcNow;
    public bool Active { get; set; }
    public Address Address { get; set; }
}
```

The preceding code contains the `Vendor` class, and its properties correspond to the `Vendor` details. These properties are explained as follows:

- `Id`: Contains a unique ID, representing the record ID of the `Vendor` model.
- `Code`: Contains the Vendor code; this code is unique for each `Vendor`.
- `Name`: Contains the name of the `Vendor`.
- `Description`: Contains a description of the `Vendor`.
- `URL`: Contains the URL of the `Vendor` website.
- `Logo`: Contains the `Base64` string of the `Vendor` logo.
- `AddedOn`: The date that the `Vendor` first came on board, in the system.

- **Active:** Contains a `True` or `False` value. If it contains `True`, that means that the `Vendor` is active; if it contains `False`, the `Vendor` is not active.
- **Address:** Contains the `Vendor` address information that represents the `Address` model.

Next, we will discuss how `Persistence` and `Services` help us implement the Aggregator pattern.

The Persistence folder

This folder contains our repositories, which provide the CRUD operations and return the aggregated data. Let's look at the following code:

```
public class OfferRepository : IOfferRepository
{
    private readonly IDealService _dealService;
    private readonly IVendorService _vendorService;
    public OfferRepository(IDealService dealService, IVendorService vendorService)
    {
        _dealService = dealService;
        _vendorService = vendorService;
    }
    public async Task<Models.Offer> Get(string dealId, string vendorId)
    {
        Deal deal = await _dealService.GetDeal(dealId);
        Vendor vendor = await _vendorService.GetBy(vendorId);
        var offer = new Models.Offer(deal, vendor);
        return offer.Get();
    }
    ...
}
```

The preceding code gives us the ability to get data from the `Deal` microservice and the `Vendor` microservice, and then we return the combined data as an object of `Offer`.

The following code registers the repositories and `Appsettings` so that we can access the config values as/when required:

```
//Configure AppSettings
services.AddOptions();
services.Configure<AppSettings>(Configuration);
//Register repository
services.AddTransient<IOfferRepository, OfferRepository>();
```

The Services folder

This folder contains our services and provides the ability to aggregate the response of these services. The following code is from the `DealService`. This service provides us with the available deals:

```csharp
public class DealService : IDealService
{
    private HttpClient _httpClient;
    private readonly IOptions<AppSettings> _settings;
    private readonly string _baseURL;
    public DealService(HttpClient httpClient, IOptions<AppSettings> settings)
    {
        _httpClient = httpClient;
        _settings = settings;
        _baseURL = $"{settings.Value.DealUrl}/api/deal";
    }
    public async Task<List<Deal>> GetDeals()
    {
        var endPoint = API.Deal.GetAllDeals(_baseURL);
        var resString = await _httpClient.GetStringAsync(endPoint);
        var response = JsonConvert.DeserializeObject<List<Deal>>(resString);
        return response;
    }
    public async Task<Deal> GetDeal(string id)
    {
        var endPoint = API.Deal.GetDeal(_baseURL, id);
        var resString = await _httpClient.GetStringAsync(endPoint);
        var response = JsonConvert.DeserializeObject<Deal>(resString);
        return response;
    }
    ...
}
```

In the preceding code, the `GetDeal` method calls the `Deal` microservices and returns the response to our repositories for further processing.

To use the remote URLs of the microservices, we have added keys to our config files, as follows:

```json
{
   "DealUrl": "http://localhost:52786",
   "VendorUrl": "http://localhost:52788",
   ...
}
```

Design Patterns and Best Practices

The preceding code has two keys, `DealUrl` and `VendorUrl`, with a remote URL. These values could be changed, as per your settings.

We mapped these keys with our `AppSettings.cs` file, as follows:

```
public class AppSettings
{
    public string DealUrl { get; set; }
    public string VendorUrl { get; set; }
}
```

We have already mapped this file to our `Startup.cs` file, so we can access the config values as follows:

```
public DealService(HttpClient httpClient, IOptions<AppSettings> settings)
{
    _httpClient = httpClient;
    _settings = settings;

    _baseURL = $"{settings.Value.DealUrl}/api/deal";
}
```

The following code is from `VendorService`:

```
public class VendorService : IVendorService
{
    private HttpClient _httpClient;
    private readonly IOptions<AppSettings> _settings;
    private readonly string _baseURL;
    public VendorService(HttpClient httpClient, IOptions<AppSettings> settings)
    {
        _httpClient = httpClient;
        _settings = settings;
        _baseURL = $"{settings.Value.VendorUrl}/api/vendor";
    }
    public async Task<List<Vendor>> GetAll()
    {
        var endPoint = API.Vendor.GetList(_baseURL);
        var resString = await _httpClient.GetStringAsync(endPoint);
        var response = JsonConvert.DeserializeObject<List<Vendor>>(resString);
        return response;
    }
    public async Task<Vendor> GetBy(string id)
    {
        var endPoint = API.Vendor.GetVendor(_baseURL, id);
        var resString = await _httpClient.GetStringAsync(endPoint);
```

```
            var response = JsonConvert.DeserializeObject<Vendor>(resString);
            return response;
        }
        ...
}
```

The `GetBy` method in the preceding code calls the `Vendor` microservice, takes the response, and returns it to `OfferRepository` for further processing.

Finally, when the client consumes the `OfferService`, we will get the aggregated data as a response from the `Offer` service. This service is created to demonstrate the Aggregator pattern, with `Composite` microservices, but without the use of the API gateway.

This section aimed to aggregate the response of two different services, also called composite services. We have discussed the Aggregator pattern, with a code example, and we implemented the code without the use of the API gateway. In the next section, we will discuss the Shared Data microservices pattern, with the implementation of two separate services that will share a common database.

The Shared Data microservices pattern

The Shared Data microservices pattern can be considered an antipattern in the context of microservices. We can also say that the Shared Data pattern is one of the most controversial patterns.

> The great concept behind this pattern is that it uses the same physical structure for data storage. This pattern can be used when there is some doubt about the structure of the data, or when the communication layer between the microservices is not well defined.

On the one hand, it is an antipattern; but, on the other hand, it is the most favorable pattern. You should bear the following points in mind about this data pattern:

- **The Shared Data pattern as an antipattern**: When we talk about this pattern in regards to microservices, then certainly this pattern would be called an antipattern. This pattern is not suitable for applications that are being developed from scratch (also called *greenfield* applications). There is a very basic concept, where, if we are developing any new application, then we should be considering the design of the application and the pattern's best practices that also take care of database design. In this scenario, if we try to implement the Shared Data pattern, we will not get any benefits; in this case, it is just an antipattern.

- **The Shared Data pattern as an appropriate pattern**: When we migrate any legacy applications (also called *brownfield* applications) to a new application while working with microservices, then this pattern is one of the appropriate patterns to use.

In this book, we have used the Shared Data pattern from the very beginning, where we started transitioning the monolith application. We then adapted the Shared Data pattern during the activities in the following ways:

- Breaking a monolithic application
- Reconsidering and developing new microservices during the transition of a monolithic application
- Data orchestration

Pros and cons of the pattern

The Shared Data pattern is considered to be both an anti-pattern and a favorable pattern, depending on the developers who implement it. In most cases, developers take it as an old concept and thus they recommend that this pattern is not used anymore. However, there are various other thoughts on this pattern, so we can say this pattern has both pros and cons, which are listed as follows:

- As technology grows, our applications should also be enhanced; there are many legacy applications that are required to be migrated or upgraded here. The Shared Data pattern is one of the favorite choices for legacy applications that require upgrading to achieve automation, scalability, and resilience.
- The positive benefit of the Shared Data pattern is that it helps to give the development team time to segregate the information from the database and to evaluate the consistency of the data.
- Moreover, it helps to reset the architecture project, as and when it is used by developers.
- Regarding the negative effects of the Shared Data pattern, the most common impact is that, with the use of this pattern, all the microservices are deposited on storage.

Best practices to be observed

Overall, there would be far fewer applications without storage. The main objective of databases is to only persist or store data. As developers, we should not store any other information in a database. But, for some reason, we might store some business rules or any information that should be part of the application code. If we are storing business rules in the database, then we are pushing our application to become dependent on our database, which hinders the process of data migration and distribution.

A common mistake is, sometimes, development teams adopt the process of using triggers with their own database resources, or workers observing changes to the information stored. The problem is that these triggers are difficult to monitor and debug, and they are also a way to create business rules for storage.

With the help of this pattern, we can make our legacy applications like greenfield applications, or, in other words, in the context of microservices, the Shared Data pattern is one of the favorable choices that helps reset the architecture project. It's also true that the Shared Data pattern is one of the most controversial patterns, and many developers consider it to be an older technique that should not be used these days. Being an anti-pattern directly indicates that this should not be used.

There are different views on this topic, and now we'll look at it in terms of our imaginary application FlixOne Store, which has been transitioned from a monolithic application. This is one of the best examples to showcase best practices and usage of the Shared Data pattern.

The problem and its solution – example in FlixOne

The FlixOne team faced a new problem while extracting order details. The team faced a scenario where two different services required them to save similar information into a database. Currently, it is duplicating information, as both the customer service and the order service use their own databases. The team found a problem when the business team came up with the idea of adding a wallet feature for customers. As per this feature, customers can have wallet credit in their FlixOne account. Whenever the customer orders/purchases any product from the FlixOne portal, then the calculation of their invoice should follow these rules:

1. The wallet balance should be checked before calculating the NetPay for the order.

2. If the wallet balance is a credit balance (a credit balance would be greater than zero), then first use the wallet balance and then calculate the NetPay.
3. Adjust the wallet balance once the NetPay is calculated.
4. The wallet balance can't be negative (less than zero).

To resolve the issue, the FlixOne team decided to use a single database for both of the services. To understand it in detail, consider the following diagram:

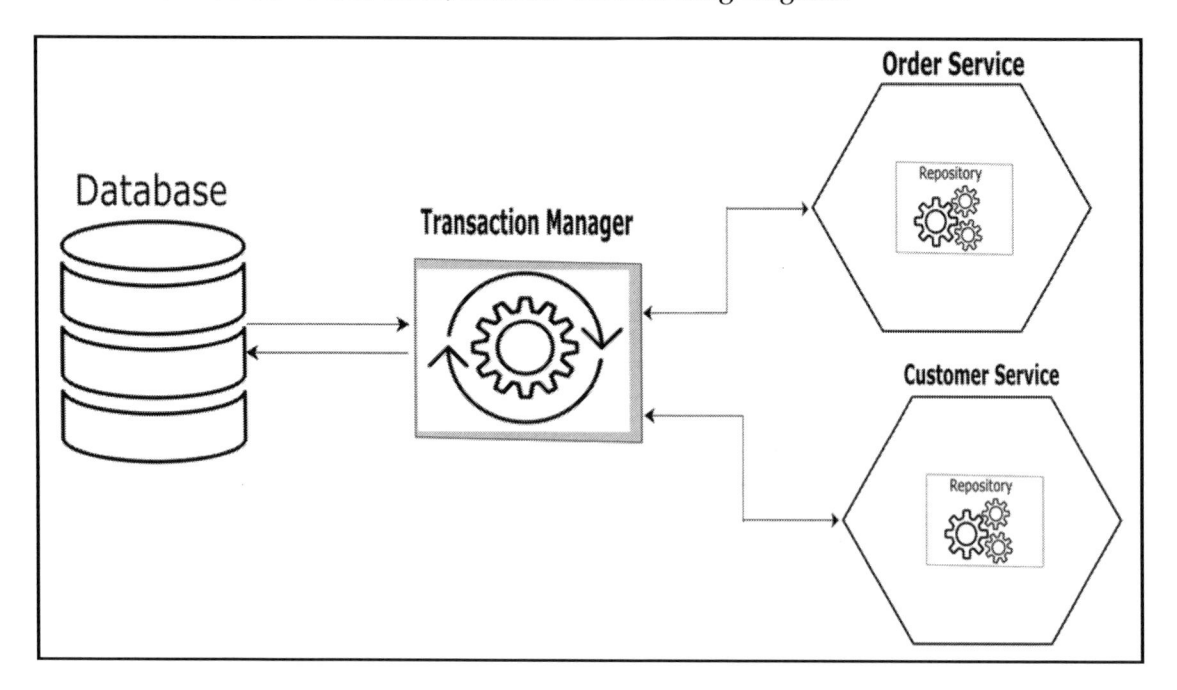

In the preceding diagram, our two services, **Order Service** and **Customer Service**, share the same database. Every interaction between these services and the database goes through the **Transaction Manager**. In this way, a service can use the correct data, which is being used by another service. For example, if our **Order Service** consumed the wallet amount (the credit), then our **Customer Service** should return the correct wallet amount (the credit), after the utilization of the amount.

Now, its time to implement this solution in our FlixOne application.

Implementing the solution

To implement the solution for the aforementioned problem, we will first create the `OrderService`:

1. Open Visual Studio.
2. Go to **Get Started** | **Create a new Project**. You can also click the **Continue without code** link from this screen. In this case, you need to click **File** | **New Project** to create a new project.
3. Select **ASP.NET Core Web Application** and then click **Next**.
4. Enter the Project name, select the path, and then click **Create**.
5. On the next screen, select an **ASP.NET Core MVC** template and then click **Create**. Make sure that you have selected **.NET Core** and **ASP.NET Core 3.1**.

To help us follow the code and its implementation, I have added files and folders and now the solution looks as follows:

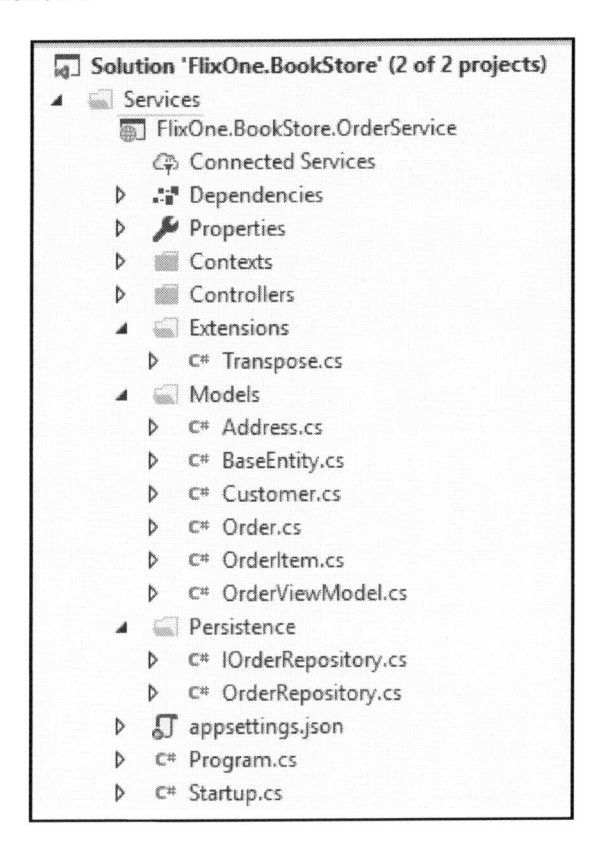

```
Solution 'FlixOne.BookStore' (2 of 2 projects)
  ▲ Services
      FlixOne.BookStore.OrderService
        Connected Services
      ▷ Dependencies
      ▷ Properties
      ▷ Contexts
      ▷ Controllers
      ▲ Extensions
          ▷ C# Transpose.cs
      ▲ Models
          ▷ C# Address.cs
          ▷ C# BaseEntity.cs
          ▷ C# Customer.cs
          ▷ C# Order.cs
          ▷ C# OrderItem.cs
          ▷ C# OrderViewModel.cs
      ▲ Persistence
          ▷ C# IOrderRepository.cs
          ▷ C# OrderRepository.cs
      ▷ appsettings.json
      ▷ C# Program.cs
      ▷ C# Startup.cs
```

Design Patterns and Best Practices

The preceding screenshot consists of several default files. Apart from these files, we added more files and folders that we will be discussing in a while. Before we go into more detail, first let's make sure we've added the NuGet packages `Microsoft.EntityFrameworkCore.SqlServer`, `Microsoft.EntityFrameworkCore.Design`, and `Microsoft.EntityFrameworkCore`. These packages will help us use the features of Entity Framework Core. Also, add the NuGet `Swashbuckle.AspNetCore` package, so that we can add documentation to our APIs.

To do so, go to **Tools** | **NuGet Package Manage** | **Package Manager Console**. Execute the following code in the **Package Manager Console**:

```
Install-Package Swashbuckle.AspNetCore
```

The preceding code installs the package for Swagger. Similarly, you should install all the other packages.

Now, let's discuss all the folders and files in detail.

The Extensions folder

This folder contains code to transpose our `Models` to `ViewModels` and vice versa. This folder contains the `Transpose.cs` file to help transpose between the `Order` and `OrderItems` models and the view model's `OrderViewModel`.

These models represent the database tables, as visualized in the following screenshot:

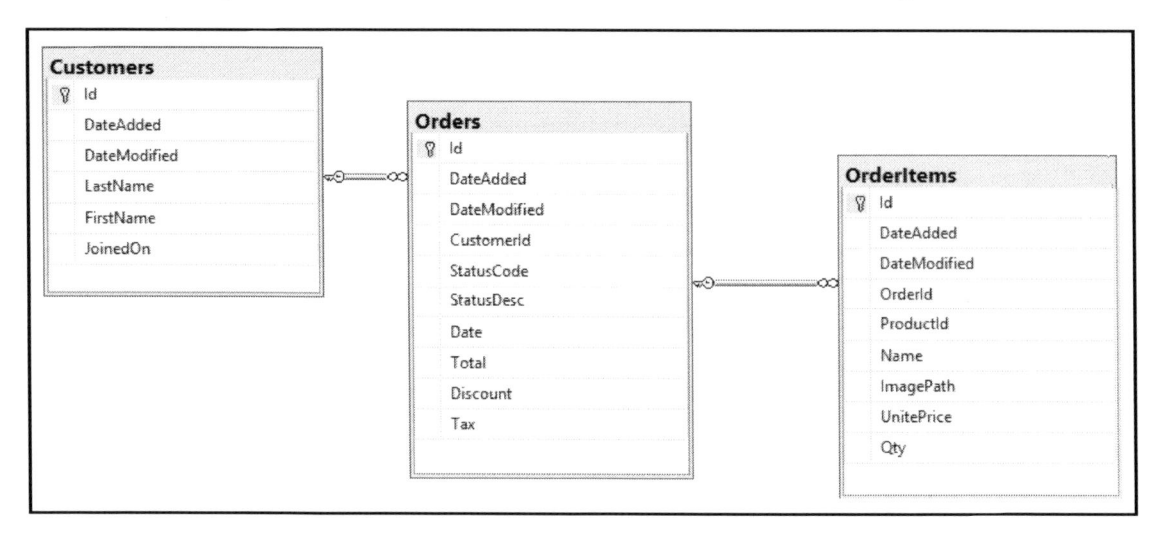

Customers
- Id
- DateAdded
- DateModified
- LastName
- FirstName
- JoinedOn

Orders
- Id
- DateAdded
- DateModified
- CustomerId
- StatusCode
- StatusDesc
- Date
- Total
- Discount
- Tax

OrderItems
- Id
- DateAdded
- DateModified
- OrderId
- ProductId
- Name
- ImagePath
- UnitePrice
- Qty

Let's discuss these models and the view models, as shown in the following code:

```
public static Models.Order ToModel(this Models.OrderViewModel vm)
{
    return new Models.Order
    {
        Id = vm.OrderId,
        CustomerId = vm.CustomerId,
        Date = vm.Date,
        StatusCode = vm.StatusCode,
        StatusDesc = vm.StatusDesc,
        Tax = vm.Tax,
        Total = vm.Total,
        NetPay = vm.NetPay,
        Items = vm.Items.ToModel()
    };
}

public static IEnumerable<Models.Order> ToModel(this
IEnumerable<Models.OrderViewModel> vm) => vm.Select(ToModel);
```

The preceding code contains the `ToModel` method. This transposes our `OrderViewModel` to the `Order` model; one method transposes into a single record, while the others transpose into a list:

```
public static Models.OrderViewModel ToViewModel(this Models.Order model)
{
    return new Models.OrderViewModel
    {
        CustomerId = model.CustomerId,
        Date = model.Date,
        OrderId = model.Id,
        StatusCode = model.StatusCode,
        StatusDesc = model.StatusDesc,
        Tax = model.Tax,
        Items = model.Items.ToViewModel()
    };
}
public static IEnumerable<Models.OrderViewModel> ToViewModel(this
IEnumerable<Models.Order> model) => model.Select(ToViewModel);
```

The preceding code contains the `ToViewModel` method. This transposes our `Order` to `OrderViewModel`; one method transposes into a single record, while the others transpose into a list.

Design Patterns and Best Practices

The Models folder

This folder contains the model classes that will help us hold and transpose our model object data. Let's look at the following code:

```
public abstract class BaseEntity
{
    [Key]
    public Guid Id { get; set; }
    public DateTime DateAdded { get; set; } = DateTime.UtcNow;
    public DateTime? DateModified { get; set; }
}
```

The previous code contains an abstract class, `BaseEntity`. This is going to be the base class for all of our models. It contains the following properties:

- `Id`: Contains a unique ID, representing the record ID of all the models that inherit this class.
- `DateAdded`: Contains the date when the record was added; its default value is the current `DateTime`.
- `DateModified`: Contains the date when the record was modified; it can also contain a null value.

Let's consider the following code, for the `Customer` model:

```
public class Customer : BaseEntity
{
    public string FirstName { get; set; }
    public string LastName { get; set; }
    public DateTime MemberSince { get; set; }
    public decimal Wallet { get; set; }
    public string FullName => LastName + " " + FirstName;
}
```

The preceding code contains the `Customer` model, which inherits the `BaseEntity` class. The `Customer` model contains the properties that are detailed as follows, including the properties of `BaseEntity`:

- `FirstName`: Contains the `FirstName` of the customer.
- `LastName`: Contains the `LastName` of the customer.
- `MemberSince`: Contains the `DateTime` when customers joined the `FlixOne` portal.

- `Wallet`: Contains the credit amount.
- `FullName`: Contains the full name, and it concatenates `LastName` and `FirstName`.

Let's consider the following code, for the `Address` model:

```
public class Address : BaseEntity
{
    public Guid CustomerId { get; set; }
    public string AddressLine1 { get; set; }
    public string AddressLine2 { get; set; }
    public string City { get; set; }
    public string State { get; set; }
    public string Country { get; set; }
    public string PIN { get; set; }
}
```

The preceding code contains the `Address` model, which inherits the `BaseEntity` class. The `Address` model contains the properties that are detailed as follows, including the properties of `BaseEntity`:

- `CustomerId`: Contains a unique ID, representing the record ID of the `Customer` model.
- `AddressLine1`: Contains the address of a customer.
- `AddressLine2`: Contains the second line (if applicable) of a customer's address.
- `City`: Contains the city of a customer.
- `State`: Contains the state of a customer.
- `Country`: Contains the country of a customer.
- `PIN`: Contains the PIN of a customer's address.

Let's consider the following code, for the `Order` model:

```
public class Order : BaseEntity
{
    public Order()
    {
        Items = new List<OrderItem>();
    }
    public Guid CustomerId { get; set; }
    public string StatusCode { get; set; }
    public string StatusDesc { get; set; }
    public DateTime Date { get; set; }
    public decimal Total { get; set; }
    public decimal Tax { get; set; }
```

```
        public decimal NetPay { get; set; }
        public IEnumerable<OrderItem> Items { get; set; }
}
```

The preceding code contains the Order model, which inherits the BaseEntity class. The Order model contains the properties that are detailed as follows, including the properties of BaseEntity:

- CustomerId: Contains a unique ID, representing the record ID of the Customer model.
- StatusCode: Contains the StatusCode of the Order.
- StatusDesc: Contains the status detail information.
- Date: Contains the Order date.
- Total: Contains the Order total.
- Tax: Contains the amount of Tax, if applied.
- NetPay: Contains the amount of NetPay for the Order.
- Items: Contains a list of the OrderItems.

Let's consider the following code, for the OrderItem model:

```
public class OrderItem : BaseEntity
{
    public Guid OrderId { get; set; }
    public Guid ProductId { get; set;
    public int Sequence { get; set; }
    public string Name { get; set; }
    public string ImagePath { get; set
    public decimal UnitePrice { get; s
    public decimal Discount { get; set
    public int Qty { get; set; }
    public decimal Total { get; set; }
}
```

The preceding code contains the OrderItem model, which inherits the BaseEntity class. The OrderItem model contains the properties, which are detailed as follows, including the properties of BaseEntity:

- OrderId: Contains a unique ID, representing the record ID of the Order model.
- ProductId: Contains a unique ID, representing the record ID of the Product model.
- Sequence: Contains the serial number of items for the order.
- Name: Contains the item's Name.

- `ImagePath`: Contains the item's image path.
- `UnitPrice`: Contains the `UnitPrice` of the item.
- `Discount`: Contains the `Discount` amount of the item, if any.
- `Qty`: Contains the `Qty` of the item.
- `Total`: Contains the item total, which is calculated as `Qty * UnitPrice - Discount`.

Apart from the discussed models, we have `OrderViewModel` and `OrderItemViewModel`, which are discussed as follows:

```
public class OrderViewModel
{
    public Guid OrderId { get; set; }
    public Guid CustomerId { get; set; }
    public string StatusCode { get; set; }
    public string StatusDesc { get; set; }
    public DateTime Date { get; set; }
    public decimal Total { get { return Items.Sum(i => i.Total); } }
    public decimal Tax { get; set; }
    public decimal WalletBalance { get; set; }
    public decimal NetPay { get { return (Total + Tax) - WalletBalance; } }
    public IEnumerable<OrderItemViewModel> Items { get; set; }
}
```

The preceding code of `OrderViewModel` contains the following properties:

- `OrderId`: Contains a unique ID, representing the record ID of the `Order`.
- `CustomerId`: Contains a unique ID, representing the record ID of the `Customer`.
- `StatusCode`: The status code of the order.
- `StatusDesc`: The status information of the order.
- `Date`: The `Date` of the `Order`.
- `Total`: Holds the `Total` of the `Order`.
- `Tax`: The `Tax` amount, if applicable.
- `WalletBalance`: Holds the credit amount, which remains in the customer's `Wallet`.
- `NetPay`: The amount due on the `Order`, after adjusting the `WalletBalance`.
- `Items`: The list of `OrderItems`.

Design Patterns and Best Practices

Let's consider the following code, for `OrderItemViewModel`:

```
public class OrderItemViewModel
{
    public Guid OrderItemId { get; set; }
    public Guid OrderId { get; set; }
    public Guid ProductId { get; set; }
    public int Sequence { get; set; }
    public string Name { get; set; }
    public string ImagePath { get; set; }
    public decimal UnitPrice { get; set; }
    public decimal Discount { get; set; }
    public int Qty { get; set; }
    public decimal Total { get { return (Qty * UnitPrice) - Discount; } }
}
```

The preceding code contains `OrderItemViewModel`, which has the following properties:

- `OrderItemId`: Contains the unique ID of the `OrderItem`.
- `OrderId`: Contains the unique ID of the `Order`.
- `ProductId`: Contains the unique ID of the `Product`.
- `Sequence`: This is the ordered item's serial number.
- `Name`: The order item name.
- `ImagePath`: The image path.
- `UnitPrice`: The unit price of the item.
- `Discount`: The discount amount of the item, if any.
- `Qty`: The quantity of the item.
- `Total`: The `Total` amount of the item, which is calculated as `Qty * UnitPrice - Discount`.

The Persistence folder

This folder contains our repositories, and these repositories provide the required **CRUD** operations, with the appropriate business rules.

> As per our requirement, we have implemented the business logic in our repository's classes, but, in most cases, we'd require separate classes that contain the business logic/business rules, and so on.

Let's consider the following code:

```
public IEnumerable<Models.Order> List() => _context.Orders.Include(o =>
o.Items).ToList();

public Models.Order Get(Guid id) => _context.Orders.Include(o =>
o.Items).FirstOrDefault(o => o.Id == id);
```

The preceding code contains two methods, `List` and `Get`. Both methods fetch the `Order` data, where `List` extracts all the available orders and `Get` extracts a single order, based on the `OrderId` from the database.

Let's consider the following code:

```
public void Add(Models.Order order)
{
    using (var transaction = _context.Database.BeginTransaction())
    {
        try
        {
            var customer = _context.Customers.Where(c => c.Id ==
order.CustomerId).FirstOrDefault();
            var walletBalance = customer.Wallet;
            if(walletBalance > 0)
            {
                if(walletBalance >= order.NetPay)
                {
                    order.NetPay = 0M; //Deduct total payment from Wallet
Balance
                    customer.Wallet = walletBalance - order.NetPay;
//Deduct amount from wallet and save the remaining amount
                }
                else
                {
                    order.NetPay = walletBalance - order.NetPay;
//partially deduct amount from wallet
                    customer.Wallet = 0M; // empty the wallet
                }
                //Update customer to reflect new/updated Wallet balance
                _context.Customers.Update(customer);
            }
            _context.Orders.Add(order);
```

[357]

```
            _context.SaveChanges();

            transaction.Commit();
        }
        catch (Exception)
        {
            throw;
        }
    }
}
```

The preceding code contains the Add method, and this method helps us to insert the new Order into the database. You'll observe that the Add method contains the business rule for the adjustment of WalletBalance (for the code explanation and demo purposes, and to make the code simpler to understand, I put these business rules here in the Add method). This method obeys the following business rules:

- Validates whether WalletBalance has a sufficient credit amount: WalletBalance > 0
- Calculates the due amount, after an adjustment of the credit amount: order.NetPay = walletBalance - order.NetPay;
- Resets the WalletBalance amount, after the adjustments are made: customer.Wallet = 0M;

The most important point to note is that the Add method, in the preceding code, operates completely within the transaction, using (var transaction = _context.Database.BeginTransaction()). During the operation of this method, there is no chance to get incorrect data for CustomerService (as and when this service required the data). The AddOrderItem method in the following code is another example of maintaining transactions:

```
public void AddOrderItem(Models.OrderItem item)
{
    using (var transaction = _context.Database.BeginTransaction())
    {
        try
        {
            var orderItemForProduct = _context.OrderItems.Where(o => o.ProductId == item.ProductId).SingleOrDefault();
            if (orderItemForProduct != null)
            {
                if (item.Discount < 0)
                {
                    //discount can't be -ve leave it
```

```
                    //if there is specific case then we can through an exception
                    //and notify the user
                }
                orderItemForProduct.Discount = item.Discount;
                if (item.Qty > 0)
                {
                    orderItemForProduct.Qty += item.Qty;
                }
                orderItemForProduct.DateModified = DateTime.UtcNow;
                _context.OrderItems.Update(orderItemForProduct);
            }
            else
            {
                var orderItem = _context.OrderItems.OrderBy(o => o.Sequence).LastOrDefault();
                item.Sequence = (orderItem != null) ? orderItem.Sequence + 1 : 1;
                _context.OrderItems.Add(item);
            }

            _context.SaveChanges();

            transaction.Commit();
        }
        catch (Exception)
        {
            throw;
        }
    }
}
```

The preceding code contains the `AddOrderItem` method, which helps us insert a newly ordered item into the table. By implementing the transaction, we make sure that the operation is successfully committed, and the complete operation would be rolled back upon any failure during the transaction.

The Controllers folder

This folder contains `OrderController` as our API controller. This `OrderController` will expose as a service. The following code explains this:

```
[Route("api/v1/[controller]")]
public class OrderController : Controller
{
```

Design Patterns and Best Practices

```
        private readonly IOrderRepository _orderRepository;
        public OrderController(IOrderRepository orderRepository) =>
_orderRepository = orderRepository;
        [HttpGet]
        public IActionResult List() => new
OkObjectResult(_orderRepository.List().ToViewModel());
        [HttpGet("{id}")]
        public IActionResult Get(Guid id) => new
OkObjectResult(_orderRepository.Get(id).ToViewModel());
        [HttpPost]
        public void Add([FromBody]OrderViewModel OViewModel) =>
_orderRepository.Add(OViewModel.ToModel());
        [HttpPost("OrderItem")]
        public void AddItem([FromBody]OrderItemViewModel item) =>
_orderRepository.AddOrderItem(item.ToModel());
}
```

The preceding code contains all the required APIs, which are detailed as follows:

- `List`: This is a `GET` resource, which fetches all the available orders from the database.
- `Get`: This is a `GET` resource, which fetches a single `Order`, based on the order ID.
- `Add`: A `POST` resource, which inserts a new `Order`.
- `AddItem`: A `POST` resource, which helps add a newly ordered item.

Notice that all the preceding resources are called from `ToModel` and `ToViewModel`, and subsequent methods are called from `OrderRepository`.

`OrderController` exposes APIs, as detailed in the following table:

HTTP method	API resource	Description
GET	/api/v1/Order	Fetches all the available orders from the database
GET	/api/v1/Order/{id}	Fetches the record of an order, based on `OrderId`
POST	/api/v1/Order	Adds a new `Order`
POST	/api/v1/Order/OrderItem	Adds a new `Order` Item

The API resources, that are listed in the preceding table, are available for all clients that are consuming `OrderServices`.

> In the solution, our `Contexts` folder contains the auto-generated files, which can be created by executing the following two commands from the Package Manager console:
> - `Add-Migration FlixOneSharedDB`
> - `Update-Database`
>
> Also, you need to register the repositories in your startup file. Tell the system where the connection string is, which needs to connect to SQLServer. You must add the following code:
> ```
> services.AddTransient<IOrderRepository, OrderRepository>();
> services.AddDbContext<VendorContext>(o =>
> o.UseSqlServer(Configuration.GetConnectionString("OrderCo
> nnection")));
> ```

At this point, we are done. The shared database helps resolve our problem and provides data consistency between the two separate services. Now, both our services will get the correct data. For example, the amount of `WalletBalance` is 500, and the total amount of `Order` is 3071. Now, whenever `Order` is processed, it will show the `NetPay` amount as 2571 and `WalletBalance` as 0. With the help of the shared database, we resolved our data consistency issue. We also got rid of the duplicating data issue, and we moved our services into separate tables.

With the implementation of a shared database, we created consistency between two separate services. However, sometimes we need to maintain two different systems to implement this. So, in the next section, we will discuss the Anti-Corruption Layer pattern.

The Anti-Corruption Layer pattern

In this pattern, two different subsystems do not share the same semantics, but they can talk to each other with the implementation of a layer (mostly with the help of the Facade or Adapter patterns). The layer works in such a way that a request made by one subsystem reaches out and talks to another subsystem. In this section, we will discuss the Anti-Corruption Layer, from the perspective of our FlixOne application.

Maintaining access to new and legacy systems requires that the new system adheres to at least some of the APIs or other semantics of the legacy system. If these legacy apps have problems with consistency, then they *corrupt* what could otherwise be a cleanly crafted modern application. These issues or problems can also arise in an existing system that you want to connect with an external/legacy system. To sort out these issues, we need to use this pattern.

Consider the following diagram, which shows a pictorial view of the Anti-Corruption Layer:

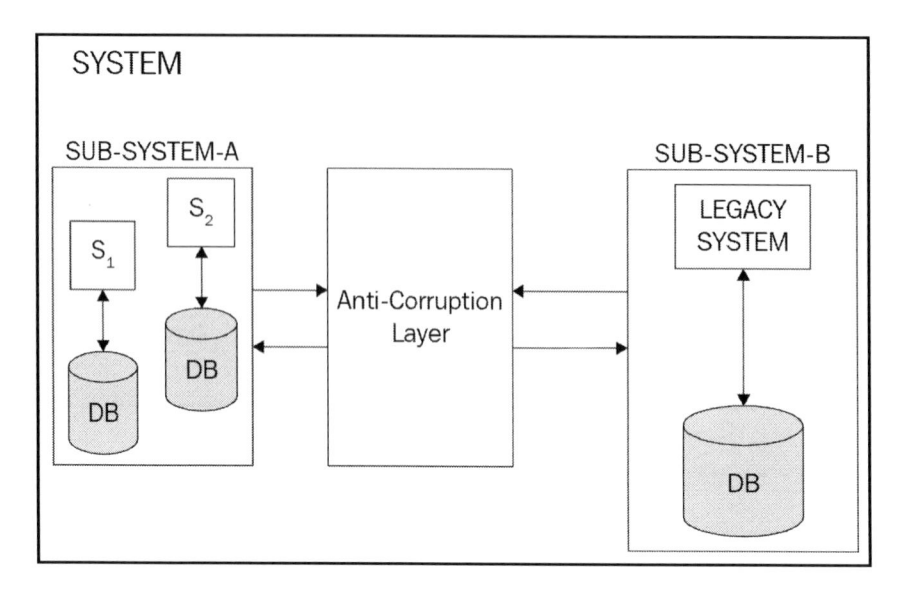

In the preceding diagram, we can see that we have two different systems: one is the **LEGACY SYSTEM (SUB-SYSTEM-B)** and the other is our growing microservices-based **SUB-SYSTEM-A (S1 and S2)**. The **Anti-Corruption Layer** works as an adapter between **SUB-SYSTEM-A** and **SUB-SYSTEM-B**.

Pros and cons

While we choose to implement the Anti-Corruption Layer pattern, we should note that the following points can be either pros or cons, depending on your requirements and implementation. Let's start with the pros:

- The Anti-Corruption Layer pattern helps to maintain both the legacy system and the new system.
- It helps to make a proper translation between the two different subsystems.

In contrast to the preceding pros, these are the cons of the Anti-Corruption Layer pattern:

- The Anti-Corruption Layer pattern may add latency to intersystem calls.
- The Anti-Corruption Layer pattern provides a function that needs to be managed and maintained.
- We need to make sure that transactions are protected and that the data integrity can be checked.

Best practices to be observed

This pattern is most useful when we need both the new system and the legacy system, and when the legacy system is going to be migrated over multiple stages. Consider the following best practices:

- Our subsystems have entirely or partially different semantics, as per the requirement that they should communicate with each other.
- This pattern may not be suitable if there are no significant semantic differences between the new system and the legacy system. We will see why we might need such a pattern in the next section.

Problem and its solution – the need for the Anti-Corruption Layer pattern

The FlixOne team found a new challenge when the team introduced the Shipment report into the system. The report depends upon the Order system and Shipment system. Both the systems are entirely different, and we need to sync them together. The team started discussing the various solutions, and, after several brainstorming sessions, they finally decided to make the implementation as simple as possible. They proposed the implementation of the Anti-Corruption Layer pattern, between both systems, so that product data will be synced and properly translated by the Shipment System.

Now it's time to implement the solution in our FlixOne application.

Implementing the solution

To implement the solution, let's first discuss the Shipment system. The following snapshot of the project visualizes the structure of the Shipment system:

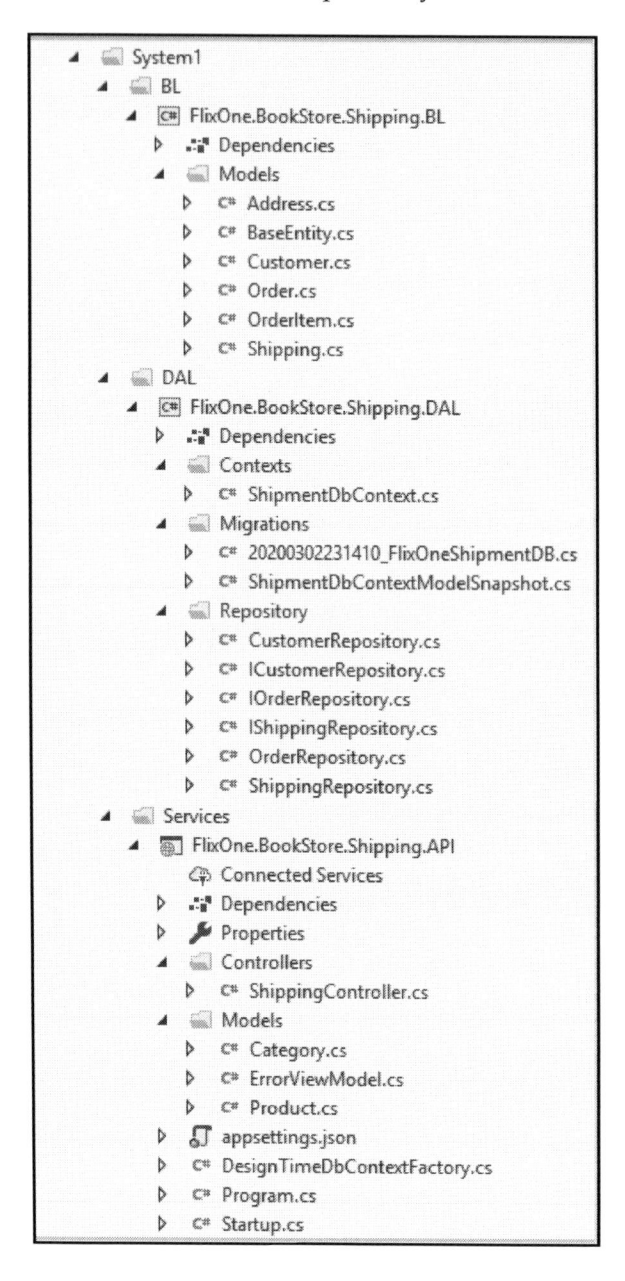

```
▲ System1
  ▲ BL
    ▲ C# FlixOne.BookStore.Shipping.BL
      ▷ ·:· Dependencies
      ▲ Models
        ▷ C# Address.cs
        ▷ C# BaseEntity.cs
        ▷ C# Customer.cs
        ▷ C# Order.cs
        ▷ C# OrderItem.cs
        ▷ C# Shipping.cs
  ▲ DAL
    ▲ C# FlixOne.BookStore.Shipping.DAL
      ▷ ·:· Dependencies
      ▲ Contexts
        ▷ C# ShipmentDbContext.cs
      ▲ Migrations
        ▷ C# 20200302231410_FlixOneShipmentDB.cs
        ▷ C# ShipmentDbContextModelSnapshot.cs
      ▲ Repository
        ▷ C# CustomerRepository.cs
        ▷ C# ICustomerRepository.cs
        ▷ C# IOrderRepository.cs
        ▷ C# IShippingRepository.cs
        ▷ C# OrderRepository.cs
        ▷ C# ShippingRepository.cs
  ▲ Services
    ▲ FlixOne.BookStore.Shipping.API
        Connected Services
      ▷ ·:· Dependencies
      ▷ Properties
      ▲ Controllers
        ▷ C# ShippingController.cs
      ▲ Models
        ▷ C# Category.cs
        ▷ C# ErrorViewModel.cs
        ▷ C# Product.cs
      ▷ appsettings.json
      ▷ C# DesignTimeDbContextFactory.cs
      ▷ C# Program.cs
      ▷ C# Startup.cs
```

System1 has the following folders: `BL`, `DAL`, and `Services`. In the forthcoming sections, we will discuss these folders.

The BL folder

This folder represents our business entities or models in a separate project, `FlixOne.BookStore.Shipping.BL`, which is detailed in the following sections.

The Models folder

This folder contains the model classes that will help us hold and transpose our model object data. Let's look at the following code of the `BaseEntity` model:

```
public abstract class BaseEntity
{
    [Key]
    public Guid Id { get; set; }
    public DateTime DateAdded { get; set; } = DateTime.UtcNow;
    public DateTime? DateModified { get; set; }
}
```

The preceding code contains the `BaseEntity` abstract class and has the following properties:

- `Id`: Contains a unique ID, representing the record ID of all the models that inherit this class.
- `DateAdded`: Contains the date when the record was added; its default value is the current `DateTime`.
- `DateModified`: Contains the date when the record was modified; it can also contain a null value.

Let's consider the following code, for the `Customer` model:

```
public class Customer : BaseEntity
{
    public string FirstName { get; set; }
    public string LastName { get; set; }
    public DateTime MemberSince { get; set; }
    public string FullName => LastName + ", " + FirstName;
}
```

The preceding code contains the Customer model, which inherits the BaseEntity abstract class. It has the following properties (including the properties of the BaseEntity class):

- FirstName: The first name of the customer.
- LastName: The last name of the customer.
- MemberSince: The date when the customer joined FlixOne.
- FullName: The full name of the customer.

Let's consider the following code, for the Order model:

```
public class Order : BaseEntity
{
    public Guid CustomerId { get; set; }
    public string StatusCode {get;set;}
    public string StatusDesc { get; set; }
    public DateTime Date { get; set; }
    public decimal Total { get; set; }
    public decimal Discount { get; set; }
    public decimal Tax { get; set; }
}
```

The preceding code contains the Order model, which inherits the BaseEntity abstract class. It has the following properties (including the properties of the BaseEntity class):

- CustomerId: Contains a unique ID, representing the record ID of the Customer model.
- StatusCode: The code that shows the status.
- StatusDesc: The status description.
- Date: The date of the order.
- Total: The total amount of the order.
- Discount: The discount amount.
- Tax: The tax amount.

Let's consider the following code, for the OrderItem model:

```
public class OrderItem:BaseEntity
{
    public Guid OrderId { get; set; }
    public Guid ProductId { get; set; }
    public string Name { get; set; }
    public string ImagePath { get; set; }
    public decimal UnitPrice { get; set; }
    public int Qty { get; set; }
}
```

The preceding code contains the OrderItem model, which inherits the BaseEntity abstract class. It has the following properties (including the properties of the BaseEntity class):

- OrderId: Contains a unique ID, representing the record ID of the Order model.
- ProductId: Contains a unique ID, representing the record ID of the Product model.
- Name: The item name that's being ordered.
- ImagePath: The item image path.
- UnitPrice: The unit price of the item.
- Qty: The quantity of the item.

Let's consider the following code, for the Shipping model:

```
public class Shipping:BaseEntity
{
    public Guid OrderId { get; set; }
    public string InvoiceNumber { get; set; }
    public DateTime Date { get; set; }
    public string TrackingNumber { get; set; }
}
```

The preceding code contains the `Shipping` model, which inherits the `BaseEntity` abstract class. It has the following properties (including the properties of the `BaseEntity` class):

- `OrderId`: Contains a unique ID, representing the record ID of the `Order` model.
- `InvoiceNumber`: The invoice number.
- `Date`: The date on which the order is shipped.
- `TrackingNumber`: The tracking number of the shipped docket.

Let's consider the following code, for the `Address` model:

```
public class Address:BaseEntity
{
    public string AddressLine1 { get; set; }
    public string AddressLine2 { get; set; }
    public string City { get; set; }
    public string State { get; set; }
    public string Country { get; set; }
    public string PIN { get; set; }
    public Guid CustomerId { get; set; }
}
```

The preceding code contains the `Address` model, which inherits the `BaseEntity` abstract class. It has the following properties (including the properties of the `BaseEntity` class):

- `AddressLine1`: The first line of the customer's address.
- `AddressLine2`: The second line of the customer's address.
- `City`: The city of the customer.
- `State`: The state of the customer.
- `Country`: The country of the customer.
- `PIN`: The Postal Index Number.
- `CustomerId`: Contains a unique ID, representing the record ID of the `Customer` model.

The DAL folder

This folder contains the `DataAccess` operations in a separate project, `FlixOne.BookStore.Shipping.DAL`, which is detailed in the following sections.

The Contexts folder

This folder contains the `ShipmentDbContext.cs` file. Entity Framework Core's `DbContext` helps query and save instances of entities. Consider the following code:

```
public class ShipmentDbContext : DbContext
{
    public ShipmentDbContext(DbContextOptions<ShipmentDbContext> options)
        : base(options) { }

    public ShipmentDbContext() { }
    public DbSet<Address> Addresses { get; set; }
    public DbSet<Customer> Customers { get; set; }
    public DbSet<Order> Orders { get; set; }
    public DbSet<OrderItem> OrderItems { get; set; }
    public DbSet<Models.Shipping> Shippings { get; set; }
}
```

The preceding code consists of the `ShipmentDbContext` class, which implements `DbContext`. `DbContext` represents a session with the database, and it further helps you interact with the database, using various `DbSet` instances. In the previous code, we have `DbSet` instances, which include `Addresses`, `Customers`, `Orders`, `OrderItems`, and `Shippings`. These `DbSet` instances represent their specific entities (also called *models*).

The Repository folder

This folder contains our repositories that provide the CRUD operations and return the aggregated data. Let's look at the following code:

```
public class CustomerRepository : ICustomerRepository
{
    private readonly ShipmentDbContext _context;
    public CustomerRepository() => _context = Context();
    public CustomerRepository(ShipmentDbContext context) => _context = context;
    public IEnumerable<Customer> Get() => _context.Customers.Include(c => c.CustomerAddresses).ToList();
    public Customer Get(Guid id) => _context.Customers.Include(c => c.CustomerAddresses).Where(c => c.Id == id).FirstOrDefault();
    ...
}
```

The preceding code has two `Get` methods; one lists all the available shipment records, while the other fetches a record of a shipment based on the shipment ID.

Design Patterns and Best Practices

> In the solution, our `Migrations` folder contains the autogenerated files, which can be created by executing the following two commands, from the Package Manager console:
> - Add-Migration FlixOneShipmentDB
> - Update-Database
>
> Also, you need to register the repositories in your startup file. Tell the system where the connection string is, which needs to connect to SQLServer. You must add the following code:
> `services.AddTransient<IOrderRepository, OrderRepository>();`
> `services.AddTransient<ICustomerRepository, CustomerRepository>();`
> `services.AddTransient<ICustomerRepository, CustomerRepository>();`
> `services.AddDbContext<ShipmentDbContext>(o => o.UseSqlServer(Configuration.GetConnectionString("ShipmentConnection")));`

The Services folder

This folder includes our business entities or models in a separate project, `FlixOne.BookStore.Shipping.API`, which is detailed in the following sections.

The Controllers folder

This folder contains our API controllers. This will be exposed as a service; the following code explains this:

```
[HttpGet]
public IEnumerable<ShippingViewModel> Get()
{
    var shippings = _repository.Get().ToViewModel();
    foreach (var shipping in shippings)
    {
        shipping.Order =
_repository.AssociatedOrder(shipping.OrderId).ToViewModel();
        shipping.Order.ShippingAddress =
_repository.ShippingAddress(shipping.Order.CustomerId).ToViewModel();
    }
    return shippings;
}
```

The preceding code contains a GET resource, and it lists all the shipping records that are available in the database.

Let's consider the following code:

```
[HttpGet("{id}")]
public ShippingViewModel Get(string id)
{
    var shipping = _repository.Get(new Guid(id)).ToViewModel();
    shipping.Order = _repository.AssociatedOrder(shipping.OrderId).ToViewModel();
    shipping.Order.ShippingAddress = _repository.ShippingAddress(shipping.Order.CustomerId).ToViewModel();
    return shipping;
}
```

The preceding code includes a GET resource, and it fetches a shipping record, based on ShippingId.

Our ShippingController exposes the APIs, as detailed in the following table:

HTTP method	Api resource	Description
GET	/api/Shipping	Fetches a list of all the shipping records that are available in the database.
GET	/api/Shipping/{id}	Fetches a shipping record for a specified ShippingId.

To get the report, we have the Anti-Corruption Layer, which provides a way to create a report that helps ensure that the product and shipping services work smoothly, without affecting each other.

In this section, we have discussed and implemented code examples to maintain two different subsystems. We saw that there is a more complex subsystem in real scenarios, and we'd implement the code in such a way so that both systems will work as they are supposed to.

Summary

In this chapter, we have covered some of the patterns that can help us build a robust microservices-based system. We have covered many examples throughout this book, which are based on the patterns discussed in this chapter. We followed the descriptions of each pattern, by looking at the roles and practices of the patterns in the microservice ecosystem.

We began with the Aggregator pattern, explaining the composite microservices, and then implementing this pattern using an example from our imaginary FlixOne store application. We then followed with the Shared Data pattern and the Anti-Corruption Layer pattern. We discussed the best practices of these patterns, in the context of the application, and we implemented solutions based on them.

In the next chapter, we will create an application that's based on a microservices architectural design.

Further reading

- *Microservice Patterns and Best Practices* (https://www.packtpub.com/in/application-development/microservice-patterns-and-best-practices)
- *Hands-On Design Patterns with C# and .NET Core* (https://www.packtpub.com/in/application-development/hands-design-patterns-c-and-net-core)
- *Hands-On Software Architecture with C# 8 and .NET Core 3* (https://www.packtpub.com/programming/hands-on-software-architecture-with-c-8)

11
Building a Microservice Application

In the application development world, developers follow various approaches, which include design patterns, design principles, and more, to delve into their problems' solutions and to make good applications. Requirements change when there's a change in a business approach, as per the demand of the business, or when developers have to follow the actual business requirements to sync the application with the business and its customers. There are a lot of challenges, when it comes to making an application that fulfills the business needs.

The world of development is a sea of evolving technologies. Each new day comes with a new buzzword that indicates the advent of new technologies. Nowadays, the microservice architectural style has become famous, and it helps us fulfill almost all our needs. In my view, we can say the following:

> *"Microservices is a culture where you follow various patterns: approaches to make sure that an application is easily available to developers and their end users. This is so that developers can work in parallel on different modules or on parts of the applications, and so the end user can use hassle-free applications."*

So far, in this book, we have discussed various examples, by looking at a variety of approaches, patterns, and so on. This chapter will walk you through how to create such a sample application. After covering all the concepts and features that we went through previously, you will be able to create a complete microservices application.

The following topics will be covered in this chapter:

- Introducing the strangler pattern
- Revisiting the application
- Understanding the business needs of an application
- Building our application

Technical requirements

This chapter contains various code examples to explain the concepts within. The code has been kept simple, and it is just for demonstration purposes. Most of the examples involve a .NET Core console application, which is written in C#.

To run and execute the code in this chapter, you will need to have the following:

- Visual Studio 2019 or later
- .NET Core 3.1 is set up

Installing Visual Studio 2019

To run the code examples in this chapter, you'll need to install Visual Studio 2019 or later (our preferred IDE). To do so, follow these instructions:

1. Download Visual Studio 2019 (Community is free) from the following link: https://docs.microsoft.com/en-us/visualstudio/install/install-visual-studio.
2. Follow the installation instructions mentioned within.
3. Multiple versions of Visual Studio will be available. We will be using Visual Studio for Windows in this chapter.

> **Setting up .NET Core:** If you don't have .NET Core 3.1 installed, you need to download it from https://dotnet.microsoft.com/download/dotnet-core/3.1.

Setting up Azure

To work with the code examples in this chapter, you'll need a valid Azure account. You can simply ignore this section, if you have a valid account. Otherwise, the following steps will help you set up your Azure account:

1. Sign up for a free Azure account at https://signup.azure.com/.
2. Follow the instructions shown on that page.
3. You will require a valid credit card to validate your payment method, just in case you want to use any paid services (you only need to use the pay-as-you-go method for this book). If you are a student or educator, an alternative free version is available at https://azure.microsoft.com/education/.

> The complete source code is available here: https://github.com/PacktPublishing/Hands-On-Microservices-with-CSharp-8-and-.NET-Core-3-Third-Edition/tree/master/Chapter%2011.

Revisiting the monolithic architecture style and SOA

In Chapter 1, *An Introduction to Microservices*, we learned that the microservice architecture removes most of the drawbacks of **service-oriented architecture** (SOA). It is also more code-oriented than SOA services. Before you move on to understanding the architecture, you need to understand two important architectures that led to its existence:

- The monolithic architecture style
- SOA

Most of us will be aware of the scenario in which, during the life cycle of an enterprise application development, a suitable architectural style is decided. Then, at various stages, the initial pattern is further improved and adapted, with changes that cater to various challenges, such as deployment complexity, large code bases, and scalability issues. This is exactly how the monolithic architecture style evolved into SOA, which then led to microservices.

> We discussed SOA and the monolithic architecture in Chapter 1, *An Introduction to Microservices*. You can skip this section if you understand this in full. However, if you want to learn more than what we have in this chapter, please refer back to the aforementioned chapter.

The monolithic architectural style is a traditional architecture type that has been widely used in the industry. The term monolithic is not new, and it is borrowed from the UNIX world:

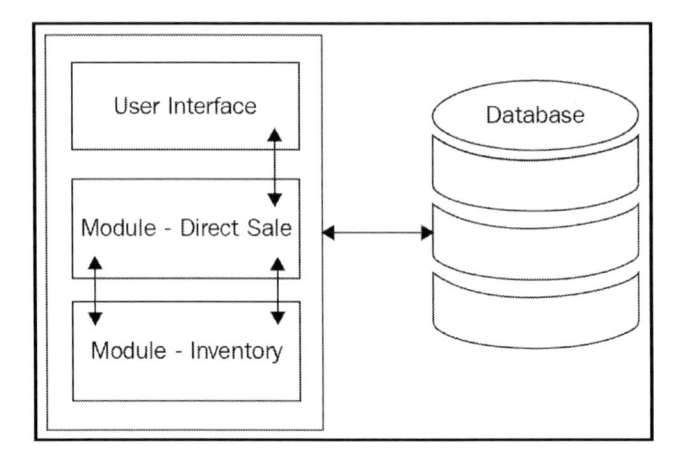

The preceding diagram shows that, in a monolithic architecture, we can have various components, including the following:

- **User interface**: This handles all of the user interactions, while responding with HTML, JSON, or any other preferred data interchange format (in the case of web services).
- **Business logic**: This includes all the business rules that are applied to the input, which is being received in the form of user input, events, and databases.
- **Database access**: This houses the complete functionality for accessing the database, for the purpose of querying and persisting objects. A widely accepted rule is that it is utilized through business modules and never directly through user-facing components.

We will be facing multiple scenarios as per our business needs and these result in a lot of challenges that we need to handle. Here, we may face the following challenges:

- **Large code base**: This is a scenario where the code lines outnumber the comments by a great margin. Since the components are interconnected, we will have to deal with a repetitive code base.
- **Too many business modules**: This is in regard to modules within the same system.
- **Code base complexity**: This results in a higher chance of the code breaking, due to the fixes that are required in other modules or services.

- **Complex code deployment**: You may come across minor changes that would require whole system deployment.
- **One module failure affecting the whole system**: This is with regards to modules that depend on each other. Apart from this, we will have modules depending on each other directly. However, we would also have *hidden dependencies* where we don't know it before it breaks (for example, if someone forgot to document it in the project documentation). On the other hand, we can have indirect dependencies. For example, we might have two virtual directories that are being run on the same IIS host, and one of them overwrites part of the root config, even though, on the surface, they are not dependent on each other.
- **Scalability**: This is required for the entire system, and not just the modules in it.
- **Intermodule dependency**: This is due to tight coupling. This results in heavy changes (if required) for an operation for any of the modules.

A system that uses a service, or multiple services, in the fashion mentioned in the preceding diagram, is called an SOA system. The main difference between SOA and monolithic is not that it produces one or multiple assemblies, but that it highlights the processes that the application runs on. Since the service in SOA runs as a separate process, SOA scales better in comparison. In this approach, services may be RESTful or ASMX web services.

> In the microservice architecture, services are small, independent units with their own persistent stores.

Going with microservice architectural-style applications, we can get a lot of benefits related to their development and the business implementation. Let's go over a few:

- **Cost-effective to scale**: You don't need to invest a lot, to make the entire application scalable. In terms of a shopping cart, we could simply load balance the product search module and the order processing module, while leaving out less frequently used operation services, such as inventory management, order cancellation, and delivery confirmation.
- **Clear code boundaries**: This action should match an organization's departmental hierarchies. With different departments sponsoring product development in large enterprises, this can be a huge advantage.
- **Easier code changes**: This is done in a way that is not dependent on the code of other modules and only achieves isolated functionality. If it were done right, then the chances of a change in one microservice affecting another microservice are minimal.

- **Easy deployment**: Since the entire application is more like a group of ecosystems that are isolated from each other, deployment could be done one microservice at a time, if required. Failure in any one of these wouldn't bring the entire system down.
- **Technology adaptation**: You could port a single microservice or a whole bunch of them overnight to a different technology, without your users even knowing about it. Hopefully, you don't expect us to tell you that you need to maintain those service contracts.
- **Distributed system**: The meaning is implied here, but a word of caution is necessary. Make sure that your asynchronous calls are used well and that your synchronous calls aren't blocking the whole flow of information. Use data partitioning well. We will come to this a little later, so don't worry about it for now.
- **Quick market response**: The world being a competitive place is a definite advantage. Users tend to quickly lose interest if you are slow to respond to new feature requests, or if you're slow to adopt new technology within your system.

> This section exists to let you revisit what we have learned about so far; you can easily skip this section if you wish.

Introducing the strangler pattern

We started our journey of learning in this book by transitioning from monolith applications to microservices-based applications. This transition follows the strangler pattern, which we will discuss in this section.

In simple words, we can define the strangler pattern as a pattern that helps us migrate a legacy application (in our case, a monolith application) continuously, by replacing specific functionality while introducing the new services/applications. Using this pattern, we replace the features of the legacy application that we identified previously, with the new system. To sum this up, a strangler pattern is all about decommissioning the old system after migrating all the required features/functionalities to the new system.

> **When should you use a strangler pattern?**
> This pattern should be used when you need to migrate your existing application, by identifying features/functionality slowly, before adding them to the new system or architecture.

Chapter 11

In this chapter, we will build our sample application, by following these topics:

1. Discussing the sample application.
2. What are the business requirements?
3. Why do we need an application?
4. Conclusion.

In the upcoming sections, we will explore these steps in more detail, and we will write a simple application that's based on microservice architectural styles.

Understanding the business needs of an application

This section is all about creating the imaginary app and the business behind the app. Let's visit our imaginary app, which we named FlixOne Store.

FlixOne Store is an on-demand store provider, based on customized software. The aim of this customized software is to expand the business, by overcoming the technical challenges that have been faced by the marketing team in the past (refer to `Chapter 1`, *An Introduction to Microservices*, for more information). The end user landed on the app, and he/she successfully met a need we have, within the store market: to buy the various items that are listed within FlixOne Store.

FlixOne Store is a software platform that matches the requirements and needs, not only of single users, but also of retailers who need an online store to sell their products/items. FlixOne is also a platform that enables online sales and purchases. This way, retailers can earn money by making extra efforts to promote their products/items. FlixOne is a solution that caters to the global market, where the two sides of the industry—the retailers and the manufacturers—create a buyer-seller relationship model:

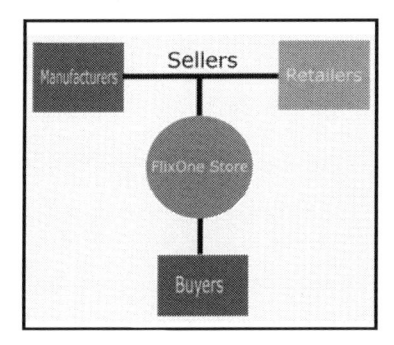

The preceding diagram shows the broader picture of the entire FlixOne software. Here, we can easily understand the business idea behind the application that **FlixOne Store** provides: a platform for both **Sellers** and **Buyers**. Both **Manufacturers** and **Retailers** can be registered as sellers, while the buyers are the end users who are going to purchase these items.

> **Business model**: FlixOne charges a commission off each transaction and provides a way for the sellers to manage products. FlixOne allows us to maintain the inventory that's uploaded by the sellers, as well as the ability to schedule deliveries, monitor product types and levels, and so on.

The following diagram shows the process of sellers within the FlixOne Store software:

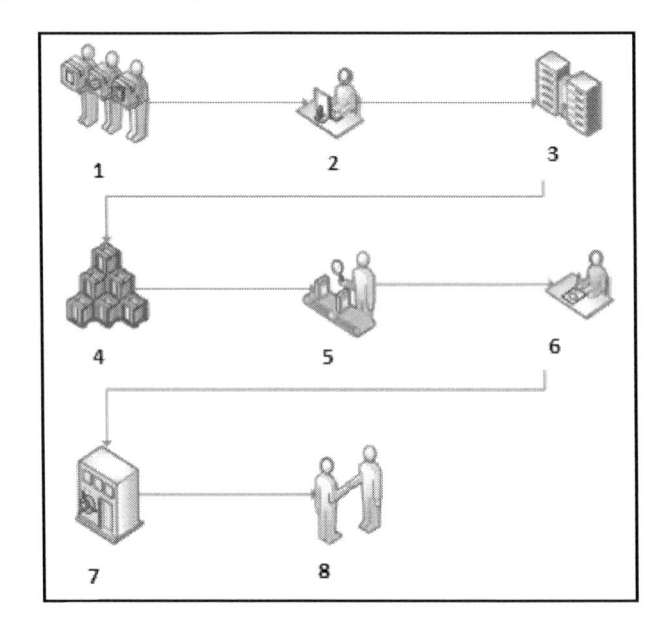

The preceding diagram defines the process workflow of sellers who use FlixOne Store, as follows:

1. The seller visits the FlixOne Store.
2. The seller registers with the FlixOne Store.
3. Then the seller registers their product types.
4. The seller creates the inventory.
5. The inventory gets validated/approved by FlixOne admins.
6. FlixOne asks the seller for approval of the inventory.

7. The seller pays the registration fees.
8. A FlixOne-seller partnership agreement is made.

The following diagram shows the process of buyers within the FlixOne Store software:

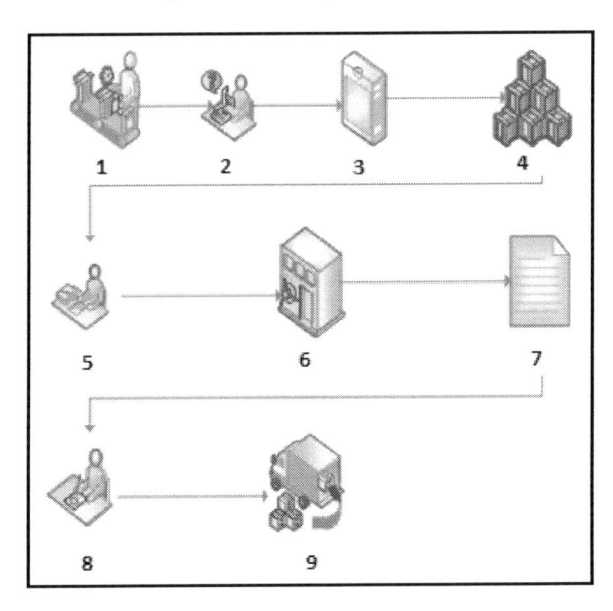

The following is the process workflow of buyers who use FlixOne Store, as follows:

1. The buyer visits the FlixOne Store.
2. The buyer registers with the FlixOne Store.
3. The available services are provided.
4. The buyer checks the available inventory for the product that they wish to purchase.
5. The buyer places an order.
6. The buyer pays for their item.
7. A smart contract process occurs.
8. Confirmation of the recent transaction is provided to the buyer.
9. The item is shipped to the desired location.

The complete picture of the FlixOne Store system contains the following:

- **Admin panel**: This is the backend that's managed by the FlixOne team.
- **Sellers panel**: This is the interface for all the sellers, so that they can manage their products and inventory, including sales and so on.

Building a Microservice Application

- **User panel**: This interface is the main interface for the end user who is going to buy the items.

The following is our imaginary user panel:

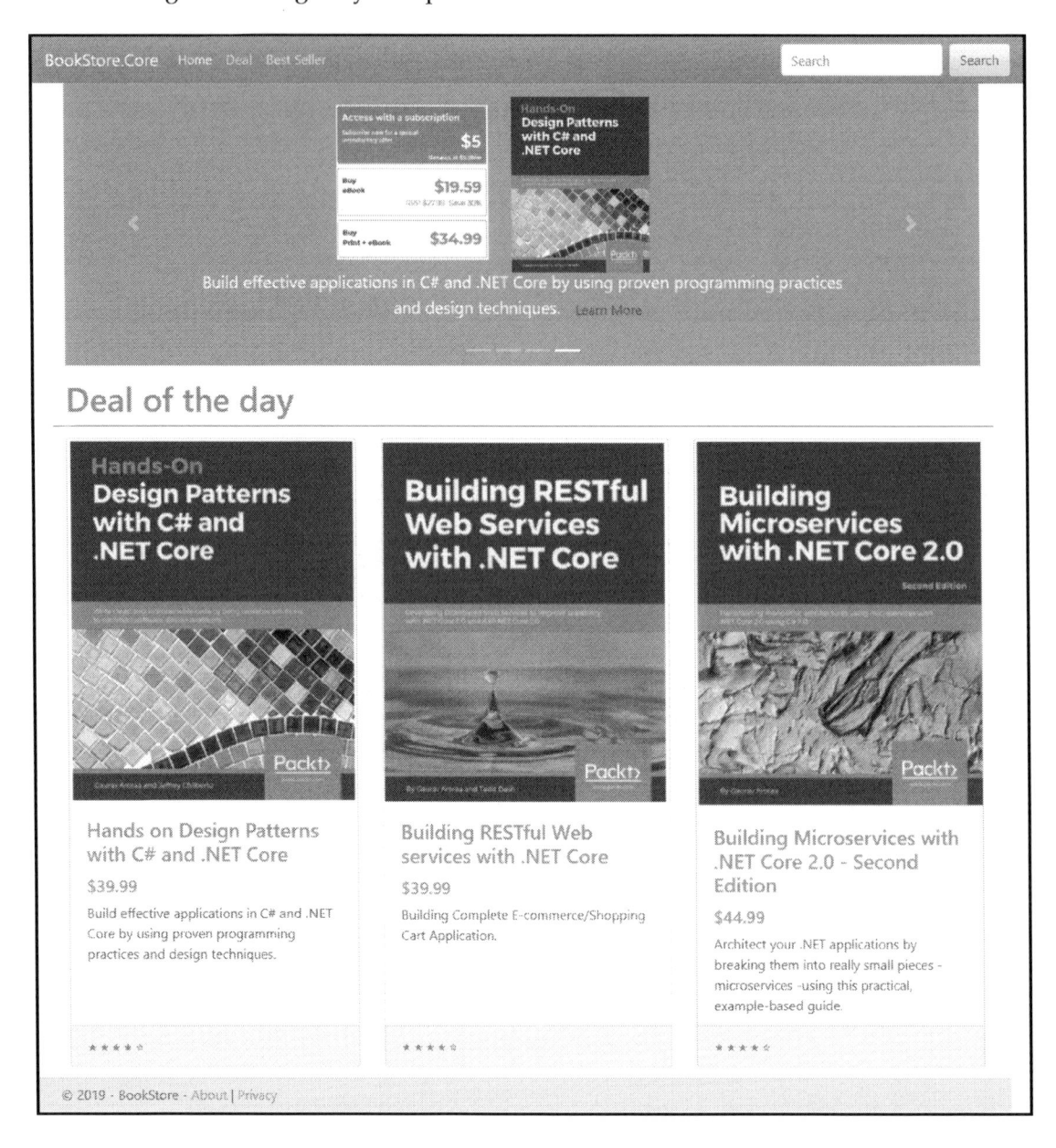

Chapter 11

The preceding screenshot is showing the imaginary user interface, where various books are available to be purchased. This snapshot is a visualization of the actual application and would have a different output.

In the next section, we will discuss the tech stack and the flow of the application.

Revisiting the application

This section will explore what we are going to develop. Throughout this book, we've used various APIs, to showcase the code examples within. In this section, we will get an overview of our sample application, which is a combination of various flows, where the end user enters the application and he/she processes the request to buy books.

The following diagram provides an overview of our application:

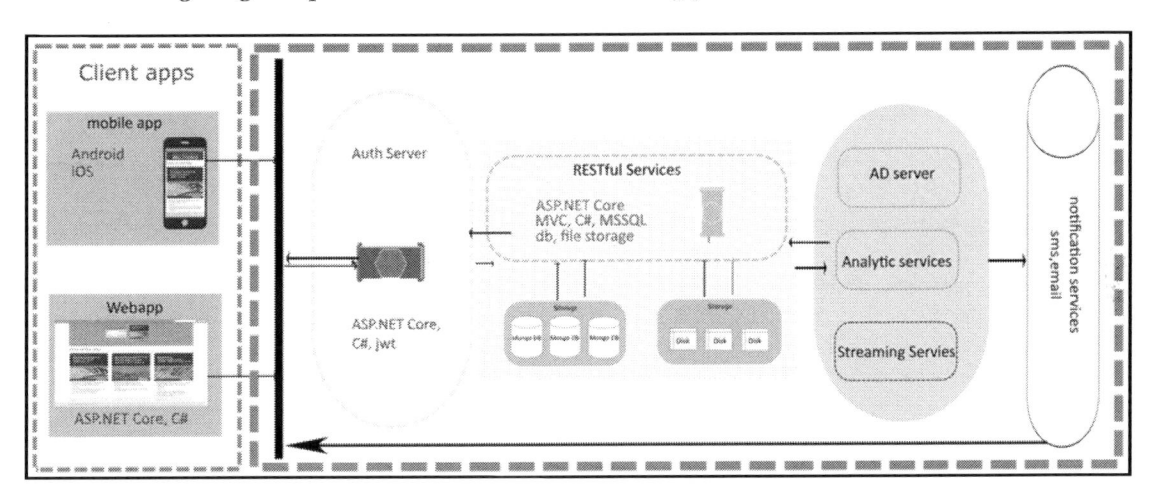

The preceding diagram is a pictorial representation of the functional overview of our sample application, and it shows the flow, which contains the following items:

- **Client apps**: Mobile and web applications are the client apps that the end user is going to use. Our code repository is shipped with the web application.
- **Auth server**: It validates the user and generates the JWT token, for further processing.
- **RESTful services**: These are the various services that are going to help our application. These services have their own databases. The file storage would be a CDN or a separate server, which would be used to store various pieces of content, including documents.

[383]

- **Notification services**: These are the external services that are used to generate a **One-Time Password (OTP)**, to authenticate the user and to notify them about the order they've generated, an item they've booked, and so on.

Apart from these, our diagram contains **Ad server**, **Analytics services**, and **Streaming services**, which are required if we need to podcast some of our videos. For this, we would require streaming services. So far, our code doesn't implement these services.

In the next section, we will discuss the **Minimum Viable Product (MVP)**, so that we can create our FlixOne application.

Building the application

In the previous sections, we discussed the complete picture of FlixOne Software. This piece of software is very big, and we aren't going to develop all of it here; instead, we will define MVP to showcase the strength of the software. This software can be extended to any level.

> By taking an MVP approach, the scope of a piece of work is limited to the smallest set of requirements, in order to produce a functioning deliverable. MVP is often combined with Agile software development by limiting requirements to a manageable amount that can be designed, developed, tested, and delivered. This approach lends itself well to smaller websites or application development, where a feature set can be progressed all the way to production in a single development cycle.

We are going to develop a FlixOne Store application that has the following functionalities:

- Login functionality
- Registration functionality
- Item search functionality
- Order functionality
- Notification functionality

Chapter 11

Let's take a look at the following diagram, which defines the flow of our search functionality:

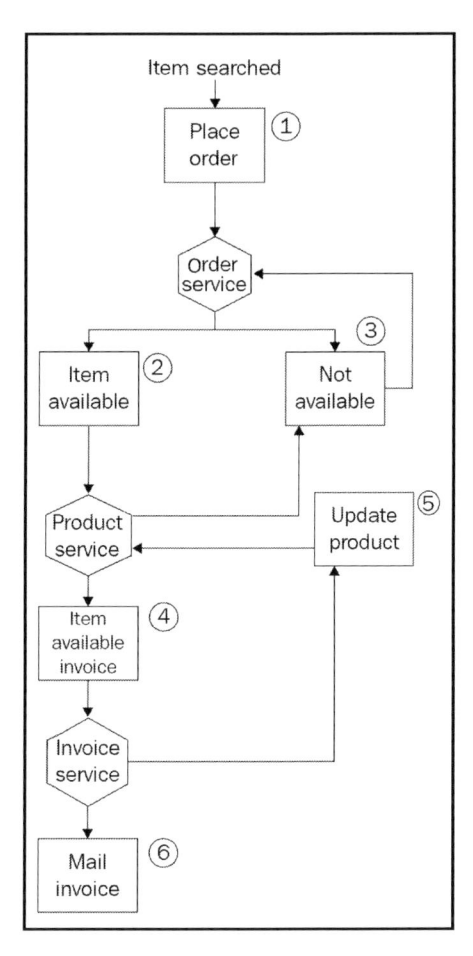

In the preceding diagram, services are depicted by hexagons, while events are represented by rectangular boxes. The flow, as shown in the preceding diagram, describes the scenario of a customer placing an order, after searching for the items he/she is looking for. This is how it goes:

1. The **Place order** event is raised to **Order service**.
2. In response to this event, our service analyzes the arguments, such as the order item and quantity, and it raises the **Item available** event to **Product service**.

3. From here on, there are two possible outcomes: either the requested product is available and has the required quantity or it is **Not available** or doesn't have the required quantity.
4. If the items are available, **Product service** raises an event called **Generate invoice** to **Invoice service**. Since raising the invoice means confirming the order, the items on the invoice would no longer be in stock; we need to take care of this and update the stock accordingly.
5. To handle this, our invoice service raises an event called **Update product quantity** to **Product service** and takes care of this requirement. For the sake of simplicity, we will not go into the details of who will handle the event of the **Mail invoice**.
6. There may be a scenario where a product is not available in the store. As per our business needs, we have to mark the product as **Notify me once available**. This purely depends upon the end user; that is, if the end user opted for this option, then he/she will get a notification when the product is available. The same action will be triggered for presales products, as per FlixOne Store's presales products means—a product has been added but isn't available to be bought yet.

This completes our MVP and shows how to create the FlixOne Store application. We haven't added any code, because we have already discussed the code we'd need (the services), throughout this book. You can get the complete application code from this book's code repository.

Summary

The aim of this chapter was to create a sample application. By doing this, we have discussed the business requirements and needs for the application. Then, we understood the flow of the application and learned about the working model of the application, by defining our MVP.

So far, in our journey of writing the application, we have passed through various phases. We explored what led to the advent of microservices, and we looked at the various advantages of utilizing them. We also discussed various integration techniques and testing strategies.

In the next chapter, we will revisit and discuss each and every aspect of our application, starting from monolith, and then we will transition to reviewing microservices applications.

12
Microservices Architecture Summary

On our journey down the lane of understanding microservices and their evolution, we passed through various phases. We explored what led to the advent of microservices and the various advantages of utilizing them. We also discussed various integration techniques and testing strategies.

In this chapter, we will revisit and discuss each and every aspect of our application, starting from the monolith through to transitioning to a microservices application, followed by a discussion of monitoring and strategies.

Let's recap all that we have talked about so far, by covering the following list of topics in this chapter:

- Understanding architectures before microservices
- Monolith transitioning
- An overview of cloud-native microservices
- Monitoring
- Monitoring strategies
- Reactive microservices

Technical requirements

This chapter contains no code examples, so there are no technical prerequisites for it.

Understanding architectures before microservices

Microservices were never designed from the ground up to be in their present form. Instead, there has been a gradual transition from other forms of prevalent architecture styles to microservices. Before microservices, we had monolithic architecture and service-oriented architecture, which reigned over the world of enterprise development.

Let's review these two architectures, before we do a quick recap of a microservices architecture and its various attributes and advantages.

Monolithic architecture

Monolithic architecture has been around for quite some time, and it results in self-contained software with a single .NET assembly. It is also fine if a monolith produces multiple assemblies, as long as it serves an isolated task. Monolithic architecture consists of the following components:

- User interface
- Business logic
- Database access

The cost paid for being self-contained is that all of the components are interconnected and interdependent. A minor change in any module could impact the entire piece of software. With all of the components so tightly coupled in this manner, it makes testing the entire application necessary. Also, another repercussion of being so tightly coupled is that the entire application has to be deployed, instead of just one part of it. Let's sum up all of the challenges we face, as a result of adopting this style of architecture:

- Large interdependent code
- Code complexity
- Scalability
- System deployment
- Adoption of a new technology

Our monolith application is a single application that has heavy interdependent code. The user interface, business logic, and database access layers are tightly coupled. This application has the challenges discussed earlier. This kind of application also creates a complex condition, when we want to write standardized code, as per the targeted framework/language. Next, we will discuss the challenges related to the .NET stack.

Challenges in standardizing the .NET stack

Technology adoption is not easy, when it comes to monolithic architecture. It poses certain challenges. Some of these challenges include security, response time, throughput rate, and technology adoption. It is not that this style of architecture does not fight back with solutions. The challenge is that in monolithic architecture, code reusability is really low or absent, which makes technology adoption difficult.

Security and technology adoption challenges exist for monolith applications, but they also suffer in terms of scaling—we will see this next.

Scaling

We also discussed how scaling is a viable option, but with diminishing returns and increasing expenses. Both vertical and horizontal scaling have their own pros and cons. Vertical scaling is seemingly easier to begin with: investing in IT infrastructures, such as RAM upgrades and disk drives. However, the return plateaus out very quickly. The disadvantage, of the downtime required for vertical scaling, doesn't exist in horizontal scaling. However, beyond a point, the cost of horizontal returns becomes too high.

Let's move ahead and discuss another widely used architecture in the industry, and that is service-oriented architecture.

Service-oriented architecture

Another widely used architecture in the industry is **Service-Oriented Architecture (SOA)**. This architecture moves away from monolithic architecture and was involved in resolving some of its challenges, mentioned in the preceding section. To begin with, it is based on a collection of services. Providing a service is the core concept of SOA.

Microservices Architecture Summary

A service is a piece of code, a program, or software that provides some functionality to other system components. This piece of code is able to interact directly with the database or indirectly through other services. It is self-contained, to the extent that it allows services to be consumed easily, by both desktop and mobile applications.

Some of the definite advantages that SOA provides over monolithic architecture, are as follows:

- Reusable
- Stateless
- Scalable
- Contract-based
- Ability to upgrade

SOA is one of the most widely used architectures, due to its benefits; this section discussed SOA and its advantages over a monolithic architecture. Next, we will discuss a microservice-style architecture.

Microservice-style architecture

Apart from some of the definite advantages of SOA, microservices provide certain additional differentiating factors that make this architecture a clear winner. At their core, microservices are designed to be completely independent of other services in the system and run in their process. The attribute of being independent requires a certain discipline and strategy in the application design. Some of the benefits they provide, are as follows:

- **Clear code boundaries**: This results in easier code changes. Their independent modules provide an isolated functionality, which leads to a change in one microservice having little impact on others.
- **Easy deployment**: It is possible to deploy one microservice at a time, if required.
- **Technology adaptation**: The preceding attributes lead to this much sought-after benefit. This allows us to adopt different technologies in different modules.
- **Affordable scalability**: This allows us to scale only the chosen components/modules, instead of the whole application.
- **Distributed system**: This is implicit, but a word of caution is necessary here. Make sure that your asynchronous calls are used well, and make sure the synchronous calls don't block the whole flow of information. Use data partitioning well. We will come to this a little later, so don't worry for now.

- **Quick market response**: In a competitive world, this is a definite advantage, as users tend to lose interest quickly if you are slow to respond to new feature requests or slow to adopt a new technology within your system.

Messaging is one of the important aspects, while discussing microservices. This section informed us about the benefits of microservices. Next, we will discuss messaging in microservices.

Messaging in microservices

This is another important area that needs its share of discussion. There are primarily two main types of messaging utilized in microservices:

- Synchronous
- Asynchronous

In microservices, communication by means of messaging is very important. Services may or may not be dependent on each other.

Microservice-style architecture has many advantages over monolith applications. This section has aimed to summarize all the benefits and advantages. These advantages are helpful when we transition a monolith to microservices, which is covered in the next section.

Understanding how monolith transitioning works

As part of our exercise, we decided to transition our existing monolithic application, FlixOne, to a microservice-style architecture. We saw how to identify decomposition candidates within a monolith, based on the following parameters:

- Code complexity
- Technology adoption
- Resource requirement
- Human dependency

There are definite advantages that it provides, with regard to cost, security, and scalability, apart from technology independence. This also aligns the application more with our business goals.

The entire process of transitioning requires you to identify seams that act like the boundaries of your microservices, along which you can start the separation. You have to be careful about picking up seams on the right parameters. We have discussed how module interdependency, team structure, database, and technology are a few probable candidates. Special care is required to handle master data. It is more a choice of whether you want to handle master data through a separate service or configuration. You will be the best judge for your scenario. The fundamental requirement of a microservice having its own database, removes many of the existing foreign key relationships. This brings forth the need to pick your transaction-handling strategy intelligently, to preserve data integrity.

Let's move ahead and discuss integration techniques.

Integration techniques

We have already explored synchronous and asynchronous ways of communicating between microservices, and we discussed the collaboration style of services. These styles were request/response and event-based. Though request/response seems to be synchronous in nature, the truth is that it is the implementation that decides the outcome of the style of integration. The event-based style, on the other hand, is purely asynchronous.

When dealing with a large number of microservices, we must utilize an integration pattern, to facilitate complex interaction among microservices. In Chapter 3, *Effective Communication Between Services*, we explored the API gateway, along with an event-driven pattern.

The API gateway provides you with a plethora of services, some of which are as follows:

- Routing an API call
- Verifying API keys, JWT, and certificates
- Enforcing usage quotas and rate limits
- Transforming APIs on the fly without code modifications
- Setting up caching backend responses
- Logging call metadata for analytic purposes

The event-driven pattern works by some services publishing their events, and by some services subscribing to those available events. The subscribing services simply react independently of the event-publishing services, based on the event and its metadata. The publisher is unaware of the business logic that the subscribers will be executing.

Integration makes sure that each part of our application is integrated; this section summarized various points that we have discussed in previous chapters. One of the important aspects of any application is smooth deployment, and we will discuss that next.

Deployment

Monolithic deployments, for enterprise applications, can be challenging for more than one reason. Having a central database, which is difficult to break down, only increases the overall challenge, along with the time to market.

For microservices, the scenario is very different. The benefits don't just come by virtue of the architecture being microservices. Instead, it is the planning from the initial stages themselves. You can't expect an enterprise-scale microservice to be managed without **Continuous Delivery (CD)** and **Continuous Integration (CI)**. Right from the early stages, the requirement for CI and CD is so strong, that without them, the production stage may never see the light of day.

Tools such as CFEngine, Chef, Puppet, Ansible, and PowerShell DSC help you to represent an infrastructure with code, and they let you easily make different environments (for example, UAT, pre-prod, prod, and so on) exactly the same. Azure could be an ally here: the rapid and repeated provisioning required could easily be met.

Containers can meet isolation requirements far more effectively than their closest rival, virtual machines. We have already explored Docker as one of the popular candidates for containerization, and we have shown you how to deploy it.

After completing the code, the application must be tested in the relevant environment, and that is possible with deployment; CI/CD works here. In this section, we summarized the deployment of an application, and next, we will summarize testing microservices.

Testing microservices

We all know the importance of unit tests and why every developer should be writing them. Unit tests are a good means of verifying the smallest functionality that contributes to building larger systems.

However, testing microservices is not a routine affair, like testing a monolith, since one microservice might interact with several other microservices. In that case, should we utilize the calls to the actual microservices, to ensure that the complete workflow is working fine? The answer is no, as this would make developing a microservice dependent on another piece. If we do this, then the whole purpose of having a microservice-based architecture is lost. To get around this, we will use the mock-and-stub approach. This approach not only makes the testing independent of other microservices, but it also makes testing with databases much easier, since we can mock database interactions as well.

Microservices Architecture Summary

Testing a small, isolated functionality with a unit test, or testing a component by mocking the response from an external microservice, has its scope, and it works well within that scope. However, if you are already asking yourself the question about testing the larger context, then you are not alone. Integration testing and contract testing are the next steps in testing microservices.

In integration testing, we're concerned about external microservices, and we communicate with them as part of the process. For this purpose, we mock external services. We take this further with contract testing, where we test each and every service call independently, and then we verify the response. An important concept worth spending time on is consumer-driven contracts. Refer to `Chapter 4`, *Testing Microservices*, to study this in detail.

Various testing was summarized in this section, and we discussed consumer-driven contracts. Security is the most important part of any application, and in the next section, we will summarize it.

Security

The traditional approach, of having a single point of authentication and authorization, worked well in monolithic architecture. However, in the case of microservices, you would need to do this for each and every service. This would pose a challenge in not only implementing a service, but in keeping it synchronized as well.

The OAuth 2.0 authorization framework, and the OpenID Connect 1.0 specifications combined, can solve the problem for us. OAuth 2.0 describes all the roles involved in the authorization process that meet our needs pretty well. We just have to make sure that the right grant type is picked up; otherwise, security will be compromised. OpenID Connect authentication is built on top of the OAuth 2.0 protocol.

Azure Active Directory (Azure AD) is one of the providers of OAuth 2.0 and OpenID Connect specifications. It is understood here that Azure AD scales very well with applications, and it integrates well with any organizational Windows Server Active Directory.

As we have already discussed containers, it is important and interesting to understand that containers are very close to the host operating system's kernel. Securing them is another aspect that can't be overrated. Docker was the tool we considered, and it provides the necessary security using the least privilege principle.

Azure Active Directory (AAD) is a good adaption to validate users and to authenticate applications, so that we do not worry about authenticating requests. But to complete the validation, we need to take some extra steps while using AAD. Apart from security, monitoring and logging are also important aspects of an application. Let's move forward and summarize monitoring our application.

Monitoring the application

The monolithic world has a few advantages of its own. Monitoring and logging are those areas where things are easier, compared to microservices. The sheer number of microservices, across which an enterprise system might be spread, can be mind-boggling.

As discussed in `Chapter 1`, *An Introduction to Microservices*, in the *Prerequisites for a microservice architecture* section, an organization should be prepared for profound change. The monitoring framework was one of the key requirements for this.

Unlike a monolithic architecture, monitoring is very much required, from the very beginning, in a microservice-based architecture. There is a wide range of ways in which monitoring can be categorized:

- **Health**: We need to preemptively know when a service failure is imminent. Key parameters, such as CPU and memory utilization, along with other metadata, could be a precursor to either the impending failure of our service, or just a flaw in the service that needs to be fixed. Just imagine an insurance company's rate engine getting overloaded and going out of service, or even performing slowly, when a few hundred field executives try to share the cost with potential clients. These days, nobody nobody can afford to wait for data.
- **Availability**: There might be a situation when the service may not perform extensive calculations, but the bare availability of the service itself might be crucial to the entire system. In such a scenario, when the system is down (known as downtime), we have to use some tools to check whether the system is back (up) or not. A frequent command used to do this is `ping`, and we have to rely on that. It might wait for a few minutes before shooting out emails to the system administrators. This solution works for monoliths, with one or two services to be monitored. However, with microservices, much more metadata comes into the picture.

- **Performance**: For platforms receiving high footfall, such as banking and e-commerce, availability alone does not deliver the service that's required. Considering the number of people converging on their platforms in very short spans, ranging from a few minutes to even tens of seconds, performance is not a luxury anymore. You need to know how the system is responding, by using its data, such as the number of concurrent users being served, and compare that with the health parameters in the background. This might provide an e-commerce platform with the ability to decide whether upgrades are required, before the upcoming holiday season. For more sales, you need to serve a higher number of people.
- **Security**: In any system, you can plan resilience only up to a specific level. No matter how well designed a system is, there will be thresholds beyond which the system will falter, which can result in a domino effect. However, having a thoughtfully designed security system in place could easily avert DoS and SQL injection attacks. This would really matter from system-to-system, when dealing with microservices. So, think ahead and think carefully when setting up trust levels between your microservices. The default strategy, that I have seen people utilizing, is securing the endpoints with microservices. Covering this aspect increases your system's security, and it is worth spending some time on.
- **Auditing**: Healthcare, financing, and banking are a few of the domains that have the strictest compliance standards, concerning associated services, and it is pretty much the same the world over. Depending upon the kind of compliance you are dealing with, you might have a requirement to keep data for a specific period of time as a record, to keep the data in a specific format to be shared with regulatory authorities, or even to sync with systems provided by the authority. Taxation systems could be another example here. With a distributed architecture, you don't want to risk losing the data recordset that's related to even a single transaction, since that would amount to a compliance failure.
- **Troubleshooting system failures**: This, I bet, will be a favorite, for a long time to come, of anybody who is getting started with microservices. I remember the early days when I used to try troubleshooting a scenario that involved two Windows services. I never thought of recommending a similar design again. But the times have changed and so has the technology.

When providing a service to other clients, monitoring becomes all the more important. In today's competitive world, a service-level agreement (SLA) will be part of any deal and has a cost associated with it, in the event of both success and failure. Have you ever wondered how easily we assumed that the Microsoft Azure SLA would stand true, come what may? I have grown so used to it that queries from clients worried about cloud resource availability are answered with a flat reply of 99.9 percent uptime, without even the blink of an eye from the customer. Keep in mind that not all components in Azure have the same SLA. With the proper design of Azure services, it will, however, beat most on-premises deployments.

So, unless you can be confident of agreeing on an SLA with your clients, when providing a service, they can't count on it to promise the same SLA going forward. As a matter of fact, no SLA might mean that your services are probably not stable enough to provide one. Next, we will summarize the various challenges of monitoring.

Monitoring challenges

There could be multiple key points that need to be addressed, before you have a successful monitoring system in place. These need to be identified, and they need to be assigned a solution. Some of these key points are discussed next.

Scale

If you have a successfully running system, with a few dozen microservices orchestrating successful transactions in perfect harmony, then you have won the first battle. Congratulations! However, you must plug in the necessary monitoring part, if you haven't done so already. Ideally, this should be part of step one itself.

Component lifespan

With the use of virtual machines and containers, we need to figure out what part is worth monitoring. Some of these components might already be nonexistent, by the time you look at the data generated by monitoring them. So, it becomes extremely important that you choose the information to be monitored wisely.

Information visualization

There are tools available, such as AppDynamics and New Relic, that will allow you to visualize the data for maybe up to 100 microservices. However, in real-world applications, this is just a fraction of the number. There has to be clarity about the purpose of this information, and we need a well-designed visualization around it. This is one area where we can opt for a reverse design. First, think about the report/visualization that you want, and then see how it is to be monitored.

We summarized monitoring and logging in this section. We also discussed various challenges of monitoring a system. Now, let's move forward and summarize various strategies to monitor a system.

Understanding monitoring strategies

To begin with monitoring, you could think of different commonly implemented strategies, as a solution to your problem. Some of the commonly implemented strategies are as follows:

- Application/system monitoring
- Real-user monitoring
- Semantic monitoring and synthetic transactions
- Profiling
- Endpoint monitoring

Just bear in mind that each one of these strategies is focused on solving a specific purpose. While one could help to analyze transaction propagation, another could be suitable for testing purposes. So, you need to pick a combination of these, when designing the whole system, since just using a single strategy won't meet your needs.

Monitoring strategies ensure and focus on serving a specific purpose, as discussed in this section. For different purposes, we would require more strategies. So, let's move ahead to that next and discuss scalability.

Understanding scalability

We have discussed in detail the scale-cube model of scalability, and we have found out what scaling at each axis means. Note that x-axis scaling is achieved through the use of load balancers, between multiple instances and the users of the microservices. We also saw how z axis scaling, based on the transaction origination, suffers from some drawbacks.

Broadly, scaling in the microservice world can be categorized into two separate heads:

- Infrastructure
- Service design

Let's study each of them in the following sections.

Infrastructure scaling

Virtual machines are an indispensable component of the microservice world. The features available, as part of the Microsoft Azure platform, enable you to perform this seemingly complex task, without breaking a sweat.

Through the scale set feature, which is integrated with Azure autoscale, we can easily manage a set of identical virtual machines.

Autoscaling lets you define thresholds for various supported parameters, such as CPU usage. Once the threshold is breached, the scale set kicks in, based on whether the parameters scale in or scale out.

This means that if the scale set predicts that it needs to add more virtual machines to cater for the increased load, it will continue to do so, until the thresholds are back to normal. Similarly, if the demand for a resource being governed falls, it will decide to remove the virtual machine from the scale set. To me, this sounds like peace for the networking team. The options around autoscaling can be explored further, as it is capable of taking care of complex scaling requirements, such as running into hundreds of virtual machines while scaling in or scaling out.

Service design

In our microservices, we have already achieved the isolation of data for each microservice. However, the model for reading and writing the database is still the same. With the underlying relational databases enforcing the ACID model, this can be a costly affair. Or we can say that this approach can be slightly modified, to implement the database read/write operation differently.

We can employ common query responsibility segregation, also referred to as CQRS, to make effective design changes in our microservices. Once the model-level separation is done, we will be free to optimize the read and write data models, by using a different strategy.

Infrastructure and service design are the two parts of scaling, and in this section, we summarized them both. The next section will help us learn about and get an overview of reactive microservices.

An overview of reactive microservices

We have progressed well, while transitioning our monolithic application to a microservice-style architecture. We have also briefly touched upon the possibility of introducing reactive traits to our services. We now know that the key attributes of reactive microservices are, namely, the following:

- Responsiveness
- Resilience
- Autonomy
- Message-driven

We also saw the benefits of reactive microservices amounting to less work on our part, when it comes to managing communication across/between microservices.

This benefit translates not just into reduced work, but the capability to focus on the core job of executing the business logic, instead of trying to grapple with the complexities of inter-service communication. So, the next section will highlight a greenfield application.

Building a greenfield application

Previous chapters have discussed monolith applications (brownfield), and then we transitioned a monolith to a new microservice application (greenfield). In this section, we will create a FlixOne bookstore from scratch.

> A brownfield application is already developed (like a monolith application), whereas a greenfield application is one created from scratch.

First, we will scope out our microservices and their functionalities, and we will identify inter-service interactions as well.

Our FlixOne bookstore will have the following set of functionalities available:

- Searching through the available books
- Filtering books on the basis of categories
- Adding books to the shopping cart
- Making changes to the shopping cart
- Placing an order from the shopping cart
- User authentication

Creating a greenfield application requires a lot of effort, to meet the business needs of the application. In the coming section, we will discuss various steps toward the creation of an application.

Scoping our services

To understand how these functionalities will map out as different microservices, we need to first understand what it would take to support it, and what can be clubbed together as a microservice. We will see how the data store would start to look, from the perspective of the microservices themselves.

Defining the scope of an application is very important, so next, we will see what the scope is, when we show the listing of our FlixOne books.

The book-listing microservice

Let's try to break down the first functionality of searching through books. To let our users browse through the store for books, we need to maintain a list of books we offer. Here, we have our first candidate being carved out as a microservice. The book-catalog service would be responsible for not just searching through the available books, but also maintaining the data store that would house all of the information pertaining to books. The microservice should be able to handle various updates that are required for the available books in the system. We will call it the book-catalog microservice, and it will have its own book data store.

The book-searching microservice

Examining the next functionality of filtering books seems to come under the purview of the book-catalog microservice itself. However, having said that, let's confirm it by questioning our own understanding of the business domain here. The question that comes to my mind is related to the impact of all of the searches that our users would perform, which would bring down the service. So, should the book-search functionality be a different service? Here, the answer lies in the fact that the microservice should have its own data store. By having the book catalog and the book-catalog search function as different services, it would require us to maintain a list of books in two different locations with additional challenges, such as having to sync them. The solution is simple: we need a single microservice, and if required, we should scale up and load balance the book-catalog microservice.

The shopping-cart microservice

The next candidate was made famous by the online shopping revolution, which was brought about by the likes of Amazon and further fueled by smartphones: the shopping-cart microservice. It should let us add or remove books from our cart, before we finally decide to check out and pay for them. There is no doubt about whether this should be a separate microservice or not. However, this brings forth an interesting question of whether it deals with the product's data store or not; it would need to do this to receive some fundamental details, such as availability (what's in stock). Accessing the data store across the service, is out of the question, as that is one of the most fundamental prerequisites for microservices. The answer to our question is inter-service communication. It is okay for a microservice to use a service that's provided by another microservice. We will call this our shopping-cart microservice.

The order microservice

Next in line is the business functionality of placing an order. When a user decides that their shopping cart has just the right books, they decide to place an order. At that moment, some information related to the order has to be confirmed/conveyed to various other microservices. For example, before the order is confirmed, we need to confirm from the book catalog that there is enough quantity available in stock to fulfill the order. After this confirmation, the right number of items is supposed to be deducted from the book catalog. The shopping cart would also have to be emptied after the successful confirmation of the order.

Our order microservice sounds more pervasive, and it seems to be in contradiction with the rules about not sharing data across microservices, but this is not the case, as we will see shortly. All of the operations will be completed, while maintaining clear boundaries, with each microservice managing its own data store.

User authentication

Our last candidate is the user-authentication microservice, which would validate the user credentials of customers who log in to our bookstore. The sole purpose of this microservice is to confirm whether or not the provided credentials are correct, to restrict unauthorized access. This seems pretty simple for a microservice; however, we have to remember the fact that, by making this functionality a part of any other microservice, it would impact more than one business functionality, if you decided to change your authentication mechanism. The change may come in the form of using JWT being generated and validated, based on the OAuth 2.0 authorization framework and the OpenID Connect 1.0 authentication.

The following is the final list of candidates for microservices:

- The book-catalog microservice
- The shopping-cart microservice
- The order microservice
- The user-authentication microservice

Microservices Architecture Summary

In the following diagram, we have visualized four services, which are catalog (Book store), shopping cart (Cart store), order (Order store), and authentication (User store):

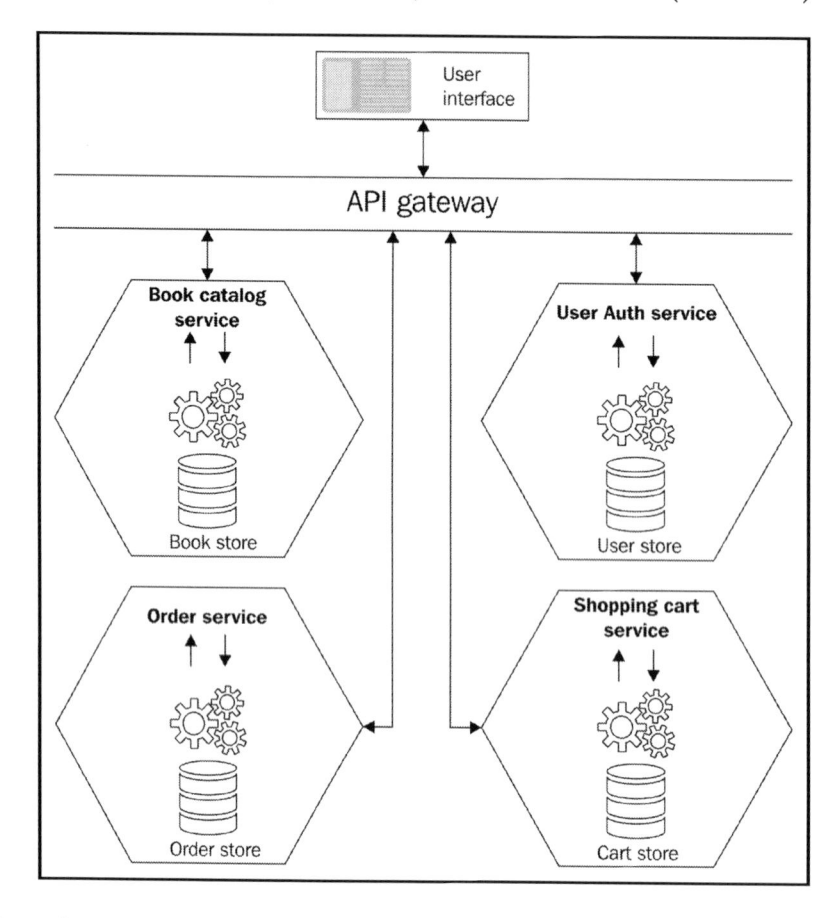

[Diagram: User interface connects to API gateway, which connects to four hexagonal services — Book catalog service (Book store), User Auth service (User store), Order service (Order store), and Shopping cart service (Cart store). The Order service and Shopping cart service are interconnected.]

The preceding diagram visualizes how a user interacts with four services: **Book catalog**, **User Auth**, **Order**, and **Shopping cart**, via the API gateway.

Synchronous versus asynchronous

Before we get started with a brief introduction of microservices, there is an important point to consider here. Our microservices will be communicating with each other, and there is a possibility that they will rely on a response to move further. This poses a dilemma for us, having gone through all of the pain of unlearning the beloved monolith, and then getting into the same situation where a point of failure could result in a cascading collapse of the system.

[404]

The book-catalog microservice

The catalog-service will be designed to list, add, and remove items from the catalog. This service will also tell us the inventory of a specific product (books).

This microservice has six main functions, which are exposed through an HTTP API component. It is the responsibility of this HTTP API component to handle all of the HTTP requests for these functions.

These functions are as follows:

API resource description	API resource description
GET /api/book	Gets a list of the available books
GET /api/book/{category}	Gets a list of the books for a category
GET /api/book/{name}	Gets a list of the books by name
GET /api/book/{isbn}	Gets a book, as per the ISBN number
GET /api/bookquantity/{id}	Gets the available stock for the intended book
PUT /api/bookquantity/{id}/{changecount}	Increases or decreases the available stock quantity for a book

The following diagram visualizes the tables of the catalog services:

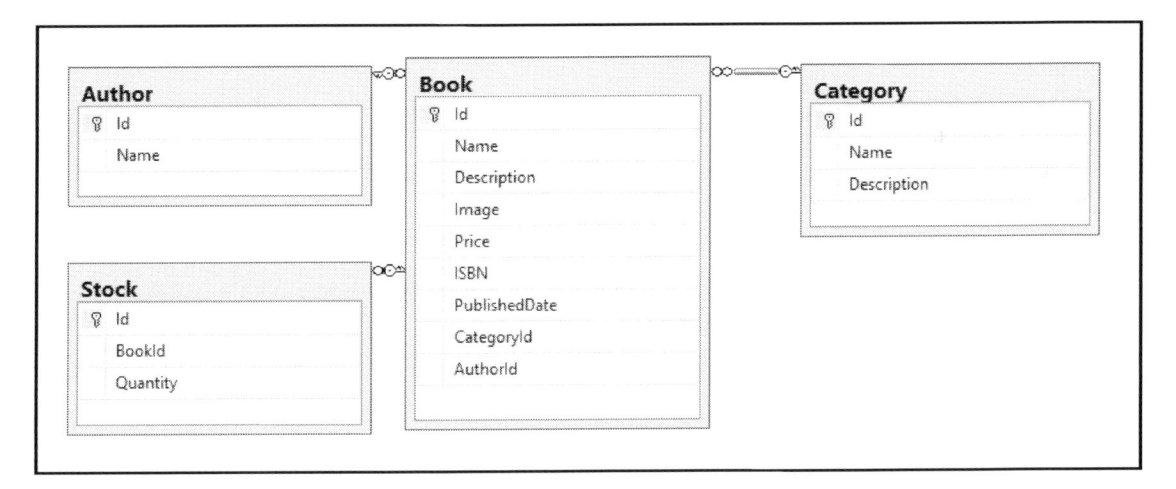

Microservices Architecture Summary

In the previous diagram, we have visualized tables of **Author**, **Stock**, **Book**, and **Category**. It also depicts the relationship between the tables. In simple words, the diagram represents the following: a book belongs to a specific category, showing its stock, and having an author.

The shopping-cart microservice

This microservice will have the following functions exposed as HTTP endpoints for consumption:

API resource description	API resource description
`POST /api/book/{customerid }`	Adds the specific book to the shopping cart of the customer
`DELETE /api/book/{customerid }`	Removes the book from the shopping cart of the customer
`GET /api/book/{customerid}`	Gets the list of books in the shopping cart of the customer
`PUT /api/empty`	Removes all of the books currently contained in the shopping cart

The following diagram visualizes both supporting tables for the shopping-cart service:

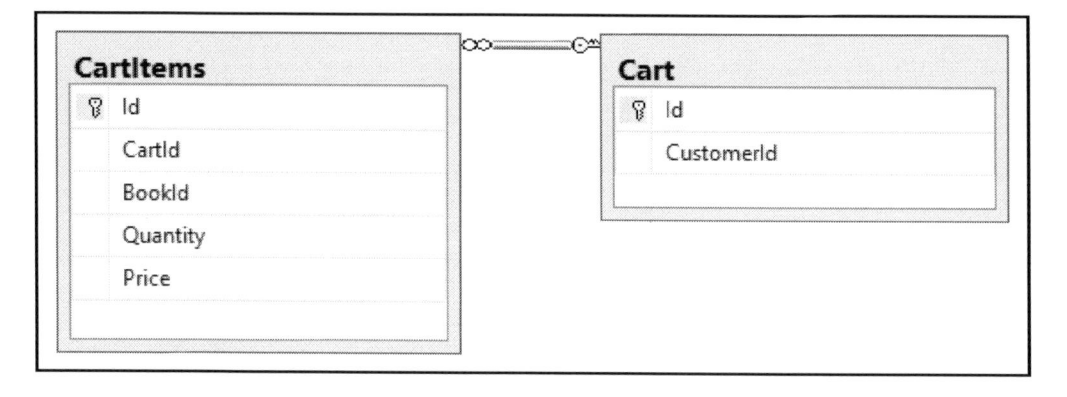

CartItems
- Id
- CartId
- BookId
- Quantity
- Price

Cart
- Id
- CustomerId

The preceding diagram visualizes the relationship between two tables, that is, **Cart** and **CartItems**. The relationship represents the one-to-many relationship between **Cart** and **CartItems**, where **CartId** is a primary key of the **Cart** table and a foreign key in the **CartItems** table.

The order microservice

This microservice will have the following functions exposed as HTTP endpoints for consumption:

API resource description	API resource description
`POST /api/order/{customerid }`	Gets all of the books in the shopping cart of the customer, and it creates an order for them
`DELETE /api/order/{customerid }`	Removes the book from the shopping cart of the customer
`GET /api/order/{orderid}`	Gets all of the books as part of the specific order

The following diagram depicts both of the tables of the order service:

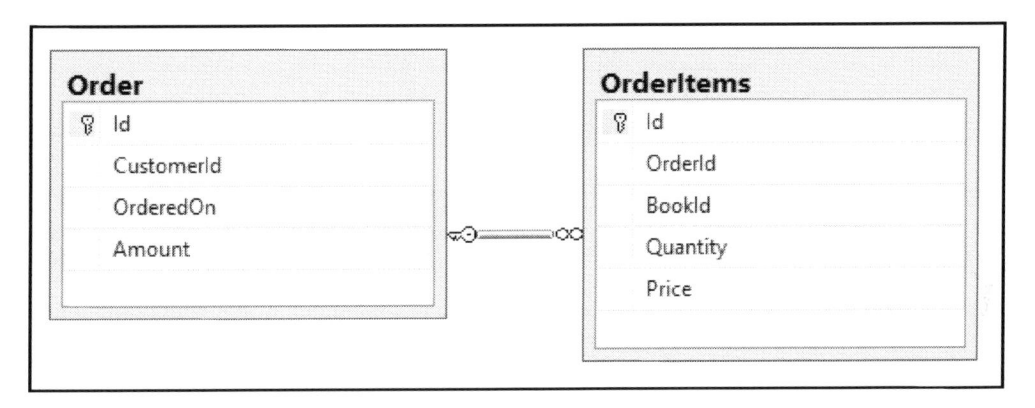

Order
- Id
- CustomerId
- OrderedOn
- Amount

OrderItems
- Id
- OrderId
- BookId
- Quantity
- Price

The previous diagram depicts the relationship between two tables, that is, **Order** and **OrderItems**. The relationship represents the one-to-many relationship between **Order** and **OrderItems**, where **OrderId** is a primary key in the **Order** table and a foreign key in the **OrderItems** table. This means one order may have multiple items.

The user-authentication microservice

This microservice will have the following functions exposed as HTTP endpoints for consumption:

API resource description	API resource description
`GET /api/verifyuser/{customerid, password}`	Verifies the user

The following screenshot shows the user table of the authentication service:

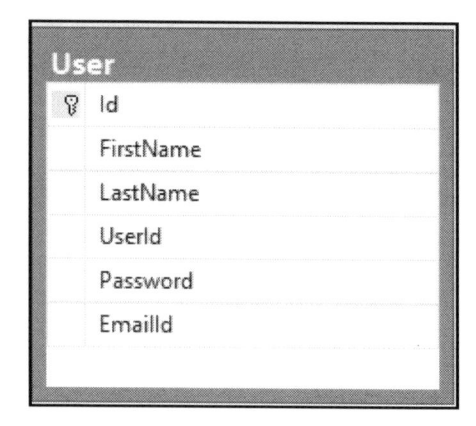

User
- Id (key)
- FirstName
- LastName
- UserId
- Password
- EmailId

You can look at the application source code and analyze it, as required.

This entire section walked us through various steps to create a greenfield application, where we discussed the Catalog and Cart services.

Next, let's move to a different topic: cloud-native microservices and how they are used in our context of microservice containers.

An overview of cloud-native microservices

The term *cloud-first*, or *cloud-native*, refers to the environment of containers, or we can say the container-based environment. In `Chapter 3`, *Effective Communication Between Services*, we discussed Azure Kubernetes Services and in `Chapter 5`, *Deploying Microservices with Docker*, we discussed Docker. Whenever we discussed containers, we were referring to the term *cloud-native*.

> The term *cloud-first* or *cloud-native* initiated a new approach to achieving complex, scalable systems.

Kubernetes, as a cloud-native platform, provides a network on top of the existing networking topologies and primitives of cloud providers. For example, in our case, we have Microsoft Azure as our cloud provider. This is similar to us working with storage that is a logically abstracted layer, of the native storage layer that is being used by developers and resource administrators lately. This is the place where deployment happens. Irrespective of the infrastructure that is being used, this may be based on physical servers or virtual machines and/or private/public clouds.

Further, cloud-native technologies are helpful, when we develop microservice applications. These applications are built with containerized services (which means services packaged in containers).

From the perspective of our system architecture, we can say that cloud-native microservices are based on the following principles:

- **Automation**: For any software system, it is best if we make it an automated system. Because with an automated system, we need to invest initially, and then, we use the system for almost nil or very little investment. An automated system would be helpful to set up infrastructure; CI/CD is also a very popular practice for an automated system. Some examples include scaling the system and monitoring the system.
- **Smart state**: This is the hardest part of any system, while architecting it. Mainly, for this, we should take care of how our data state will store user data.
- **Managed services**: Azure provides many managed services, so it is not just an infrastructure provider.
- **An evolving system**: The improvement and refinement of any system helps to develop it to be the best system. These systems are always evolving, and improvements happen throughout the life of these systems. On the same note, our cloud-native system should evolve.

In this section, we saw how a cloud-first or cloud-native system is one that always evolves, and hence, this is important for its overall growth.

Summary

In this chapter, we revisited our entire journey from a monolithic application to a microservices-based application. We revisited problems that are related to our legacy application. (Our monolithic application is now a legacy application, because, before this chapter, we transitioned our monolithic application to a microservices-based application.) We then discussed business cases, communication between services, the testing of services, the monitoring of services, and so on. We also discussed reactive microservices. Finally, we discussed `Order` microservices and `Shopping-Cart` microservices.

We hope that this book was able to introduce you to the fundamental concepts of a microservice-styled architecture, and we hope it helped you dive deeply into the fine aspects of microservices, with clear examples of the concepts. The final application is available for you to take a closer look at, in order to analyze what you have learned so far, at your own pace. We wish you luck in utilizing the skills learned in this book and in applying them to your real-world challenges.

Appendix

This section will walk you through how to implement your own API Gateway. The examples that we discussed in this book are used in Azure API Management. If you would like to set up your own API Gateway apart from Azure API Management, then please refer to this appendix.

> You can find all the working examples related to the API Gateway in the `Chapter 10` folder of this book's GitHub repository, which is located here: `https://github.com/PacktPublishing/Hands-On-Microservices-with-CSharp-8-and-.NET-Core-3-Third-Edition/tree/master/Appendix`.

To stick with the implementation of the API Gateway, we will be concentrating on implementing the API Gateway and summarizing the code examples that were provided in this book.

API Gateway pattern

The API Gateway is the only one at the center level of UI (client) and services, which means the UI can use it to collaborate with microservices. It provides us with an easier way to manage and expand these services. It gives us another degree of granularity regarding various clients (apps) as required (the application and its scope).

> Simply put, granularity describes *a framework that is separated into little sections. Huge frameworks can also be separated or divided into better, more appropriate sections.*

Appendix

The role of the API Gateway in microservices is to provide an intermediate, direct connection between the client and the hosted services with a specific arrangement and interpretation. This way the client only concentrates on what is required of it, without focusing on the server-side.

> The API Gateway exemplifies the framework's design and gives us a service that is custom-fitted to every client. It may serve different operations – for instance, validating incoming requests.

Adapting the API Gateway on the basis of its pros and cons

The implementation of the API Gateway pattern has some benefits for us developers. For example, an API Gateway allows us to hide the actual endpoints of the services from the client (UI/end-users), and it also allows us to handle business logic at one place for multiple clients (UI). The API Gateway has its own pros and cons.

Here are the pros of implementing the API Gateway pattern:

- The client (UI) can get complete data by making minimal requests to the services.
- We can handle multiple-format responses, such as JSON, XML, and so on. Authentication and logging can also be managed with the implementation of the API Gateway pattern.
- We can reduce round trips between the client and the application.
- It helps us access different APIs in one place, as exposed by the gateway.

The API Gateway provides many other advantages but still has some disadvantages, such as the following:

- There are chances of performance degradation, as most of the manipulation and transposing of responses happens at the API Gateway itself.
- There are chances of having single points of failure. If any issue occurs in terms of the API Gateway, then the client would experience failure.
- It needs extra attention and coding to manage routes.
- It adds more complexity to the system.

Preferred practices while implementing the API Gateway

We should follow these best practices, if we want to implement this pattern:

- We should implement logging and monitoring at a central place of the API Gateway. By doing this, we're saving a lot of effort that we would be investing in implementing, logging, and monitoring individual services. There may be scenarios where you want to log independent services. In that case, your code implementation should be very clean, so that you do not log the same data at multiple places.
- For aggregate services, it is good to have a combined logic in API Gateway to return client-specific responses. However, when the aggregate service has complex business logic or you have a specific requirement (such as not using the API Gateway), then you can proceed without the API Gateway. For instance, in Chapter 10, *Design Patterns and Best Practices*, in the *Aggregator pattern* section, we implemented aggregate services without the use of the API Gateway, due to our requirements, and because our code contained less complex business logic.
- While implementing security, make sure you are doing so in the right way. This means assessing if you need security for individual services or a group of services. You can also create policies for security. For instance, let's say you have a policy that requires login and password details from all the incoming requests. You can apply this policy to the services or a group of services, where you want to authenticate services using their login and password.

This is the basic list of best practices that we will adhere to in our code examples, which we are going to discuss later.

Implementing the API Gateway

With respect to our FlixOne application, we have different services, and all of these services are fine-grained and use their own databases. It is a bit complex to consume these services clients (any web or mobile device), as these services are hosted on different servers. This makes it hard to manage so many different endpoints from all the different clients. This also requires effort from the client to make changes in code, if any changes are made on the server-side, such as the server changing. Also, if any of the servers that host these APIs go down/offline, our end users (clients) would suffer, and this may have an impact on the client application.

Appendix

The following are the main reasons why we'd want to implement our own API Gateway:

- There should be a single endpoint for all clients. Currently, we do not have such a facility.
- There is no way to get the combined output from `ProductService` and `VendorService`. Currently, this is achieved with explicit calls to individual services.
- Logging and monitoring should be done at a central level. Currently, we are logging individual service levels.
- Security should be done at a central level, before requests come to the actual services. Currently, all the services have their own security implementations.

Creating an API Gateway from scratch is time-consuming and requires a lot of effort. Due to this, for the FlixOne application, we will go with Ocelot. There are a couple of reasons to go with the Ocelot API Gateway. Let's talk about these now.

Preferring Ocelot

The main reason why we selected Ocelot as our API Gateway implementation, is that Ocelot is open source for .NET Framework and .NET Core. It also supports .NET Core 3.1 (the current version of .NET Core for our application). Being an open source project, we have the liberty to customize the code and use it as per our requirements.

> The source code for Ocelot can be found at `https://github.com/ThreeMammals/Ocelot`.

More importantly, Ocelot has various features that we need in order to meet our requirements of using an API Gateway on-premises. A few of these required features are as follows:

- It allows us to define our own routes. For example, if we have `api/product/listproduct`, which is the route of our `product` service, then by using this feature, we can make it something similar to `/product/list`. In this case, the client/consumer would need to use `/product/list` to get the product listing.
- It provides us with security, so that we can apply authentication and authorization.

- With the caching feature, it reduces subsequent calls and data can be managed from the available cache, as per our requirements.
- We can set a retry policy. This will help if any of the requested services are down or not responding.
- With logging and monitoring, we can resolve one of the crucial problems of logging requests and response data.

Initial steps

To get started with the Ocelot API Gateway, we need to set up our project. This requires following these steps:

1. Open **Visual Studio**.
2. Go to **Get Started** | **Create a new Project**. You can also click **Continue** regarding continuing without a code link from this screen. In this case, you need to click **File** | **New Project** to create a new project.
3. Select **ASP.NET Core Web Application** and click **Next**.
4. Enter the project name, select the path, and click **Create**.
5. On the next screen, select an **Empty** template and click **Create**; make sure that you have selected **.NET Core** and **ASP.NET Core 3.1**.
6. Right-click **Add** | **New Item**.
7. On the next dialog, select **JSON File**, name it `apiroute.json`, and click **Add**.
8. Next, we add support for Ocelot. To do so, Go to **Tools** | **NuGet Package Manage** | **Package Manager Console**. Execute the following code in the **Package Manager Console**:

    ```
    Install-Package Ocelot
    ```

9. Now, open the **apiroute.json** file. This file is a configuration file that is required for **Ocelot**. Add the following **JSON** data:

    ```
    {
      "ReRoutes": [
        {
          "DownstreamPathTemplate": "/api/product/productlist",
          "DownstreamScheme": "https",
          "DownstreamHostAndPorts": [
            {
              "Host": "localhost",
              "Port": 44338
            }
          ],
    ```

Appendix

```
      "UpstreamPathTemplate": "/product/list",
      "UpstreamHttpMethod": [ "GET" ]
    },
    ...
  ],
  "GlobalConfiguration": {
    "BaseUrl": "https://localhost:44340"
  }
}
```

In the preceding code example, there are two sections: `ReRoutes` (an array) and `GlobalConfiguration`. The main functionality of `ReRoutes` is where all incoming requests are taken and then forwarded to the relevant services (also called downstream services). Then, the route identifies the relevant services (also called upstream services) so that it can pass the request. `GlobalConfiguration`, as its name suggests, is a configuration that applies to all the routes. It also allows us to override the `ReRoutes` settings. Our configuration file has the following properties:

- `DownstreamPathTemplate` is the route where the request is being forwarded.
- `DownstreamScheme` is the place where you can define the HTTP or HTTPs scheme for your downstream services.
- `DownstreamHostsAndPorts` is a collection of hosts and ports for downstream services. We used a single entry for this collection, but we can have multiple entries if we are implementing a load balancer to our downstream services.
- `UpstreamPathTemplate` is the URL that the requests have to pass through. The URL belongs to a specific upstream service.
- `UpstreamHttpMethod` allows us to identify what type of method is this. To set this, we use HTTP verbs. We can set a specific list of HTTP methods (`GET`, `POST`, `PUT`, `DELETE`, and so on) for the same URL. If it is empty, then it picks any of them.
- `BaseUrl` is part of the `GlobalConfiguration` section and tells us the base URL of all the upstream services.

Appendix

10. Before we start calling these APIs via the API Gateway, we have to make a few more changes to our code so that Ocelot works smoothly. Open the `Program.cs` file and replace the `CreateHostBuilder(string[] args)` method with the following code:

```
public static IHostBuilder CreateHostBuilder(string[] args) =>
    Host.CreateDefaultBuilder(args)
    .ConfigureAppConfiguration((hc, config) =>
    {
        config.AddJsonFile("apiroute.json");
    })
    .ConfigureServices(oc =>
    {
        oc.AddOcelot();
    })
    .ConfigureWebHostDefaults(webBuilder =>
    {
        webBuilder
        .UseStartup<Startup>()
        .Configure(app =>
        {
            app.UseOcelot().Wait();
        });
    });
```

In the preceding code, we are enabling Ocelot's dependency by adding `AddOcelot()`. This includes middleware for when we use `UserOcelot().Wait()` to handle all requests. This helps our application work as an API Gateway. Now that we are ready to test our basic implementation of API Gateway, press *F5* (it is assumed that the product and vendor services are running).

With that, we have implemented the Ocelot API Gateway with basic support. In the next section, we will add more features to our API Gateway, as follows:

- Aggregation
- Logging
- Rate-limit
- Security

[417]

Appendix

Aggregation

We need API Gateway aggregation, in order to get a combined result from two different services. The following diagram visualizes how aggregation works:

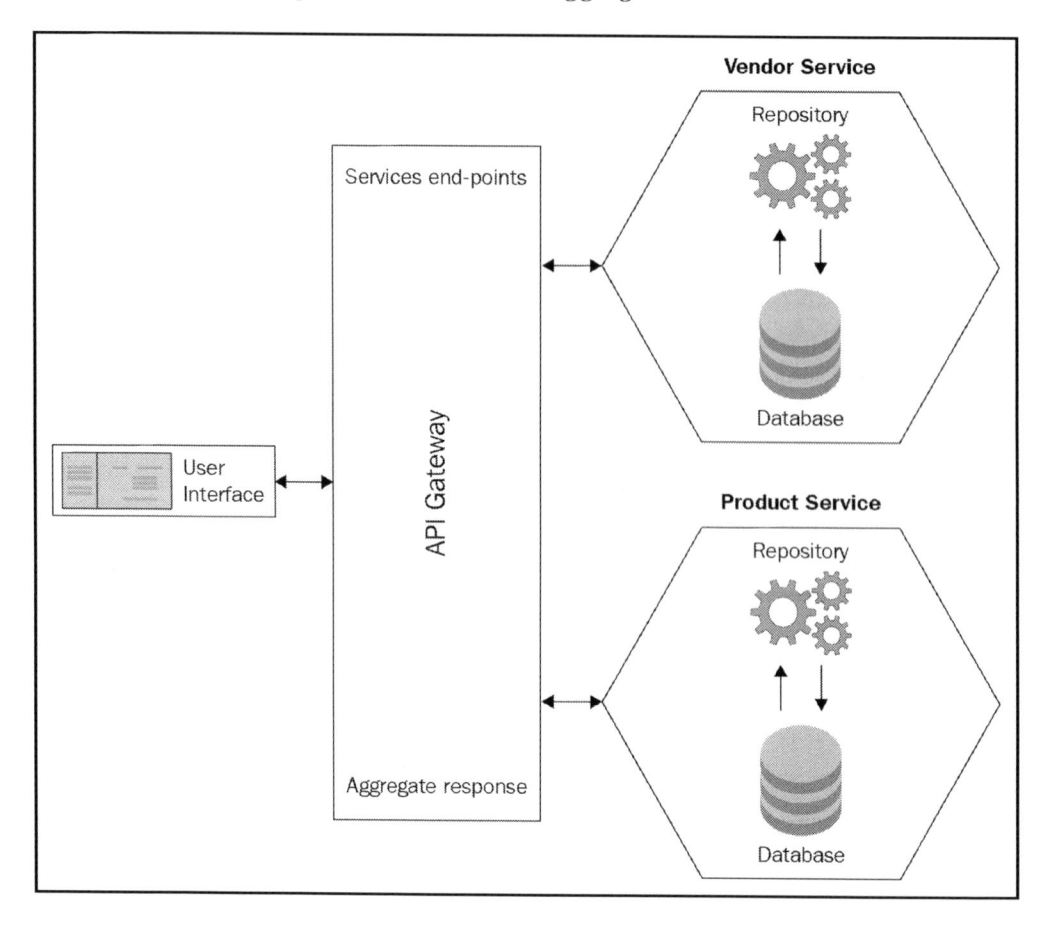

The preceding diagram is a pictorial view of our solution. The **API Gateway** is a single point of contact that receives the requests from the **User Interface** and forwards them to **Vendor Service** and **Product Service**. Furthermore, **API Gateway** provides a **User Interface** with **Service endpoints** and an **Aggregate response**.

Appendix

Open the `apiroute.json` file and update the JSON document using the following code:

```
{
  "ReRoutes": [
    //Product Service Routes
      ...
      "UpstreamPathTemplate": "/product/single/byvendorid/{id}",
      "UpstreamHttpMethod": [ "GET" ],
      "Key": "product"
    },
    ...
    //Vendor Service Route
    {
      ...
      "UpstreamPathTemplate": "/vendor/{id}",
      "UpstreamHttpMethod": [ "GET" ],
      "Key": "vendor"
    }
  ],
  "Aggregates": [
    {
      "ReRouteKeys": [
        "product",
        "vendor"
      ],
      "UpstreamPathTemplate": "/productlist/{id}"
    }
  ],
  ...
```

In the preceding code, we have added a `Key` property to the `ProductService` and `VendorService` routes. In `ReRouteKeys`, we're instructing our gateway to aggregate the collection represented by the `product` and `vendor` keys.

> You can also run all the service projects by executing the `runprojects.bat` file, which is available under the `Api Gateway pattern| Aggregation` folder of the `Chapter 10` folder in this book's GitHub repository.

To make the code implementation simple and as per its scope, which is to describe services, we are going to verify the response using Postman. To do so, launch the Postman application, enter the `/productlist/{id}` resource, and click **Send** from the Postman interface.

Appendix

Logging

Logging is one of the required features of an API Gateway, with respect to our `FlixOne` application. We will implement logging at the **API Gateway** level. The following diagram will help us visualize API Gateway logging:

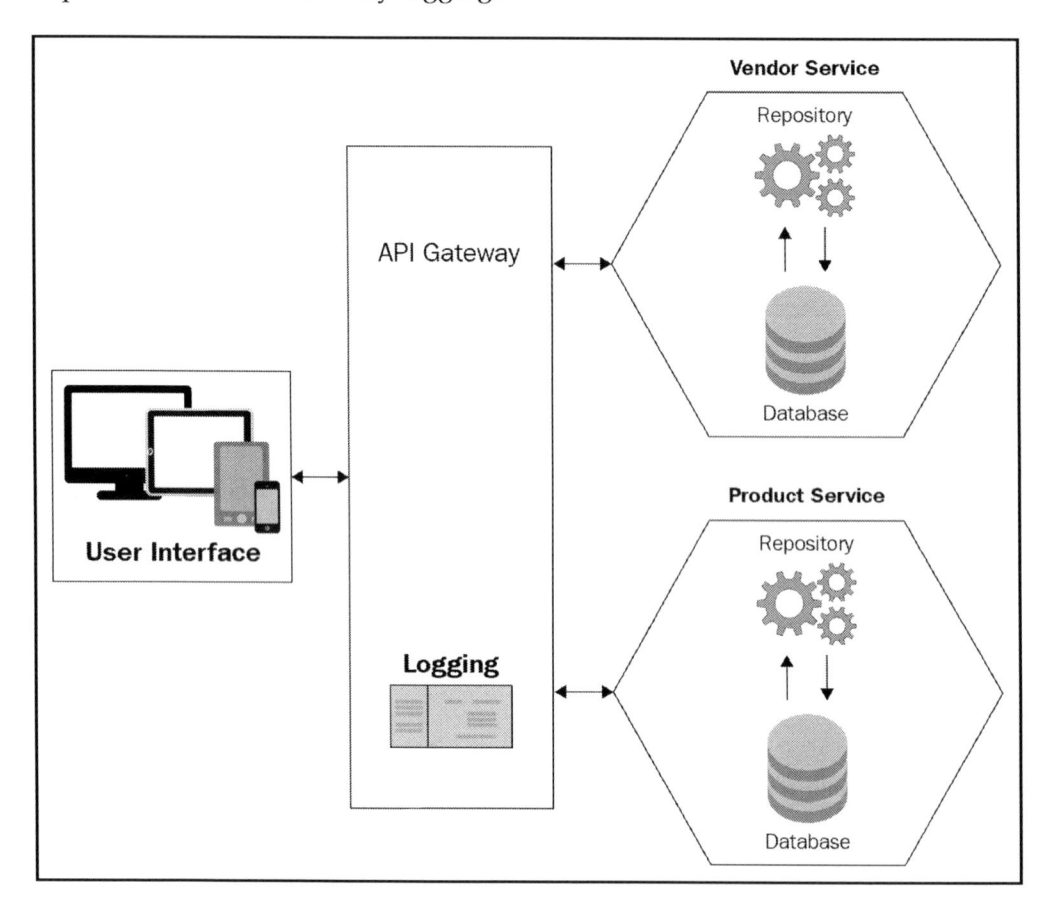

The preceding diagram is a pictorial representation of our implementation in the FlixOne application, where we are putting **Logging** at the **API Gateway**. With this, we've avoided adding the logging code to each and every service.

> `Log4Net` is a logging library that allows us to log the preferred operations of the application. The log data can be available in various sources, such as `Console`, `File`, `DB`, and so on. Moreover, `Log4Net` is open source, which means you can take advantage of it to customize the source code and use it as per your requirements.

Appendix

Open the `FlixOne.BookStore.ApiGateway` project and add support for `Log4Net` by executing the following command in `Package Console`:

```
Install-Package Microsoft.Extensions.Logging.Log4Net.AspNetCore
```

Now, we need to instruct our API Gateway to log the output to a file. For this, add a new file, name it `Log4Net.config`, and update the file with the following code:

```xml
<?xml version="1.0" encoding="utf-8" ?>
<log4net>
...
  <appender name="RollingFile" type="log4net.Appender.RollingFileAppender">
    <file value="FlixOneLog.log" />
     <appendToFile value="true" />
    <maximumFileSize value="10MB" />
    <maxSizeRollBackups value="3" />
...
  </appender>
  <root>
    <level value="ALL"/>
    <appender-ref ref="DebugAppender" />
    <appender-ref ref="RollingFile" />
  </root>
</log4net>
```

In the preceding code, we are configuring our `Log4Net` in order to log the output using `DebugAppender` and `RollingFile`. These appenders are defined to log messages in a specific format, which is mentioned in `ConversionPattern`. You'll observe that the output format for `DebugAppender` and `RollingFile` is different in the preceding code. We also configured our `RollingFile` appender in such a way so that the log file size will not increase from 10 MB and the maximum numbers of files will be 3. These files will be stored under the name `FlixOneLog.log`. We configured our logging system in order to log everything by setting the level value to `ALL`. This value can be changed as per your environment; for example, you wouldn't be interested in logging `DEBUG` in the production environment.

The following are the various levels of `Log4Net`:

- `All`: Log everything.
- `Debug`: Log only the debug operations. For example, if the logger is an instance of `Log4Net`, then `Logger.Debug("This is a Debug log!");` would be logged.

[421]

- **Info**: Log only information operations. For example, if the logger is an instance of `Log4Net` then `Logger.Info("This is an Info log!");` would be logged.
- **Warn**: Log only warning messages. For example, if the logger is an instance of `Log4Net`, then `Logger.Warn("This is a Warn log!");` would be logged.
- **Error**: This mainly logs exceptions or custom error messages. For example, if the logger is an instance of `Log4Net`, then `Logger.Debug("This is an Error log!");` would be logged.

Next, open the `Startup.cs` file and update the `Configure` method using the following code:

```
public void Configure(IApplicationBuilder app, IWebHostEnvironment env,
ILoggerFactory loggerFactory)
{
    ...
    loggerFactory.AddLog4Net();
    app.UseOcelot().Wait();
}
```

In the preceding code, we added `loggerFactory.AddLog4Net();` just before `app.UseOcelot().Wait()`. By doing this, we are saying that our API Gateway will log the output of every request/response based on our configuration, which is provided in the `Log4Net.config` file.

> You can also run all the projects by executing the `runprojects.bat` batch file, which is available under the `Api Gateway pattern | Logging` folder of the `Chapter 10` folder, in this book's GitHub repository.

Protecting services from attacks by defining rate-limits

Protecting an application from external attacks is one of the most important tasks we will need to perform. We can do this with the help of the API Gateway, which will control the requests coming to our API Gateway for APIs. Attackers can send numerous requests – sometimes in the thousands – in a fraction of a second. This is known as a **Distributed Denial of Service (DDoS)** attack. Here, attackers target a specific machine or application and send multiple requests. To handle this problem, we need to set the rate-limit for requests. We will implement the same in our `FlixOne.BookStore` application.

Appendix

Take a look at the following diagram to understand what we are trying to implement as a solution to our aforementioned problem:

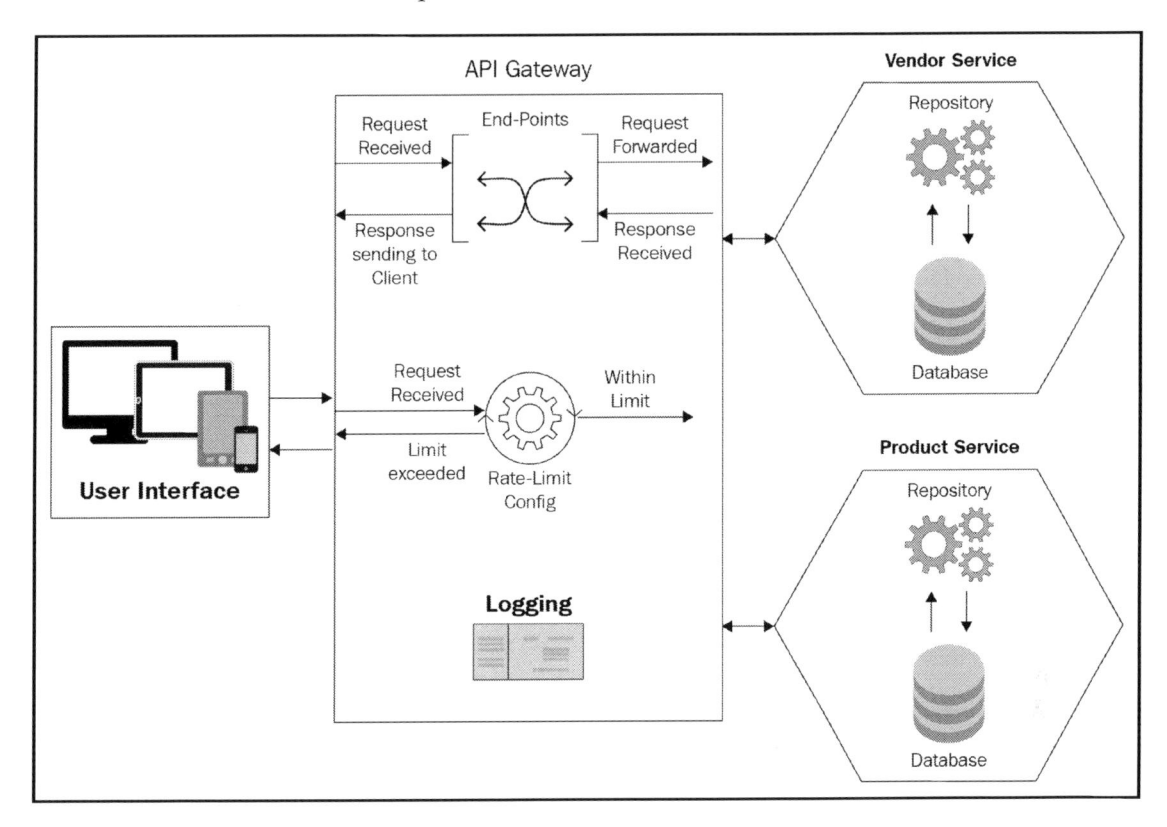

The preceding diagram clearly shows that, whenever a request is received at the **API Gateway**, the **Rate-Limit Config** from within the **API Gateway** analyzes the quota of the request for the client, and requests are either forwarded to the relevant service at the server-side or returned to the client with a *specified quota exceeded* message.

Appendix

To implement rate-limits in the API Gateway, open the `FlixOne.BookStore.ApiGateway` project and restrict one of our services so that it makes a request within 3 seconds. To do this, update the product service with the following code:

```
{
     "DownstreamPathTemplate": "/api/product/productlist",
     "DownstreamScheme": "https",
     "DownstreamHostAndPorts": [
       {
         "Host": "localhost",
         "Port": 44338
       }
     ],
     "UpstreamPathTemplate": "/product/list",
     "UpstreamHttpMethod": [ "GET" ],
     //Setting up a limit for 1-request within 3second, retry in 5seconds
     "RateLimitOptions": {
       "ClientWhitelist": [],
       "EnableRateLimiting": true,
       "Period": "3s",
       "PeriodTimespan": 5,
       "Limit": 1
     }
}
```

In the preceding code, we are configuring our `Upstream` service's `/product/list`, which is a `GET HttpMethod`, to restrict 1 request within 3s by providing the following `RateLimitOptions`:

- `ClientWhitelist`: Consists of an array of client IPs and considers whitelisted clients. This means that the incoming requests coming from these whitelisted clients will not fall under the rule of whitelist IPs.
- `EnableRateLimiting`: Consists of a `true/false` value. This indicates whether we are instructing our API Gateway to enable/disable endpoint rate limiting. In our case, we are enabling rate-limiting for the `/product/list` endpoint.
- `Period`: Consists of the time period in the format of `{number}{unit}`, where number would be *1* to *n* based on the unit, and unit would be `s` for seconds, `m` for a minutes, `h` for hour, and `d` for days. In our case, we have provided `3s` for the value of `Period`, which means 3 seconds.

- `PeriodTimespan`: This is actually a waiting period (in seconds) if the limit is exceeded within a specified `Period`. In our case, we have to wait for 5 seconds before making a second request.
- `Limit`: This indicates the number of maximum requests that we can make within a specified `Period`. In our case, we can only make one request within 3 seconds, and we need to wait for 5 seconds before making a second request.

> You can also run all the projects by executing the `runprojects.bat` batch file, which is available under the `Api Gateway pattern | Rate-Limit` folder of the `Chapter 10` folder in this book's GitHub repository.

Run the API Gateway project and press the `/product/list` endpoint in your preferred browser. You will get the expected results. Now, hit *F5* as many times as you want. You'll see that you're unable to make the request but will be able to see a rate-limit message, as shown in the following screenshot:

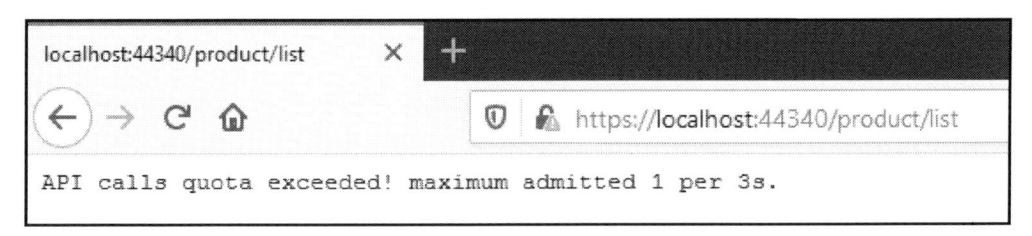

```
API calls quota exceeded! maximum admitted 1 per 3s.
```

The preceding screenshot shows that we are trying to make more than one request within 3 seconds, which isn't possible.

> When we set `EnableRateLimiting` to `true`, we are actually adding the `X-Rate-Limit` and `Retry-After` headers with the specified requests.

Implementing security services

Security is one of the biggest concerns these days. To handle this, we will implement security in our API Gateway. We will mark all our services as secure so that the client will get an unauthorized error message if they try to make a direct request to backend services.

Appendix

Consider the following diagram to understand what we are trying to implement as a solution to our problem:

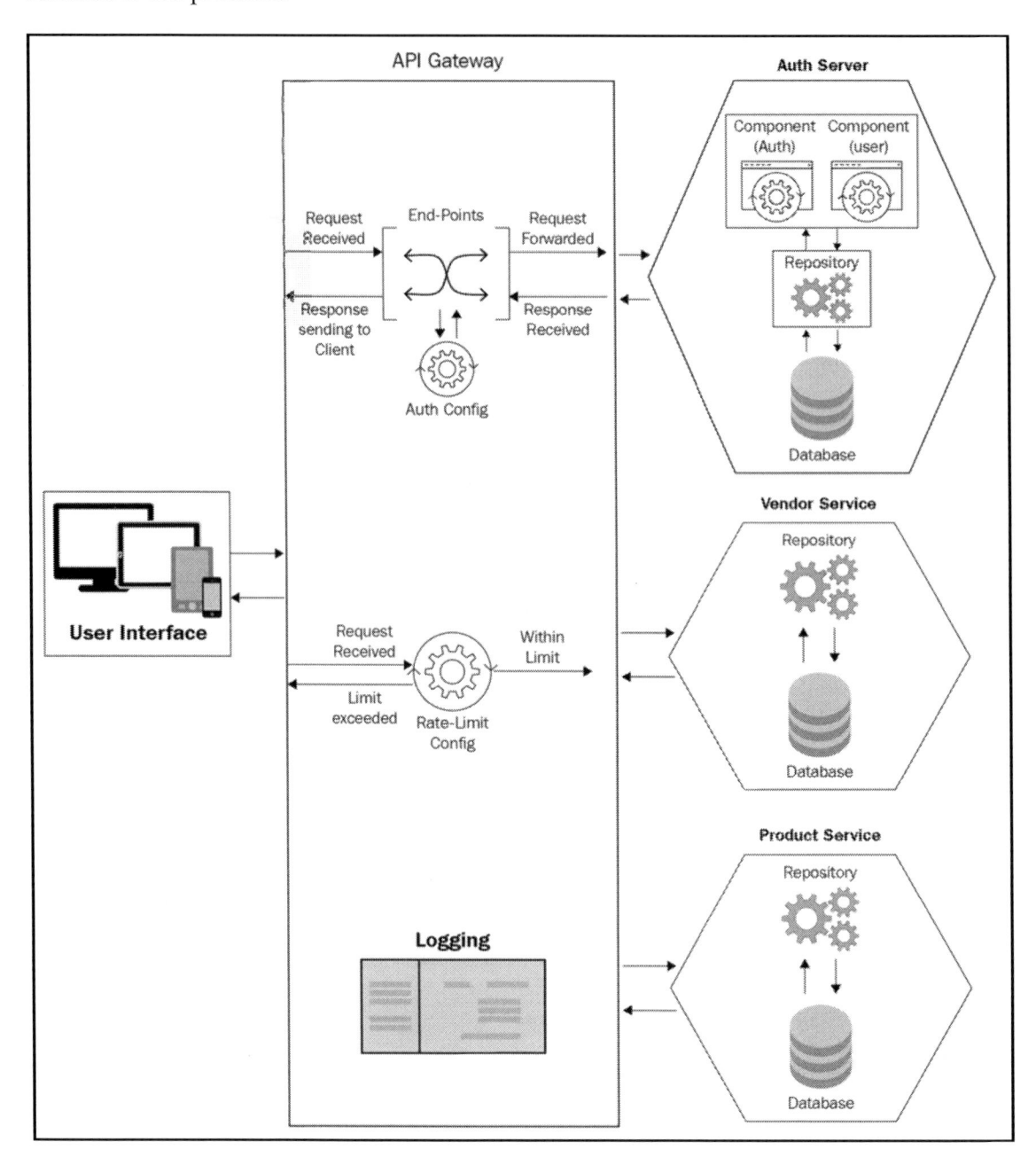

In the preceding diagram, we added the **Auth Config** component to our API Gateway with a new **Auth Server**. Now, whenever the API Gateway receives a request, the **Auth Config** component will check if the request meets the specified authentication mechanism or not. The API Gateway will deny or forward this request to the backend services accordingly. Our **Auth Server** generates a **JWT token**. It also handles user registration operations.

> If you are writing a production-ready application, do not create and validate tokens in the same place; you can secure and validate it by adding another layer.

Now that we have added the required features to our API Gateway, we have to take care of one more point, which is exposing the service endpoints per client. This means the clients of mobile devices will have different service endpoints than that of the clients of web applications. Now that we have implemented the API Gateway pattern, let's think of a scenario where our clients need specific content as per their target devices. We can do this with the help of **Backend for Frontend** (BFF) patterns. This will be like creating a client-specific API Gateway. In the next section, we will learn how to implement backends for frontends.

Backends for Frontends pattern

The Backends for Frontends pattern helps us to create separate backend services for all, or for specific, frontend applications (user interfaces), with the user interfaces sending a request to their specific backend services. This pattern is useful if you want to avoid having a multi-interface customization for a single backend.

Appendix

The following diagram depicts what we are trying to achieve:

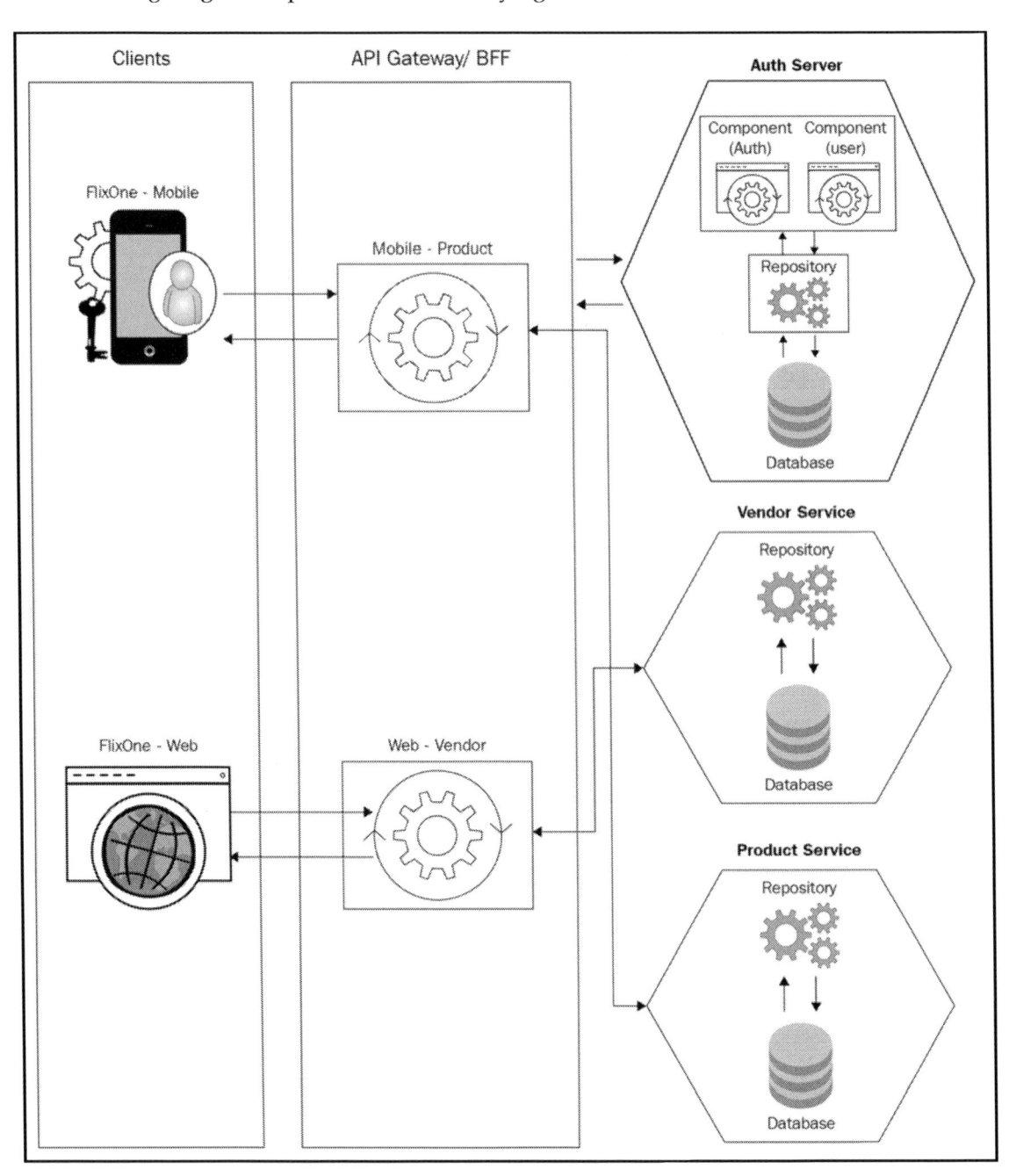

The preceding diagram tells us that we have two **API Gateway** blocks. One is **Mobile - Product**, which provides the endpoints of `Product Service` to the clients of mobile devices, and the other is **Web-Vendor**, which provides the endpoints of `Vendor Service` to all the web clients.

> We have created two new projects for this: `FlixOne.BookStore.Web.ApiGateway` and `FlixOne.BookStore.Mobile.ApiGateway`.

Consider the following code of the `apiroute.json` file from the `FlixOne.BookStore.Web.ApiGateway` project:

```
{
  "ReRoutes": [
    //Vendor Service Route
    {
      "DownstreamPathTemplate": "/api/Vendor/{id}",
      "DownstreamScheme": "https",
      "DownstreamHostAndPorts": [
        {
          "Host": "localhost",
          "Port": 44339
        }
      ],
      "UpstreamPathTemplate": "/vendor/{id}",
      "UpstreamHttpMethod": [ "GET" ],
      "Key": "vendor"
    }
  ],
  "GlobalConfiguration": {
    "BaseUrl": "https://localhost:44340"
  }
}
```

The preceding code is self-explanatory. Here, we are configuring the endpoints for the API Gateway to get a vendor response from `Vendor Service`.

Appendix

Consider the following code of the `apiroute.json` file from the `FlixOne.BookStore.Mobile.ApiGateway` project:

```json
{
  "ReRoutes": [
    //Product Service Route

    {
      "DownstreamPathTemplate": "/api/product/{productid}",
      "DownstreamScheme": "https",
      "DownstreamHostAndPorts": [
        {
          "Host": "localhost",
          "Port": 44338
        }
      ],
      "UpstreamPathTemplate": "/mobile/product/{productid}",
      "UpstreamHttpMethod": [ "GET" ],
      "Key": "product"
    }
  ],
  "GlobalConfiguration": {
    "BaseUrl": "https://localhost:44341"
  }
}
```

In the preceding code, we configured the **Mobile API Gateway** to get a response from `Product Service`.

By implementing BFF, we're serving separate APIs for relevant clients. In this way, we are achieving the following:

- A single contact for all the endpoints. This was achieved when we implemented the API Gateway.
- Now, the client of the mobile device and the client of the web interface have their own specific APIs. These APIs serve them the relevant content.

Now, we have the required services available for our clients via the API Gateway.

Assessments

Chapter 1

What are microservices?

A microservices architecture is a bunch of services, where each service is independently deployed and should implement a single business capability.

Can you define Azure Service Fabric?

Azure Service Fabric is a platform that helps us with easily packaging, deploying, and managing scalable and reliable microservices (the container is also like Docker, and so on). Sometimes, it is difficult to focus on your main responsibility as a developer due to complex infrastructural problems, and so on. With the help of Azure Service Fabric, developers need not worry about the infrastructural issues. It provides various technologies and comes as a bundle that has the power of Azure SQL Database, Cosmos DB, Microsoft Power BI, Azure Event Hubs, Azure IoT Hub, and many more core services.

What is database sharding?

In general, database sharding is simply defined as a shared-nothing partitioning scheme for large databases. This way, we can achieve a new level of high performance and scalability. The word sharding comes from the term shard and spreading, which means dividing a database into chunks (shards) and spreading it into different servers.

What is TDD and why should developers adopt this?

With TDD, a developer writes the test before coding it so that they can test their own code. The test is another piece of code that can validate whether the functionality is working as intended. If any functionality is found to not satisfy the test code, the corresponding unit test fails. This functionality can easily be fixed; as you already know, this is where the problem is. In order to achieve this, we can utilize frameworks such as MS tests or unit tests.

Can you elaborate on dependency injection (DI)?

Dependency injection (DI) is a design pattern and provides a technique so that you can make a class independent of its dependencies. This can be achieved by decoupling an object from its creation.

Chapter 2

What are all of the factors we should consider while refactoring a monolith application?

In respect to microservices, refactoring a monolith application plays an important role. This is not just something like refactoring code but thinking of it as a whole system. This refactoring further helps transition monolith applications into microservices. There may be many factors to think of while refactoring or preparing our monolith application for a microservces architecture. The following are the important factors we should keep in mind (these are based on our imaginary application and the discussion we had in this chapter) while refactoring a monolith:

- **Technical consideration**: Considerations such as segregating the features, technology stack, and team and team skills should be taken into account. These help us make a decision about refactored components.
- **Commercial consideration**: Considerations for a go-to market plan is the most important factor if we decide to refactor the monolith.

What are the default interface methods of C# 8.0?

The default interface methods are the methods in the interfaces that implement interface members. Take a look at the following code for a better understanding of this feature:

```
public interface IProduct
{
  public int Id { get; set; }
  public string Name { get; set; }
  public decimal Price { get; set; }
  public string ProductDesc() => $"Book:{Name} has Price:{Price}";
}
```

Let's implement the `IProduct` interface to our `Product` class. Consider the following code:

```
public class Product : IProduct
{
  public Product(int id, string name, decimal price)
  {
    Id = id;
    Name = name;
    Price = price;
  }
  public int Id { get; set; }
  public string Name { get; set; }
  public decimal Price { get; set; }
}
```

`ProductDesc` is the default method of our interface and always produces a result. In our case, it will return a string as a result of this method. Also, this method is available to all the classes that implement the `IProduct` interface. In a similar manner, we have implemented the `IProduct` interface in our `Product` class.

Why do we use Swagger?

Swagger provides documentation about APIs based on the Open API Specification (former Swagger specifications). Swagger also provides a facility for testing APIs. We use Swagger so that we can provide proper documentation to the end user.

Chapter 3

What is synchronous and asynchronous communication?

Synchronous communication is where a client makes a request to the remote service (called a service) for specific functionality and waits until it gets a response. Asynchronous communication is where clients make a request to the remote service (called a service) for specific functionality and don't wait, although it does care about the response.

What is an integration pattern?

An integration pattern is where two or more services read and write data out of one data store.

What is an event-driven pattern and why it is so important for microservices?

In an event-driven pattern, we implement a service in such a way that it publishes an event whenever a service updates its data and another service (dependent service) subscribes to this event. Whenever a dependent service receives an event, it updates its data. This way, our dependent services can get and update their data if required. The preceding diagram shows an overview of how services subscribe to and publish events. Here, Event-Manager could be a program running on a service or a mediator helping you manage all the events of the subscribers and publishers. It registers an event of the Publisher and notifies a Subscriber whenever a specific event occurs/is triggered. It also helps you to form a queue and wait for events.

Assessments

What is the CAP theorem?

The CAP theorem is also known as Brewer's theorem and stands for **Consistency, Availability, (network) Partition tolerance**. According to this theorem, in a distributed system, we can only choose two out of these three:

- Consistency (C)
- Availability (A)
- Partition tolerance (CA)

Consider that we have an imaginary system that is highly available (A) and highly consistent (C) but there is no partition (CA). When we require and do the partitioning (P), we partition our system up to n number of partitions or say we are continuously partitioning our system. In this case, it is a very complex scenario and data might not be able to reach/cover all the partitions. This is the reason why we either make the system highly available (AP) or highly consistent (CP).

Chapter 4

Write a short note on unit testing.

Unit tests are tests that typically test a single function call to ensure that the smallest piece of the program is tested. These tests are meant to verify specific functionality without considering other components. Unit tests can be of any size; there is no definite size for a unit test. Generally, these tests are written at the class level.

Why should developers adhere to test-driven development?

With TDD, a developer writes the test before the actual code so that they can test their own code. This test is another piece of code that can validate whether the functionality is working as intended. If any functionality is found to not satisfy the test code, the corresponding unit test fails. This functionality can easily be fixed since you know this is where the problem is. In order to achieve this, we can utilize frameworks such as MS tests or unit tests.

What are stub and mock objects?

Stub objects do not depend on the input, which means the response or result does not hamper due to correct or incorrect input. Initially, we created stubs as objects. A mock object is not real and may always be a fake object. By using a mock object, you can test methods that can be called and tell us whether a unit test has failed or passed. In other words, we can say that mock objects are just a replica of our actual object.

What is the testing pyramid?

The testing pyramid is a strategy or a way to define what you should test in microservices. In other words, we can say it helps us define the testing scope of microservices. The concept of the testing pyramid was created by Mike Cohn (`http://www.mountaingoatsoftware.com/blog/the-forgotten-layer-of-the-test-automation-pyramid`) in 2009. There are various flavors of the testing pyramid; different authors have described this by indicating how they had placed or prioritized their testing scope.

What are consumer tests?

Contract testing is an approach where each service call independently verifies the response. If any service is dependent, then the dependencies are stubbed. This way, the service functions without interacting with any other service. Consumer-driven contracts refer to a pattern that specifies and verifies all the interactions between clients/consumers and the API owner (application). Here, consumer-driven means that the client/consumer specifies what kind of interactions it is asking for in the defined format. On the other hand, the API owner (application services) must agree to these contracts and ensure that they are not breaking them.

How can we use consumer tests in a microservices-based application?

In the case of microservices, it's a bit more challenging to implement a consumer-driven test than for a .NET monolithic application. This is because, in monolithic applications, we can directly use any unit test framework, such as MS tests or NUnit, but we can't do this directly in the microservice architecture. In microservices, we would need to mock not only method calls but also the services themselves, which get called via either HTTP or HTTPs. To implement a consumer-driven test, we need to use a variety of tools. One famous open source tool for .NET frameworks is PactNet; another for .NET Core is known as Pact.Net Core. These are based on Pact (`https://docs.pact.io/`) standards.

Assessments

Chapter 5

What is a Docker image and why it is so important?

A Docker image is a kind of a template that contains instructions for creating a Docker container. You can only read the instructions; you can't add your own instructions to this template since this a read-only template. It consists of a separate filesystem, associated libraries, and so on. Here, an image is always read-only and can run exactly the same abstracting, underlying, host differences. A Docker image can be composed of one layer on top of another. This composability of the Docker image can be compared to the analogy of a layered cake. Docker images that are used across different containers can be reused. This also helps reduce the deployment footprint of applications that use the same base images.

What is the Docker repository?

The Windows Registry is a database that stores information for the internal or low-level settings of the Microsoft Windows operating system.

What is a Docker container?

An instance of a Docker image that's currently running is called a Docker container.

What is Docker hub?

This is a public registry and stores images. It is located at `http://hub.docker.com`.

Can I use JSON instead of YAML in Docker files? If so, how?

Yes, we can use a JSON file instead of a YAML file. Please note that YAML is a superset of JSON. In this way, when we use a JSON file, it is implicitly a valid YAML file. We need to specify the file name to use JSON files; for example, `docker-compose -f jsoncomposefile.json up`.

Here, we used `up` to tell the system that we can to start or restart all the services defined in the `jsoncomposefile.json` file.

Explain these words in regard to containers: `FROM, COPY, WORKDIR, EXPOSE, ENTRYPOINT`.

To understand these terms, let's consider the following code snippet:

```
FROM mcr.microsoft.com/dotnet/core/aspnet:3.0-nanoserver-1903
 AS base WORKDIR /app
 EXPOSE 80 EXPOSE 443
 FROM mcr.microsoft.com/dotnet/core/aspnet:3.0 AS runtime
 WORKDIR /app
 COPY ${source:-obj/Docker/publish} .
 ENTRYPOINT ["dotnet", "FlixOne.BookStore.ProductService.dll"]
```

`FROM` it is some kind of a message that tells Docker to pull the base image on the existing image and call `microsoft/aspnetcore:3.0`. `COPY` and `WORKDIR` copy content to a new directory inside the called/app container and set it to the working directory for subsequent instructions. To expose our Product service on port 80 of the container, we can use `EXPOSE` and `ENTRYPOINT`, which specify the command to execute when the container starts up. For our example, we have `ProductService`, and our entry point is `["dotnet", "FlixOne.BookStore.ProductService.dll"]`.

Write a simple ASP.NET Core web application to display `Add`, `Delete`, **and** `Update` **products in a tabular view with the help of our** `Product Services`.

Refer to the code example of our imaginary FlixOne book store application.

Chapter 6

What is software security?

Security is one of the most important cross-cutting concerns for web applications. Unfortunately, data breaches of well-known sites seem commonplace these days. Taking this into account, information and application security has become critical to web applications. For the same reason, secure applications should no longer be an afterthought. Security is everyone's responsibility in an organization. If we were to define security, then we can say that this is a way to implement code so that we can protect our software from malicious attacks and hacker risks so that we can provide a secure application with uninterrupted functionality.

What are the security challenges of monolithic applications?

Refer to the *Security in monolithic applications* section for more information.

Assessments

Create a demo application and elaborate on OAuth.

Refer to the example application we discussed in the *Working with OAuth 2.0* section of this chapter.

What is an authorization server and how does it work?

The **authorization server** validates the credentials and redirects the user back to the client with an **authorization** code.

What is Azure API Management and why do we need an API gateway for microservices?

The **Azure API Management (APIM)** service comes with an easy-to-follow user interface and good documentation. Azure API management also comes with a REST API, hence all the capabilities of the Azure APIM portal can be programmatically achieved using the Azure REST API endpoints that are available for Azure APIM.

Chapter 7

What is monitoring?

Monitoring provides information around the behavior of an entire system or different parts of a system in their operational environment. This information can be used for diagnosing and gaining insight into the different characteristics of a system.

What is the need for monitoring?

Microservices are complex, distributed systems. Microservice implementation is the backbone of any modern IT business. Understanding the internals of the services along with their interactions and behaviors will help you make the overall business more flexible and agile. The performance, availability, scale, and security of microservices can directly affect a business and its revenue. Hence, monitoring microservices is vital. It helps us observe and manage the quality of the service's attributes.

What is health monitoring?

With health monitoring, we monitor the health of a system and its various components at a certain frequency, which is typically a few seconds. This ensures that the system and its components behave as expected. With the help of an exhaustive health monitoring system, we can keep tabs on the overall system's health, including the CPU, memory utilization, and so on. It might be in the form of pings or extensive health monitoring endpoints, which emit the health status of services along with some useful metadata at that point in time.

Assessments

What are the challenges of monitoring?

Microservice monitoring presents different challenges. There will be scenarios where one service could depend upon another service, or a client sends a request to one service and the response comes from another service that would make the operation complex; hence, scaling a microservice would be a challenging task here. Similarly, process implementation – let's say, DevOps – would be a challenging job while implementing a huge enterprise microservice application.

What are the main logging and monitoring solutions from Microsoft Azure?

There is no single, off-the-shelf solution or offering in Azure – or any cloud provider, for that matter – when it comes to the monitoring challenges presented by microservices. Microsoft Azure Diagnostics, Application Insights, and Log Analytics are the logging and monitoring solutions offered by Azure.

Chapter 8

What is caching and what is the importance of caching in microservices applications?

Caching is the simplest way to increase the application's throughput. The principle is very easy. Once the data is read from the data storage, it is kept as close as possible to the processing server. In future requests, the data is served directly from the data storage or cache. The essence of caching is to minimize the amount of work that a server has to do. HTTP has a built-in cache mechanism embedded in the protocol itself. This is the reason it scales so well.

What is service discovery and how does it play an important role in a microservices application?

Refer to the *Service discovery* section for more information.

Define the Azure Redis Cache by implementing a small program.

Azure Redis gives you access to a secure, dedicated Redis cache that's managed by Microsoft and accessible from any application within Azure. For the required implementation steps, please refer to the *Azure Redis Cache* section.

What is a circuit breaker?

A circuit breaker is a safety feature in an electronic device that, in the event of a short-circuit, breaks the electricity flow and protects the device, or prevents any further damage to the surroundings. This exact idea can be applied to software design. When a dependent service is not available or not in a healthy state, a circuit breaker prevents calls from going to that dependent service and redirects the flow to an alternate path for a configured period of time.

Chapter 9

What are reactive microservices?

There are certain fundamental attributes that a piece of software must possess in order to be considered reactive. These attributes are responsiveness, resilience, elasticity, autonomy and, above all, being message-driven.

What is message-level security?

Message-level security is the most fundamental method available if you wish to secure your individual request messages. After the initial authentication has been performed, the request message itself may contain the OAuth bearer token or the JWTs, based on the implementation. This way, each and every request is authenticated, and the information related to the user can be embedded within these tokens. The information could be as simple as a username along with an expiration timestamp indicating token validity. After all, we don't want to allow a token to be utilized beyond a certain time frame.

What is AutoRest?

AutoRest is a tool that helps us generate client libraries so that we can access RESTful web services. AutoRest fetches the API definition from the Open API Specification (Swagger).

Other Books You May Enjoy

If you enjoyed this book, you may be interested in these other books by Packt:

Hands-On Software Architecture with C# 8 and .NET Core 3
Francesco Abbruzzese, Gabriel Baptista

ISBN: 978-1-78980-093-7

- Overcome real-world architectural challenges and solve design consideration issues
- Apply architectural approaches like Layered Architecture, service-oriented architecture (SOA), and microservices
- Learn to use tools like containers, Docker, and Kubernetes to manage microservices
- Get up to speed with Azure Cosmos DB for delivering multi-continental solutions
- Learn how to program and maintain Azure Functions using C#

Other Books You May Enjoy

Learn ASP.NET Core 3 - Second Edition
Kenneth Yamikani Fukizi, Jason De Oliveira, Et al

ISBN: 978-1-78961-013-0

- Delve into basic and advanced ASP.NET Core 3 concepts with the help of examples
- Build an MVC web application and use Entity Framework Core 3 to access data
- Add web APIs to your web applications using RPC, REST, and HATEOAS
- Create a fully automated continuous integration and continuous delivery (CI/CD) pipeline using Azure DevOps
- Use Azure, Amazon Web Services, and Docker to deploy and monitor your applications

Leave a review - let other readers know what you think

Please share your thoughts on this book with others by leaving a review on the site that you bought it from. If you purchased the book from Amazon, please leave us an honest review on this book's Amazon page. This is vital so that other potential readers can see and use your unbiased opinion to make purchasing decisions, we can understand what our customers think about our products, and our authors can see your feedback on the title that they have worked with Packt to create. It will only take a few minutes of your time, but is valuable to other potential customers, our authors, and Packt. Thank you!

Index

.NET Core 3.0
  features 56, 57, 58, 59, 60, 61
  installation link 198
.NET Core
  download link 374
  reference link 203
.NET stack
  standardizing, challenges 389

A

Active Directory Federation Services (ADFS) 217
advantages, microservices
  alignment, with business goals 47
  cost benefits 47
  data management 48
  easy scalability 47
  interdependency removal 46
  security 48
  technology independence 46
Aggregator pattern solution
  implementing, in FlixOne application 334, 335, 336
Aggregator pattern
  about 332, 333
  advantages 333
  best practices 334
  disadvantages 333
ambassador pattern
  about 150, 151
  best practices 152
  using 151
Anti-Corruption Layer pattern solution
  implementing, in FlixOne application 364, 365
Anti-Corruption Layer pattern
  about 361, 362

advantages 362
best practices 363
disadvantages 363
need for 363
API gateway
  about 118, 120
  beneficial, for microservices 83
  benefits 121
  versus API management 84
API management
  versus API gateway 84
AppKey
  generating, for FlixOne.BookStore.Web 225, 227
Application Insights 261
application performance management (APM) 261
application/system monitoring 249
applications
  integration techniques 392
  monitoring 395
  running 230, 231
Aqua
  URL 236
architectures
  before microservices 388
ASP.NET Core web application
  creating 200, 201, 202, 203, 205
ASP.NET WebHooks
  reference link 122
asynchronous communication 114
asynchronous messaging 19
atomicity, consistency, isolation, and durability (ACID) 26
authentication 209
authorization 209
AutoRest 328
autoscaling 293, 294

availability monitoring 244
Azure Active Directory (Azure AD) 217, 394
Azure AD tenant
  ProductService applications, registering with 219, 220, 222, 224, 225
Azure API management (Azure APIM), parts
  developer portal 233
  publisher portal 233
Azure API management (Azure APIM)
  about 233
  managing, as API gateway 232, 233, 235
  security-related concepts 234
Azure API Management, capabilities
  reference link 84
Azure API management
  about 118
  reference link 119
Azure Cloud
  monitoring 255
Azure DevOps 188, 197
Azure Kubernetes Service (AKS)
  about 145
  ambassador pattern 150, 151
  concepts 146
  microservices, deploying 146, 148
  microservices, managing 146, 148
  overview 145
  sidecar pattern 148, 149
Azure message queues 133
Azure portal
  URL 134
Azure Redis Cache 298
Azure Resource Manager (ARM) 218, 293
Azure Service Bus, service types
  brokered communication 132
  non-brokered communication 132
Azure Service Bus
  about 131
  reference link 132
Azure Service Fabric
  about 50, 51, 127
  configuration settings, adding 140, 141
  container application, creating on Windows 144
  information, implementing on 133
  information, implementing on competing

    consumers 131
  information, implementing on containers 143
  messages, receiving from queue 142, 143
  messages, sending to queue 138, 139
  orchestrator, discussing 130
  prerequisites 133, 135, 136
  programming models, overview 130
  references 51
  Service Fabric architecture 127
Azure storage schema
  for diagnostic data 259
Azure storage
  used, for storing diagnostic data 257
Azure subscription
  reference link 133
Azure
  reference link 259
  setting up 375

B

Backend For Frontend (BFF)
  about 232
  reference link 118
baseline figures 289
big database, monolithic application
  single schema 31
  stored procedures 31
blob storage container
  wad-control-container 260
book-catalog microservice 405
book-listing microservice 402
book-searching microservice 402
Brewer's theorem 125
brokered communication 132

C

C# 54
C# 8.0
  default interface methods 70, 71
  features 56, 63, 64
  indices 65, 66, 67, 68
  ranges 65, 66, 67, 68
  readonly members 69
CacheCow 297
caching mechanism

  about 296, 297
  Azure Redis Cache 298
  CacheCow 297
centralized logging 253
challenges, in standardizing .NET stack
  fault tolerance 26
CHECKOUT-SERVICE 123
circuit breakers
  about 299
  closed state 301
  half-Open state 301
  open state 301
client certificates
  generating, on IIS Express 229
cloud-native microservices
  automation 409
  evolving system 409
  managed services 409
  overview 408
  smart state 409
code maintainability
  improvements 39
code reactive
  making 310, 311
code reusability 39
Command Line Interface (CLI)
  using 57
Common Query Responsibility Segregation
  (CQRS) 296
communication mechanisms, Azure Service Bus
  notification hubs 133
  queues 133
  relays 133
  topics 133
Communication subsystem 129
compensating transactions 126
competing consumers
  about 126
  Azure message queues 133
  Azure Service Bus 131
  information, implementing 131
component testing 163
concept, of seam
  about 75
  database 77, 78, 79, 80

  master data 80, 81
  module interdependency 75
  team structure 76, 77
  technology 76
  transaction 81
Consistency, Availability (network), Partition
  tolerance (CAP) theorem 125
consumer contract 165
consumer-driven contracts 164, 165
consumer-driven test
  implementing 165
container application, on Windows
  execution points 144
  prerequisites 144
container application
  creating, on Windows 144
container scaling
  with Docker Swarm 294
container security 236, 237
containers
  about 192, 194, 195
  information, implementing on 143
  versus virtual machines 192, 193
continuous deployment (CD) 186
continuous integration (CI) 44, 186, 393
contract testing
  about 164
  consumer-driven contracts 164
correlation ID
  used, in logging 254
critical business transactions
  auditing 246
CUSTOMER-SERVICE 123

D

data persistence model design 295, 296
data
  managing 314, 316, 317
database partitioning 41, 42
database refactoring
  about 40, 41
  schema correction 40
database sharding 41, 42
decomposition candidates
  identifying, within monolith 45

dependency injection (DI) 35, 36, 37, 38
dependent service 122
deployment paradigm
  need for 191, 192
deployment terminology 186, 187
deployment terminology, steps
  build 186
  build and deployment pipelines 187
  continuous delivery 187
  continuous deployment (CD) 186
  continuous integration (CI) 186
  deployment 186
  release 187
designer issue, solving
  reference link 62
DevOps culture 43
diagnostic data
  Azure portal, using 258
  Azure storage schema 259
  storage account, defining 259
  storing, with Azure storage 257
Docker compose 196
Docker container 196
Docker hub 196
Docker image 196
Docker registry 196
Docker Swarm
  about 196
  used, for container scaling 294
Docker, for Windows
  about 144
  installation link 144
Docker
  about 197
  application deployment 197
  prerequisites 198, 199
  setting up, on machine 198
  URL 195
  used, for Microservice deployment 198
Dockerfile 196
domain model design 73
Domain-Driven Design (DDD)
  significance, for microservices 73, 74
domain-driven model
  characteristics 73

E

ELK stack
  about 277, 280
  Elasticsearch 277
  Kibana 278
  Logstash 277
end user monitoring 246
end-to-end tests 167
endpoint monitoring 251
enterprise service bus (ESB) 23, 72
Entity Framework (EF) 85
Entity Framework Core (EF Core)
  about 55
  reference link 55
event communication, security
  about 312
  message-level security 312
event communication
  about 311, 312
  communication resilience 313, 314
  scalability 313
event sourcing pattern 124
Event Store 124
Event Tracing for Windows (ETW)
  about 254
  reference link 254
event-driven pattern
  about 122
  dependent service 122
  independent services 122
Event-Manager 123
eventual consistency pattern 125

F

fault tolerance 299
Federation subsystem 128
FlixOne 32
FlixOne application, Aggregator pattern solution
  Common folder 337
  Controllers folder 338, 339
  Models folder 340, 341, 342
  Persistence folder 342
  Services folder 343, 344, 345
FlixOne application, Anti-Corruption Layer pattern

solution
  BL folder 365
  BL folder, Models folder 365, 366, 367, 368
  DAL folder 368
  DAL folder, Contexts folder 369
  DAL folder, Repository folder 369
  Services folder 370
  Services folder, Controllers folder 370, 371
FlixOne application, Shared Data microservices pattern solution
  Controllers folder 359, 360, 361
  Extensions folder 350, 351
  Models folder 352, 353, 355, 356
  Persistence folder 356, 358, 359
FlixOne application
  monitoring 262, 264, 267, 274, 275, 276
FlixOne bookstore application
  better monolith applications, making 35
  deployment problems, handling 35
  functional overview 33
  solution, for current challenges 34
FlixOne case study, migrations
  code migration 87, 88
  EF Core DbContext 99, 100, 101
  EF Core migrations 101, 102
  EF Core support, adding 99
  model, adding 91, 92, 93, 94
  product controller, adding 97, 98
  ProductService API 98
  project, creating 88, 90, 91
  repositories, registering 96
  repository, adding 94, 95, 96
FlixOne case study
  controller 102, 103
  database migration 102
  migrations 87
  overview 84
  prerequisites 85
  ProductController 105
  repositories 102, 103
  transitioning, to product service 85, 86
  ViewModel 103, 104
FlixOne Store 379
FlixOne Store application
  building 384, 386

business needs 379, 380, 381, 383
  overview 383, 384
FlixOne.BookStore.Web
  AppKey, generating for 225, 227
framework-based strategy 249
functional tests 167

G

Globally Unique Identifier (GUID) 93
Grafana-type
  reference link 242
granularity
  reference link 83
Greenfield application
  book-catalog microservice 405
  building 401
  order microservice 407
  services, scoping 401
  shopping-cart microservice 406
  user-authentication microservice 407

H

health monitoring 243
hired service 132
horizontal scaling 28, 285, 286, 389
Hosting subsystem 129
Hotfix 185

I

IIS Express
  client certificates, generating on 229
independent services 122
information
  implementing, on Azure Service Fabric 133
  implementing, on competing consumers 131
instrumentation 241, 242
Integrated Development Environment (IDE)
  about 55, 144
  reference link 55
integration patterns
  API gateway 118, 120, 121
  compensating transactions 126
  competing consumers 126
  event sourcing pattern 124
  event-driven pattern 122, 123

[449]

learning 118
integration testing 163
integration tests
  implementing 175
Internet of Things (IoT)
  about 152
  used, for building microservices apps 152, 153
inversion of control (IoC) 36, 96
Invoice service 117
IoT Edge
  overview 155
IoT Hub
  overview 154
isolated unit tests
  about 168
  versus sociable tests 168
issues, monolithic architecture style
  .NET stack standardization, challenges 25, 26
  about 24
  big database 31
  modularity 30
  organizational alignment 29
  scaling 27

J

JSON padding (JSONP) 235
JSON Web Tokens (JWT)
  about 212, 213
  example 213
  reference link 213

K

KataCoda
  URL 195
Katas
  reference link 162
Kibana 278
Kubernetes
  microservices, using with 145
  reference link 146
Kusto query
  reference link 275

L

learning phase 29
load testing 167
logging
  about 252
  centralized logging 253
  challenges 252
  correlation ID, using in 254
  semantic logging 254
  strategies 253
Logstash 277

M

Managed Service Identity (MSI)
  reference link 227
Management subsystem 129
mean time between failures (MTBF) 185
mean time to recover (MTTR) 185
microservice application
  about 169
  implementing 176, 178, 179, 180
  integration tests, integrating 175
  testing 169, 170, 172
  unit tests, implementing 172
microservice architecture
  about 16, 17, 18, 390
  benefits 20, 21, 390
  prerequisites 23, 24
  working 20
microservice Auth example
  with Azure AD 218
  with OAuth 2.0 218
  with OpenID Connect 218
Microservice deployment, isolation
  build stage isolation 189
  deploy stage isolation 189
  release stage isolation 189
  service teams 189
  source control isolation 189
Microservice deployment
  isolation requirements 189, 191
  prerequisites 188
  with, Docker 198
Microservice deployments, practices

  CI and CD 188
  cloud computing, utilizing 188
  infrastructure as code 188
  self-sufficient teams 188
microservice monitoring solutions
  about 277
  ELK stack 277
  Splunk 278, 279
microservice scalability 286
microservice tests
  about 162
  component (service) testing 163
  contract testing 164
  end-to-end tests 167
  functional tests 167
  integration testing 163
  mocks 168, 169
  performance testing 167
  sociable unit test, versus isolated unit test 168
  stubs 168, 169
  unit testing 162
microservices apps
  building, with IoT 152, 153
microservices, high-level isolation
  considerations 72
  size 72
microservices, messaging mechanism
  about 18
  asynchronous messaging 19
  synchronous messaging 18
microservices
  about 9, 10
  advantages 21, 22, 46
  API gateway, benefits 83
  challenges, handling 159, 160
  communicating, between 82, 83
  Domain-Driven Design (DDD), significance 73, 74
  messages 391
  messages formats 19
  origin 8, 9
  prerequisites 31, 32, 33
  reference link 9
  security 210
  size 71

  synchronous, versus asynchronous 404
  testing 158, 393, 394
  testing, challenges 159
  used, for integrating monolithic applications 49, 50
  using 20
  versus SOA 22, 23
  with Kubernetes 145
Microsoft Azure Diagnostics 256
Microsoft SQLServer (MSSQL) 55
Microsoft Visual Studio 2019
  installation link 198
Minimum Viable Product (MVP) 384
mocks 169
monitoring, challenges
  about 397
  component lifespan 397
  data flow visualization 248
  DevOps mindset 248
  information visualization 398
  issues, scaling 247
  monitoring tools, testing 249
  scale 247, 397
monitoring, in Azure Cloud
  about 255
  Application Insights 261
  diagnostic data, storing with Azure storage 257
  Microsoft Azure Diagnostics 256
monitoring, strategies
  about 249
  endpoint monitoring 251
  profiling 250
  semantic monitoring 250
  synthetic transactions 250
monitoring
  about 395
  availability monitoring 244
  end user monitoring 246
  health monitoring 243
  need for 243
  performance monitoring 245
  reasons 395, 396
  security monitoring 245
  SLA monitoring 244
  strategies 398

system failures, troubleshooting 246
monolith architecture
  challenges 45
monolith transitioning
  working 391
monolithic applications
  deployment challenges 185, 186
  integrating, with microservices 49, 50
  security 209, 210
monolithic architecture style
  about 375
  benefits 377, 378
  challenges 376
  components 376
  issues 24
monolithic architecture, components
  business logic 10
  database access 10
  user interface 10
monolithic architecture
  about 388
  challenges 12, 46
  contract-based 15
  decomposition candidates, identifying 45
  exploring 10, 11
  reusability 15
  scalability 15
  security 394, 395
  SOA 12
  stateless 15
  upgradeability 15
monolithic deployments
  for enterprise applications 393

N

non-brokered communication 132

O

OAuth 2.0 Roles
  client 214
OAuth 2.0
  roles 214
  working with 214, 215, 216
object-oriented programming (OOP) 20
Object-Relational Mappers (ORMs) 55

observable 309
Observer Design Pattern 309
observers 309
One-Time Password (OTP) 384
Open Web Application Security Project (OWASP) 213
OpenID Connect
  exploring 216
orchestrator
  discussing 130
order microservice 403, 407
Order service 117
ORDER-SERVICE 124

P

Pact.Net Core
  reference link 165
  used, for achieving goal 165
Pact
  expectations, defining 166
  expectations, verifying 166
  reference link 165
PactNet
  reference link 165
Password Hash Synchronization (PHS) 218
patch 185
Path-Through Authentication (PTA)
  reference link 218
performance monitoring 245
performance testing
  load testing 167
  soak testing 167
  spike testing 167
  stress testing 167
Plain Old CLR Objects (POCOs) 88
policies 234
postal index number (PIN) 340
Product service 117
ProductController 105
ProductService applications
  registering, with Azure AD Tenant 219, 220, 222, 224, 225
profiling 250
programming models, Azure Service Fabric
  Container 130

Guest Executable 130
Reliable Actors 131
Reliable services 130
Progressive Web Apps (PWAs) 211
provider contract 165

Q

Quickfix 185
quota policy
  example 235, 236

R

rate limit
  example 235, 236
reactive microservices project
  communication, between application and
    database 325, 327
  creating 318, 320, 322, 325
  web client, creating 328, 329
reactive microservices, attributes
  autonomy 308
  message-driven 309
  resilience 308
  responsiveness 307
reactive microservices
  about 307
  coding 317
  overview 400
real user monitoring 250
Redis
  reference link 298
reduced module dependency 39
redundancy 299
replication controller 146
Root Cause Analysis (RCA) 244

S

scalability, types
  about 27
  horizontal scaling 28
  vertical scaling 27
scalability
  about 27, 399
  deployment challenges 28, 29
  infrastructure 399

overview 284
service design 400
scalable microservice
  characteristics 289, 290
Scale Cube model of scalability
  about 286, 287
  scaling of the x axis 287
  scaling of the y axis 288
  scaling of the z axis 288
scale sets
  used, for scaling virtual machines 292
scaling 389
scaling infrastructure
  about 284
  horizontal scaling 285, 286
  implementing 291
  vertical scaling 285
security monitoring 245
security token service (STS) 217
security, in microservices
  about 210
  best practices 237
  JSON Web Tokens (JWT) 212, 213
security
  in monolithic applications 209, 210
self-organizing phase 29
semantic logging 254
semantic monitoring 250
sensitive data
  auditing 246
server-side caching, types
  distributed caching, for persisted data 297
  response caching 297
servers 194
service design
  scaling 295
service discovery 301, 302
Service Fabric architecture
  about 127
  application types 127
Service Fabric SDK and Tools
  about 144
  download link 144
service testing 163
service-level agreements (SLA) 244

[453]

service-oriented architecture (SOA)
  about 12, 389
  advantages 390
  overview 375, 377
  services 13, 14, 15
  versus microservices 22, 23
services
  asynchronous communication 114
  communicating 112
  loose coupling 73
  standard communication protocol 73
  standard data formats 73
  styles of collaboration 114, 117
  synchronous communication 113
Shared Data microservices pattern solution
  implementing, in FlixOne application 347, 348, 349, 350
Shared Data microservices pattern
  about 345, 346
  advantages 346
  best practices 347
  disadvantages 346
shared nothing principle 189
shopping-cart microservice 402, 406
sidecar pattern
  about 148, 149
  best practices 150
  using 149
SLA monitoring 244
soak testing 167
sociable tests
  versus isolated unit tests 168
solutions, for making better monolith applications
  automated testing 43
  automation 43
  database partitioning 41, 42
  database refactoring 40, 41
  database sharding 41, 42
  dependency injection (DI) 35
  deployment 44
  DevOps culture 43
  versioning 44
spike testing 167
Splunk
  about 278, 279
  altering functionalities 279
  reporting functionality 279
SQL Server 2019
  reference link 56
strangler pattern 378, 379
stress testing 167
Structured Query Language (SQL)
  about 55
  reference link 55
stubs 169
styles of collaboration
  about 117
  event-based 116
  request/response 114, 115
subsystems, Service Fabric architecture
  Communication subsystem 129
  Federation subsystem 128
  Hosting subsystem 129
  Management subsystem 129
  Reliability subsystem 128
  Testability subsystem 129
  Transport subsystem 128
survival phase 29
Swagger support
  adding, to web API documentation 106, 107, 108
Swagger
  URL 106
swarm 294
synchronous communication 113
synchronous messaging 18
synthetic transactions 250
system failures
  troubleshooting 246

T

Team Foundation Online Services (TFS) 188
TeamCity 188
technology stack
  about 54
  using 54
telemetry 241, 242
test project
  setting up 170, 172
test-driven development (TDD) 43, 162

Testability subsystem 129
testing pyramid
  about 161
  service tests 161
  system tests 161
  unit tests 161
testing strategies
  about 160
  reactive 160
traditional .NET auth mechanism
  shortcomings 210, 212
Transport subsystem 128
Twistlock
  URL 236

U

unit testing 39, 162
unit tests
  implementing 172, 173, 174, 175
  reference link 168
user-authentication microservice 403, 407

V

vertical scaling 27, 285, 389
ViewModel 103, 104
virtual machines (VMs)
  about 247
  versus containers 192
virtual machines
  scaling, with scale sets 292
  versus containers 193
virtualization 191
Visual Studio 2019
  about 55
  download link 306
  installing 306, 374
Visual Studio solution projects
  configuring 227, 228
Visual Studio Team Services (VSTS) 147, 197
Visual Studio
  features, reference link 55
  version, reference link 55

W

web services 26
Windows Presentation Foundation (WPF) 59
Windows
  container application, creating 144

Z

Zookeeper
  URL 302

Printed in Great Britain
by Amazon